The Capitals of Spanish America

William Eleroy Curtis

Alpha Editions

This edition published in 2024

ISBN : 9789364732314

Design and Setting By
Alpha Editions
www.alphaedis.com
Email - info@alphaedis.com

As per information held with us this book is in Public Domain.
This book is a reproduction of an important historical work. Alpha Editions uses the best technology to reproduce historical work in the same manner it was first published to preserve its original nature. Any marks or number seen are left intentionally to preserve its true form.

Contents

MEXICO. THE CAPITAL OF MEXICO. ....- 1 -
GUATEMALA CITY. THE CAPITAL OF GUATEMALA. - 48 -
COMAYAGUA. THE CAPITAL OF HONDURAS. ....- 90 -
MANAGUA. THE CAPITAL OF NICARAGUA. ....- 112 -
SAN SALVADOR. THE CAPITAL OF SAN SALVADOR. ....- 140 -
SAN JOSÉ. THE CAPITAL OF COSTA RICA. ....- 162 -
BOGOTA. THE CAPITAL OF COLOMBIA. ....- 184 -
CARACAS. THE CAPITAL OF VENEZUELA. ....- 213 -
QUITO. THE CAPITAL OF ECUADOR. ....- 246 -
LIMA. THE CAPITAL OF PERU...- 299 -
LA PAZ DE AYACUCHO. THE CAPITAL OF BOLIVIA. ....- 344 -
SANTIAGO. THE CAPITAL OF CHILI. ....- 373 -
PATAGONIA. ....- 418 -
BUENOS AYRES. CAPITAL OF THE ARGENTINE REPUBLIC. ....- 439 -
MONTEVIDEO. THE CAPITAL OF URUGUAY. ....- 476 -
ASUNCION. THE CAPITAL OF PARAGUAY. ....- 500 -
RIO DE JANEIRO. THE CAPITAL OF BRAZIL...............- 532 -

MEXICO.

THE CAPITAL OF MEXICO.

WITH the exception of Buenos Ayres and Santiago, Chili, the city of Mexico is the largest and the finest capital in Spanish America; but unfortunately the shadow of the sixteenth century still rests upon it. It wounds the pride of the Yankee tourist to discover that so little of our boasted influence has lapped over the border, and that the historic halls of the Montezumas are only spattered with the modern ideas we exemplify. The native traveller still prefers his donkey to the railroad train, and carries a burden upon his back instead of using a wagon. Water is still peddled about the capital of Mexico in jars, and the native farmer uses a plough whose pattern was old in the days of Moses. Nowhere do ancient and modern customs come into such intimate contrast as in the city of Mexico.

The people are highly civilized in spots. Besides the most novel and recent product of modern science, one finds in use the crudest, rudest implement of antiquity. Types of four centuries can be seen in a single group in any of the plazas. Under the finest palaces, whose ceilings are frescoed by Italian artists, whose walls are covered with the rarest paintings, and shelter libraries selected with the choicest taste, one finds a common *bodega*, where the native drink is dealt out in gourds, and the *peon* stops to eat his *tortilla*. Women and men are seen carrying upon their heads enormous burdens through streets lighted by electricity, and stop to ask through a telephone where their load shall be delivered.

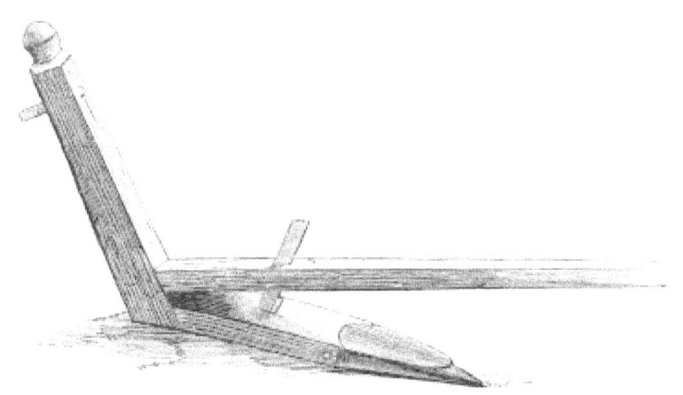

IT WAS USED IN THE DAYS OF MOSES.

The correspondence of the Government is dictated to stenographers and transcribed upon type-writers; and every form of modern improvement for the purpose of economizing time and saving labor is given the opportunity of a test, even if it is not permanently adopted. There is no Government that gives greater encouragement to inventive genius than the administration of President Diaz, and it has been one of the highest aims of his official career to modernize Mexico. The twelve years from 1876, when he came into power, until 1889, when his third term commenced, may be reckoned the progressive age of our neighborly republic; but the common people are still prejudiced against innovations, and resist them. In all the public places, and at the entrance of the post-office, are men squatting upon the pavement, with an inkhorn and a pad of paper, whose business is to conduct the correspondence of those whose literary attainments are unequal to the task. Such odd things are still to be seen at the capital of a nation that subsidizes steamship lines and railways, and supports schools where all the modern languages and sciences are taught, and has a compulsory education law upon its statute-books. In the old Inquisition Building, where the bodies of Jews and heretics have been racked and roasted, is a medical college, sustained by the Government for the free education of all students whose attainments reach the standard of matriculation; and bones are now sawn asunder in the name of science instead of religion.

A WATER-CARRIER.

The country within whose limits can be produced every plant that grows between the equator and the arctics, and whose mines have yielded one-half of the existing silver in the world, is habitually bankrupt, and wooden effigies of saints stolen from the churches are sold as fuel for locomotives purchased with the proceeds of public taxation. What Mexico needs most is peace, industry, and education. The Government now pays a bounty to steamships upon every immigrant they bring, and is importing coolie labor to develop the coffee and sugar lands. Since 1876 there has not been a political revolution of any importance, and the prospect of permanent peace is hopeful.

The political struggle in Mexico, since the independence of the Republic, has been, and will continue to be, between antiquated, bigoted, and despotic Romanism, allied with the ancient aristocracy, under whose encouragement Maximilian came, on the one hand, and the spirit of intellectual, industrial, commercial, and social progress on the other. The pendulum has swung backward and forward with irregularity for sixty years; every vibration has been registered in blood. All of the weight of Romish influence, intellectual, financial, and spiritual, has been employed to destroy the Republic and restore the Monarchy, while the Liberal party has strangled the Church and stripped it of every possession. Both factions have fought under a black flag, and the war has been as cruel and vindictive on one side as upon the other; but the result is apparent and permanent.

RUINS OF THE COVERED WAY TO THE INQUISITION.

No priest dare wear a cassock in the streets of Mexico; the confessional is public, parish schools are prohibited, and although the clergy still exercise a powerful influence among the common people, whose superstitious ignorance has not yet been reached by the free schools and compulsory education law, in politics they are powerless. The old clerical party, the Spanish aristocracy, whose forefathers came over after the Conquest, and reluctantly surrendered to Indian domination when the Viceroys were driven out and the Republic established, have given up the struggle, and will probably never attempt to renew it. They were responsible for the tragic episode of Maximilian, and still regret the failure to restore the Monarchy. The Aztecs sit again upon the throne of Mexico, after an interval of three hundred and fifty years, and the men whose minds direct the affairs of the Republic have tawny skins and straight black hair.

MEXICAN MULETEER.

Several of the aristocrats have left the country and reside in Paris, receiving enormous revenues from their Mexican estates, which they visit biennially, but will not live upon. Others are friends of Diaz, sympathize with the progressive element, and will turn out full-fledged Republicans when the issue is raised again. The finest houses in Mexico are unoccupied, and the palatial villas of Tacubaya, the aristocratic suburb, are in a state of decay. They are too large and too costly for rental, and the owners are too obstinate and indifferent to sell them. Perhaps these haughty dons still have a hope of coming back some time to rule again as they did years ago, but they will die as they have lived since Maximilian's failure, impotent but unreconciled.

The beautiful castle of Chapultepec, which was dismantled during the last revolution, but has been restored and fitted up as a beautiful suburban retreat for the Presidents of Mexico, was occupied by Maximilian and Carlotta in imitation of the Montezumas, whose palace stood upon the rocky eminence. Around the place is a grove of monstrous cypress-trees, whose age is numbered by the centuries, and whose girth measures from thirty to fifty feet. It is the finest assemblage of arborial monarchs on the continent, and sheltered imperial power hundreds of years before Columbus set his westward sails. Before the Hemisphere was known or thought of, here stood a gorgeous palace, and its foundations still endure. Here the rigid ceremonial etiquette of Aztec imperialism was enforced, and human sacrifice was made to invoke the favor of the Sun.

SHOPS.

In Mexican society one meets many notable people; some are remarkable for talent, or their birth, etc., and others for the strange vicissitudes of their lives. For example, in an obscure little house lives a well-educated gentleman who is, by lineal descent from Montezuma II., the legal heir to the Aztec throne, and should be Emperor of Anahuac. This Señor Montezuma, however, indulges in no idle dream of the restoration of the ancient Empire, and quietly accepts the meagre pension paid him by the Government. In contradistinction to this scion of the house of Montezuma, the heirs of Cortez receive immense revenues from the estates of the "Marquis del Valle" (Cortez), live in grand style, and are haughty and influential. There is also a lineal descendant of the Indian emperor Chimalpopoca. This young man is a civil engineer, industrious, and quite independent.

The acknowledged heir to the throne of Mexico is young

CASTLE OF CHAPULTEPEC.

TILE FRONT.

Augustin Yturbide, according to the feelings of the few and feeble remnants of the Monarchical party; but it may be said to the young man's credit that he entirely repudiates their homage, although he is the heir to two brief and ill-starred dynasties. He is the grandson of the Emperor Augustin Yturbide, and the adopted heir of Maximilian and Carlotta. The Yturbide they call "Emperor" was an officer in the Spanish army when Mexico was a colony, and during the revolution headed by the priest Hidalgo, in 1810, he fought on the side of the King. But, being dismissed from the army in 1816, he retired to seclusion, to remain until the movement of 1820, when he placed himself at the head of an irregular force, and captured a large sum of money that was being conveyed to the sea-coast. With these resources he promulgated what is known in history as "the plan of Iguala," which proposed the organization of Mexico into an independent empire, and the election of a ruler by the people. The revolution was bloodless, and in May, 1822, Yturbide proclaimed himself Emperor, declared the crown hereditary, and established a court. He was formally crowned in the July following, but in December Santa Anna proclaimed the Republic, and after a brief and ignominious reign Yturbide left Mexico on May 11, 1822, just a year, lacking a week, from the date he assumed power. The Congress gave him a pension of $25,000 yearly, and required that he should live in Italy; but impelled by an insane desire to regain his crown, in May, 1824, he returned to Mexico, and was shot in the following July.

THE TREE OF MONTEZUMA.

He left a son, Angel de Yturbide, who came to the United States with his mother, and was educated at the Jesuit College at Georgetown, District of Columbia, the Government having given them a liberal pension. There he fell in love

PRINCE YTURBIDE.

with Miss Alice Green, the daughter of a modest but prosperous merchant of the town, and married her. They had one child, the so-called Prince Augustin, who, when three years old, with the consent of his ambitious mother, was adopted by the childless Maximilian and Carlotta, in the vain hope that the act might in a measure increase their popularity among the Mexicans.

Meanwhile Maximilian's fate was fast overtaking him. When he saw the catastrophe was at hand, he determined to save the young Yturbide, and with the assistance of the Archbishop of Mexico notified Madame Yturbide that her child would be placed on a certain steamer reaching Havana at such a date; and it was there the mother was united to him after a separation of two years. Maximilian and Carlotta had surrounded the young prince with all the elegancies of royalty, and he retained many of their royal gifts. His father was then dead, and his mother had sole charge of his education. He was educated at Washington, where Madame Yturbide lived in a fine house on the corner of Nineteenth and N streets. When her son came of age she sold her house and returned with him to Mexico. His intention was to enter the army at once, but by the advice of his Mexican friends he entered the national military college for a course of study before taking his commission. He is a handsome young man, very quiet and prepossessing. His abilities can scarcely be judged so far, but he has always conducted himself with great good-sense. Madame Yturbide is now with him in Mexico. One of the most promising signs of the permanency of the Republic is the presence in the party of progress of this young man, whose name represents all the ancient aristocracy desires to restore. He has inherited two worthless crests; but, whether from policy or principle, has added his youthful strength and the traditions that surround his name to the support of the Diaz administration.

The widow of General Santa Anna is a woman who played a prominent part in the political tragedies that have succeeded one another with such great rapidity upon the Mexican stage. Until her death in the autumn of 1886, she was an object of interest to all visitors to the capital, and always welcomed cordially strangers who called upon her, provided they would permit her to smoke her cigarettes, and talk about her beauty and the attentions she had received in the past.

Santa Anna is not so highly estimated in Mexico as in some other parts of the world where people are not so familiar with his eccentric and adventurous career. He was a man of remarkable natural abilities, force of character, energy, and personal courage, but devoid of principle, education, culture, and mindful only of his own interests. He served all political parties in turn. She was his second wife, and was only thirteen years old when he married her, in the fifth term of his presidency, and when he was trying to set himself up as an absolute monarch. For twenty years her life was spent in a camp, surrounded by the whirl of warfare. Her husband was five times President of Mexico, and four times Military Dictator in absolute power. He was banished, recalled, banished again, and finally died, denounced by all as a traitor. She had seen much "glory," and had received unlimited adulation, but she hardly ever enjoyed one thoroughly peaceful month in her life.

It created a sensation in Mexico when the pretty peon girl, Dolores Testa, was suddenly raised from abject poverty to affluence. The Dictator ordered all to address his bride as "Your Highness," ladies-in-waiting were appointed in order to teach the bewildered little Dolores how to play her rôle in the great world, and then the President organized for her a body-guard of twenty-five military men, who were uniformed in white and gold, and were styled "los Guardias de la Alteza" (her Highness's Body-guard). When the President's wife attended the theatre these guards rode in advance of and at the sides of the coach, each bearing a lighted torch. During the performance they remained in the *patio* or *foyer* of the theatre, and then escorted her Highness back to the palace in the same order. Such was the power of

General Santa Anna in those days that even the clergy bent before him; and when

GENERAL GRANT ON A BANANA PLANTATION.

his young wife went to mass, the priests, attended by their acolytes, actually used to leave the cathedral to meet her on the pavement, and with cross and lighted tapers escort her from her carriage to her seat within the church, and at the conclusion of the mass accompanied her to her coach.

Her last days were quite in contrast with the glory of her youth. She owned a residence in the city and a lovely country-seat in Tacubaya, the aristocratic suburb; her wardrobes and chests were filled with rich robes of velvet, satin, and silk, costly laces, and magnificent jewels; but she was too listless to interest herself in anything. No stranger who by chance might see her exhighness at home, with her pretty feet thrust into down-trodden old leather shoes, and her unkempt hair covered by a common cotton *rebosa*, could ever, by the greatest effort of imagination, possibly fancy her to be the same person who once dazzled Mexico by a display of pomp that exceeded even that of the Empress Carlotta. Mrs. Santa Anna was an estimable woman, but was almost forgotten by the generation that once bent before her. Her family plate, and the diamond snuffbox which was presented her husband when he was Dictator, and cost twenty-five thousand dollars, were, during the latter years of her life, and still are, in the National pawn-shops of Mexico, and his wooden leg, captured in battle during our war with Mexico, is in the Smithsonian Institute.

The family of the great Juarez, the Washington of Mexico, an Aztec peon, who overthrew the empire of Maximilian as Cortez had overthrown the ancient dynasty of his ancestors, live in good style in the city of Mexico, the daughters being well married, and the son the secretary of the Mexican legation at Berlin. They all talk English well, and are very highly educated. Every American who visits their city is handsomely entertained by them.

But time spent in conjecturing the future of the aristocratic or clerical party is wholly wasted. No priest, no bishop, is allowed by law to hold real estate; titles vested in religious orders are worthless; the Church is forbidden to acquire wealth, and has been stripped of the accumulated treasures of three centuries. The candlesticks and altar ornaments are gilt instead of gold, and the heavy embroideries in gold and silver have been replaced by tinsel. A solid silver balustrade which has stood in one of the churches since the time of Cortez was torn down not long ago and taken to the mint, and a chandelier in the cathedral of Puebla, when it was melted, made sixty thousand silver dollars.

There still stands in the cathedral at Guadalupe, on the spot where the Mother of Christ appeared to a poor shepherd and stamped her image in beautiful colors upon his cotton *serape*, a double railing from the altar to the choir, perhaps sixty feet long and three feet high, which is said to be of solid silver, with considerable gold. This is the only one of the remnants of pontifical magnificence which remains undespoiled, for the superstition which pervades all classes of society has protected it; but the altars have been stripped of the jewels which were bestowed by grateful people who had received the protection of the Virgin, who watches over those in distress, and the veneering of gold which once covered the altar carvings has all been ripped off. It is said that an enterprising American offered to replace the solid silver railing with a plated one, and give a bonus of three hundred thousand dollars to the Church, but the proposition was rejected.

This Guadalupe shrine is the most sacred spot in Mexico, and to it come, on the 12th of each December, the anniversary of the appearance of the Virgin, thousands upon thousands of pilgrims, bringing their sick and lame and blind to drink of the miraculous waters of a spring which the Virgin opened on the mountain-side to convince the sceptical shepherd of her divine power. The waters have a very strong taste of sulphur, and are said to be a potent remedy for diseases of the blood. In testimony of this the walls of the chapel, which is built over the spring, are covered with quaint, rudely written certificates of people who claim to have been miraculously cured by its use. In the cathedral are multitudes of other testimonials from people who have been preserved from death in danger by having appealed for protection to the Virgin of Guadalupe; but nowadays, instead of sending jewels and other articles of value as they did when the Church was able to protect its property, they hang up gaudily painted inscriptions reciting specifically the blessings they have received. On the crest of the hill is a massive shaft of stone, representing the main-mast of a ship with the yards out and sails spread. This was erected many years ago by a sea-captain who was caught in a storm at sea, and who made a vow to the Virgin that if she would bring him safe to land he would carry his main-mast and sails to Guadalupe, and raise them there as an evidence of his gratitude for her mercy. He fulfilled his vow, and within the double tiers of stone are the masts and canvas.

CHURCH OF GUADALUPE.

In the cathedral is the original blanket, or *serape*, which

ISTACCIHUATL.

the shepherd wore when the Virgin appeared to him, and upon which she stamped her portrait. It is preserved in a glass case over the altar, and may be seen by paying a small fee to the priest. Copies of the Guadalupe Virgin are common and familiar; one can scarcely look in any direction in Mexico without seeing the representation upon the walls of a house, or pendent from the watch-chain of a passer-by; but the average reproduction is a great improvement upon the original, which is a dull and heavy daub, without any evidences of skill in its execution, or even the average degree of accuracy in drawing. According to the story, the portrait was stamped upon the *serape* or blanket of the shepherd, and this all Catholics in Mexico devoutly believe; but a close examination reveals the fact that it is done in ordinary oil colors, upon a piece of ordinary canvas, and that the pigments peel off like those of any poorly executed piece of work.

In the ancient town of Guadalupe, in a house near the cathedral, was signed the famous treaty determining the boundary line between Mexico and the United States, while in a cemetery on the hill General Santa Anna lies buried.

The Mexican people, like all the Spanish race, are fond of ceremony, but the inauguration of their President is not attended with so much display or interest as is shown on similar occasions on this side of the Rio Grande. Perhaps it is because the event occurs so often. During the two hundred and eighty-six years between the fall of the Empire and the establishment of the Republic, there were but sixty-four Viceroys; but during the sixty-three years that followed there have been thirty-two Presidents, seven Dictators, and two Emperors. Although the constitutional term of the presidency is four years, but two in the long list were permitted to serve out their time, and they were the last, which at least shows improvement in the political condition of the country.

I witnessed the inauguration of President Diaz on the 1st of December, 1884. The ceremonies, which were simple enough to satisfy the most critical of Democrats, took place in the handsome theatre erected in 1854, and named in honor of the Emperor Yturbide. It is now called the Chamber of Deputies, and is occupied by the lower branch of the National Legislature, a body of some two hundred and twenty-seven men. The Senate, composed of fifty-six members, meets in a long, narrow room in the old National Palace which was formerly used as a chapel by the Viceroys. The viceregal throne, a massive chair of carved and gilded rosewood, still stands upon a platform opposite the entrance, under a canopy of crimson velvet, but upon its crest is carved the American eagle, with a snake in its mouth, the emblem of Republican Mexico. Maximilian hung a golden crown over the eagle; Juarez tore it down and placed the broken sword of the Emperor in the talons of the bird. The Aztecs say that the founders of their empire, whose origin is lost in the mists of fable, were told to march on until they found an eagle sitting upon a cactus with a snake in its mouth, and there they should rest and build a great city. The bird and the bush were discovered in the valley that is shadowed by the twin volcanoes, and there the imperishable walls were laid which are now bidding farewell to their seventh century.

EX-PRESIDENT GONZALES.

The old Theatre Yturbide has not been remodelled since it became the shelter of legislative power, and all the natural light it gets is filtered through the opaque panels of the dome, so that during the day sessions the Deputies are always in a state of partial eclipse. It is about as badly off for light as our own Congress. The members occupy comfortable arm-chairs in the parquet, arranged in semicircular rows. The presiding officer and the secretaries sit upon the stage, and at either side is a sort of pulpit from which formal addresses are made, although conversational debates are conducted from the floor. The orchestra circle and galleries are divided into boxes, and are reserved for spectators, but are seldom occupied, as the proceedings of the Congress are not regarded with much public interest.

PRESIDENT PORFIRIO DIAZ.

The members of both Houses have no regular seats, but sit where they please. As they have few constituents to write to, they use no desks. There are some that might be used, but never are. The members vote themselves no stationery, postage-stamps, or incidentals, as our Congressmen do, but are paid two hundred and fifty dollars a month during the two years for which they are elected. Habit and the exercise of military power have reversed the constitutional relations of the executive and legislative branches of the Government, and the business of the Congress sometimes is not to pass bills for the approval or disapproval of the President, but to enact such legislation as he recommends. The members of the Cabinet have seats in both houses of the Congress, participate in the debates, and submit measures for consideration, but have no vote; and the President himself often exercises his constitutional right to meet and act with the Legislature. Very seldom is a law passed that does not come prepared and approved by the Executive Department, and to oppose the policy of the administration is usually fatal to the ambition of Mexican statesmen.

In appearance the members will compare favorably with those of our Congress, and they are far in advance of the average State Legislature in ability and learning. The first features that strike a visitor familiar with legislative bodies in the United States is the decorum with which proceedings are conducted, and the scrupulous care with which every one is clothed. On certain formal occasions it is usual for all of the members to appear in evening dress, which gives the body the appearance of a social gathering rather than a legislative assembly. Nine-tenths of the members are white, and the other tenth show little trace of Aztec blood. There is never anything like confusion, and the laws of propriety are never transgressed. One hears no bad syntax or incorrect pronunciation in the speeches; no coarse language is used, and no wrangles ever occur like those which so often disgrace our own Congress. The statesmen never tilt their chairs back, nor lounge about the chamber; their feet are never raised upon the railings or desks; there is no letter-writing going on; the floor is never littered with scraps of paper; no spittoons are to be seen, and no conversation is permitted. Extreme dignity and decorum mark the proceedings, which are always short and silent, and the solemnity which prevails gives a funereal aspect to the scene.

THE DOME.

But everybody smokes. The secretary lights a cigarette at the end of a roll-call, and the chairman blows a puff of smoke from his lips before he announces a decision. The members are constantly rolling cigarettes with deft fingers, and the people in the galleries do the same, so that a cloud of gray vapor always hangs over the body, and in the dark corners of the chamber one can see the glow of burning tobacco like the flash of fire-flies. But cigars are never used, nor pipes, and no one chews tobacco.

Whole sessions pass away with nothing but formal business, such as receiving communications from the Executives of the States or petitions from the people, which are rarely acted on. Occasionally a bill is passed, but it passes almost as a matter of course, some of the members giving a delicate little wave of the hand to the secretary as he calls their names by sight, others merely smiling at him, some paying no attention whatever to him, but none of them taking the trouble to open their mouths or rise, as the rules require. Weeks and months pass away without a speech of any kind, or even a point of order.

In the presence of this body, and with a similar indifference, Profirio Diaz was inaugurated President of the United States of Mexico. He had been President once before, having seized the government by force of arms from Lerdo, but was so just and wise a ruler, and possessed the confidence of the people so thoroughly, that he was allowed to serve out a full term, being one of the few Mexican Presidents to enjoy that privilege. He would have been re-elected at the expiration of his administration but for a constitutional provision prohibiting it. Four years passed and he was restored to power by the votes of the people against a man whose administration was a saturnalia of corruption and extravagance, that ended with a bankrupt treasury and an impoverished people.

The last days of the term of Gonzales were stormy. His attempt to secure certain unpopular financial legislation created great excitement, and the students of the universities, who numbered six or seven thousand, made a protest which would have ended in violence and assassination but for the overpowering military guard that surrounded the palace. The students would have resisted any attempt of Gonzales to prevent the inauguration of his successor, and kept up a demonstration against the existing Government until that event occurred.

SAN COSME AQUEDUCT, CITY OF MEXICO.

It was nine o'clock on the morning that the ceremonies were to occur. Long lines of bayonets and sabres glittered in the streets around the theatre, regiments of cavalry and infantry were drawn up in the Alameda and Plaza, squads of police, on foot and mounted, were marching here and there. Bands of students yell "*Viva!*" and "*Mira!*" Some were fired into, and several students wounded. The shops were nearly all closed early in the day; huge iron padlocks and bolts that would resist a sledge-hammer for half a day hung on doors that but a few days ago were thronged with customers, and the few that remained open were merely ajar, ready to be slammed shut in a minute, and the ponderous bars swung into place.

The attendance at the theatre was not large, and consisted almost entirely of officials, foreign ambassadors, and the personal friends of the President, who, like the members of the Congress, were nearly all in full dress, but carried revolvers in their pockets for use if the occasion demanded. In a gilded box over the stage was the wife of General Diaz, of girlish years and striking beauty, attended by a party of lady friends and two military officers resplendent in gold lace. There was no crush, no confusion, but a suppressed excitement and anxiety, made intense by the recollection that such incidents in the history of Mexico had been usually attended by war. The outgoing President was regarded as the enemy of his successor, and the Congress was about equally divided in its allegiance. The former was not present, and his movements and intentions were unknown.

The members of the Senate sat in a double row of chairs which had been placed around the sides of the parquet for their accommodation, and all of them wore white kid gloves. The members of the Lower House, the Deputies, sat in their accustomed seats, and their chief officer presided. Promptly at nine o'clock General Diaz, in full evening dress, with white gloves, was escorted to the platform by a committee of Senators, took the oath of office with his back to the audience, and passed rapidly out of the building. The whole proceeding did not last more than five minutes, and when the clerk announced that the oath of office had been taken in accordance with the law, and declared Diaz "Constitutional President," the audience quietly left the chamber as if nothing more than the ordinary routine had taken place.

But the excitement was not abated. The oath had been taken, but the outgoing administration by its absence from the ceremonies had intensified the anxiety lest the admission of Diaz to the Palace might be denied. Accompanied by a committee of Senators and an escort of cavalry. President Diaz drove half a mile to the Government building, and to his gratification the column of soldiers which was drawn up before the entrance opened to let him pass. The plaza which the building fronts was crowded with thousands of people, who announced the arrival of the new President by a deafening cheer, and the chimes of the old cathedral rang a melodious welcome.

THE PALACE OF MEXICO.

In the centre of the old palace, which stands upon the foundations of the heathen temple Cortez destroyed, is an enormous court, in which the President's party alighted and ascended the marble stairs. The sentinels which lined the staircase saluted them respectfully, and this omen relieved their minds. At the entrance of the Executive chamber, where relics of the luxurious taste of Maximilian still remain, Diaz was received by an aide-de-camp of Gonzales, who ushered him into the presence of the retiring administration. Surrounded by his Cabinet, Gonzales stood, and as Diaz entered stepped forward to welcome him, and according to the ancient practice, handed him an enormous silver key, which is supposed to turn the bolts that protect authority. Short formal addresses were made upon either side, and after wishing the new administration a peaceful and prosperous term, Gonzales and his ministers retired.

General Porfirio Diaz, the foremost man in Mexico to-day, and one whose public career will fill pages in the history of that Republic, is the representative of mixed Aztec and Spanish ancestry, like all of the famous native leaders of the last half century. He is tall and dark, his muscular figure impressing one as the very incarnation of health and endurance. He has a military, yet nonchalant air, his brown eyes meet you squarely with the glance of one born to command, and his voice is peculiarly pleasant as in deep tones he rolls off the musical dialect of his mother-tongue.

His career, like that of all Mexican leaders, is full of romantic adventure. He was born in the rich State of Oaxaca, which was also the birthplace of Juarez, Mejia, Romero, Mariscal, and others famed in politics and literature. Don Porfirio's parents designed him for the law and sent him to the Literary Institute, in Puebla, the City of the Angels, which celebrated institution has graduated many of Mexico's most eminent men. But Diaz, at the age of twenty-four, enlisted as a private in the National Guard against the government of Santa Anna. Again, in the so-called war of reform—in 1858 and 1861—he won more substantial honors than the straps of an officer, and when his country was convulsed by the French invasion of 1862, Diaz, then a general, took a prominent part in the struggle. Once during those wars, when a prisoner at Puebla, he escaped by letting himself down from the tower in which he was confined by means of a rope spliced out with his clothing. Another of his numerous hair-breadth escapes was during the bloody struggle by which he made himself President for the first time. Having captured Matamoras by daring strategy, he was seized on shipboard by the Lerdists, and saved himself only by leaping into the sea, assisted by the connivance of a French captain, whom he afterwards made consul at Saint Nazaire.

In 1871 General Diaz was one of the three candidates for the Presidency, and being defeated by Juarez, issued his celebrated manifesto known as the "Plan of Noria," repudiating all existing powers, and proposing to retain military command. Being thoroughly whipped by the Indian President, after more than a year's hard fighting and the loss of thousands of lives, the general left Mexico for a time, along with a number of his fellow-partisans.

After Juarez died in office, his successor, Don Sebastian Lerdo de Tejada, recalled all political exiles by issuing a general amnesty, which act Diaz hastened to repay by rushing again to arms and speedily deposing his rival. Although the Electoral College had declared Lerdo the legally elected ruler by a vote of 123 to 49, Diaz proceeded to issue a pronunciamento from Palo Blanco, State of Tamaulipas, denouncing the President, Congress, and all recognized authorities, and at the head of the Constitutional army took possession of the capital and usurped the Executive chair, driving the incumbent into exile, and holding his position by force of arms.

When the term was over for which Diaz had thus elected himself, he retired temporarily to fulfil the law he had so strenuously advocated, Article 28 of the amended constitution. Next he set about paving the way to permanent success by placating all opposing factions. First, he forever laid any restless ghost of Lerdist sentiment that might arise and shake its gory locks in the future, by marrying in the very midst of the enemy's camp. His young and beautiful wife is the daughter of Romero Rubio, who was President Lerdo's most influential adviser, and his bosom friend and companion in exile. Señor Rubio has since been President of the Senate, and Minister of the Interior.

No man since the Indian Juarez, who was the Abraham Lincoln of Mexican history, has achieved the popularity that Diaz enjoys, or has won the confidence of the people to so great a degree. The ballad-singers at Santa Anita, an Indian village in the suburbs of the capital, on the romantic canal that leads to the far-famed Floating Gardens, where the populace swarm on Sundays to drink *pulque* and dance fandangoes, carol many a long-drawn refrain to twanging guitars in praise of Porfirio D-i-i-iaz, while the dedications of their myriad *pulquerias* are about equally divided between Diaz, Montezuma, and the Mother of God.

The old Capitol, or Palace, as it is called, which Cortez raised upon the ruins of the Aztec temple is still occupied as the seat of government, and shelters the Executive departments. Here, too, is the National Museum, with its collection of antiquities, and in its centre, near the Sacrificial Stone of the Aztecs, is the imperial coach in which the ill-fated Emperor rode. Public business is conducted very much as in the United States; the officials are usually accomplished linguists, and well read in political economy. The science of government is studied there more than with us, and public life is a profession, like law or engineering. There still exists, however, and many generations will come and go before it can be eradicated, a caste that divides the people into three classes—the peon, the aristocrat, and the middle class. The prejudice that separates them is usually overcome by military force. The peon, who like Diaz becomes a political and a social leader, must win the place by military skill, or wear a *sarepa* forever.

Among the upper classes of Mexico will be found as high a degree of social and intellectual refinement as exists in Paris, as quick a reception and as cordial a response to all the sentiments that elevate society, and a knowledge of the arts and literature that few people of the busy cities of the United States have acquired.

THE CATHEDRAL, CITY OF MEXICO.

Their wealth is lavishly displayed, their taste is exercised to a degree equal to that of any people in the world, and the interior of many of their dwellings furnishes a glimpse of happiness and cultured elegance that, with their less active temperament, they enjoy more than their northern neighbors. Yet the people who receive the latest Paris fashions and literature by every steamer, and who would rather wear a shroud than a garment out of style, still cling to some ancient customs as eagerly as they seize some modern ideas. Social laws restrict intercourse between the sexes, as in the Latin nations of Europe, and Pedro makes love to Mercedes through his father and hers. Marriage is often a commercial contract for pecuniary or social advantages, and a parent chooses his son-in-law as he selects his partners or the directors of a bank. It is an impropriety for men and women to be alone together, even if they are closely related, and no woman of the higher caste goes upon the streets without a duenna.

The funeral customs of Mexico are a source of constant interest to strangers in that land, as the burial of the dead is a ceremony of great display. The poor rent handsome coffins which they have not the means to buy, and transfer the body from its temporary casket to a cheap box before it is laid in the grave. Invitations are issued by messenger, and advertisements of funerals are published in the newspapers or posted at the street corners like those of a bull-fight or a play. Announcements are sent to friends in big, black-bordered envelopes, and are usually decorated with a picture of a tomb. The information is conveyed in faultless Spanish, that Señor Don Jesus San a Maria Hidalgo died yesterday at noon, and that his bereaved wife, who mourns under the name of "Donna Maria José Concepcion de los Angelos Narro Henriandos y Hidalgo," together with his family, desire you to honor them by participating in the ceremonies of burial, and in supplicating the Mother of God and the Redeemer of the world to grant the soul of the dead husband a speedy release from the pains of Purgatory, and eternal bliss in Paradise.

The oddities of Mexican life and customs strike the tourist in a most forcible manner. The first thing he observes among the common people is that the men wear extremely large hats, and the women no hats at all. The ordinary sombrero costs fifteen dollars, while those bearing the handsome ornaments so universally popular run in price all the way from twenty-five to two hundred and fifty dollars. The Mexican invests all his surplus in his hat. Men whose wages are not more than twelve dollars a month often wear sombreros which represent a whole quarter's income. A servant at the house of a friend was paid off one day for the three months his employer had been absent. He got forty-two dollars, of which he paid thirty-five dollars for a hat and gave seven dollars to his family.

STYLES OF ARCHITECTURE.

The next thing that you notice is that every block on the same street has a different name, and when you start out on foot to make a visit you become bewildered at once, and have to call a carriage. Take the chief street, for example, which begins at the Grand Plaza, where the Palace stands, and runs to the statue of Charles IV. of Spain. Each of the seventeen blocks has a name of its own, and the names that are used are quite as striking as this perplexing custom. Here is a list of some of the principal blocks or streets translated into English: "Crown of Thorns Street," "Fifth of May Street," "Holy Ghost Street," "Blood of Christ Street," "Body of Christ Street,"

"Mother of Sorrows Street," "Street of the Sacred Heart," "The Heart of Jesus Street," "Street of the Love of God," "Jesus Street," and "John the Baptist Street." Nearly every saint in the calendar has a street named after him or her, and nine-tenths of the city has the religion of the people thus illustrated.

Another thing that surprises you greatly is that nearly every man you meet makes you a present of a residence. He grasps your hand with ardent cordiality when he leaves you, and says, "My house is yours; it stands numero tres—Calle," and so on, "and is at your service." The next man tells you that your house is such and such a number, and he shall be angry if you do not occupy it. As neither of them has enjoyed the honor of your acquaintance for more than five minutes, and both are only casually introduced, this excessive generosity is quite embarrassing. An English lord told me he met fourteen men at the Jockey Club one evening, and was presented with thirteen houses. The other man lived in Cuba. But it is only the Mexican way of saying, "I'm pleased to meet you." It often leads to comical adventures, however, for the gentleman who tenders such profuse hospitality seldom remembers you the next morning. People have accepted these ardent invitations and been met with a cold welcome. Another amusing and puzzling peculiarity is that everybody lives over a shop. Even the millionaires rent out the first floor of their residences for purposes of business, and live in the third story. The handsomest house in all Mexico has a railway ticket-office on one side of the entrance and a cigar shop on the other. Everybody smokes: women as well as men. They smoke in the street-cars, in the shops, at the opera, everywhere. I have often seen a man upon his knees in a chapel muttering his prayers with a lighted cigar in his hand.

The street-cars run in groups. Instead of starting a car every ten minutes from the terminus, three are started together every half hour. One car is never seen alone, nor two together, but always three in a row, less than half a block apart. It requires two conductors to run a car. One approaches a passenger and sells him a ticket; the second one then comes in and takes it up. In some respects it is an improvement on the bell-punch system. There are first-class cars and second-class cars. The former are of New York manufacture, and similar to those used in that city; the latter are of domestic construction, have but few windows, and look like the cabooses used on railroad freight trains. First-class fares are sometimes as high as twenty-five cents, but are more often a *medio* (six and a quarter cents), being governed by the distance. Second-class fares are always one-half the amount of first-class fares. Street-car drivers carry horns, and blow them when they approach street crossings. The conductors usually carry revolvers. Nearly everybody, in truth, carries a revolver.

Horseback riding is the national amusement, and the streets are full of horsemen, particularly in the cooler hours of the morning and evening. The proper thing to wear is a wide sombrero, very tight trousers of leather or cassimere, with rows of silver buttons up and down the outer seam, a handsomely embroidered velvet jacket, a scarlet sash, a sword, and two revolvers, not to mention spurs of marvellous size and design, and a saddle of surpassing magnificence. A Mexican caballero often spends one thousand dollars for an equestrian outfit. His saddle costs from fifty dollars to five hundred dollars, his sword fifty dollars, his silver-mounted bridle twenty-five dollars, his silver spurs as much more, the solid silver buttons on his trousers one hundred dollars, his hat fifty dollars, and the rest of his rig in proportion. The Mexican small boy, if he has wealthy parents, is mounted after a similar fashion, even to the revolver and sword. An equestrian costume for a boy of ten years can be purchased for about fifty dollars, not including saddle and bridle.

A MEXICAN CABALLERO.

The Mexican ladies do not ride any more than their sisters in the United States. Social etiquette prohibits this recreation, unless they have brothers to go with them. The señoras and señoritas take their exercise in closed carriages. You never see a phaeton or wagon in Mexico. When they go shopping they sit in their carriages and have the goods brought out to them. It is a common thing to see a row of carriages before a fashionable store with a clerk at the door of each one exhibiting silks or gloves or ribbons. In some of the stores are parlors in which a señora can sit if she likes and have the goods brought to her. None but foreigners and the common people stand at the counters and buy. Mexican merchants never classify their goods. They have no system in arranging them. Silks and cottons are indiscriminately mixed on the shelves. There is no place for anything, and nothing is ever in place. Hence shopping requires the exercise of a vast deal of patience. I went to buy a pair of gloves one day. The clerk pulled open a drawer in which were shoes, corsets, and ribbons. He found some gloves, but there being none in the box to fit, he hunted around on the shelves and in the drawers until he discovered another lot. Nor are goods ever delivered at the residences of purchasers. If your package is too bulky to carry in your hands or in your carriage it is sent to your house by a licensed carrier, similar to the district messenger boy of New York, to whom you pay a fee. Each carrier has a brass badge like a policeman's, bearing a number, and if he does not deliver the goods promptly and in good order you report him at police headquarters, where he is heavily fined. On the other hand, if he cannot find your residence, or there is a mistake in the directions, he takes the goods to police headquarters, and you can find them there, and discover the reasons why they were not delivered.

On pleasant afternoons—and except in the rainy season all afternoons are pleasant here—everybody who owns a carriage, or is able to hire one, drives on the boulevard which Maximilian made from the city to the Castle of Chapultepec, a distance of two and a half miles. As most of the carriages are closed, the scene is not so interesting as it might be, but you can occasionally catch a glimpse of a beautiful face through the carriage windows. The horses are indifferent. Some of the handsomest equipages are drawn by mules.

There are more public hacks and carriages in Mexico than in any other city in the world in proportion to its population, and few cities have worse pavements. Most of the vehicles are coupés, but there are a few victorias. There are no hansoms. The public carriages are all under police regulation, and the rates are fixed by law, according to the condition of the vehicle and the horses. Each carriage has a small tin flag attached to the top. A green flag means that you have to pay a dollar and a half an hour, for the carriage is new, the horses are good, and the harness is handsomely trimmed. A blue flag means a dollar an hour, with a little less style; a white flag, seventy-five cents. The latter class are about the toughest-looking outfits that can be found anywhere.

Each of the other sort of carriages has a footman as well as a coachman, without additional price, although generous people give him a tip to the extent of a *real* (twelve and a half cents). The footman is called a *mozo*, and acts as a sort of apprentice or private secretary to the *cochero*, or driver. When you hire a hack the *mozo* rushes off to the nearest store, looks at the clock, and brings you back a card upon which the hour is written. When you finish your ride he hands you the card again, and you pay from the time you started. On feast-days charges are doubled, and as feast-days are frequent, when all the stores are closed, the hackmen make a good thing of it. They drive in a most reckless manner, and as the pavements are rough the passengers are bounced about.

The Spaniards drink cognac and sour wines. Whiskey is not a safe beverage for the climate. American mixed drinks are not popular, and the scarcity of ice makes juleps and that sort of thing expensive. The stranger in Mexico is always very thirsty; the rapid evaporation makes the mouth and throat dry, and water furnishes only temporary relief. The most refreshing drink is lime-juice in Apollinaris water.

Pulque (pronounced *poolkee*) is the national drink, and is

NOCHE TRISTE TREE.

the fermented milk of the cactus. Eighty thousand gallons are said to be sold in Mexico every day, and double that amount on Sundays and saints' days. It is a sort of combination of starch and alcohol, looks like well-watered skim-milk, and tastes like yeast. It costs but a penny a glass, or three cents a quart, so that it is within the reach of the humblest citizen, and he drinks vast quantities of it. Five cents' worth will make a peon (as all the natives are called) as happy as a lord, and ten cents' worth will send him reeling into the arms of a policeman, who secures him an engagement to work for the Government for ten days without compensation. But it leaves no headache in the morning, and is said to be very healthful. In the moist climates one might drink large quantities without injury, but all the usual intoxicants are harmful in this altitude.

The police system of Mexico is admirable. At every street corner there is a patrolman night and day—not a patrolman either, for he never moves. He stands like a statue during the day, occasionally leaning against a lamp-post, and answers inquiries with the greatest urbanity. Whenever there is a row two or three policemen are instantly present, and if their clubs cannot suppress it they use revolvers. At night the policeman brings a lantern and a blanket. He sets the lantern in the middle of the street, and all carriages are compelled to keep to the right of the row of lanterns, which can be seen glimmering from one end of the street to the other. As long as people are passing he stands at the corner, but when things quiet down he leaves his lantern in the road, retires to a neighboring door-way, wraps his blanket around him, and lies down to pleasant dreams. As all the windows in the city of Mexico have heavy prison-like gratings before them, and all the doors are great oaken affairs that could not be knocked in without a catapult; as there are never any fires, and everybody goes to bed early, the policeman's lot is usually a happy one. He is numerous because of revolutions, and because the Government always wants to know what is going on. There is a popular belief in Mexico that no stranger ever comes to town without having his past history and future plans recorded at police headquarters. One never reads of robberies or pocket-picking, or assault and battery cases, in the city of Mexico. Common thieves have no chance there. The only disturbances are political revolutions, and the Government alone is robbed.

All the ice that is used in Mexico comes from the top of Popocatepetl. It is brought down the mountain on the backs of the natives, and then sixty miles on the cars to the city, where it is sold at wholesale for ten cents a pound. At the bar-rooms iced drinks are very expensive, and ice is seldom seen anywhere else. The people all use a jug of porous earthenware made by the Indians in which water is kept cool by rapid evaporation. The stranger should always squeeze a little lime-juice into his glass before he drinks water, to get a pleasant flavor, and escape evil effects from alkaline properties.

From the top of the cathedral spire you can see the entire city, and the most striking feature of the view is the absence of chimneys. There is not a chimney in all Mexico; not a stove, nor a grate, nor a furnace. All the cooking is done with charcoal in Dutch ovens, and, while the gas is sometimes offensive, one soon becomes used to it. Coal costs sixteen dollars a ton, and wood sixteen dollars a cord. All the coal was formerly imported from England, but now comes from Cohahuila, and the wood is all brought from the mountains.

As formerly, bull-fighting is at present the most popular amusement in Mexico, and a matador is more distinguished in the eyes of the common people than a prima donna or a president. The Mexican Government has of late years become humanized to the extent of prohibiting these brutal spectacles within the city limits, and they now take place at what is called the "Plaza de Toros," or Bull Park, on the plains five or six miles from the city. Here the people gather on every Sunday and saint-day to witness the butchery of three or four bulls and twice as many horses, under the official patronage of the Governor of the State, who always is present with his family and official staff, and from a decorated platform directs the entertainment, giving his orders through a trumpeter.

Back of the Castle of Chapultepec is the battle-field of Molino del Rey (The Mill of the King), where General Scott met stubborn resistance when he attempted to enter Mexico, but drove the Mexicans up the hill. The old earthworks erected by the latter still stand as they were at the time of the battle, and are usually visited by tourists. On the plain beyond the battle-field stands an amphitheatre enclosed within a massive wall of adobe—the mud bricks which are used for building material in all the rainless region of this continent. The amphitheatre is arranged in the usual form, except that the shady side is divided up into boxes to be occupied by the grandees, while the sunny side has plain board benches for the barefooted Castilians whose mild eyes and pathetic deference give no key to the cruelty of which their race has been guilty. The centre of the amphitheatre is enclosed by a board wall, perhaps eight feet in height, surmounted at a point two feet higher by a heavy cable strung through stalwart iron rods. The top of this fence appeared to be the favorite eyrie from which to survey the field, and upon it for the entire length sat a row of urchins, with here and there a bearded man, all poised upon the edge, with their legs hanging over into the bull-ring, and their arms clinging to the rope.

The Governor, a tall, swarthy man, with a wide sombrero, mustache and goatee, the very picture of the "haughty Don," sat in a decorated box, with the flag of his country profusely draped around him. He had two aides-de-camp, his three children, and an orderly, who with a trumpet sounded a blast now and then to convey his excellency's desires. We happened luckily to have the adjoining box, from which we could watch him closely and hear his comments upon the performances.

The audience was very large, and composed of all classes, from the proud Castilian who came behind his four-in-hand, with a retinue of outriders, to the poor peon who had been saving his scanty earnings for a week, and walked five miles to witness the ghastly spectacle. There were perhaps ten thousand people, and one-fifth of them were women in silks and satins, in jewels and rare laces, who hid their eyes behind their fans when the spectacle was too repulsive, but encouraged the matadors with applause at the end of each act.

A band of music played lively airs, and played them well, to entertain the people until the Governor came, whose presence being recognized, the people gave a cordial cheer by way of welcome. Then the herald in the Governor's box blew a signal which sounded like the "water call" of the United

THE PICADORS.

TEASING THE BULL.

States Cavalry, the doors of the pit were opened, and in marched a dozen or so of matadors, in the same sort of jackets and breeches which they wear in the pictures of Spanish life so familiar to all. Each wore a plumed hat, a scarlet sash, a poniard, and the gold lace upon the black velvet showed their lithe and supple forms to advantage. They looked as Don Juan looks in the opera, while the leader, Bernardo Cavino, "del decano de los toreros," I was a veritable Figaro, in appearance at least. Each carried a scarlet cloak upon his arm, and in the other hand a pikestaff. Behind them came a troop of eight horsemen upon gayly caparisoned steeds, with the usual amount of silver and leather trappings in which the Mexicans delight. The procession tailed up with a team of four mules hitched abreast, dragging a whiffletree and a long rope. These, we are told, were for the purpose of dragging out the dead. The cavalcade made a circuit of the amphitheatre, like the grand entrée at a circus, and upon reaching the Governor's box stopped, saluted him, and received a short address in Spanish, which probably was simply one of approval and congratulation at their fine appearance. There was a rack in front of the Governor's box upon which hung several rows of darts, gayly decorated with paper rosettes and paper fringes of gold and other brilliant tints. Upon these racks the matadors hung their plumed hats, and stood a while to give the ladies and gentlemen of the audience an opportunity to see and admire.

THE ENCORE.

The gay horsemen then rode out, and were followed by the mules, but the horsemen soon returned upon an entirely different style of animals—poor, broken-down, lean, lame, and mangy hacks, which looked as if they had been turned out of some street-car stable as bait for vultures. They were covered with a sort of leathern armor, and this concealed their fleshless ribs; but nothing could disguise the shambling and uncertain gait with which they painfully ambled across the arena under the savage spurring of their riders. They managed to get across, and that was all. The first set of horses were intended for show, and the second for slaughter. Public opinion appears to demand that something besides a bull be sacrificed, and the matadors not being amiable enough to afford this gratification, a pair of animated clothes-racks are turned in to be gored. The poor beasts are blindfolded, which is about the only humane feature of the show.

The Governor's herald gave another blast, at which the entire audience, who were on the *qui vive*, arose and shouted. A door across the pit opened, and a large, clumsy, long-horned bull poked his head out into the arena. The crowd yelled, and matadors posed at different parts of the ring—ten of them—and the two horsemen pretended to get ready for the fray. The bull looked up, the only frightened being in the entire multitude. The posters described him as "a valiant and arrogant animal." He was a fine piece of beef, but he didn't want to fight. Somebody behind spurred him, and he ran into the ring. The doors were closed behind him, and there was no way of escape. He plunged one way, but was met by three matadors, who flapped their cloaks in his eyes; he turned in the other direction, but was met by three more; then he made a bolt between them, and darting towards the other side of the ring, gave a great leap, as if he would go over the eight-foot wall. Of course he failed, but he struck the planks with tremendous force, tumbling forty or fifty fellows who were perched on the top into a heap on the other side. It was the only amusing feature of the whole show. There was a grand crash, a loud howl, forty or fifty pairs of legs were in the air, and the audience shouted with laughter. The bull turned around frightened at the noise, ran to the other side of the ring, and sought in vain for a place to get out. Then one of the horsemen rode up in front of the animal and jammed a spear into his face. The bull plunged at his assailant, bellowing with pain, lifted the poor horse upon his horns, raised him from the ground, and threw him with great force against the side of the arena.

The rider, expecting the attack, was prepared for it, and leaped with great agility from the saddle just as the two animals came in contact. There was very little left of the horse. There was not much of him when he was dragged into the ring, but the long horns of the bull penetrated his bowels and tore them out. The bull jams the horse against the planks, two, three, four times, and then withdraws. The horse lies a bleeding, disembowelled mass, and the crowd cheers the dreadful spectacle.

The bull having given up all idea of escape, plunges at everything he sees, and the second horse is ridden up before him. No attempt is made to get the animal out of the way. He was brought there to be slaughtered, and took his turn. Both horses having been disposed of, and the bull being completely exhausted, the bugle gives the signal, the matadors enter the arena, and tease him with their scarlet cloaks. At frequent intervals around the ring are placed heavy planks, behind which the matadors run for protection when they were pursued. The bull had no chance at all; he was there simply to be teased and killed by slow degrees. One matador more agile than the rest baits the animal with his lance, and when the bull turns upon him, vaults over the down-turned horns by resting his lance upon the ground. Then they bring out the ornamented darts, and thrust them into the bull's hide. The animal jumps and plunges with pain, and tries to shake them off, but the barbs cling to the hide, and the more he struggles the farther they penetrate the flesh. His shoulders are covered with them, and the crimson blood trickles down his sides. He stands panting with distress, his tongue hanging out, and is thoroughly exhausted.

MEXICAN BEGGAR.

The Governor's trumpet sounds the bull's death-warrant. It means that the cruel sport has lasted long enough, and the chief matador comes forward with a red blanket and a sword. He approaches the bull, and flaps the blanket in his eyes; the animal plunges at him, and with great dexterity the matador whirls and thrusts the sword into the animal's heart. The bull plunges with pain, and throws the sword out of his body into the air. He staggers and falls upon the ground, the chief matador runs up, pierces his brain with a poniard, and the mules are brought in to drag the dead animals out. The band plays, the crowd cheers, and the first act is over. The matadors bow to the Governor, bow to the crowd, and rest, while a clown dances in the ring to amuse the people in the interim. Pretty soon the trumpet blows again, two more old crow-baits are ridden in, and another bull is brought from the corral. The same scenes recur; the horses are always killed, but the men are seldom injured. Four bulls are usually disposed of each Sunday afternoon before the appetite for blood is satiated.

This cruel sport in Mexico is in its decadence. It grew out of the lack of other entertainment. Until two years ago there was no horse-racing in Mexico, and this class of sport is unknown outside of the capital. The young men are not allowed to visit the girls, are not permitted to walk with them in the parks, and have, in short, no amusements but billiards, cock-fighting, and bull-baiting. The exodus of foreigners into the Republic will break many of the barriers down. While the "Gringos," as foreigners are called, generally conform to the customs of the country, they refuse to accept all of them, and the Mexican people are gradually tending towards a more modern civilization.

The ancient volcano, Popocatepetl, has got into the courts. Not that it has been bodily transported into the halls of litigation, but it is the subject of a novel suit at law. For many years General Ochoa has been the owner of the volcano, the highest point of land in North America, together with all its appurtenances. The crater contains a fine quality of sulphur, which the general has been extracting, giving employment to Indians who cared to stay down in the vaporous old crater. The property was at one time fairly profitable; the volcano was, some time ago, mortgaged to Mr. Carlos Recamier, who brings suit of foreclosure. The papers have been joking about the matter, some asking what Mr. Recamier intends to do with his volcano when he gets legal possession. He has been solemnly warned that the law forbids the carrying out of the country ancient monuments and objects of historical interest.

Good-Friday is observed as a sort of May festival. The *Paseo de las Flores* (Flower Promenade) is held along the Viga, the picturesque canal which stretches away between willows and poplars to the far-famed Floating Gardens of the ancient Aztecs. The scene along the historic causeway is astonishing to foreigners, and as charmingly peculiar as it is typical of a poetic and pleasure-loving people. For miles along the tree-lined avenue a constant procession of vehicles, horsemen, and pedestrians pack the space between green booths on either side, while the canal is crowded with canoes and Venetian-like gondolas. Everything imaginable on wheels is seen—the stately closed carriage of the Mexican millionaire, open barouches, coupés, victorias, dog-carts, wagonettes, even velocipedes and tricycles, while thousands of horsemen gallop gayly between.

The festivities are kept up, though in diminishing scale, until late Sunday night. During all these days the shrill, discordant rattle of ten thousand *matracas* rises above the babel of human voices. These little instruments of torture are made of tin, iron, ivory, wood, even of gold and silver, and in all imaginable shapes. Some are in the form of humming-birds, birds-of-paradise, chickens, parrots; others are like gridirons, frying-pans, musical instruments, fruits, flowers, or reptiles. Everybody must have one, from the dignified grandparent to the baby in arms, and by twirling them rapidly a most unearthly, rasping, grinding sound is produced by wooden springs inside. The noise is intended to typify and ridicule the cries of the Jews, "Crucify him! crucify him!" as they followed Christ to His death.

On Easter-Sunday the strangest of all Mexican ceremonies takes place in the burning of the traitor. During all Holy-week men are continually perambulating the streets, holding high above the heads of the multitude long poles encircled by hoops, upon which are suspended the most grotesque figures, in every conceivable color, shape, and degree of deformity, and all with horns and crooked backs and twisted limbs. These are filled with fire-crackers, the mustache forming the fuse, and millions of them are annually exploded. Many are life-size, some having faces to represent politicians who are unpopular at the time. Some are hung by the neck to wires stretched across the streets, or to the balconies of houses. Every horse-car and railroad engine and donkey-cart is decked with one, and even every mule-driver has one or more tied on his breast. At ten o'clock on Easter-Sunday, when the cathedral bells peal forth in commemoration of Christ's resurrection, they are all touched off at once, and the air is filled with flying traitors everywhere over the length and breadth of Mexico.

ON MARKET-DAY.

SUNDAY AT SANTA ANITA.

An American who is married in Mexico finds that he must be three times married: twice in Spanish and once more in Spanish or English, as he prefers, besides having a public notice of his intention of marriage placed on a bulletin-board for twenty days before the ceremony. This is the law. The public notice can be avoided by the payment of a sum of money, but a residence of one month is necessary. The three ceremonies are the contract of marriage, the civil marriage—the only marriage recognized by law since 1858—and the usual, but not obligatory, Church service. The first two must take place before a judge, and in the presence of at least four witnesses and the American consul. The contract of marriage is a statement of names, ages, lineage, business, and residence of contracting parties. The civil marriage is the legal form of marriage. These ceremonies are necessarily in Spanish. Most weddings are confirmed by a church-service.

A MEXICAN BELLE.

At a Mexican church wedding it is the custom for the groom to pass coins through the hand of the bride, as typical of the fact that she is to keep the money of the household. A very pretty feature, as the couple kneel at the altar with lighted candles in their hands—an emblem of the light of the Christian faith—is the placing of a silken scarf around the shoulders of the bridal couple, and then the binding them together with a yoke of silver cord placed around the necks of both. That "thy people shall be my people" is an accepted fact, for it is a common thing for members of the bride's family to take up their permanent residence with the husband, and make it their home.

One of the most singular, and, to the foreigner, most interesting of the institutions of Mexico is the *Monte de Piedad*. The phrase means "The Mountain of Mercy." It is the name given to what is in reality a great national pawnshop, which has branches in all the cities of the country, is exclusively under Government control, and is not managed, as in the United States, by guileless Hebrew children. The central office of the Monte de Piedad occupies the building known as the Palace of Cortez, which stands on the site of the ancient Palace of Montezuma, on the Plaza Mayor. It was founded in 1775 by Conde de Regla, the owner of very rich

CACTUS, AND WOMAN KNEADING TORTILLAS.

mines, who endowed it in the sum of three hundred thousand dollars. His charitable purpose was to enable the poor of the city of Mexico to obtain loans on pledges of all kinds of articles, and for very low rates of interest. He thus relieved the poorer classes from usurious rates of interest which had been previously charged them by rapacious private pawnbrokers. At first no interest was charged, the borrower only being asked, when he redeemed his pledge, to give something for the carrying on of the charitable work which the institution had in hand. But as this benevolence was greatly abused, it was found necessary to charge a rate of interest which was very low, and yet sufficient to yield a revenue equal to necessary expenses. The affairs of this institution have been wisely managed, and it has been kept true to the purpose of its benevolent founder. When pledges come to be sold, if they bring a price greater than the original valuation, the difference is given back to the original owners. The Monte de Piedad has survived all revolutions, and its ministry of relief to the sufferers by these revolutions and other misfortunes has been incalculably great and blessed. Its average general loans on pledges amount to nearly a million dollars, and the borrowers whom it yearly accommodates number from forty to fifty thousand. From the time when it was founded, in 1775, down to 1886—a little more than the first century of its existence—it made loans to 2,232,611 persons, amounting in the aggregate to nearly $32,000,000, and during the same period it gave away nearly $150,000 in charity.

There is nothing in which the Mexican character appears to better advantage than in the provisions made for the sick and unfortunate. There are in the city of Mexico alone ten or a dozen hospitals, some of which are large, well endowed and equipped, and managed in a way to compare favorably with the best appointed hospitals in any country. This for a city of three hundred thousand inhabitants is a more liberal provision than many larger cities in our own country have. A lying-in hospital was founded by the Empress Carlotta, who, after her return to Europe, sent the sum of six thousand dollars for its support. Besides the hospitals there is a foundling asylum capable of accommodating two hundred inmates: an asylum for the poor, which is a very large and important charity; a correctional school; an industrial school for orphans, having thirteen hundred scholars; an industrial school for women; another for men; schools for deaf-mutes and for the blind; and an asylum for beggars.

The Church of England has been established in Mexico for twelve or fifteen years, having been induced to hold services there by the large number of English residents in the city; but no missionary work has been done by that denomination. The Presbyterian Board of Foreign Missions several years ago commenced to labor in the Republic under the patronage of Diaz, who was then President, and who gave them substantial

FIRST PROTESTANT CHURCH IN MEXICO.

encouragement. Among other things, he presented the American Board with an old Catholic church, where the school is now held daily, and a printing-office, for the purpose of the publication of a weekly newspaper and religious literature, is carried on. There are now at work in Mexico six Protestant clergymen and two lady missionaries from the United States, twenty-four regularly ordained Mexican ministers, six native licentiates, and three native helpers. Seventy-five congregations have been organized, and meet for worship every Sunday, and the number of native members is about three thousand. There is also a Theological Seminary, with two professors from the United States and one native instructor, having a total attendance of twenty-seven young men preparing for the ministry. Fourteen of these are studying theology, and thirteen are in the preparatory department. There is also a school for girls, with two American and one native lady teacher, which has a large attendance. A missionary paper called *El Faro* (The Light-house) is conducted at the Theological Seminary. The work is rapidly increasing, seven churches having been organized in 1885 and as many more in 1886.

THE FIRST CHRISTIAN PULPIT IN AMERICA—
TLAXCALA.

The missionaries are very often interfered with by the country people, instigated by the priests, and several of the native preachers have been shot or injured. These attacks have usually been attributed to highwaymen, but after investigation have proven to be the work of assassins employed by the priests. One white missionary was murdered some two years ago while passing along the road at night, but his assassins were brought to speedy justice, and wholesome examples made of them.

In July, 1885, the Romanists of a small town in the interior entered a Protestant church, carried off all of the valuables, smashed the organ into fragments, emptied kerosene oil upon the benches, and set the place on fire. The furniture of the interior was destroyed, but the walls of the building, being of adobe, and the roof of tiles, the house was not destroyed. For some weeks afterwards several shots were fired at people who were on their way to evening service, and a missionary was attacked in the dark by armed assassins who would have been murdered but for the courageous use of his revolver. Subsequently all the other churches in the neighborhood were similarly treated, and when appeals were made to the local authorities for protection, and for the punishment of those who had committed the outrages, it was decided that it was the work of highwaymen, and a reward was offered for the arrest of the perpetrators. This opinion was thought to be a subterfuge, and it is believed that the authorities were in sympathy with the acts.

The matter was carried to President Diaz, who ordered an investigation, and promised an effectual protection to the missionaries wherever there was need of it. Several days after he issued a proclamation which was addressed to the commandants of the several departments of the Republic, and ordered that it should be read before the troops on parade, and kept posted in conspicuous places for the information of the public. In this proclamation, among other things, President Diaz said: "These acts of intolerance, apart from their injustice, are the data by which people of other lands judge of the nature and degree of our civilization, and for this reason especially I command that you give especial attention to prevent such outrages, and to secure to all believers in any religion the liberty which the constitution and laws concede to them. Catholics shall be protected in the same way as Protestants, and those who attempt to interfere with the exercise of any religious ceremony shall be punished severely. If troops are needed to carry this order into effect, they will be supplied upon request."

FONT IN OLD CHURCH OF SAN FRANCISCO.

GUATEMALA CITY.

THE CAPITAL OF GUATEMALA.

GUATEMALA has had three capitals, all called Guatemala City, since the Conquest. The first was founded by Alvarado in 1524, and buried under a flood of sand and water in 1541. The second capital was founded the same year, a few miles eastward of the old site, and was destroyed by an earthquake in 1773. The present capital is the largest and by far the finest city in Central America, and is more modern in its appearance than any other. It is situated in what is called the *tierra templada*, or temperate zone, about forty-five hundred feet above the level of the sea, at the northern extremity of an extensive and beautiful plain, and has a climate that is very attractive. The plain upon which it stands is by no means as fertile as many other portions of the country, and is deficient in water. The supply which is used by the people is brought for a distance of fifteen miles in an aqueduct, which has the honor of having been described by Charles Dickens in his sketch of "The Flying Dutchman." These water-works were commenced as far back as 1832, and involved an expenditure of over two million dollars, but without them the city could not have prospered.

Guatemala City is not favorably situated for commerce, as it is a considerable distance from both seas, and is shut out from the most productive portions of the country by walls of mountains. The city is laid out in quadrilateral form, and formerly was surrounded by a great wall through which it was entered by gates opening in various directions. It covers a vast area of territory for a place of its population, as the houses, like those of other Central American cities, are very

VIEW OF GUATEMALA CITY.

large, and enclose attractive gardens. During the last twelve years, under the presidency of General Barrios, Guatemala has made rapid progress, and but for the low and commonplace appearance of the houses would resemble the more modern cities of Europe. All the streets are paved, with gutters in the centre, and have broad paths of flag-stones on each side for foot-passengers.

Antigua Guatemala, the old capital, thirty miles to the westward of the new, is still a place of considerable importance, and in its time was far superior to the present capital in size and appearance. Previous to its destruction in 1773 there were but two cities on the American hemisphere which compared with it in population, wealth, and magnificence. These were the City of Mexico, and Lima, Peru. New York was then a commercial infant, Boston a mere village, and Chicago yet unknown. But here was a city in which were centred the ecclesiastical and political interests of the Central American colonies, where millions of dollars were spent in erecting churches, convents, and monasteries, which covered acres of ground, and beautiful residences whose shattered portals still bear the escutcheons of the noble families who ruled the city and cultivated the plantations of coffee, sugar, and cochineal.

Antigua, as it is now called (properly old Guatemala), was not only the scene of wealth and influence, and the commercial metropolis of the country, but the home of the most learned men of all Spanish America, the seat of great schools of theology, science, and art, for two hundred years the Athens and Rome of the New World, the residence of the university, as well as the Inquisition, and the headquarters of those untiring apostles of evil, the

Jesuits. The population is said to have been about one hundred and fifty thousand. It is not known that a census was ever taken, and this estimate is based upon the size of the city and number of inhabitants its ruined walls could have contained. It is situated in the centre of a great valley, between the twin volcanoes Agua and Fuego; and as the old Spanish chroniclers used to say, had Paradise on one side and the Inferno on the other. The beauty of its position and the richness of the adjacent country, the grandeur of the scenery that surrounds it, have called forth the most extravagant admiration from travellers, and have made it the theme of the native poets. Mr. Stephens, who wrote the most elaborate sketch of Central America we have, some forty years ago, says that Antigua Guatemala is surrounded by more natural beauty than any location he had ever seen during the whole course of his travels. The city is watered by a stream bearing the poetical name of El Rio Pensativo, which encircles the mountains and winds about through the plain in most graceful curves. It has for its tributaries many rivulets that water the plain, and finally falls over a cataract and flows through the valley below to the sea.

This valley was formerly famous for the culture of cochineal, and much wealth was derived from this source before aniline dyes drove it out of the market. The cochineal is a little insect which clings to the leaves of a species of the cactus, known as the nopal, and in the natural state the white hair upon its body causes the leaves to look as if they were covered with hoar-frost. Before the rainy season sets in the leaves of the nopal are cut close to the ground and hung up under a shed for protection. Then they are scraped with a dull knife, and the insects are killed by being baked in a hot oven or dipped into boiling water. If the first process is used, the insects become a brownish color, and furnish a scarlet or crimson dye. Those killed by baking are black, and are used for blue and purple dyes. They are then packed up in little casks, covered with hides to keep out the moisture, and sent to market, being valued at several dollars a pound. The great part of the expense is due to the time and trouble required to detach the insects from the nopal, two ounces being considered a fair result of a day's labor; and it is said that it requires seventy thousand to make a pound. When they are dried they look like coarse powder.

The first capital was founded by Alvarado, the Conqueror. The exploits of Cortez in Mexico had become known among

RUINS OF THE OLD PALACE AT ANTIGUA GUATEMALA.

the Indian tribes in the south, and the native kings sent an embassy to him offering their allegiance to the crown of Spain. Cortez received the embassy with distinction, and sent Alvarado back with them to take possession of the country. In 1523 Alvarado left the City of Mexico with three hundred Spanish soldiers and a large body of natives, and nearly a year later arrived at a place at the foot of the volcano Antigua, called by the Indians Almolonga, meaning in their language "a spring of water." On the 25th of July, 1524, the festival of St. James, the patron saint of Spain, Alvarado, under a tree which is still standing, assembled his horsemen, the Mexican Indians who had accompanied him, and as many of the natives of the country as could crowd around, when the chaplain, Juan Godinez, said mass, invoking the protection of the apostle, and christening the city he intended to build there with the name of San Diego de los Cabeleleros—the City of St. James, the Gentleman. After these religious services, Alvarado assumed authority as governor, and appointed his subordinates.

For fifteen years thousands of Indians were kept at work building the city. A church was the first structure raised; but in September, 1541, there came a calamity which entirely destroyed the place, and buried more than half the inhabitants under the ruins, among whom was the Donna Beatrice de la Queba, the wife of Alvarado. It had rained incessantly for three days, and on the fourth the fury of the wind, the incessant lightning and dreadful thunder, were indescribable. At two o'clock in the morning the earthquake shocks became so violent that the people were unable to stand. Shortly after an enormous body of water rushed down from the mountain, forcing with it large pieces of rock, trees, and entirely overwhelming the town with an avalanche of earth and ashes.

It has generally been assumed, and is believed by the people, that this flow of water was a real eruption, and for that reason the volcano was named Agua. The theory of some scientists is, that the water flowed from an accumulation of rain and snow in the extinct crater, the walls of which were broken through by the pressure during the earthquake. Such a thing is not only doubtful, but almost impossible; and unless the situation of the crater has changed, there is no evidence of it. Any torrent of water cast from the crater would have gone down on the other side of the mountain, and there are ashes upon the slope near the summit which must have lain there for hundreds of years. About three thousand feet from the summit there is evidence of a terrible struggle between a storm and the earth. Great trees were uprooted, rocks were hurled from their places, and a vast fissure is seen, fifteen or sixteen hundred feet deep, extending directly to the buried city, growing in depth and width until it reaches the valley. From this gorge came the mass of ashes and sand which buried the first Guatemala, like Sodom and Pompeii, and it must have been carried down by a water-spout or some agent of that sort.

The cathedral was buried to the roof; but years afterwards, when the sand was dug away, it was found uninjured, with all its contents preserved, because of the interposition of St. James. The palace, being in the immediate path of the torrent, was undermined and overthrown by its force. The ruins, half covered by sand, are the only remaining evidences of the massive grandeur of the building, one of whose angles points in the direction from which the water came. Many excavations have been made in search of treasure, as Alvarado had the reputation of keeping there stores of silver and gold. They have resulted in no remunerative discovery, but have disclosed some fine carvings, wonderful frescos, and other evidences of the beauty which the place is said to have possessed. Over its ruins to-day stands a low-browed house, with an inscription over its door reading, "*Complimetaria Escula Para Ninos*"—A Free School for Girls.

The tree under which tradition says Alvarado and his soldiers first camped, and where Padre Godinez sanctified the city by religious services, is still standing. When I visited it, the most noticeable things about the place were a wagon made by the Studebaker Brothers, of South Bend, Indiana, and several empty beer bottles, bearing the brand of a Chicago brewer.

ALVARADO'S TREE.

The fountain of Almolonga, which first induced Alvarado to select this spot as the site of his capital, is a large natural basin of clear and beautiful water shaded by trees. It has been walled up and divided off into apartments for bathing purposes and laundry work; and here all the women of the town come to wash their clothing. The old church was dug out of the sand, and is still standing. In one corner is a chamber filled with the skulls and bones that were excavated from the ruins. The old priest who was responsible for the spiritual welfare of the people showed us over the ruins, and told us stories of Alvarado and his piety. He said that the pictures, hangings, and altar ornaments in the church were the same that were placed there in Alvarado's time, and unlocking a great iron chest he showed us communion vessels, incense urns, crosses, and banners of solid gold and silver. Among other things was a magnificent crown of gold, which was presented to the church by one of the Philips of Spain. It was originally studded with diamonds, emeralds, and other jewels, but they have been removed, and the settings are now empty. Yankee-like, we tried to buy some of these treasures, for they were the richest I had seen at any place, but the old priest refused all pecuniary temptations, and crossed himself reverently as he put the sacred vessels away. The only people who patronize this church are the Indians, who, to the number of two or three thousand, live in the neighborhood, and the ancient vessels are never used in these days, but are kept as curiosities.

ANCIENT ARCHES.

The second city of Guatemala was built about three miles

THE OLD AND THE NEW.

from the original one, a little farther down, and nearly at the foot of the volcano Fuego. Both of these ruined cities offer the greatest attractions to the antiquarian, but few have ever visited them, and very little has been written of either place. In Antigua, as the second Guatemala is called, is the most extensive collection of ruins that can be found in this hemisphere. From a tower of the cathedral one can see on either side the ruins of many churches, monasteries, convents, and miles of public and private residences, large and costly; some with walls still standing, liberally ornamented with stucco or carved stone, but roofless, without doors or windows, and trees growing within them.

The ruins of forty-five churches can be counted, and nearly every one of them had a convent or monastery attached. Some cover several acres, and have cells for five or six hundred monks or nuns. Several of the churches are as large as the cathedral in New York. They are not so much ruined but that their outlines can be traced, showing the noble architecture and costly work by which they were built. The force of the earthquake can be seen by broken pillars of solid stone five or six feet in diameter; walls of ten or fifteen feet thickness were shaken into fragments, and buildings with foundations of stone as deep and solid as those of the Capitol at Washington were crumbled into dust. About ten per cent. of the houses have been rebuilt, but the remainder are still in ruins. The inhabitants occupy the old residences that have been restored, but appear to know little of the place as it was before the earthquake. They have forgotten what their fathers told them, and no attempt has ever been made to secure a permanent and accurate record of the antique conditions.

In the centre of the town is a great plaza, which, as usual in all of the Central American capitals, is surrounded by public buildings and the cathedral. In the centre stands a noble fountain, which is surrounded every morning by market-women selling the fruit and vegetables of the country. The old palace has been partially restored, and displays upon its front the armorial bearing granted by the Emperor Charles the Fifth to the loyal and noble capital in which the Viceroy of Central America lived. Upon the crest of the building is a statue of the Apostle St. James on horseback, clad in armor, and brandishing a sword. The majestic cathedral, 300 feet long, 120 feet broad, 110 feet high, and lighted by fifty windows, has been restored, and within it services are held every morning, the faithful being called to mass by a peon pounding upon a large and resonant gong.

HOW THE OLD TOWN LOOKS NOW.

Without warning, on a Sunday night in 1773, the disaster came, and the proudest city in the New World was forever humbled. The roof of the cathedral fell; all the other churches were shaken to pieces; the great monasteries, which had been standing for centuries, and were thought to be useful for many centuries more, crumbled in an instant. The dead were never counted, and the wounded died from lack of relief. Those who escaped fled to the mountains, and the earthquake continued so violent that few returned to the ruins for many days. The volcano, whose single shudder shook down the accumulated grandeur of two hundred and fifty years, has since been almost idle, but is smoking constantly, and emitting sulphurous vapors which tell of the furnace beneath. As if satisfied with its moment's work, it stands at rest, tempting man to try again to build another magnificent city, as firm as he can make it, for another test of strength. The people, like the dwellers over the buried Herculaneum, seem to have no fear of ruin or disaster, because, as very respectable citizens will tell you, the volcano which did the damage has since been blessed by a priest.

FRAGMENT OF A RUINED MONASTERY.

In one of the old monasteries, established by the Franciscan Friars, is a tree from which four different kinds of fruit may be plucked at one time—the orange, lemon, lime, and a sweet fruit called by the Spanish the limone. It was a horticultural experiment of the Friars many hundred years ago, and still stands as a monument of their experimental industry. It was they who first introduced the cultivation of coffee from Arabia into these countries, and who discovered the use of that curious insect the cochineal. The latter used to be an extensive article of commerce, but the cheapness of the aniline dyes has driven it out of the market. Now it is cultivated only for local consumption, and is extensively used by the natives, whose cotton and woollen fabrics are gayly dyed in colors that will endure any amount of water or sunshine. Thirty years ago two million tons were exported annually, but now very little goes out of the country.

JOSÉ RUFINO BARRIOS.

The progress of Guatemala during the last twelve years, and the advancement of the country towards a modern standard of civilization, has been very rapid, and it is due to the energy and determination of one man, José Rufino Barrios, who stands next, if not equal, to Morazan as a patriot and benefactor of his country. President Barrios studied the conditions of social and political economy in the United States and European nations, and used a remarkable amount of energy to introduce them among his own people. There has been no man in Central or South America with more progressive ideas or more ardent ambition for the advancement of his countrymen.

The prevailing opinion of President Barrios is that he was a brutal ruffian. He drove out of the country many political opponents who occupied themselves by telling stories of his cruelty, some of which were doubtless true. The methods which he habitually used to keep the people in order would not be tolerated in the more civilized lands. But in estimating his true character, the good he accomplished should be considered as well as the evil. Until the history of Central America shall be written years hence, when the mind can reflect calmly and impartially upon the scenes of this decade, when public benefits can be accurately measured with individual errors, and the strides of progress in material development can be justly estimated, the true character of General Barrios will not be understood or appreciated even by his own countrymen. Like all vigorous and progressive men, like all men of strong character and forcible measures, he had bitter, vindictive enemies, who would have assassinated him had they been able to do so, and repeatedly tried it. There was nothing too harsh for them to say of him, living or dead, no cruelties too barbarous for them to accuse him of, no revenge too severe for them to visit upon him or his memory. But, on the other hand, people who did not cherish a spirit of revenge, who had no political ambition, and no schemes to be disconcerted, who are interested in the development of Central America, and are enjoying the benefits of the progress Guatemala has made, regard Barrios as the best friend and ablest leader, the wisest ruler his country ever had, and would have been glad if his life could have been prolonged and his power extended over the entire continent. They are willing to concede to him not only honorable motives, but the worthy ambition of trying to lift his country to the level with the most advanced nations of the earth. Ten more years of the same progress that Guatemala made under Barrios would place her upon a par with any of the States of Europe, or those of the United States. While he did not furnish a government of the people, by the people, it was a government for the people, provided and administered by a man of remarkable ability, independence, ambition, and extraordinary pride. While his iron hand crushed all opposition, and held a power that yielded to nothing, he was, nevertheless, generous to the poor, lenient to those who would submit to him, and ready to do anything to improve the condition of the people or promote their welfare.

FRANCISCO MORAZAN.

That a man of his ancestry and early associations should have brought this republic to the condition in which he left it when he died is remarkable. Without education himself, he enacted a law requiring the attendance at school of all children between the ages of eight and fourteen years, and rigorously enforced it. People who refused to obey this law, or sent their children to private schools, or educated them at home, were compelled to pay a heavy fine for the privilege. He established a university at Guatemala City and free schools in every city of the republic, to the support of which a larger proportion of the public revenues were appropriated than in any one of the United States or the nations of Europe. He founded hospitals, asylums, and other institutions of charity with his own means, or supported them by appropriations from the public treasury. He compelled physicians to be educated properly before they were allowed to practise; he punished crime so severely that it was almost unknown; he regulated the sale of liquors, so that a drunken man was never seen upon the streets; he enforced the observance of the Sabbath by closing the stores and market-places, which in other Spanish-American republics are always open, and was active for the material as for the moral welfare of the people. During the twelve years he was in power the country made greater progress, and the citizens enjoyed greater prosperity, than during any period of all the three centuries and a half of previous history.

His ambition to reunite the five Central American republics in a confederacy was not successful; but it was inspired by a desire to do for the neighboring States what he had done for Guatemala. His ambition was for the advancement and development of Central America; and while the means he used cannot be entirely approved, his purpose should be applauded. His crusade was quite as important in the civilization of this continent as the bloody work England attempted to accomplish in Egypt and the Soudan. He was better than his race, was far in advance of his generation, and while he did not succeed in lifting his people entirely out of the ignorance and degradation in which they were kept by the priests, what he did do cannot but result in the permanent good, not only of Guatemala, but of the nations which surround that republic.

CHURCH OF SAN FRANCESCA, GUATEMALA LA ANTIGUA.

After the independence of the Central American colonies the priests ruled the country. Their excesses awakened a spirit of opposition, which finally culminated in a revolution. The famous Morazan became dictator, and might have been successful but for a decree he issued abolishing the convents and monasteries, and confiscating the entire property of the Church. This was in 1843. Led by the priests, the people rose in rebellion; but Morazan retained his power until an unknown man, tall, dark, and blood-thirsty, came out of the mountains—an Indian without a name, who could neither read nor write, whose occupation had been that of a swineherd, like Pizarro, who had graduated in the profession of a bandit, and led a gang of murderous outlaws in the mountains. Urged by a greed for plunder, this remarkable man, Rafael Carera, came out from his stronghold and joined the Church party in their war against the Government.

His successes as a guerilla were so great that what was a small, independent band became the main army of the opposition, and he led a horde of disorganized plunderers towards the capital. The priests called him the

Chosen of God, and attributed to him the divinely inspired mission of restoring the Church to power. The pious churchmen rushed to his standard, and fought by the side and under the command of the savage, whose only motive was plunder. He drove Morazan into Costa Rica, and proclaimed himself Dictator. The Church party were amazed at the arrogance of the bandit, but had to submit, and he soon developed into a full-fledged tyrant, ruling over Guatemala until his death for a period of thirty years.

When Carera died there was no man to take his place, and the Church party began to decay. The Liberals gathered force and began a revolution. In their ranks was an obscure young man from the borders of Mexico, from a valley which produced Juarez, the liberator of Mexico, Diaz, the president of that republic, and other famous men. He began to show military skill and force of character, and when the Church party was overthrown and the Liberal leader was proclaimed President, Rufino Barrios became the general of the army. He soon resigned, however, and returned to his coffee plantation on the borders of Mexico. But the revival of the Church party shortly after caused him to return to military life, and when the Liberal president died, he was, in 1873, chosen his successor.

ONE OF FIFTY-SEVEN RUINED MONASTERIES.

From that date until 1885 there was but one man in Guatemala, and he was Barrios. He began his career by adopting the policy that Morazan had failed to enforce. He expelled the monks and nuns from the country, confiscated the Church property, robbed the priests of their power, and, like Juarez in Mexico, liberated the people from a servitude under which they had suffered since the original settlement of the colonies. Then he visited the United States and Europe to study the science of government; sent men abroad to be educated, at Government expense, in the arts and sciences and political economy, and upon their return placed them in subordinate positions under him. He offered the most generous inducements to immigrants, and the country filled up with agricultural settlers, merchants, and mechanics. The population increased, and the country began to grow in prosperity with the development of its natural resources, and there was a "boom" in Guatemala the like of which was never before witnessed on that continent.

Although he found Guatemala in a condition of moral degradation and commercial stagnation, he educated the people in a remarkable degree to an appreciation of his own ideas, and by introducing many modern improvements succeeded in inspiring them with his own ambition, so that they co-operated with him in any measure for the welfare of the country. He secured the enactment of laws which have been of great benefit, and compelled the natives to submit to what they first regarded as hardships but now accept as blessings. Roadways were constructed from the sea-coast to the interior, so that produce could get to market; diligence lines were established at Government expense; liberal railroad contracts were made, telegraph lines were erected, and all the modern facilities were introduced. The credit of the country was restored by a careful readjustment of its finances, and encouragement from the Government brought in a large amount of European capital. So that to-day, while the other Central American States are still in the condition that they were one hundred years ago, or have retrograded, Guatemala has stepped to the front, rich, powerful, progressive, and but for the peculiar appearance of the houses, the language of the people, and the customs they have inherited from their ancestors, Guatemala is not different from the new States of our great West.

Under a compulsory education law free public-schools have

FAÇADE OF AN OLD CHURCH.

been established in every department of the republic, at an expense aggregating one-tenth of the entire revenues of the Government, an amount larger in proportion than is paid by any of the United States. Not only is tuition free, but textbooks are furnished by the Government. In 1884 the total number of schools in the republic was 934, with an attendance of 42,549 pupils, supported at a cost of $451,809, being an average cost to the public treasury of about ten dollars per pupil. Of this aggregate 850 were public graded schools with 39,642 pupils, 55 were private schools with 1780 pupils, 20 were academies for the education of teachers and others desiring education in the higher branches. In addition to these the Government supports a university, with a faculty of high reputation, some of them imported from Germany and Spain, who are paid salaries of four thousand dollars a year each, a compensation greater than is received by instructors in the colleges of the United States, except in rare instances. Under this university are two law-schools with fifty-two pupils, one school of engineering with eleven pupils, a music-school with sixty-six pupils, a school of arts and drawing with one hundred and seventeen pupils, and a commercial college with fifty pupils, besides a deaf and dumb asylum with nine inmates. It is required that students in this university shall study the English language, and in a female college adjacent to it nothing but American textbooks are used. No language but English is spoken by the pupils residing in the institution, and the teachers as well as the principal are from the United States. This system of education was established about ten years ago, but has gradually improved until it has reached its present importance, and cannot but have a wholesome influence in the elevation of the people and the development of the State.

Having overthrown the religion in which the people had been reared, Barrios recognized the necessity of providing some better substitute. He therefore, through the British minister, invited the Established Church of England to send missionaries to Guatemala; but owing to the disturbed condition of the country it was not considered advisable to commence work at that time, and the opportunity was neglected. In 1883 President Barrios visited New York, where he had conferences with the officers of the Presbyterian Board of Foreign Missions, which resulted in diverting the Rev. John C. Hill, of Chicago, who was *en route* to China, into this field of labor. Mr. Hill returned with the President to Guatemala, receiving a cordial welcome, and the President not only paid the travelling expenses of himself and family from his own pocket, but the freight charges upon his furniture, and purchased the equipment necessary for the establishment of a mission and school.

A REMNANT.

The reception of the President on his return to the country after an absence of nearly two years was a royal one, and the journey from San José, the Pacific seaport, to the capital of Guatemala was a triumphal march. Of all the honors, of all the attentions General Barrios received, he insisted that Mr. Hill should have a share, and the blushing young parson found himself again and again on public platforms, with the President of Guatemala leaning upon his shoulder and introducing him to the people as his friend. This demonstration had its purpose, and resulted precisely as General Barrios intended it should. He meant that the people should know that he had taken the missionary and the cause he represented under the patronage of the Government, and expected them to show the same respect and honor he bestowed himself. He went still further. He placed Mr. Hill in one of his own houses, and there the school and chapel were opened. He sent his own children to the new Sunday-school, and notified members of his Cabinet to follow his example. He issued a decree to the Collectors of Customs to admit free of duty all articles which Mr. Hill desired to import, and in every possible manner showed his interest in the success of the work. The Protestant Mission became fashionable, and was known as the President's "pet."

The encouragement President Barrios gave to the Presbyterian Mission was an example the people were glad to follow, and the mission met with nothing but the most cordial and respectful treatment. The Catholics looked very sour at the rapidity with which the breach was widened in the walls they were nearly four hundred years in erecting, but they dared not utter even a remonstrance against those favored by the potent force behind the military guard. They saw the monks and nuns expelled, the churches sold at public auction for the benefit of the public treasury, and with a muttered curse against the power by which all these things were done, submitted servilely to his will for fear of losing what they had been able to retain.

Mrs. Barrios was the loveliest woman in Guatemala; beautiful in character as well as person, socially brilliant and graceful, charitable beyond all precedent in a country where the poor are usually permitted to take care of themselves, generous and hospitable, a good mother to a fine family of children, and a devoted wife, loyal to all the President's ambitions, and an enthusiastic supporter of all his schemes. Like a wise man who knows the perils which constantly surround him, and the uncertainty of the head which wears a crown in these countries, he had made ample provision for his family by purchasing for Mrs. Barrios a handsome residence in Fifth Avenue near Sixty-fifth Street, New York, and investing about a million dollars in her name in other New York real estate. His life was also insured for two hundred and fifty thousand dollars in New York companies, which, it must be said, carried a hazardous risk, as there were hundreds of men who lived only to see Barrios buried. Very few of them were in Guatemala, however, during his lifetime. They did not find the atmosphere agreeable there. They were exiles in Nicaragua, Costa Rica, Mexico, California, or elsewhere, waiting for a chance to give him a dose of dynamite or prick him with a dagger.

FORT OF SAN JOSÉ, GUATEMALA.

Mrs. Barrios and her children talk English as well as if they had always lived in New York. While the President himself could not speak the language fluently, he could understand what was said to him, and apologized for what he called a misfortune, on the ground that he did not have the opportunity to learn it until he was too old to master its intricacies. But he required English to be taught in all the common-schools, and the children use nothing but American text-books. I talked with him one day, with his little girl as an interpreter. She was a beautiful child, about ten years of age, and when she said she was an American (which means a citizen of the United States) the President patted her fondly upon the head and cried "bueno" (good).

Several years ago there was a conspiracy to assassinate the President. A woman, who was the Mrs. Surratt of the plot, and at whose house the conspirators were in the habit of meeting, did not like the arrangement, and on the afternoon of the night on which the plan was to be carried into execution revealed the whole thing to the President. He had the conspirators arrested, and ordered the men shot who proposed to ravish his wife, but he pardoned his treacherous private secretary. The latter rewarded the President's generosity by forging an order to the commandant of the prison to release the condemned men. He was arrested again, confessed his crime, even boasted of it, and was shot also. Several other attempts were made to assassinate Barrios. The last came very near being successful. He was on his way to the theatre, when three men, who had been employed by an ambitious politician for the purpose, threw a bomb at him. He coolly stepped on the fuse, extinguished it, picked up the dose of death that had been prepared for him, and remarked to his companion,

"The rascals don't know how to kill me!"

The leader of the plot was sent into exile, but his tools were pardoned, and are walking the streets of the city of Guatemala to-day.

The prettiest and most picturesque of the native costumes to be found in Spanish America is worn by the women of Guatemala, who are of a dark complexion, nearly that of the mulatto type, but are famous for their beauty of form. A Guatemala girl in her native costume makes as pretty a picture as one can find anywhere. Her face is bright and pretty, her figure as perfect as nature unaided by art can be, and her movements show a supple grace and elasticity that cannot be imitated by those of her sex who are encumbered by modern articles of feminine apparel. Her head is usually bare, in-doors and out, and her thick black tresses hang in braids often reaching to her heels.

YNIENSI GATE, GUATEMALA.

Her garments are only two—a *guipil* and a *sabana*. The first is a square piece of cotton of coarse texture, covered with embroidery of brilliant colors and simple but artistic designs. In the centre of the *guipil* is an aperture like that in the ordinary poncho, through which her head goes, and it is usually wide enough to constitute, when worn, a low-neck waist. The ends are tucked in her skirts at the belt. Her bare arms come through the open folds of her *guipil*, and when she raises them her side is exposed. Her skirt is a straight piece of plaid cotton of brilliant colors, like the Scotch plaids, and is wound tightly around her limbs. It is secured at the waist by a sash, usually of scarlet, woven by her own hands of the fibres of the *pita* grass, and executed in the most skilful manner. These belts in their texture resemble the Persian camel's-hair shawl, and often cost months of labor. Very often the name of the owner, and sometimes mottoes, are woven into the texture, and they are brought away from the country as curiosities by travellers.

Every article the Guatemala girl wears she makes with her own hands, and the natives of that country are as ingenious, industrious, and intelligent as are found in Spanish America. Even her sandals are home-made, and her little stockingless feet look very pretty in them. The small size of the hands and feet of the men and women is always noticed by those who visit Guatemala, and they are usually very shapely and delicately formed.

The costume which has been described is worn only by the peasants. The upper classes dress just as they would in New York, and the fashions are followed quite as closely. The women are very pretty, but have the habit of plastering their faces over with a paste or rouge that makes them look as if they had been poking their heads into a flour-barrel. This cosmetic is made of magnesia and the whites of eggs, stirred into a thick paste, and plastered on without regard to quantity. The natural beauty of complexion is thus concealed, and in time totally ruined. There is a Swiss lady at the head of a large seminary in Guatemala City to which the daughters of the aristocracy are sent. She has forbidden the use of this plaster by the young ladies under her charge to prevent the boarding pupils from destroying their fair skins, but over the day-scholars she has no control out of school-hours. Every morning she stands at the entrance with a basin of water, a sponge, and a towel, and puts the girls through a system of scrubbing that arouses their indignation.

The natives are fond of bright colors, and have a remarkable deftness in their fingers, which hold the embroidery-needle as well as the hoe and machete. The *guipils* are embroidered in gay tints and artistic patterns, and a group of peons

A VOLCANIC LAKE.

returning from or going to market looks as quaint and picturesque as the peasants of Normandy or Switzerland. The women are short, squarely built, and very muscular, and carry as much load as a mule. Their cargo is always borne upon their heads in a large basket, and they seldom walk, but move in a jog-trot, with a swaying, graceful motion, swinging their arms and carrying their shoulders as erect as a West Point cadet. They travel up hill and down without changing this gait, and make about six miles an hour, being able to outstrip any ordinary horse or mule not only in speed but in endurance. It is a common thing to see a woman not more than twenty-five or twenty-eight years of age coming to town with a hundred pounds of meat or vegetables upon her head, a baby slung in a *reboso* or blanket fastened around her hips, and several children from six to twelve years of age, each heavily laden, trotting along by her side. Almost as soon as they are able to walk, the children receive loads to carry, and the little ones come seven, eight, and ten miles to market every day or so, thinking nothing of bearing on their heads a weight that would be a burden to the ordinary man of North America.

The men do not carry their loads upon their heads, but upon their backs in a pannier, which is held by bands around the shoulders and across the forehead. They are wonderfully strong and fleet of foot. "If you are going to buy wood or hay," said a friend who has lived long in the country, "always take the man's load. You will get more than if you bought the load of a mule." These men come into town driving ahead of them three or four pack-mules loaded with coffee, sugar, corn, hay, or wood, which they sell to the commission merchants or at the market. When they return at night to their homes in the country they never ride, but drive the unladen mules ahead of them, and many of them are so accustomed to a weight upon their backs that they place a great stone in the pannier to give them a proper balance.

Some are very fleet of foot. Barrios had a runner attached to his retinue of whom some tall stories are told. He was sent as a courier into the country with messages, and his average speed was ten miles an hour. This runner was kept pretty busy in war times, and was constantly in motion. Once he carried a despatch thirty-five leagues into the interior and returned with the answer in thirty-six hours, making the two hundred and ten miles over the mountains at six miles an hour, including detentions and delays for food and sleep.

These men wear short trousers, like bathing-trunks, and a white cotton shirt, with sandals made of cowhide. The shirt is kept for occasions of ceremony, and is worn only in town. While on the road they are naked except for the trunks.

When Barrios issued his decree that the peasants should wear clothing the country narrowly escaped a revolution; but policemen were stationed on all the roads leading into the city, and confiscated all the cargoes borne by those who did

ON THE ROAD TO THE CAPITAL.

not comply with the regulations and put on a shirt or a *guipil*. The peons pleaded poverty, when Barrios, who was as generous as he was tyrannical, furnished the cloth to make the garments.

It is a novel sight to see a native policeman wearing a uniform like that worn by the policemen of New York—helmet, club, badge, and all. Here extremes meet. Quite as significant and striking a contrast is often furnished in the picture of one of these peons, laden down with his pannier, leaning for a moment's rest upon a letter-box like those used in the United States, attached to a telephone-pole; or one of the gayly dressed women, with a load of vegetables upon her head, dodging a still more gayly painted mail-wagon, the exact counterpart of those used in our postal service, except that the coat of arms of Guatemala appears in the place of the American eagle.

Barrios imported a sergeant of the New York police force two years ago, bought a lot of uniforms, and organized a patrol system that is remarkably successful. He put letter-boxes on nearly every street-corner, and had the mail carried to and from the railroad-station in wagons made by the same man and after the same pattern as those in use in the United States. He introduced the letter-carrier system also. It is not successful, because the natives object to have their correspondence carried through the streets, preferring to send for it themselves.

The military law of Guatemala requires the enrolment in the militia of every able-bodied man between the ages of eighteen and forty, and when Barrios issued his pronunciamento they were all called out for service. Even the hotels were stripped of servants, the business houses of porters, and all industries of laborers. Jesus Maria was the name of a male chamber-maid at the Grand Hotel, where all the work is done by men. Jesus was very patriotic, and made many vows, he said, for the success of Barrios, but he did not want to go to war, and appealed to all the boarders who had influence with the Government to secure him an exemption-paper. He could say a few words of English, and expressed his sentiments concerning the pending struggle in the words, "La union much grande; la guerra no good." That exactly describes the attitude the United States took in the contest.

When the conscripts come in from the country, rag-tag and bob-tail, in all kinds of costumes, and usually barefooted, they are sent to the garrison, where each receives a uniform made of white drilling from the United States. About every twelfth one bears across the seat of his trousers or between his shoulders the legend, "Best Massachusetts Drillings XXXX Mills." This rather adds to the beauty of the uniform, and there is quite a strife among the volunteers to secure trousers or blouses so marked. Each is given a straw hat, a cartridge-box, a gun, and a blanket, with which they were marched to the front at the rate of five or six hundred a day, while the streets were lined with tearful women giving parting words to sons, husbands, and sweethearts. The Guatemalatacos, as the inhabitants are called, are said to be the best fighters in Central America, and were inspired with an intense admiration for Barrios, who had never shown anything but a fatherly solicitude for the welfare of the common people. He may have been cruel to his political enemies, and arbitrary in his treatment of aspiring rivals, but to the masses, the poor, he was always generous and kind. Much of his strength came from the fact that he always shared the shelter and food of the common soldier. He never took any camp equipage with him, but slept on the ground, and ate beans and tortillas (corn-cakes), which constitute the ordinary soldier's rations.

Although the hotels are clean, and have better beds and food than are found elsewhere in Spanish America, there is one peculiarity which is decidedly objectionable—the bill of fare is never changed. One gets the same dinner and the same breakfast every day. There is enough and a variety at both tables, but there is always the same amount and the same variety. First, at breakfast, there is always soup; there is an omelette, or eggs cooked as you want them; next comes cold beef or mutton left from the previous day; then beefsteak, usually with onions; then beans and fritters. For dinner, soup is first served; second, rice with curry; next, boiled beef with cabbage; then turkey or chicken; then roast beef, salad, fruit, and cheese in order. All the native food (beef, fowls, fruit, and vegetables) is cheap, but flour and other imported products are very expensive. The hotel-keepers are usually Frenchmen or Germans. You seldom find a native keeping a hotel, but if you do, avoid it.

The people of Guatemala have a peculiar way of preparing their coffee for the table. Every week or so a quantity of the berry is ground and roasted, and hot water is poured upon it. The black liquid is allowed to drip through a porous jar, and when cool is bottled up and set upon the table like vinegar or Worcestershire sauce. Pots of hot water or milk, with which the coffee-drinker can dilute the cold, black syrup to such a weakness as he likes, are set before him. This plan has its advantages, but it takes a long time to become accustomed to it.

The laundry work of the city is never done at home, but always at the public fountains, which are scattered over the city, and have basins of stone for the purpose. The wet clothes are placed in a basket and carried home on the head of the laundress to be dried. Every morning and evening, Sundays included, there is a long procession of washer-women going to and from these fountains, with baskets of soiled or wet garments upon their heads.

Sunday is observed in Guatemala more than in any other Spanish-American city. Usually, in all these nations, Sunday is the great market-day of the week, when all the denizens of the country dress in their best suits to come to town to trade and have a little recreation; but in Guatemala there is a law, which is respected and generally enforced, requiring the market and all other places of business to remain closed on the Sabbath. Sometimes a cigar shop or a saloon will be found open, and the hotel bar-rooms, or "canteens," as they are called, do more business than on any other day but there is no more general business done on Sunday than in the cities of the United States.

All the city stores sell what is known in the slang of trade as "general merchandise;" that is, they keep all sorts of goods. You buy your canned fruit or sardines where you get your shoes or hat, and can fill an order for every variety of edible or apparel in the same establishment. An exception should be made of drugs, for the apothecary shops are usually kept by the physicians, who compound their own prescriptions, and the drug-stores in Guatemala, as in every other city of Central and South America, are usually fine establishments. But when you send for a "doctor" a lawyer comes. If you are sick, always ask for an apothecary or a physician. When you see a man alluded to as Dr. Don So-and-so, you may know that he is an attorney of distinction. The notaries draw all legal documents, as in Europe. Nobody ever asks a lawyer to draw a contract or a will.

The photographers of Central and South America are almost invariably from the United States, and there is usually one in every town of importance. The people are vain of their personal appearance, hence photography is a lucrative business. But customs differ. In Venezuela, or Havana, or the Argentine Republic, if a gentleman possesses the photograph of a lady, he is either a near relative or is engaged to marry her. Otherwise her brother or father has good cause to thrash him, or challenge him to fight a duel. If the photographer sold the picture, or gave it away, he is liable to be punished by fine and imprisonment.

In Guatemala, on the other hand, as in Peru, the pictures of the belles of the city, whether married or maidens, can be purchased by any one who wants them at the photographers', and often at the shops, and the rank and popularity of the subject is usually estimated by the number of her portraits so disposed of. Codfish is a luxury. It is served at fashionable dinners in the form of a stew or patties, or a salad, and is considered a rare and dainty dish. They call it *bacalao* (pronounced "backalowoh"), and the shop-windows contain handsomely illuminated signs announcing that it is for sale within. It costs about forty cents a pound, and is therefore used exclusively by the aristocracy.

TILED HOUSE-TOPS.

The railroads in Guatemala are run on the credit system. Freight charges are seldom paid upon the delivery of the goods, but merchants and others expect three or four months' time, and sometimes more. If a package arrives with your address upon it, the railroad company is expected to deliver it at your residence, unless it happens to be very bulky, and a few weeks after a collector comes around for the freight money.

The cars came into Guatemala for the first time in August, 1884, and have not yet ceased to be a novelty. There is always a large crowd of spectators at the station upon the arrival and departure of every train, and among these are the best people of the place. Twice a week, at train time, the National Band plays in the plaza fronting the station, to entertain the people who are waiting.

The Government owns the telegraph line, and charges low tariffs, the cost being twenty-five cents for a message to any part of the republic. But the cable rates are very high—$1.15 per word to the United States, and $1.50 per word to Europe.

The literary people here always spell general with a "J." Barrios was the "Jeneral Presidente," but after his pronunciamento "Supremissimo Jefe Militar"—Most Supreme Military Chief.

When a letter is addressed to a person of distinction the envelope reads, "Exmo y' Illustra Señor Don John Smith"—The Most Excellent, or His Excellency, the Illustrious Señor Don, etc. One is apt to feel very highly complimented when he gets a letter bearing this inscription.

Everybody is named after some saint, usually the one whose anniversary is nearest the hour of their birth, and the saint is expected to look after them. When a man comes here who doesn't happen to be christened after a saint, the ignorant people express their surprise, and ask, "Who takes care of him? Who preserves him from evil?"

General Barrios was always dramatic. He was dramatic in the simplicity and frugality of his private life, as he was in the displays he was constantly making for the diversion of the people. In striking contrast with the customs of the country where the garments and the manners of men are the objects of the most fastidious attention, he was careless in his clothing, brusque in his manner, and frank in his declarations.

MARKET-PLACE, GUATEMALA.

It is said that the Spanish language was framed to conceal thoughts, but Barrios used none of its honeyed phrases, and had the candor of an American frontiersman. He was incapable of duplicity, but naturally secretive. He had no confidants, made his own plans without consulting any one, and when he was ready to announce them he used language that could not be misunderstood. In disposition he was sympathetic and affectionate, and when he liked a man he showered favors upon him; when he distrusted, he was cold and repelling; and when he hated, his vengeance was swift and sure. To be detected in an intrigue against his life, or the stability of the Government, which was the same thing, was death or exile, and his natural powers of perception seemed almost miraculous. The last time his assassination was attempted he pardoned the men whose hands threw the bomb at him,

IN THE RAINY SEASON.

but those who hired them saved their lives by flight from the country. If caught, they would have been shot without trial. He was the most industrious man in Central America; slept little, ate little, and never indulged in the siesta that is as much a part of the daily life of the people as breakfast and dinner. He did everything with a nervous impetuosity, thought rapidly, and acted instantly. The ambition of his life was to reunite the republics of Central America in a confederacy such as existed a few years after independence. The benefits of such a union are apparent to all who understand the political, geographical, and commercial conditions of the continent, and are acknowledged by the thinking men of the five States, but the consummation of the plan is prevented by the selfish ambition of local leaders. Each is willing to join the union if he can be Dictator, but none will permit a union with any other man as chief.

MAGUEY PLANT.

Diplomatic negotiations looking to a consolidation of the five Central American republics extended over a period of several years, but were fruitless because of local jealousies. The leading politicians in the several States feared they would lose their prominence and power, and distrusted Barrios, although he assured them that he was not ambitious to be Dictator. He thought he was the right man to carry out the plan, but as soon as it was consummated he proposed to retire and permit the people to frame their Constitution and elect their Executive, promising that he would not be a candidate. As he told me shortly after his *coup-d'état*, he desired to retire from public life and reside in the United States, which he considered the paradise of nations. He had already purchased a residence in New York, and invested money there, and was educating his children with that intention.

Sending emissaries into the several States to study public sentiment, he became assured that the time was ripe for the consummation of his plans. He believed that the masses of the people were ready to join in a reunion of the republics, and had the assurance of Zaldivar, the President of San

Salvador, and Bogran, the President of Honduras, that they would consent to his temporary dictatorship. He determined upon a *coup-d'état*. Moral suasion had failed, so he decided to try force, with the co-operation of San Salvador and Honduras, which with Guatemala represented five-sixths of the population of Central America. He believed he could persuade Nicaragua and Costa Rica to accept a manifest destiny and voluntarily join the union.

Realizing how impressionable the people he governed were, and knowing their love for excitement, he always introduced his reforms in some novel way, with a blast of trumpets and a gorgeous background.

The union of Central America was announced in the same way, and came upon the people like a shock of earthquake. On the evening of Sunday, the 28th of February, 1885, the aristocracy of Guatemala were gathered as usual at the National Theatre to witness the performance of "Boccaccio" by a French opera company. In the midst of the play one of the most exciting situations was interrupted by the appearance of a uniformed officer upon the stage, who motioned the performers back from the foot-lights, and read the proclamation issued by Rufino Barrios, the President of Guatemala, who declared himself Dictator and Supreme Commander of all Central America, and called upon the citizens of the five republics to acknowledge his authority and take the oath of allegiance. The people were accustomed to earthquakes, but no terrestrial commotion ever created so much excitement as the eruption of this political volcano. The actresses and ballet-dancers fled in surprise to their dressing-rooms, while the audience at once organized into an impromptu mass-meeting to ratify the audacity of their President.

Few eyes were closed that night in Guatemala. Those who attempted to sleep were kept awake by the explosion of fireworks, the firing of cannon, the music of bands, and shouts of the populace, who, crazy with excitement, thronged the streets, and forming processions marched up and down the principal thoroughfares, rending the air with shouts of "Long live Dictator Barrios!" "Vive la Union!" A people naturally enthusiastic, and as inflammable as powder, to whom excitement was recreation and repose distress, suddenly and unexpectedly confronted with the greatest sensation of their lives, became almost insane, and turned the town into a bedlam. Although every one knew that Barrios aspired to restore the old Union of the Republic, no one seemed to be prepared for the *coup-d'état*, and the announcement fell with a force that made the whole country tremble. Next morning, as if by magic, the town seemed filled with soldiers. Where they came from or how they got there so suddenly the people did not seem to comprehend. And when the doors of great warehouses opened to disclose large supplies of ammunition and arms, the public eye was distended with amazement. All these preparations were made so silently and secretly that the surprise was complete. But for three or four years Barrios had been preparing for this day, and his plans were laid with a success that challenged even his own admiration. He ordered all the soldiers in the republic to be at Guatemala City on the 1st of March; the commands were given secretly, and the captain of one company was not aware that another was expected. It was not done by the wand of a magician, as the superstitious people are given to believing, but was the result of a long and carefully studied plan by one who was born a dictator, and knew how to perform the part.

But the commotion was even greater in the other republics over which Barrios had assumed uninvited control. The same night that the official announcement was made, telegrams were sent to the Presidents of Honduras, San Salvador, Nicaragua, and Costa Rica, calling upon them to acknowledge the temporary supremacy of Dictator Barrios, and to sign articles of confederation which should form the constitution of the Central American Union. Messengers had been sent in advance bearing printed official copies of the proclamation, in which the reasons for the step were set forth, and they were told to withhold these documents from the Presidents of the neighboring republics until notified by telegram to present them.

The President of Honduras accepted the dictatorship with great readiness, having been in close conference with Barrios on the subject previous to the announcement. The President of San Salvador, Dr. Zaldivar, who was also aware of the intentions of Barrios, and was expected to fall into the plan as readily as President Bogran, created some surprise by asking time to consider. As far as he was personally concerned, he said, there was nothing that would please him more than to comply with the wishes of the Dictator, but he must consult the people. He promised to call the Congress together at once, and after due consideration they would take such action as they thought proper. Nicaragua boldly and emphatically refused to recognize the authority of Barrios, and rejected the plan of the union. Costa Rica replied in the same manner. Her President telegraphed Barrios that she wanted no union with the other Central American States, was satisfied with her own independence, and recognized no dictator. Her people would protect their soil and defend their liberty, and would appeal to the civilized world for protection against any unwarranted attack upon her freedom.

The policy of Nicaragua was governed by the influence of a firm of British merchants in Leon with which President Cardenas has a pecuniary interest, and by whom his official acts are controlled. The policy of Costa Rica was governed by a conservative sentiment that has always prevailed in that country, while the influence of Mexico was felt throughout the entire group of nations. As soon as the proclamation of Barrios was announced at the capital of the latter republic, President Diaz ordered an army into the field, and telegraphed offers of assistance to Nicaragua, San Salvador, and Costa Rica, with threats of violence to Honduras if she yielded submission to

Barrios. Mexico was always jealous of Guatemala. The boundary-line between the two nations is unsettled, and a rich tract of country is in dispute. Feeling a natural distrust of the power below her, strengthened by consolidation with the other States, Mexico was prepared to resist the plans of Barrios to the last degree, and sent him a declaration of war.

A NATIVE SANDAL.

In the mean time Barrios appealed for the approval of the United States and the nations of Europe. During the brief administration of President Garfield he visited Washington, and there received assurances of encouragement from Mr. Blaine in his plan to reorganize the Central American Confederacy. Their personal interviews were followed by an extended correspondence, and no one was so fully informed of the plans of Barrios as Mr. Henry C. Hall, the United States minister at Guatemala.

Unfortunately the cable to Europe and the United States was under the control of San Salvador, landing at La Libertad, the principal port of that republic. Here was the greatest obstacle in the way of Barrios's success. All his messages to foreign governments were sent by telegraph overland to La Libertad for transmission by cable from that place, but none of them reached their destination. The commandant of the port, under orders from Zaldivar, seized the office and suppressed the messages. Barrios took pains to inform the foreign powers fully of his plans, and the motives which prompted them, and to each he repeated the assurance that he was not inspired by personal ambition, and would accept only a temporary dictatorship. As soon as a constitutional convention of delegates from the several republics could assemble he would retire, and permit the choice of a President of the consolidated republics by a popular election, he himself under no circumstances to be a candidate. But these messages were never sent. In place of them Zaldivar transmitted a series of despatches misrepresenting the situation, and appealing for protection against the tyranny of Barrios. Thus the Old World was not informed of the motives and intentions of the man and the situation of the republics.

The replies of foreign nations and the comments of the press, based upon the falsehoods of Zaldivar, had a very depressing effect upon the people. They were more or less doctored before publication, and bogus bulletins were posted for the purpose of deceiving the people. The inhabitants of San Salvador were led to believe that naval fleets were on their way from the United States and Europe to forcibly prevent the consolidation of the republics, that an army was on its way from Mexico overland to attack Guatemala on the north, and that several transports loaded with troops had left New Orleans for the east coast of Nicaragua and Honduras.

The United States Coast Survey ship *Ranger*, carrying four small guns, happening to enter at La Union, Nicaragua, engaged in its regular duties, was magnified into a fleet of hundreds of thousands of tons; and when the people of San Salvador and Nicaragua were convinced that submission to Barrios would require them to engage the combined forces of Europe and the United States, they rose in resistance and supported Zaldivar in his treachery.

The effect in Guatemala was similar, although not so pronounced. There was a reversion of feeling against the Government. The moneyed men, who in their original enthusiasm tendered their funds to the President, withdrew their promises; the common people were nervous, and lost their confidence in their hero; while the Diplomatic Corps, representing every nation of importance on the globe, were in a state of panic because they received no instructions from home. The German and French ministers, like the minister from the United States, were favorable to the plans of Barrios; the Spanish minister was outspoken in opposition; the English and Italian ministers non-committal; but none of them knew what to say or how to act in the absence of instructions. They telegraphed to their home governments repeatedly, but could obtain no replies, and suspected that the troubles might be in San Salvador. Mr. Hall, the American minister, transmitted a full description of the situation every evening, and begged for instructions, but did not receive a word.

ORNAMENTAL, BUT NOISY.

The Government at Washington had informed Mr. Hall by mail that its policy in relation to the plan to reunite the republics was one of non-interference, but advised that the spirit of the century was contrary to the use of force to accomplish such an end; and acting upon this information, Mr. Hall had frequent and cordial conferences with the President, and received from him a promise that he would not invade either of the neighboring republics with an army unless required to do so. If Guatemala was invaded he would retaliate, but otherwise would not cross the border. In the mean time the forces of Guatemala, forty thousand strong, were massed at the capital, the streets were full of marching soldiers, and the air was filled with martial music, while Zaldivar was raising an army by conscription in San Salvador, and money by forced loans. His Government daily announced the arrival of so many "volunteers" at the capital, but the volunteering was a very transparent myth. A current anecdote was of a conscript officer who wrote to the Secretary of War from the Interior: "I send you forty more volunteers. Please return me the ropes with which their hands and legs are tied, as I shall need to bind the quota from the next town."

In the city of San Salvador many of the merchants closed their stores, and concealed themselves to avoid the payment of forced loans. The Government called a "Junta," or meeting of the wealthy residents, each one being personally notified by an officer that his attendance was required, and there the Secretary of War announced that a million dollars for the equipment of troops must be raised instantly. The Government, he said, was assured of the aid of foreign powers to defeat the plans of Barrios, but until the armies and navies of Europe and the United States could reach the coast the republic must protect itself. Each merchant and *estancianado* was assessed a certain amount, to make the total required, and was required to pay it into the Treasury within twenty-four hours. Some responded promptly, others procrastinated, and a few flatly refused. The latter were thrust into jail, and the confiscation of their property threatened unless they paid. In one or two cases the threat was executed; but, with cold sarcasm, the day after the meeting the *Official Gazette* announced that the patriotic citizens of San Salvador had voluntarily come to the assistance of the Government with their arms and means, and had tendered financial aid to the amount of one million dollars, the acceptance of which the President was now considering.

Barrios, knowing that the army of Salvador would invade Guatemala and commence an offensive campaign, so as to occupy the attention of the people, ordered a detachment of troops to the frontier, and decided to accompany them. The evening before he started there was what is called "a grand *funcion*" at the National Theatre. All of the military bands assembled at the capital—a dozen or more—were consolidated for the occasion, and between the acts performed a march composed by a local musician in honor of the Union of Central America, and dedicated to General Barrios. A large screen of sheeting was elaborately painted with the inscription,

"*All hail the Union of the Republic!*"
"*Long live the Dictator and the Generalissimo,*"
"*J. Rufino Barrios!*"

This was attached to heavy rollers, to be dropped in front of the stage instead of the regular curtain at the end of the second act of the play, for the purpose of creating a sensation; and a sensation it did create—an unexpected and frightful one.

As the orchestra commenced to play the new march the curtain was lowered slowly, and the audience greeted it with tremendous applause, rising to their feet, shouting, and waving their hats and handkerchiefs. But through the blunder of the stage carpenter the weights were too heavy for the cotton sheeting; the banner split, and the heavy rollers at the bottom fell over into the orchestra, severely wounding several of the musicians. As fate would have it, the rent was directly through the name of Barrios. The people, naturally superstitious, were horrified, and stood aghast at this omen of disaster. The cheering ceased instantly, and a dead silence prevailed, broken only by the noise of the musicians under the wreck struggling to recover their feet. A few of the more courageous friends of the President attempted to revive the applause, but met with a miserable failure. Strong men shuddered, women fainted, and Mrs. Barrios left the theatre, unable to control her emotion. The play was suspended; the audience departed to discuss the omen, and everybody agreed that Barrios's *coup-d'état* would fail.

The President left the city at the head of his army for the frontier of San Salvador, his wife accompanying him a few miles on the way. A few days later a small detachment of the Guatemala army, commanded by a son of Barrios, started out on a scouting expedition, and were attacked by an overwhelming force of Salvadorians. The young captain was killed by the first volley, and his company were stampeded. Leaving his body on the field, they retreated in confusion to headquarters. When Barrios heard of the disaster he leaped upon his horse, called upon his men to follow him, and started in pursuit of the men who had killed his son. The Salvadorians, expecting to be pursued, lay in ambush, and the Dictator, while galloping down the road at the head of a squadron of cavalry, was picked off by a sharpshooter and died instantly. His men took his body and that of his son, which was found by the roadside, and carried them back to camp. A courier was despatched to the nearest telegraph station with a message to the capital conveying the sad news. It was not unexpected; since the omen at the theatre, no one supposed the Dictator would return alive. All but himself had lost confidence, and it transpired that even he went to the front with a presentiment of disaster, for among his papers was found this peculiar will, written by himself a few moments before his departure.

THE WILL OF BARRIOS.

"I am in full campaign, and make my declaration as a soldier.

"My legitimate wife is Donna Francisca Apaucio vel Vecusidario de Quezaltenanzo.

"During our marriage we have had seven children, as follows: Elaine, Luz, José, Maria, Carlos, Rufino, and Francisca.

"Donna Francisca is the sole owner of all my properties and interest whatsoever. She will know how much to give our children when they arrive at maturity, and I have full confidence in her.

"She may give to my nephew, Luciano Barrios, in two or three instalments, $25,000, for the kindness which this nephew has rendered to me, and which I doubt not he will continue to render to my wife Donna Francisca.

"She will continue to provide for the education of Antonio Barrios, who is now in the United States of America.

"She is empowered to demand and collect all debts due to me in this country and abroad. The overseers and administrators of my properties, wherever they may be, shall account only to Donna Francisca or the person whom she may name.

"It is five o'clock in the morning. At this moment I start forth to Jutiapa, where the army is.

"J. RUFINO BARRIOS.

"MONDAY, *March 23, 1885.*"

The attempt to reunite the republic ended with the death of the Dictator, and the whole country was thrown into confusion. In Guatemala City anarchy prevailed. The enemies of Barrios did not fear a dead lion, and kicked his body. They came out in force, stoned his house, and his beautiful wife was forced to seek the protection of the United States minister, whose secretary escorted her to San José, where she took a steamer for San Francisco, and has since resided in New York.

Señor Sinibaldi, the Vice-president of the republic, called the Congress together, and a new election was ordered, at which Señor Barrillas, a man of excellent ability and wise discretion, was chosen President of the republic.

COMAYAGUA.

THE CAPITAL OF HONDURAS.

IN 1540 Cortez, the Conqueror of Mexico, directed Alonzo Caceres, one of his lieutenants, to proceed with an army of one thousand men to the Province of Honduras, which had been subdued by Alvarado a few years before, and select a suitable site for a city midway between the two oceans. Caceres was a pioneer of most excellent discretion, and so good a judge of distance was he that if a straight line were drawn from the Atlantic to the Pacific, the centre would be just three miles north of the plaza of Comayagua. A modern engineer, with all the scientific appliances at his disposal, could not have obeyed instructions more accurately; and as for location, there are few finer sites in the world than the elevated plain upon which the little capital of Honduras stands. A semicircle of mountains enclose it, with a wall of peaks six and seven thousand feet high upon one side, while upon the other a great plain stretches away nearly forty miles, gradually sloping to the eastward. The altitude of the city is about twenty-three hundred feet above the sea, and the climate is a perpetual June, the thermometer seldom varying more than twenty degrees during the entire year, and averaging about 75° Fahrenheit. The soil is deep, rich, and fertile, and the productions of the plain are tropical; but beyond the city, in the foothills of the mountains and upon their slopes, corn, wheat, and other staples of the temperate zones can be raised in enormous quantities with a minimum of labor. The pineapple and the palm tree are growing within two hours' ride of waving wheat-fields, while orange and apple orchards stand within sight of each other.

A CONSPICUOUS LANDMARK.

Comayagua is said to have at one time contained nearly thirty thousand inhabitants, but at present it has no more than one-fifth of that number; for, like all of the Central American cities, its population has been reduced since the independence of the country, and, like the most of them, it is in a state of decay. Everything is dilapidated, and nothing is ever repaired. No sign of prosperity appears anywhere. Commercial stagnation has been its normal condition for sixty years, and the indolence and indifference of the people has not been disturbed for that period, except by political insurrections. No one seems to have anything to do. The aristocrats swing lazily in their hammocks, or discuss politics over the counters of the *tiendas*, or at the club, while the poor beg in the streets, and manage to sustain life upon the fruits which Nature has so profligately showered upon them. Nowhere upon the earth's surface exist greater inducements to labor, nowhere can so much be produced with so little effort; and the vast resources of the country present the most tempting opportunity for capital and enterprise, for nearly every acre of the land is susceptible to some sort of profitable development.

THE TRAIL TO THE CAPITAL.

The area of Honduras is about the same as that of Ohio, and the inhabitants number from three to four hundred thousand, according to the guess of the well informed, but no census has been taken for a quarter of a century, and the last enumeration was so inaccurate as to discredit itself. In ancient times the population must have been very dense.

It is as difficult and as long a journey to reach the capital of Honduras from New York as the capital of Siam or Siberia. One must go by steamer to Truxillo, the chief Atlantic port, or to Amapala, on the Bay of Fonseca, on the Pacific side—a voyage of from fifteen to twenty days by either route—and then ride for twelve days on mule-back over the mountains, without any of the accommodations or comforts known to modern travel, and not even one clean or comfortable inn. When the capital is reached there is no hotel to stop at, and one must trespass upon the hospitality of the citizens, or seek some boarding-place through the aid of a local merchant or priest.

A GLIMPSE OF THE INTERIOR.

The President is General Bogran, a man who came into power by a peaceful revolution in 1885, to succeed Marco A. Soto, who fled that year to San Francisco, and from there sent his resignation to Congress. Bogran is a man of brains and progressive ideas, possessing more of the modern spirit

VIEW OF THE CAPITAL.

and broader views than most of his contemporaries, and if he is permitted to carry out his plans Honduras will make rapid speed in the development of her great natural resources. He is offering tempting inducements to foreign capital and immigration, has given liberal concessions to Americans who desire to enter the country, and is wisely endeavoring to induce some one to construct the Interoceanic Railway, which was surveyed fifty years ago, and twenty-seven miles of which has already been built and at intervals operated. But the discontented element in the country, in league with his predecessor, who now lives in New York, are surrounding him with obstacles and harassing him with all sorts of embarrassments, so that his success is made doubtful. Bogran spends very little of his time at Comayagua, and the seat of government has been removed to Tegucigalpa, the largest town in the country, as well as its commercial metropolis. Here the Congress sits also, and the place is to all intents and purposes the capital.

A POPULAR THOROUGHFARE.

The cathedral of Comayagua is by far the finest building in the country, being an excellent specimen of the semimoresque style, which was so popular among the Spanish provinces. Its walls and roof are of the most solid masonry, but are considerably marred by the revolutions through which the country has passed, for in nearly all of them the cathedral has been used as a fortress and subjected to a shower of lead. Near the cathedral stands a monument originally intended to honor one of the Spanish kings, but after the independence of the country was established the royal symbols were erased by the order of one of the Presidents, the inscription was chiselled off, and the obelisk now stands to commemorate independence. This monument is the place of public execution, and criminals sentenced to death are made to sit blindfolded at its base, where they are shot by the soldiers.

CHURCH OF MERCED AND INDEPENDENCE MONUMENT, COMAYAGUA.

In November, 1886, General Delgrado, the leader of a revolution, with four of his comrades, was executed here. It was the desire of President Bogran to spare Delgrado's life, and any pretext would have been adopted to save him if the honor of the country could have been vindicated, but he was convicted of treason, and sentenced by the courts to die. The President offered to pardon him if he would take the oath of allegiance and swear never to engage in revolutionary proceedings again; but the old soldier would not even accept life on these terms, and much to the regret of the President,

RUBBER HUNTERS.

against whom he had conspired, and the better portion of the people, the sentence had to be executed. On the morning of the day fixed by the courts, the five men were led from the prison to the Church of La Merced, where the last rites were administered to them, and were then conducted to the Peace Monument, where a file of soldiers was drawn up with loaded rifles. The last word of Delgrado was a request that he might give the command to fire, and he did so as coolly as if he had been on dress parade.

THE PITA PLANT.

The residents of Comayagua are chiefly the owners of haciendas situated in the neighborhood, or small tradesmen, with four or five thousand lazy and worthless half-breeds, who live upon *tortillas*, or corn-cakes, and the fruits in which the country abounds. The most conspicuous feature of their life is the filth that surrounds them, and the freedom with which their pigs and chickens enjoy the shelter of the dwelling. A few stone jars of native make, a few rude calabashes, a couple of hammocks, and a few broken articles of furniture, constitute the equipment of a peon's house. The man of the house swings in a hammock while his spouse brings water from the stream in a large stone jar upon her head, and the pigs and chickens and children lie upon the floor indiscriminately mixed. The pigs take the tortillas out of the mouths of the children, and the compliment is returned, while the chickens forage upon every article of food within their reach.

Both cotton and silk grow upon trees, the vegetable silk being of very fine and soft fibre, and frequently used by the natives in the manufacture of robosas, serapas, and other articles of wear, while the product of the cotton-tree is utilized in a similar manner.

HARVESTING ONE OF THE STAPLES.

There is said to be a greater variety of medicinal plants in Honduras than in any country on the globe, and the botany of the country contains nearly every tree and shrub and flower that is known to man. They are all of spontaneous growth, and might be made a prolific source of wealth, but are entirely neglected. There is one famous weed, called by the natives *el agrio*, which is a certain cure for sunstroke, or for prostration from exposure to the sun or over-exertion, and is used for both men and animals. As it is excessively bitter, the leaf of the plant is wound about the bit of the bridle of a sunstruck horse, and the animal gradually sucks the juice from it. The leaves are dried in the shade, and a tea made of them by the natives to cure sunstroke and other diseases of the brain or blood.

The interior of the country is beyond the reach of markets, because of the absence of transportation facilities. In this respect the people are no further advanced than they were two hundred years ago. The only wagon-roads in the country are one built by a party of Americans near San Pedro, in the west, and a few miles of a national highway that a century ago was begun for the purpose of connecting Amapala, the Pacific port, with Tegucigalpa.

THE FLOATING POPULATION.

Honduras has the finest fluvial system in Central America. There are few countries with such available water facilities, both for transportation and manufacturing powers, and it has the finest harbors on both coasts—all wasted because of the indolence of the people. The Government has given several liberal concessions in timber and agricultural lands to secure the opening of its rivers to navigation, and for the construction of railways from the coast to the interior. Some of these grants are in the hands of responsible and capable companies, and if the peace of the country is assured, and immigrants can be induced to settle there, a rapid development of its resources is promised.

Ten years ago the telegraph was unknown, and there was no postal system in the interior. All communications were transmitted from place to place by messengers, who were famous for their endurance and swiftness of foot. The letter or package to be conveyed was first wrapped in cloth and then fastened around the loins of the carrier. This system is still in vogue for the transmission of letters, packages, and money. The couriers, or *cozeos*, are noted for being trusty and courageous; they travel long distances over the mountains and through the forest, generally by routes known only to themselves.

BRANCH OF THE RUBBER-TREE.

Within the last eight years every town of importance has been connected with the capital by lines of telegraph. Before its construction information of the utmost importance could not reach the capital from the remote points in less than ten or twelve days. The Government saw the necessity of some better and quicker method for transmitting information, and constructed these lines. They are owned and operated entirely by the Government, and from them a considerable revenue is realized. For the purpose of sending a message, you must first purchase of the proper Government officer a stamped telegraphic blank, which varies in price from one real (twelve and a half cents) to one or two dollars, in proportion to the number of words which it is to contain. The distance the message is to travel makes no difference in the price, provided its destination is within any of the republics of Central America. When the message is written on the blank it is taken to the telegraph-office, and if the charge for the number of words contained in the message corresponds with the stamped blank it is forwarded.

A MODERN TOWN.

Every department of Honduras possesses more or less mineral wealth, and within the limits of the country almost every metal known to man is found. The discoveries of gold and silver were made by the aborigines, who possessed much treasure when the Spaniards conquered them, and ever since the Conquest the mines have been worked with great profit; but their development was greater under the viceroys than since the independence of the republic, as this branch of industry has suffered more from civil wars than any other. As a consequence, mine after mine has been abandoned, and the districts where the best mineral deposits exist are marked with depopulated towns and villages.

UP THE RIVER.

The lack of roads renders it impossible to transport machinery to the mining districts. The mines are seldom worked to any depth, and the waste is enormous. But even under this system, rude and primitive as it is, much wealth has been acquired, and millions of dollars in silver and gold have been taken out annually for hundreds of years. Of late a good deal of attention has been given to the Honduras mines by American experts, and much capital has been invested in purchasing and prospecting them, but the hope of realizing upon the investment lies in the improvement of transportation facilities, for nothing that cannot be carried on the back of a mule can either reach the mines or come from them. And imported labor is quite as necessary, as the native of Honduras cannot be induced to do anything in other than the way to which he has been accustomed, and looks upon labor-saving machinery as the invention of the evil one.

A MINING SETTLEMENT.

The city of Tegucigalpa, the commercial metropolis and the actual capital of the country, stands upon both banks of the Rio Cholutica in an amphitheatre of mountains, and has twelve thousand inhabitants. The river is spanned and the two divisions of the town connected by an ancient bridge with some fine arches of stone. The suburb is called Comayaguaita (Little Comayagua). The streets are well paved, in the same manner as other Spanish American cities, with a gutter in the centre, to which they slope from both sides. This gutter is always full of weeds and dust and filth, but seldom of water; and although the hills which half surround the city are full of running streams, with a fall sufficient to force water to the tower of the cathedral, it has never occurred to the inhabitants to utilize them. Every drop of water used for any purpose in the city is carried, in an earthen jar on the top of some woman's head, from the river at the bottom of a gorge a hundred feet deep.

VIEW IN NICARAGUA.

The houses in Tegucigalpa show much more evidence of prosperity than those of Comayagua, and are kept more tidy and in better repair. They are usually painted either a dead white or pink, blue, yellow, green, or some other very pronounced color, while often a native amateur artist tries his hand at exterior decoration, and endeavors to make the walls of adobe look as if they were made of marble.

AN INTERIOR PLAIN.

Somehow or another Tegucigalpa always looks new. The grass is growing in the streets, and there are many other indications of commercial stagnation, but the people do not let their houses show how poor and indolent they are. These two national characteristics, moreover, do not appear in any form in the city. It is not only the present headquarters of the Government and of commercial affairs, but it is the centre of fashionable life and the residence of the aristocracy of Honduras. Two-thirds of the white people in the republic live here, and the other third come here to get their clothes, so that the city is by comparison gay.

The numerous farms surrounding the city are capable of enormous production, and some of them are still profitably operated, while many have gone to waste. The staples are sugar, coffee, cocoa, and other tropical products, which require and receive little attention. The buildings upon these plantations are all very old, but are still in good condition. The chief dwelling is commonly large and comfortable, built of adobe and roofed with imported tiles, and located where it can secure a good natural water supply. There is usually but one floor, no ceiling, nor glass in the windows, for the climate does not require it, and glass is expensive. The windows are protected with iron bars and heavy mahogany shutters. As little timber as possible is used, because all dry wood is subject to destruction from a little insect called the *comojeu*, which honey-combs every rafter, joist, and beam in a building as soon as the sap is exhausted, and the interiors of the houses have to be restored at intervals of a few years.

Most of the churches are in a dilapidated condition, and have been divested of their former ornaments and riches by the hands of vandals during revolutions. The cathedral was erected at the expense of a devout and wealthy padre, and was once a fine building, but is now in a sad state of decay.

What will impress the traveller at once in Tegucigalpa is the entire absence of carriages. I do not believe there is one in the country, any more than there is a chimney or an overcoat, and for the same reason—the people do not need them. All roads, it was said, lead to Rome, but no roads lead to the capital of Honduras except a few short ones, narrow and stony, like the way of salvation, and hedged about with divers trials and pitfalls, from the neighboring plantations, and are used only by rude ox-carts. Everybody goes on horseback, and all the transportation is done on the backs of mules and men. Long caravans of pack animals are coming and going to and from the sea-coast daily over the mountain trails, and there is a class of Indians called Cargadors who carry a cargo of a hundred pounds or so upon their backs, and run at a jog-trot for hours at a time, making the same journey twice as rapidly as a mule. Their loads are strapped to their backs on a wicker frame, and by a broad band passing around the forehead.

ONE OF THE BACK STREETS.

At breakfast chocolate often takes the place of coffee, and it is prepared from the cocoa-bean in a manner different from that in use in other countries. A handful or two of cocoa-beans, with a few vanilla-beans or sticks of cinnamon, and a much larger amount of raw sugar, are ground up together by the *matete*—that is, by being rubbed between two stones—and moistened until it is reduced to paste; then it is rolled out in little balls as large as a chocolate cream, and allowed to harden. A plate of these is placed upon the table, each member of the family takes as many as he or she chooses, drops them in a cup, and pours boiling milk upon them. They soon dissolve, and are very palatable.

The shops, or *tiendas*, of Tegucigalpa display very few goods that are pretty or costly, and are usually "general merchandise" stores, such as are found in the country villages of the United States—a few drugs and dry goods, a little hardware, patent-leather boots and elaborately stitched kid shoes for ladies— often white or pink or blue, for the ladies affect bright-colored foot-gear— some cutlery and crockery, and other household articles. Nearly all sales are on credit, even if the purchaser have the money in his pocket, for the custom of the country is not to do anything to-day that can be postponed.

PLAZA OF TEGUCIGALPA.

The ladies usually do their shopping in the morning before breakfast, which is served at eleven o'clock, for the afternoons are given up to siestas. Most of the business of the city is done before breakfast, and from eleven o'clock until four in the afternoon the streets are empty and most of the stores are closed. Activity is resumed at the latter hour, and continues until eight or nine o'clock in the evening.

MAKING TORTILLAS.

Every woman goes to mass at seven in the morning, but a man is seldom seen to enter a church except on feast-day or to attend a funeral. All their religion is crammed into Holy-week, when they are very pious.

The schools of the republic are nominally free, but there are few of them; education is compulsory, but the law is not enforced. The school funds have usually been stolen, or diverted to other purposes, and only in the cities, where public sentiment demands it, are schools sustained. There is a university at Tegucigalpa which is said to have been once an institution of some importance, but is such no longer. It has a few students and a small faculty, but those who can afford it, and who are anxious to secure an education, go to Guatemala or to Europe.

INDIGO WORKS.

Tegucigalpa is famous for having been the birthplace of Morazan, the Washington of Central America, and his descendants still reside there. He was undoubtedly the greatest man any of these republics ever produced, and had the broadest vision as well as the broadest views as to the nature of a republic. The fires of liberty were enkindled by him, and he led the fight against Spain which resulted in the overthrow of the Viceroys and the establishment of the confederacy. He was born in 1799; his father was a native of Porto Rico and his mother a lady of Tegucigalpa. He prided himself on the fact that his ancestors came from the birthplace of Napoleon, and his descendants, to whom strangers are usually introduced, seldom fail to forget that circumstance

THE TLACHIGUERO.

in conversation. Before Morazan was of age he was prominent in Honduras, and became the governor of the city in 1824, when he was but twenty-five. For fourteen years thereafter his career was one of singular activity and success, and the people of the entire continent followed him with feelings akin to idolatry. He was so far ahead of them in ideas and enterprise that his counsels were not followed, and he was overthrown by a combination of priests, who took up a cruel Indian of Guatemala named Rafael Carera, and succeeded in overthrowing the power of Morazan, not only in Honduras, but throughout the entire confederacy. The patriot and liberator was afterwards assassinated at Cartago, Costa Rica, by men whom he trusted as his friends.

MANAGUA.

THE CAPITAL OF NICARAGUA.

A STRANGER landing at the port of Corinto, Nicaragua, asked the men who were taking him ashore in a *bongoe* the name of the capital of the republic. There were three of them. The quickest of wit answered promptly, "Grenada;" both the others disputed it, one of them contending for the city of Managua, and the other for Leon. So animated did the controversy become that all three dropped their oars, and nearly upset the boat by their gesticulations. This question is, and always has been, a dangerous one, and thousands of lives and hundreds of thousands of money have been wasted in repeated attempts to determine it. If it were the only excuse for the blood that has been shed in the little republic during the last sixty-five years, its history would be a nobler and a prouder one; for bitter wars have been waged for less, and brother has fought brother to settle questions not only involving a preference for cities but for men. There is no spot of equal area upon the globe in which so much human blood has been wasted in civil war, or so much wanton destruction committed. Nature has blessed it with wonderful resources, and a few years of peace and industry would make the country prosperous beyond comparison; but so much attention has been paid to politics that little is left for anything else. Scarcely a year has passed without a revolution, and during its sixty-five years of independence the republic has known more than five times as many rulers as it had during the three centuries it was under the dominion of Spain. It was seldom a question of principle or policy that brought the inhabitants to war, but usually the intrigue of some ambitious man. It is a land of volcanic disturbance, physical, moral, and political, and the mountains and men have between them contrived to almost compass its destruction.

VIEW OF LAKE FROM BEACH AT MANAGUA.

For sixty years the country has been going backward. Its population is less than when independence was declared, and its wealth has decreased even more rapidly. Its cities are heaps of ruins, and its commerce is not so great as it was at the beginning of the century. There is, however, a commercial elasticity, owing to the extreme productiveness of the fields and the ease with which wealth is acquired, that has kept the little republic from bankruptcy, and promises great prosperity if political order can be preserved.

Most of the people live in towns, and waste much time in going and coming between their homes and the plantations upon which they labor. This is owing to the frequency of revolutions and the milder forms of destruction and murder that are practised by highwaymen and other robbers. None but the very poor live along the roadside, and they have nothing to tempt assault.

CORINTO.

Everybody rides on horseback, and the animals are plenty and fine. The horses of Nicaragua resemble those of Arabia, being small but fleet, spirited, and capable of much endurance. Great care is taken in training them, and they are taught an easy gait, half trotting and half pacing, called the *paso-trote*. A well-broken animal will take this as soon as the reins are loosened, and continue it all day without fatigue to himself or his rider, making five or six miles an hour. The motion is so gentle that an experienced rider can carry a cup of water for miles in his hand without spilling a drop.

There is only one road in the country suitable for carriages, and that is seldom used except by carts. It runs from Grenada, the easternmost city of importance on the shore of Lake Nicaragua, to Realjo, or Corinto, the principal seaport; and over this road, which was built three hundred years ago by the Spaniards, all the commerce of the country passes. There is now a railroad along this highway; the Government has several times made loans to construct it, but the money was wasted in revolutions, and the track was not completed till recently. The road belongs to the Government, and is managed by a citizen of the United States. The cart road passes through Managua, and thus unites the three principal cities of the land. Over it have passed hundreds of armies and no end of insurgent forces, and the whole distance has been washed with blood, shed in public and private quarrels. Wherever a man has been slain a rude cross is usually erected, and it is common to see wreaths of flowers hanging upon it, placed there by some interested or, mayhap, loving hand. At these places pious passengers breathe a prayer for the soul that has been released, and they are so numerous that it keeps them praying from one end of a journey to the other.

HIDE-COVERED CART.

The carts which furnish transportation are rude contrivances of native manufacture, and the design has not been improved upon since the conquest. The body consists of a very heavy framework of wood, and the wheels are solid sections cut from some large tree, usually of mahogany. They are not sawed, but chopped into shape, and are generally about eight or ten inches thick and five feet in diameter, and weigh several hundred pounds. The oxen do not wear yokes, but the pole of the cart is fastened to a bar of tough wood, usually lignum vitæ, which is lashed by cowhide thongs to the horns. There are always two pair of oxen—one to haul the cart and the other to haul the load, for the vehicle is twice the weight of its cargo. Two men are required to navigate the craft; one goes ahead armed with a gun or a machete, which is a long knife, and answers for many purposes—a weapon as well as an agricultural implement—and the oxen are supposed to follow him, while the other sits on the load and yells as he prods the animals with an iron-pointed goad long enough to reach the leaders. The man ahead assists his colleague by uttering constant admonitions to the oxen without turning his face, and between the two, and the squeaking of the cart-wheels, which are never greased, there is noise enough to deafen the whole neighborhood. The approach of one of these vehicles can be anticipated half an hour.

Each cart contains five or six days' forage for the animals, as well as rations for the *carreteros*. They camp whenever night overtakes them, even if it is only a mile from the end of their journey. The oxen are fastened to the cart and given their fodder, while the men light a fire, make their coffee, and either lie under the cart or upon it to sleep. Most of the carts have covers or awnings of cured hides, which are lashed over boughs to protect the loads in the rainy season. The average rate of speed is about a mile an hour over a good road, but ten miles a day is fast travelling, owing to the amount of time wasted by the roadside.

The cartmen are invariably honest in dealing with their employers, and always render a strict account of their cargoes, whether they are composed of silver or coffee, but

AN INTERIOR TOWN.

consider it a privilege, which they have inherited from their ancestors, to plunder along the road. Nothing is too hot or too heavy for them to carry away, and accordingly precautions are taken for the protection of whatever is likely to tempt them. They have an unorganized union to protect themselves, and permit no impositions to be practised upon any of their number, or underbidding or other irregularities among themselves. They charge so much a journey, no matter what their load is, and persons having small parcels to be carried have to club together to make up a cargo, or pay a high rate for transportation. Many of the carts and oxen are owned by those who drive them, but others are leased to the carreteros by capitalists who possess a large number. The cattle come from the savannas in the southwestern portion of the republic, where there are immense and nutritious pastures extending over the line into Costa Rica.

THE INDIGO PLANT.

THE KING OF THE MOSQUITOES.

Although the mineral resources of the country are undoubtedly rich, its future wealth will come, if peace can ever be made permanent, from the development of the agricultural and timber lands. Beyond the mining district down to the Mosquito coast there extends a forest of immense area, filled with the finest woods, and it has scarcely been touched. The most useful timber is the mahogany, although there are kindred varieties quite as good, but not so popular or well known. It is more easily obtained too, as it grows upon the ridges and keeps out of the swamps, which are full of miasma and mosquitoes. The tree is one of the most beautiful, as well as one of the largest, that are found in tropical lands, commonly reaching a height of sixty or seventy feet, and being from twenty-five to forty feet in circumference. Timbers forty feet long and eight feet square are frequent, although so heavy that they are difficult to handle; and the only way fine timber can be obtained is by taking saw-mills into the forest and cutting up the timber into sizes suitable for transportation. This is difficult, however, owing to the lack of roads. Logs five and six feet in diameter are common, and it is said that the largest trees have the finest color and grain.

The mahogany is one of the few trees in the tropical forests whose leaves change color with the season, and the Carrib Indians, who are employed to cut them, discover their presence by this peculiarity. They climb the highest tree they can find, sight the mahoganies, locate their position with great skill, and lead the choppers to them with unerring accuracy. When the tree is found, the underbrush around it and the lower limbs are first cleared away before the trunk is attacked. When it falls, the branches are chopped off; then the log is hewn into shape, after which it is dragged by oxen—sometimes a hundred yoke being employed—to the nearest water-course, the choppers going ahead and clearing away with their machetes the underbrush and small trees to make a road. When the timber is rolled into the river, it is branded and allowed to lie there until the rainy season, when the waters rise and carry it down to the sea.

There are other trees of great value in the forests, and not for timber alone. The caoutchouc, or rubber-tree—a name which when properly pronounced sounds like the plunge of a frog into the water—kachunk—is very plentiful in the Nicaragua forests, although this resource, like most of the others, is comparatively idle. The Mosquito Indians gather some, however, which is shipped from Blewfields and Greytown in small quantities. The quality is not so good as that which comes from Brazil, as the sap is not reduced with any skill or care.

The average North American supposes that the rubber is obtained like pitch, and comes from the exuded gums of the tree, but the process is altogether different, resembling our method of making maple sugar. When the sap begins to rise from the roots to the branches of the tree, expeditions of thirty or forty men are organized, who are furnished by the exporting merchants with an outfit of buckets, axes, machetes, pans, and provisions, and start into the woods. The *uleros*, as the rubbermen are called, from the term *ule*, which is the native name for the tree, are always paid a small sum in advance, ostensibly for the support of their families during their absence, but which is always exhausted in debauchery before they start. When they reach the forest of the ule-trees they build a shanty of palms and brush, if there is not one already standing, on the bank of some stream, as a great deal of water is required for the manufacture of the gum. There they distribute their large cans and buckets through the forest at convenient intervals and proceed to business. When the *ulero* selects his tree, he clears the trunk of vines and creepers and climbs it to the branches. Then he descends, cutting diagonal channels through the bark with a single blow of his machete, or knife, left and right, left and right, all meeting at the angle. At the bottom of the lowest cut an iron trough about six inches long and four inches wide is driven into the tree, which catches the milk as it flows from the wound, and conducts it into a bucket on the ground below. This is done with great speed and skill by an expert; and necessarily so, to prevent waste, as the sap springs out instantly, and by the time the spout is driven into the tree is flowing at the rate of four gallons an hour. A large tree will produce twenty gallons of sap, and will run dry in a single day. The *ulero* having tapped a dozen or eighteen trees has all the work he can attend to emptying the buckets into the ten-gallon cans that are provided for the purpose. In the evening the cans are carried to the camp, and the sap strained through sieves into barrels. In Brazil it is boiled, but in Nicaragua the natives have a peculiar system of reducing it. There is a plant or vine called the Achuna, whose sap when mixed with that of the rubber-tree has the singular property of coagulating it in a few minutes. By whom, or how, or where this process was discovered no one can tell. Undoubtedly it was an accident, for the vine hangs from all the trees in the *ule* forest, and probably a cutting dropped into a bucket of sap some time or another produced the result for which it is now used. Having their barrels full, the *uleros* cut short

A MAHOGANY SWAMP.

A MAHOGANY SWAMP.

pieces of this vine, soak it in water, and small bunches are thrown into pans upon which the sap is poured. In the morning the rubber has turned to gum—about two pounds to every gallon of sap. At the top of the pan is a quantity of dark brown liquid, like a weak solution of licorice. This is poured off, and then the gum is rolled under heavy weights of wood into long flat strips called tortillas, which are hung over poles under the shed to drip and dry. At first they are white, like the vulcanized rubber, but with exposure they turn black and become hard after a few days. Then the tortillas are stacked up under cover until the end of the season, and shipped to market.

INTERNAL COMMERCE.

The cocoa or chocolate tree grows wild in the forests of Nicaragua, and when cultivated yields the most profitable crop that can be produced; but the republic furnishes but little, comparatively, for export, although its possibilities in this direction are almost unlimited. The most of the world's supply of cocoa comes from Ecuador and Venezuela.

There always has been a prejudice in Nicaragua against foreign immigration, inspired and stimulated by the priests, who inveterately oppose all progress and every innovation. A number of German families are settled throughout the country, engaged in mercantile pursuits. Most of the large commission houses and exporters are English, while the hotel or posada keepers are Frenchmen. England furnishes most of the money to move the crops, as the natives are impoverished by wars or their own extravagance. The country will never be prosperous until its peace is assured and its population increased by the introduction of foreign labor and capital.

HOW THE PEONS LIVE.

Like other Spanish-American countries, the national vices are indolence and extravagance. The common people never get ahead, and have no need of purses, much less of savings-banks. They might make good wages, as they are naturally good producers, but they always spend their earnings before they receive them, and are encouraged to keep in debt to those who employ them, as, under the law, no laborer can leave a job upon which he is employed as long as he owes his employer a penny. This system of credit, although it amounts to only a few dollars in each case, is equivalent to slavery, a peonage which is permanent; for if the laborer really aspires to be a free man, he is persuaded or threatened or swindled into renewing the obligation under which his life is spent.

The aristocracy are equally extravagant. It is a part of their religion, apparently, to spend their incomes, even if they do not anticipate them; and the latter is generally the case. Nearly every crop is mortgaged to the commission man before it is harvested, and the planter is compelled to take the price that is offered. The peon is in debt to the planter, the planter to the merchant, the merchant to the commission-house, and the latter conducts his business on borrowed money; and so it goes on, year after year, without cessation, each person involved spending as much or more than he makes, and conducting his business on paper, like speculators in the stock market, the country growing poorer each year, with no possible hope of redemption except by an influx of fresh blood and capital. The climate is delightful, the land is wonderfully productive, and the products always in active demand in the markets of the world.

The chief cities are pictures of desolation, and along the roads in the country are the ruins of *estancias* that were the abode of wealthy planters years ago. Much of the destruction was caused by earthquakes, but more by civil war. The population in 1846 was 257,000; in 1870 it had been reduced to less than 200,000, and since then there have been disturbances in which thousands of men were slaughtered or driven into exile by fear or force. The whites, or those of pure Spanish blood, number about 30,000; the negroes about half as many; the mixed races, Mestizos and Ladinos—the former of Spanish and Indian and the latter Negro and Indian blood—are probably 8,000; and there are supposed to be about as many pure-blooded Indians upon the Atlantic coast and scattered throughout the republic. The education of the common people is neglected and left to the priests, who teach them nothing but superstition and their obligations to the Church. In 1868 a decree was passed making education compulsory and free, and providing for the diversion of a liberal amount of the public revenue each year for the support of the schools; but the law is a dead letter, and in no year has the amount assigned to the Department of Education been appropriated. At present there are but sixty schools, with a normal attendance of twenty-five hundred, or an average of forty pupils to thirty thousand inhabitants. There is a university at Leon, with an average of fifty students, and another at Grenada, with a few more, at which law, medicine, and theology are taught, under the direction of the bishop; but most of the sons of wealthy families are sent to Europe to be educated.

A FAMILIAR SCENE.

The city of Leon is the commercial metropolis, and was the ancient capital. In 1854 the seat of government was removed to Grenada, during the great revolution, which lasted for five years, and in which our famous filibuster, Walker, figured; and the people of the latter city would not permit its return to the capital of the viceroys. After fighting over the question for several years, shedding much blood and destroying much property, a compromise was effected by locating the headquarters temporarily at Managua, a smaller place half way between the two, where, since 1863, the President has resided, and the Congress has assembled every year. The public buildings in Leon remain as they were at the time of the removal of the capital, and most of the archives are there, the expectations of the citizens being that they will be needed for the Government again in the near future; but Grenada keeps a threatening look in that direction, and any attempt to disturb the present situation would result in another war, so bitter is the rivalry.

A COUNTRY CHAPEL.

Leon is one of the oldest cities in America, having been founded in 1523 by Fernandez Cordova. Two years before, Pedrarias Divilla, who was Governor at Panama, sent to Leon, on a tour of exploration, a lusty old buccaneer, named Gil Gonzalez, with a few hundred men. He landed at about the centre of the Pacific coast, and marched across to the present city of Rivas. Here he found on the borders of the lake a vast population of Indians under a cacique named Nicaro, and called the country in his reports *Nicaro's Agua*, or waters; hence the name. The Indians regarded the Spaniards with awe and amazement. They had heard of their appearance at Panama and on the Atlantic coast, but believed that the stories of their presence, which came from their ancient enemies, the Carribs, were false and intended to frighten them. Seeing the chief surrounded by such a multitude of savages, Gonzalez approached with great caution, and having captured a native, sent him to Nicaro with this bombastic message:

THE UNITED STATES CONSULATE.

"Tell your chief," said Gonzalez, "that a valiant captain cometh, commissioned to these parts by the greatest king on earth, to inform all the lords of these lands that there is in the heavens, higher than the sun, one Lord, Maker of all

CATHEDRAL OF ST. PETER, LEON.

things, and that those believing on Him shall at death ascend to that loftiness, while disbelievers shall descend into the everlasting fire that burns in the bottomless pit. Tell your chief that I am coming, and that he must be ready upon my arrival at his camp to accept these truths and be baptized, or prepare for battle."

The cacique surrendered, and, with all his warriors and their women, to the number of nine thousand, was baptized. In his report to the King of Spain, the pious old Bombastes Furioso claimed the credit of having converted more heathens than any other man that had ever lived.

In the days of the Spaniards Leon was a splendid city, and there are still existing numerous monuments of its opulence and grandeur. The public buildings are constructed upon a magnificent scale and without regard to cost, and the private dwellings are built in imitation of them, being of imposing exteriors and luxurious in their equipment and adornment. There were seventeen fine churches to a population of fifty thousand, chief of which was the Cathedral of St. Peter, which cost five millions of dollars, and was over thirty-seven years in course of erection. It was finished in 1743, and is still in a good state of preservation, being built of most substantial masonry, with walls of stone eighteen or twenty feet thick. It is of the Moorish style of architecture, resembling the great cathedral at Seville, Spain, and is by far the largest and finest church in Central America. During the frequent revolutions it has always been used as a fortress, and its walls, although still firm and enduring, are much battered by the assaults that have been made upon it.

In 1823, during the first revolution after independence between the aristocrats and the Indians, there was a fire at Leon which destroyed more than a thousand of the finest buildings; and the flames were aided in the work of devastation by thousands of Indian soldiers, who plundered and murdered the inhabitants. This part of the city has never been restored, and long streets, whose pavements are overgrown with weeds and underbrush, are still lined with ruined walls that disclose rich marble columns and artistic carvings. In mockery of the former magnificence which their ancestors destroyed, the Indian peons are living in bamboo huts, enclosed by cactus hedges, on the sites where once lived the proudest hidalgos in Central America. There is a tradition that the town was once cursed by the Pope, because of the murder of an archbishop there, and this accounts for the succession of calamities from which it has suffered.

THE PACIFIC COAST OF NICARAGUA.

The ladies of the aristocracy are in youth usually pretty, and at whatever age are always proud. For some reason or other they consider their country far above and beyond criticism, and themselves superior to the rest of Adam's race. Ancestral pride is so conspicuous as to be ofttimes offensive, and the fact that a person born out of Nicaragua seems to them to have been a misfortune for which no other circumstances can compensate. This is true among both sexes of the upper caste, but more especially among the ladies, whose exalted opinion of their own importance in the universe has never been tarnished by travel. This feeling has gone far to excite the existing prejudice against foreigners, and while the tourists are always most hospitably received, the fact that their stay is only temporary adds to the pleasure of entertaining them. The most rigid restrictions prevent the social intercourse of the sexes, and nowhere in the world is a woman's honor protected with such great precaution; and for excellent reasons. No lady of caste would think of receiving a call from a gentleman alone, except a priest; and the clergy make the most of their privileges, according to common report.

ANTICS ON THE BRIDGE.

The ladies are always idle. To do any sort of work other than embroidery is beneath them, and the number of servants they employ is regulated not by their necessities but by their means. They are all uneducated, the privilege of a few years in a convent only being allowed them; and those are spent in learning the lives of the saints, a little embroidery, to drum on the piano, and to dance. There is no distinctive national costume. The aristocracy imitate the Parisian fashions, while the common masses wear whatever they can get. The Nicaraguans are much more social in disposition than the citizens of the other Central American countries. They have *tertulias*, which is a near relation of a "high tea," and balls more frequently, and are much more given to dinner-parties, at which one of the greatest of imported luxuries is codfish.

The great annual holiday of the people is known as *El Paseo al Mar*, (the Excursion to the Sea), but is often alluded to as the festival of St. Venus, because of the excesses that are committed there by the people, who are most discreet when at home. But as nobody cares what occurs at the carnivals at Rome, so can a party of fashionable Nicaraguans be allowed liberties at their watering-places. In the latter part of March, when the dry season is far advanced and everything is buried in dust, after the harvests are gathered and the crops are sold and carried to Corinto, the seaport, everybody feels like taking a little relaxation. Preparations are made long in advance, but as soon as the March moon comes carts are packed with a little furniture and a good many trunks, and the exodus begins. It is only about fifteen miles to the beach, but the journey occasions as much planning and preparation, and is anticipated with as much pleasure, as a tour through Europe. Everybody goes, the peon as well as the hidalgo, and for two weeks during the full moon the city is deserted. There are no hotels, but each family takes a tent or builds a hut of bamboo, and lives *à négligé* under the shade of the forest trees, which extend almost to the ocean. The Government sends down a battalion of troops, ostensibly to keep order and do police duty, but really as an excuse for giving the officers and soldiers a holiday. Social laws are very much relaxed during the *Paseo*, and it is really the only time when lovers can do their billing and cooing without the interfering presence of a duenna. Flirtations are the order of the day, and Cupid is king.

IN THE UPPER ZONE.

There are no bathing-houses, and no bathing-dresses are worn. The people go into the surf as Nature equipped them—the women and the girls on one side of a long spit of land that reaches into the sea, and the men and boys on the other. This annual Paseo is the perpetuation of a semi-religious Indian custom.

Another peculiar Nicaraguan religious custom is the baptism of the volcanoes, a ceremony which is believed by the superstitious to be very effective in keeping them in subjection and making them observe the proprieties of life. This observance is said to be as old as the Conquest, having originated after the first eruption succeeding the invasion of Nicaragua by the Spaniards, and is repeated on the anniversary of the last disturbance caused by each particular volcano. The priests of the nearest city take the affair in charge, and, followed by a large company of the faithful, ascend to the crater, and with great ceremony sprinkle holy water into it. Each of the volcanic peaks in Nicaragua has been repeatedly sanctified in this way except Momotombo, the grandest but most unregenerate of them all, who has never permitted a human foot to reach his summit or a human eye to look into his crater. Two hundred years ago, after old Tombo, as the master is familiarly called, had been acting very badly, three brave monks determined to try the effect of holy water upon him, and started for the summit with a large cross which they proposed to erect there; but they were never heard of again, and the people look upon the mountain with greater reverence.

VOLCANOES OF AXUSCO AND MOMOTOMBO, FROM THE CATHEDRAL.

VOLCANO OF COSEQUINA, FROM THE SEA.

From the tower of St. Peter's Cathedral in the city of Leon thirteen volcanoes can be seen, several of which are active. There are eighteen standing in a solemn procession around the lakes of Nicaragua and Managua. They are not so high as certain peaks in Guatemala or Costa Rica, but look higher from the fact that they rise immediately from the level of tide-water, and can be seen from the sea in their full grandeur, old Tombo looking to be about the height of Pike's Peak as seen from Colorado Springs. This gigantic mountain rises boldly out of the waters of Lake Nicaragua, its bare and blackened summit, which has forbidden all attempts to scale its sides, being always crowned with a light wreath of smoke, attesting the perpetual existence of the internal fires which now and then break forth and cover its sides with burning floods. At its base are several hot sulphur springs, and at frequent intervals heavy rumbling sounds can be heard from within its walls. In the middle of the lake, only a few miles away, is an exact duplicate of the mountain; in miniature, however, being but one-fourth its size. This is called Momotombita, the three last letters expressing the diminutive. It forms an island, from which its peak rises a perfect cone. Its crater has been extinct for hundreds of years; but the island was a sacred place to the aborigines. In the forests which now cover it are the ruins of vast temples and gigantic idols hewn out of the solid rock. The last serious earthquake, in 1867, occurred without much damage to the city, whose walls have been several times shaken down in the three centuries and a half since it was founded.

LA UNION AND VOLCANO OF CONCHAGUA.

The most fearful eruption on record in Nicaragua, and one of the most serious the world ever saw, was that of the volcano Cosequina, near Grenada, in 1835. It continued for four days, and covered the country for hundreds of miles around with ashes and lava, causing a panic from which the people did not recover for many years, and resulting in great destruction of life and property. The explosions were of such force that ashes fell in the city of Bogota, Colombia, fifteen hundred miles away in a direct line, and at an altitude eleven thousand feet above the sea. Ashes fell in the West India islands, also far in the interior of Mexico, and showers of them that obscured the sun caused great consternation in Guatemala and the neighboring republics, while the people in Nicaragua thought the end of the world had come. Vessels sailing in the Pacific had their decks covered with lava and ashes, and several sailors were injured by falling stones; while the ocean for a hundred and fifty miles was so strewn with floating ashes and pumice-stone that the surface of the water was concealed. The anniversary of this horrible catastrophe is always observed by the people as a great fast-day, business being suspended throughout the whole republic, and the people gathering in the churches to pray for deliverance from further eruptions. Since that date the volcano has continued active, but has caused no damage.

A great part of the surface of the country is covered with beds of lava and scoria, lakes of bitter water that have no bottom, yawning craters surrounded with blistered rocks, and pits from which sulphurous vapors are constantly rising that the people appropriately call *infernillos*.

THE FATE OF FILIBUSTERS.

The city of Grenada stands at the eastern end of the inhabited valley of Nicaragua, as Leon does at the western end, the two rival cities being about seventy miles apart. Until its almost total destruction by Walker and his filibusters in 1857, it was a beautiful town, filled with fine mansions, and proud of its appearance. The population was reduced during the civil war, in which the American adventurers played so conspicuous a part, from thirty-five thousand to fifteen thousand; and although that was nearly thirty years ago it has scarcely begun to recover. Grenada was the seat of the "aristocratic" government which Walker and his allied Nicaraguans overthrew, and was besieged for two years, during which time the inhabitants endured not only great hardships, many dying of starvation and epidemics which broke out among them, but suffered the destruction of almost their entire property. During the days of Spanish dominion it was one of the most wealthy and prosperous cities in Central America, and its commerce was enormous. The old chronicles relate that nearly every day caravans of eighteen hundred mules laden with bullion and merchandise arrived from the surrounding country, and carried away European goods in exchange.

One of the largest monasteries on the continent was situated here, erected and occupied by the Franciscan Friars, who owned extensive estates in the surrounding country, and continued to acquire great wealth until they were expelled and their property confiscated in 1829. It is still standing in a good state of preservation.

The actual capital of Nicaragua, the city of Managua, sits on the southern shore of the lake of the same name, about sixty miles from the Pacific Ocean, and is reached by an overland journey of three days from Leon, which is connected with Corinto, the chief seaport, by a railroad. The population of Managua is about eight or ten thousand, at a guess, for no census has been taken since 1870. It has increased since that date, when the inhabitants numbered six thousand seven hundred. The rich residents are mostly planters who have estancias in the neighborhood, and live in houses of one or two stories without any pretension to architectural beauty or elegance. They are more modern in construction than those of Leon and Grenada, for it is only since the seat of government was located at Managua that it has been of any commercial or political importance. A large portion of the standing army of the republic, consisting of two thousand men, is stationed at Managua, occupying an old monastery as a barracks, and the streets are always crowded with military men in resplendent uniforms. There are about three officers to every ten privates in the army, and positions in the military service are actively sought by the sons of the aristocratic families, who prefer them to professional or commercial careers. The privates are exclusively Indians or half-breed peons, who wear a uniform of dirty white cotton drilling with a blue cap. They are supposed to be voluntarily enlisted, but when troops are needed they are secured by sending squads of impressarios into the country, who seize as many peons as they want, bring them, bound with ropes, to the capital, and then compel them to sign the enlistment rolls.

A FARMING SETTLEMENT.

The National Palace is a low, square edifice, with balconies of the ordinary Spanish styles, and was formerly the home of one of the religious orders. The only handsome rooms are the headquarters of the President and the chambers in which the two Houses of Congress meet annually. They are fitted up with fine imported furniture, and the walls are covered with portraits of men distinguished in the history of the republic.

The peons live in the outskirts of the city, in huts of bamboo thatched with palm-leaves and straw, surrounded with curious-looking fences or hedges of cactus. They are apparently very poor, and are surrounded with filth and squalor; but the real, which is worth twelve and a half cents, will sustain a whole family for a week, for they need little more than nature has supplied them with—the plantains and yams that grow profusely in their little gardens. They seldom eat meat, and never wash themselves. They appear to be perfectly happy, and sit at the doors of their huts, women and men, both nearly naked, smoking cigarettes, and chatting as contentedly as if all their wants in life were fully supplied. Densely ignorant and superstitious, they know nothing of the world beyond their own surroundings, and care less.

THE QUESAL.

The environs of Managua are very picturesque. On one side is the beautiful lake, sixty miles long and thirty miles wide, surrounded by volcanoes, and on the other are fertile slopes, on which are coffee plantations and cocoa groves, both yielding prodigious crops. The peons of the city work upon the estancias when there is anything to be done, travelling five or six miles each day in going to and returning from the scene of their labor. The country about Managua must have been densely populated by the aborigines, and is full of most curious and puzzling relics of a prehistoric race, which the natives regard with great veneration. The geologist, as well as the ethnologist and antiquarian, finds here one of the most abundant fields for investigation, which was explored and described by Stephens, Squier, and many earlier writers.

The Government consists of a President, who receives a salary of two thousand five hundred dollars, and is elected for four years, during which time, if he is not overpowered by some political rival, he usually manages to amass an immense fortune. A common argument in favor of re-electing presidents is that they are able to steal all they want during their first term. There are two Vice-Presidents, generally the President of the Senate and the Speaker of the Lower House, and either of them may be designated to perform the duties of the Executive when he so elects. There is a cabinet, or council, of four ministers. One has the finances in charge; another foreign affairs, agriculture, and commerce; a third military affairs and public works; and a fourth justice, public instruction, and ecclesiastical affairs.

The Senate is composed of fourteen members, two from each of the Departments, or Provinces, elected for four years; and the House of Deputies of twenty-four members, or one for each ten thousand of population, elected for two years. They are paid one dollar and fifty cents per diem during the sessions of Congress. No Senator or Deputy can be elected more than two consecutive terms, and no official of the Government or member of Congress can be a candidate for election or appointment to any other office during his constitutional term of service. Ecclesiastics are ineligible for civil positions, and all candidates for every post of honor under the Government must have proper qualifications; while all persons accepting pensions from the Government, and performing the duty of house or body servants, are denied the right of suffrage or of holding office. There are three courts, State or Department judges being elected by the people. District Federal judges and members of the Supreme Court being appointed by the House of Representatives and confirmed by the Senate, to serve during life unless impeached and convicted by the Deputies before the Senate for malfeasance in office. It requires a two-thirds vote in the House to enact legislation, but only a majority vote in the Senate. The President has the power of issuing decrees during the recess of Congress, which decrees have the force of law, but must be affirmed or reversed by Congress at its next session.

Since the charter of the Interoceanic Canal Company by the Congress of the United States, and the actual commencement of work upon the long-projected enterprise, under the direction of Chief-engineer Menocal, the republic of Nicaragua assumes a position of more prominence among nations, and of greater interest to the public at large, than it has ever had before. The failure of the Panama Canal Company, and the apparent impossibility of piercing the Isthmus at its narrowest part, has also given the Nicaragua Company increased importance, but Mr. Menocal and the company of capitalists who stand behind him feel no doubt of ultimate success.

SAN SALVADOR.

THE CAPITAL OF SAN SALVADOR.

WHOEVER visits the little republic of San Salvador, and lands at La Libertad, its principal seaport, must expect to undergo a novel and alarming experience. There is no harbor in the country, although it has one hundred and fifty-seven miles of sea-coast. The shore of the Pacific is a line of bluffs, with a fringe of beach at the bottom, and upon the sand a mighty surf is always beating. Ships anchor several miles off the coast, to avoid being driven ashore by the winds that sometimes rise very suddenly, and no boat can survive the breakers. An iron pier, or mole, twice as long and twice as high as the famous pier at Coney Island, extends from the bluff for three-quarters of a mile into the sea. A tramway runs from the town of La Libertad, connecting its monster warehouses with the pier, and cars loaded with coffee, sugar, and other products of the country are shoved out by peons or drawn by mules. The freight is piled upon the pier until the steamer arrives, when it is carried out to the anchorage in large lighters rowed by a dozen naked boatmen. The cargo is hoisted and lowered by means of a huge iron crane and derrick, operated by a small steam-engine. Bags and boxes are tumbled into great nets of cordage holding two tons or more, which are jerked up into the air by the derrick, swung around to be clear of the pier, and then dropped into the lighter.

Live cattle are hoisted and lowered by the horns, a lasso being thrown, one end of which is attached to the derrick, and the animal finds himself suddenly jerked into the air, and hangs kicking and struggling until his feet touch the bottom of the lighter, when he shakes himself to see if he is still alive. It is a wicked way to treat beasts, but under the circumstances there seems to be no other method. Sometimes, when the rope is carelessly adjusted, and the animal is young and heavy, his horns are torn out by the roots, and he falls sixty or seventy feet into the lighter, breaking his neck or legs, when one of the boatmen, drawing a knife from his belt, severs the jugular, and hangs his head over the side of the boat to let his life-blood run into the sea.

Horses are lifted and lowered with greater care by means of a strong harness of wide leather, with an iron ring in the saddle to which a rope's end is hooked.

Humankind are treated with less consideration. When passengers arrive by a vessel they come to the pier on a lighter with freight, which rises and sinks with the heavy swell in a manner that is not only very alarming, but is almost certain to cause sea-sickness. One may have come all the way from New York or Europe to Aspinwall, and then from Panama up the coast, without a symptom of the distressing malady, but he is pretty sure to succumb to the rocking of the lighter at La Libertad, as it rubs and pounds against the iron trestle of the pier, while he is awaiting his turn to land. The officers of the vessels, accustomed to the motion, spring from the gunwales of the boat to the rounds of ladders that hang down the sides of the mole, and climb them as the boatmen do; but ladies and gentlemen unacquainted with this method, and untrained to clamber among the rigging of a ship, are treated to a sensation that is apt to make a timid person apprehensive.

An iron cage, capable of holding six persons, is lowered to the lighter, and you are invited to step in. As soon as it is full a boatman shuts the door and gives a signal to the engineer above. There is a sudden, startling jerk, you shut your eyes, cling to the bars of the cage, and feel your heart in your throat. The cage stops as suddenly as it started, whirls around swiftly for an instant or two, then swings over the pier, and drops with a thump. The door is opened, you step out,

LANDING AT LA LIBERTAD.

uninjured, but trembling like a frightened bird, and register an unuttered vow that you will never land at La Libertad again. But this feeling leaves you when you enjoy a laugh at the demonstrations of alarm made by your fellow-passengers who have to follow you, and when you are assured, as people always are, that thousands have landed and embarked in the same manner without receiving a bruise or having a bone broken. It is not so pleasant, but quite as safe, as scrambling up a gangway from a dock to the deck of a vessel.

EN ROUTE TO THE INTERIOR.

Although San Salvador is the smallest in area of the group of republics, and only a little larger than Connecticut, it is the most prosperous, the most enterprising, and the most densely populated, having even a greater number of inhabitants than the land of wooden nutmegs. The population averages about eighty to the square mile—almost twenty times that of its neighbors. The natives are inclined to civilized pursuits, being engaged not only in agriculture, but quite extensively in manufacture. They are more energetic and industrious than the people in other parts of Central America, work harder, and accomplish more, gain wealth rapidly, and are frugal, but the constantly recurring earthquakes and political disturbances keep the country poor. When the towns are destroyed by volcanic eruptions, they are not allowed to lie in ruins, as those of other countries are, but the inhabitants at once clear away the rubbish and begin to rebuild. The city of San Salvador has been twice rebuilt since Leon of Nicaragua was laid in ruins, but the débris in the latter city has never been disturbed.

San Salvador has always taken the lead in the political affairs of Central America. It was the first to throw off the yoke of Spain, and uttered the first cry of liberty, as Venezuela did among the nations of the southern continent. The patriots of San Salvador received the cordial co-operation of the liberal element in the cities of Grenada, Nicaragua, and San José of Costa Rica, but were suppressed by the Imperial power. Its provisional congress was driven from place to place, but remained intact; it had the sympathy and support of the people, and defied the invaders of the country. Finally, as a last resort, the congress, by a solemn act passed on the 2d of December, 1822, resolved to annex their little province to the United States, and provided for the appointment of commissioners to proceed to Washington and ask its incorporation in the body politic of "La Grande Republica." Before the commissioners could leave the country the revolution in the other Central American States had become too formidable to suppress, as the example of San Salvador had spread like an epidemic among the people, and its demand for liberty had found an echo from every valley and from every hill, from the Rio Grande to the Chagres. The five States joined in a confederacy one year after the act of annexation to the United States was passed, and the resolution was never officially submitted to our government. This was before the days of the Monroe Doctrine, and if the rise of Liberalism in Central America had not been so rapid, the political divisions of the North American continent might have been different now, and the destiny of several nations changed.

THE PEAK OF SAN SALVADOR.

Some time before the organization of the confederacy the people of San Salvador had adopted a constitution and formed a State government, being always foremost, and their example was followed seven months later by Costa Rica, then by Guatemala, Honduras, and Nicaragua in succession. Salvador was the first of the republics also to throw off the shackles of the Church. Indignant at the interference of the archbishop of Guatemala, who had charge of the Church in Central America, they defied his authority and elected a liberal bishop of their own. The archbishop denounced the act and appealed to the Pope, who threatened to excommunicate the entire population. But the threat was received with indifference, and the example of the Salvadorians was shortly after imitated by the people of Costa Pica, in like disregard of the will of the successor of St. Peter.

The President is elected for four years, the members of the Senate for three, and of the House of Deputies for one, all of them directly by the people. There is a senator for every thirty thousand of the population, and a deputy for every fifteen thousand. The exercise of suffrage is guarded by some wholesome restrictions. All married men can vote, except those who are engaged in domestic service, those who are without stated occupation, those who refuse to pay their legal debts, those who owe money past due to the Government, those who have accepted pay for any service from foreign powers, and those who have been convicted of felony. Unmarried men, to exercise the right of citizens, must be property owners, and be able to read and write. All voters have to show receipts for the payment of taxes the year previous if they are property owners, and bankrupts are entirely disfranchised, the idea being that none but a producer—one who adds to the wealth of the State or pays taxes—shall have a voice in its government. None but property owners are eligible to office.

The President has a cabinet of four ministers. They have in charge the Departments of Finance, War, and Public Works, Internal Affairs and Public Instruction, and Foreign Affairs. The Judiciary are appointed by the Deputies and confirmed by the Senate. Education is free and compulsory. There is a school for every two thousand inhabitants, supported by the general government, and a University at the capital with three hundred and fifty students, studying law, medicine, and the applied sciences, and one hundred and forty pursuing a classical course.

The standing army consists of twelve hundred men, but all able-bodied citizens between the ages of eighteen and forty are organized as a militia, and are subject to be called upon for service at the will of the President.

The capital, San Salvador ("The City of our Saviour"), is

THE PLAZA.

eighteen miles from the sea-coast, and has an elevation of 2800 feet. It is surrounded by a group of volcanoes, two of which are active, one, Yzalco, discharging immense volumes of smoke, ashes, and lava at regular intervals of seven minutes from one year's end to the other. San Salvador is reached by coaches over a picturesque mountain-road, but the journey is not pleasant in the dry season on account of the dust, nor in the rainy season on account of the mud. The city was founded in 1528 by George Alvarado, a brother of the renowned lieutenant of Cortez, who was the discoverer, conqueror, and the first viceroy of Central America. The situation it occupies is one of the most beautiful that can be imagined, being in the midst of an elevated *mesa*, or tableland, which overlooks the sea to the southward, and is surrounded by mountains upon its three other sides. As the prevailing winds are from the ocean, the climate is always cool and healthful, and the mountain streams are so abundant that the foliage is fresh during the entire year. Through each street runs an *asequia*, or irrigating ditch, which is always filled with water. Pipes lead from it into the gardens of the people, and supply hydrants for their use.

SPANISH-AMERICAN COURTSHIP.

There is very little architectural taste shown in the construction of the dwellings or of the public buildings. This is because of the frequency of earthquakes. The walls are of thick adobe, with scarcely any ornamentation, and the streets are dull and unattractive; but within the houses are gardens of wonderful beauty, in which the people spend the greater portion of the time, more often sleeping in a hammock among the trees in the dry season than under the roofs of their houses.

The public buildings are of insignificant appearance, and even the cathedral and the other churches are painfully plain and commonplace compared with those of other cities of its size. All this is owing to the fact, as has been stated, that the danger of their destruction at any moment forbids a lavish expenditure in construction or unnecessary display.

The women of San Salvador are neater in appearance, more careful in their dress, and are therefore more attractive than their sisters in Nicaragua, where, if there is any difference between the sexes, they are less tidy than the men. The girls in the rural districts always bathe in the *asequias* every morning at daylight, and the traveller who starts out early generally surprises groups of Naiads disporting in the streams. They plunge into the bushes or keep their bodies under the water until the intruder passes by, but do not hesitate to exchange a few words of banter with him, and good-naturedly bid him godspeed.

There is more freedom between the sexes in San Salvador than in the sister republics; and it is not at the cost of morals, for, as a rule, in countries where social restrictions are the most severe there is the greatest amount of licentiousness. The education of the masses has proved to be the greatest safeguard, and the number of illegitimate births is reduced as the standard of intelligence is elevated. The constitutional provision in San Salvador which confers superior advantages upon married men, together with a law limiting the marriage fees of the priests, have proven to be wise and effective policy. The girls marry at fifteen and over, and very few peons reach their majority without taking a lawful wife.

There is a public theatre, subsidized by the Government, at which frequent entertainments are given, and nearly every season an opera company comes from Italy or France. The performances are liberally patronized, at high prices of

A HACIENDA.

admission. But the most popular *funcions*, as they are called, are by local amateurs, the programmes being made up of vocal and instrumental music, recitations, and original poems and orations. The latter are always the popular features of the occasion, and the *funcions* are usually arranged to give some young orator an opportunity to show his talents before the foot-lights. There is a great deal of rivalry, too, among the local poets, each aspirant for honors having his clique of admirers, or *faccions*, who feel it their duty to applaud no one else, however meritorious, and to hiss all others down. When two of these popular idols appear upon the platform on the same evening, as they often do, there are scenes of sensational excitement and sometimes mob violence. The subjects of all the orations and poems are usually patriotic— the praise of San Salvador—for the love of country is a theme of which the people never tire. The programmes of all public entertainments are mostly composed of local compositions, national airs, and patriotic songs. The musicians prefer the scores of their own composers, and everything foreign is to a degree offensive, to be tolerated only as a matter of variety.

INTERIOR OF A SAN SALVADOR HOUSE.

The Salvadorians have a dozen or more "Fourths of July"—memorial days—sometimes two patriotic celebrations occurring in a month, on the anniversary of historical events. All classes of people join in the demonstrations, closing their places of business, decorating the streets, attending high-mass in the morning, engaging in processions and hearing patriotic orations during the day, and in the evening closing the festivities with fireworks, banquets, and balls. But the two great days of the year are Christmas and the Feast of San Miguel (St. Michael), the patron saint of the republic. The latter is celebrated very much like our Independence Day was in ancient times, except that the hours from sunrise to noon are devoted to solemn religious services in all the churches, the bishop himself officiating at the cathedral, and the rest of the time to the next morning to holiday festivities. There is much powder wasted in fire-crackers, or *bombas*, as they are called, fireworks, and salutes by the artillery.

The annual fair of St. Miguel, which is held in February, is always a notable event, being not only a national anniversary, but the greatest market season of the year, and the occasion of general and prolonged festivities. It lasts about two weeks, and is attended by buyers and sellers from all parts of Central America. The importing houses always have their representatives present on such occasions. The days are occupied with trading, and the nights with balls, concerts, theatrical performances, and gambling. Everybody plays cards, and no one, man or woman, ever sits down to a game without stakes. Women play at their residences with or without their gentlemen friends, and large sums of money often pass across the table. At the fairs, and in fact on all occasions which bring people together, the peons are entertained with cock-fights and bull-fights, although the latter cruel sport is nominally forbidden by law. The bull-rings and cock-pits are invariably crowded every Sunday afternoon, and always on saints' days, and often the best people are found among the spectators, particularly the young men, who ruin themselves with reckless betting. It is the fashion for the swells to keep gamebirds, and employ professional cock-fighters to train and handle them.

The Christmas festivities commence about midnight, and the explosions of cannon and fireworks always begin as soon as the clock in the cathedral tower strikes twelve. Everybody is up and dressed before daylight to attend early mass, and when the sun rises the streets are full of people saluting each other by exchanging the compliments of the day, and throwing egg-shells filled with perfumed water. From morning till night the air is full of the noise of fireworks, cannonades, the shouts of people, and the music of military bands, while processions are continually passing through the principal streets. In nearly every house preparations have been going on for weeks, not for the exhibition of Christmas-trees or the exchange of gifts, but for the representation of the *naciamiento*, or birth of Christ. The best room in the house is often fitted up to resemble a manger, asses being brought in from the stable to make the scene more realistic. Several incidents in the life of the Saviour are portrayed in a like manner. In other residences are different representations. Sometimes the parlor is arranged like a bower, filled with tropical plants and flowers, moss-covered stones and sea-shells, and draped with vines. Within the bower are figures of the Virgin and Child, surrounded by the kneeling Magi and the members of the Holy Family.

A TYPICAL TOWN.

It is the ambition of the mistress of the house to surpass all her friends and neighbors in the realism of her representation and in the elegance with which the puppets are dressed. During the day there is a general interchange of calls to see the displays, to criticise them, and make comparisons. The grandest display is always made in the cathedral, the cost often amounting to many thousands of dollars, while the subordinate churches enter into an active and expensive rivalry, raising funds for the purpose by soliciting subscriptions in the parish. The ceremonies usually begin before daylight, and last for a couple of hours, high-mass being sung by the leading vocalists of the country, assisted by orchestras and military bands.

WHAT ALARMS THE CITIZENS.

The favorite incident for portrayal is the Adoration of the Magi, and human figures are usually trained by the priests to play the various characters. The most beautiful woman in the city is selected to act the part of the Virgin, and some young infant is volunteered to represent the baby Christ. The church is always crowded, and illuminated by thousands of candles. At the proper moment the curtain is drawn, and the choir breaks out in a glorious anthem; the bells of the churches ring, and the vast audience, rising to their feet, join in the exultant song, "Jubilate! jubilate! Christ is born!" Processions of priests enter, and at the close of the anthem the bishop sings high-mass to a living representation of the Virgin and Child.

The people are not so priestridden as those of some of the Spanish-American countries, being naturally more self-reliant and independent. They know what liberty is, and insist upon being allowed to enjoy it, both civil and religious. They choose their own priests, and the latter elect their own bishop, without regard to the Pope or the College of Cardinals. The clerical party in politics, or the Serviles, as they were called, because of their slavery to the Church, has long been extinct in San Salvador, and the political struggles are more personal than over abstract issues. There is a considerable degree of superstition among the people, and they believe in all sorts of signs and omens, but the priests do not attempt to humbug them with bogus miracles or wonder-working images.

Much of this superstition relates to the earthquakes and volcanic disturbances to which the country is so subject. Within view of the capital are eleven great volcanoes, two of which are unceasingly active, while the others are subject to occasional eruptions. The nearest is the mountain of San Salvador, about eight thousand feet high, and showing to great advantage because it rises so abruptly from the plain. It is only three miles from the city, to the westward, very steep, and its sides are broken by monstrous gorges, immense rocky declivities, and projecting cliffs. The summit is crowned by a cone of ashes and scoriæ that have been thrown out in centuries past, but since 1856, subsequent to the greatest earthquake the country has known, the crater has been extinct, and is now filled with a bottomless lake. Very few people have ever ascended to the summit, because of the extreme difficulty and peril of making the climb, while even a smaller number have entered the chasm in which the crater lies. Some years ago a couple of venturesome French scientists went down, but became exhausted in their attempts to return. Their companions who remained at the top lowered them food and blankets by lines, and they were finally rescued, after several days of confinement in their rocky prison, by a detachment of soldiers, who hauled them up the precipice by ropes.

The two active volcanoes, or *vivos*, as the people call them, are San Miguel and Yzalco, and there are none more violent on the face of the globe. They present a magnificent display to the passengers of steamers sailing by the coast, or anchored in the harbor of La Libertad and Acajutla, constantly discharging masses of lava which flow down their sides in blazing torrents, and illuminating the sky with the flames that issue from the craters at regular intervals. Yzalco is as regular as a clock, the eruption occurring like the beating of a mighty pulse every seven minutes.

It is impossible to conceive of a grander spectacle than this monster. It rises seven thousand feet, almost directly from the sea, and an immense volume of smoke, like a plume, is continually pouring out of its summit, broken with such regularity by masses of flame that rise a thousand feet that it has been named *El Faro del Salvador*—"The Light-house of Salvador." Around the base of the mountain are fertile plantations, while above them, covering about two-thirds of its surface, is an almost impenetrable forest, whose foliage is perpetual and of the darkest green. Then beyond the forest is a ring of reddish scoriæ, while above it the live ashes and lava that are cast from the crater so regularly are constantly changing from livid yellow, when they are heated, to a silver gray as they cool.

Yzalco is in many respects the most remarkable volcano on earth; first, because its discharges have continued so long and

YZALCO FROM A DISTANCE.

with such great regularity; again, because the tumult in the earth's bowels is always to be heard, as the rumblings and explosions are constant, being audible for a hundred miles, and sounding like the noises which Rip van Winkle heard when he awakened from his sleep in the Catskills; and, finally, it is the only volcano that has originated on this continent since the discovery by Columbus.

It arose suddenly from the plain in the spring of 1770, in the midst of what had been for nearly a hundred years the profitable estate of Señor Don Balthazar Erazo, who was absent from the country at the time, and was greatly amazed upon his return to discover that his magnificent coffee and indigo plantation had, without his knowledge or consent, been exchanged for a first-class volcano. In December, 1769, the peons on the hacienda were alarmed by terrific rumblings under the ground, constant tremblings of the earth, and frequent earthquakes, which did not extend over the country as usual, but seemed to be confined to that particular locality. They left the place in terror when the tremblings and noises continued, and returning a week or two after, found that all the buildings had been shaken down, trees uprooted, and large craters opened in the fields which had been level earth before. From these craters smoke and steam issued, and occasionally flames were seen to come out of the ground. Some brave *vaqueros*, or herdsmen, remained near by to watch developments, and on the 23d of February, 1770, they were entertained by a spectacle that no other men have been permitted to witness, for about ten o'clock on the morning of that day the grand upheaval took place, and it seemed to them, as they fled in terror, that the whole universe was being turned upside down.

First there were a series of terrific explosions, which lifted the crust of the earth several hundred feet, and out of the cracks issued flames and lava, and immense volumes of smoke. An hour or two afterwards there was another and a grander convulsion, which shook and startled the country for a hundred miles around. Rocks weighing thousands of tons were hurled into the air, and fell several leagues distant. The surface of the earth was elevated about three thousand feet, and the internal recesses were purged of masses of lava and blistered stone, which fell in a heap around the hole from which they issued. These discharges continued for several days

YZALCO.

at irregular intervals, accompanied by loud explosions and earthquakes, which did much damage throughout the entire republic; the disturbance was perceptible in Nicaragua and Honduras. In this manner was a volcano born, and it has proved to be a healthy and vigorous child. In less than two months from a level field arose a mountain more than four thousand feet high, and the constant discharges from the crater which opened then have accumulated around its edges until its elevation has increased two thousand feet more. Unfortunately, the growth of the monster has not been scientifically observed or accurately measured, but the cone of lava and ashes, which is now twenty-five hundred feet from the foundation of earth upon which it rests, is constantly growing in bulk and height by the incessant discharges of lava, ashes, and other volcanic matter upon it.

The capital of San Salvador has been thrice almost entirely, and eleven times in its history partially, destroyed by earthquakes and volcanic eruptions coming together. These catastrophies occurred in 1575, 1593, 1625, 1656, 1770, 1773, 1798, 1839, 1854, 1873, and 1882. The most serious convulsions took place in 1773 and 1854, when not only the City of Our Saviour, but several other towns were entirely ruined, and nearly every place suffered to a greater or less degree; but the restoration was rapid and complete.

The chief products of the country are coffee, cocoa, sugar, indigo, and other agricultural staples, which are raised by the same process that prevails in other States, with the addition of a balsam that is very valuable, and is grown exclusively on a little strip of land lying along the coast between the two principal seaports, La Libertad and Acajutla. Lying to the seaward of the volcanic range is a forest about six hundred square miles in extent that is composed almost exclusively of balsam-trees, and is known as the "Costa del Balsimo." It is populated by a remnant of the aboriginal Indian race, who are supported by the product of their forest, and are permitted to remain there undisturbed, and very little altered from their original condition.

The forest is traversed only by foot-paths, so intricate as to baffle the stranger who attempts to enter it; and it is not safe to make such an attempt, as the Indians, peaceful enough when they come out to mingle with the other inhabitants of the country, violently resent any intrusion into their

IN THE INTERIOR.

strong-hold. They live as a community, all their earnings being intrusted to the care of *ahuales*—old men who exercise both civil and religious offices, and keep the common funds in a treasure-box, to be distributed among the families as their necessities require. There is a prevailing impression that the tribe has an enormous sum of money in its possession, as their earnings are large and their wants are few. The surplus existing at the end of each year is supposed to be buried in a sacred spot with religious ceremonies. Both men and women go entirely naked, except for a breech-clout, but when they come to town they assume the ordinary cotton garments worn by the peons. They are darker in color, larger in stature, more taciturn and morose, than the other Indians of the country, but are temperate, industrious, and adhere to their ancient rites with great tenacity. They are known to history as the Nahuatls, but are commonly spoken of as "Balsimos."

HAULING SUGAR-CANE.

Agriculture is carried on by them only to an extent sufficient to supply their own wants, and usually by the women, while the men are engaged in gathering the balsam, of which they sell about twenty thousand dollars' worth each year. They number about two thousand people, and including what they spend at their festivals, which are more like bacchanalian riots than religious ceremonies, and are accompanied by scenes of revolting bestiality, their annual expenses cannot be more than one half of their incomes.

The balsam is obtained by making an incision in the tree, from which the sap exudes, and is absorbed by bunches of raw cotton. These, when thoroughly saturated, are thrown into vats of boiling water and replaced by others. The balsam leaves the cotton, rises to the surface of the water, and at intervals is skimmed off and placed in wooden bowls or gourds, where it hardens, and then is wrapped in the leaves of the tree and sent to market. In commerce it is known as Peruvian balsam, because in early times Callao was the great market for its sale, but the product comes exclusively from San Salvador.

There is one railroad in San Salvador, extending from Acajutla to the city of Sonsonate, the centre of the sugar district, and it is being extended to Santa Ana, the chief town of the Northern Province. It is owned by a native capitalist, and operated under the management of an American engineer. The plan is to extend the track parallel with the sea through the entire republic, in the valley back of the mountain range, with branches through the passes to the principal cities. It now passes two-thirds of the distance around the base of the volcano Yzalco, and from the cars is furnished a most remarkable view of that sublime spectacle. The entire system when completed will not consist of more than two hundred and fifty miles of track, and the work of construction is neither difficult nor expensive.

SAN JOSÉ.

THE CAPITAL OF COSTA RICA.

NEARLY four hundred years ago an old sailor coasted along the eastern shore of Costa Rica in a bark not much bigger than a canal-boat, searching for a passage to the western sea. He had a bunk built in the bows of his little vessel where he could rest his weary bones and look out upon the world he had discovered. There was little left of him but his will. He had explored the whole coast from Yucatan to Trinidad, and found it an unbroken line of continent, a contradiction of all his reasoning, a defiance of all his theories, and an impassable obstacle to the hopes he had cherished for thirty years. The geography of the New World was clear enough in his mind. The earth was a globe, there was no doubt of it, and there must be a navigable belt of water around. So he groped along, seeking the passage he felt should be there, cruising into each river, and following the shorelines of each gulf and bay. Instinctively he hovered around the narrowest portion of the continent, where was but a slender strip of land, upheaved by some mighty convulsion, to shatter his theories and defy his dreams. It was the most pathetic picture in all history. Finally, overcome by age and infirmity, he had to abandon the attempt, and fearing to return to Spain without something to satisfy the avarice of his sovereign, surrendered the command of his little fleet to his brother Bartholomew, and wept while the carnival of murder and plunder, that was to last three centuries, was begun.

Among other points visited for barter with the Indians was a little harbor in which were islands covered with limes, and Columbus marked the place upon his chart "Puerto de

CRATER OF A VOLCANO.

Limon." To-day it is a collection of cheap wooden houses and bamboo huts, with wharves, warehouses, and railway shops, surrounded by the most luxurious tropical vegetation, alive with birds of gorgeous plumage, venomous reptiles, and beautiful tiger-cats. Here and there about the place are patches of sugar-cane and groups of cocoa-nut trees, with the wide-spreading bread-fruit that God gave to the tropical savage as He gave rice and maize to his Northern brother, and the slender, graceful rubber-tree, whose frosty-colored mottled trunk looks like the neck of a giraffe. It scarcely casts a shadow; but the banana, with its long pale green plumes, furnishes plenty of shelter for the palm-thatched cabins, the naked babies that play around them, and the half-dressed women who seem always to be dozing in the sun.

Surrounding the city for a radius of threescore miles is a jungle full of patriarchal trees, stately and venerable, draped with long moss and slender vines that look like the rigging of a ship. Their limbs are covered with wonderful orchids as bright and radiant as the plumage of the birds, the Espiritu Santo and other rare plants being as plentiful as the daisies in a New

England meadow. There is another flower, elsewhere unknown, called the "turn-sol," which in the morning is white and wax-like, resembling the camellia, but at noon has turned to the most vivid scarlet, and at sunset drops off its stem. This picture is seen from shipboard through a veil of mist—miasmatic vapor—in which the lungs of men find poison, but the air plants food. It reaches from the breasts of the mountains to the foam-fringed shore, broken only by the fleecy clouds that hang low and motionless in the atmosphere, as if they, with all the rest of nature, had sniffed the fragrance of the poppy and sunk to sleep.

But in the mornings and the evenings, when the air is cool, Limon is a busy place. Dwarfish engines with long trains of cars wind down from the interior, laden with coffee and bananas. Half-naked roustabouts file back and forth across the gangplanks, loading steamers for Liverpool, New York, and New Orleans. The coffee is allowed to accumulate in the warehouses until the vessels come, but the bananas must not be picked till the last moment, at telegraphic notice, the morning the steamer sails. Trains of cars are sent to the side-tracks of every plantation, and are loaded with the half-ripe fruit still glistening with the dew. There are often as many as fifty thousand bunches on a single steamer, representing six million bananas, but they are so perishable that more than half the cargo goes overboard before its destination is reached. The shipments of bananas from Costa Rica are something new in trade. Only a few years since all our supply came from Honduras and the West Indies, but the development of the plantations around Limon has given that port almost a monopoly. This is due to the construction of a railway seventy miles into the interior, intended to connect the capital of the country and its populous valley with the Atlantic Ocean. The road was begun by the Government, but before its completion passed into the hands of Minor C. Keith, of Brooklyn, who has a perpetual lease, and is attempting to extend it to San José, from and to which freight is transported in ox-carts, a distance of thirty miles.

RUBBER-TREES.

Along the track many plantations have been opened in the jungle, and produce prolifically. Numbers of the settlers are from the United States, from the South particularly, and it being the fashion to christen the plantations, the traveller finds over the entrances sign-boards that bear familiar names. Over the gate-way to one of the finest haciendas, as they are called, is the inscription "Johnny Reb's Last Ditch," a forlorn and almost hopeless ex-Confederate having drifted there, after much buffeting by fortune, and taken up Government land, on which he now is in a fair way to make a fortune.

From the terminus of the railway the ride to the capital is over picturesque mountain passes and through deep gorges and cañons whose mighty walls never admit the sun. There are no coaches, but the ride must be made on mule-back, starting before sunrise so as to reach the city by dark. San José is found in a pretty valley between the two ranges of the Cordilleras, and surrounded by an entertaining group of volcanoes, not less than eight being in sight from any of the housetops. Ordinarily they behave very well, and sleep as quietly as the prophets, but now and then their slumbers are disturbed by indigestion, when they get restless, yawn a little, breathe forth fire and smoke, and vomit sulphur, lava, and ashes. One would think that people living continually in the midst of danger from earthquakes and eruptions would soon become accustomed to them; but it is not so. The interval since the last calamity, when the city of Cartago was destroyed, has been forty years—so long that the next entertainment is expected to be one of unusual interest; and as no announcements are made in the newspapers, the people are always in a solemn state of uncertainty whether they will awake in a pile of brimstone and ashes or under their ponchos as usual. This gives life a zest the superstitious do not enjoy.

It is the theory of the local scientists that there is a subterranean connection between the group of volcanoes, and that prodigious fires are constantly burning beneath. Therefore it is necessary for at least one of them to be always doing business, to permit the smoke and gases to escape through its crater, for if all should suspend operations the gases would gather in the vaults below, and when they reached the fires

THE ROAD FROM PORT LIMON TO SAN JOSÉ.

would shake the earth by their explosion. It is said to be a fact that the total cessation of all the volcanoes is followed by an earthquake, and if Tierra Alba, which is active now, should cease to show its cloud of smoke by day and its pillar of fire by night, the people would leave their houses and take to the fields in anticipation of the impending calamity. All the buildings in the country are built for earthquake service, being seldom more than one story in elevation, and never more than two, of thick adobe walls, which are light and elastic.

A PEON.

The city has about thirty thousand inhabitants—nearly one-seventh of the entire population of the republic—and seems quaint and queer to the North American traveller because of its unlikeness to anything he has seen at home. The climate is a perpetual spring. The flowers are perennial; the foliage fades and falls in autumn, dying from exhaustion, but never from frost. The days are always warm and delightful, and the nights cool and favorable to sweet rest. Winter is not so agreeable as summer, for when it is not raining the winds blow dust in your eyes, and you miss the foliage and fruits. There is not such a thing as an overcoat in the place—the storekeepers do not sell them—and the natives never heard of stoves. One can look over the roofs of the town from the tower of the cathedral and not see a chimney anywhere. The mercury seldom goes above eighty, and never below sixty, Fahrenheit. The thick walls of the houses make an even temperature within, scarcely varying five degrees from one year to another, and it never rains long enough for the dampness to penetrate them. There is no architectural taste displayed, and a never-ending sameness marks the streets. It is only in the country that picturesque dwellings are found, and usually Nature, not man, has made them so. The shops differ from the residences only in having wider doors and larger rooms, while the warehouses are usually abandoned monasteries or discarded dwellings.

The merchants are mostly foreigners—Frenchmen or Germans; the professional men and laborers are natives. The people are more peaceful and industrious than in the other Central American States, and have the reputation for greater honesty, but less ingenuity, than their neighbors. They take no interest in politics, seldom vote, and do not seem to care who governs them. There has not been a revolution in Costa Rica since 1872, and that grew out of the rivalry of two English banking houses in securing a government loan. The prisons are empty; the doors of the houses are seldom locked; the people are temperate and amiable, and live at peace with one another. The national vice is indolence—*mañana* (pronounced manyannah), a word that is spoken oftener than any other in the language, and means "some other time." It is a proverb that the Costa-Rican is "always lying under the mañana-tree," and that is why the people are poor and the nation bankrupt. The resources of the country, agricultural, mineral, pastoral, and timber, are immense, but have not even been explored. Ninety per cent. of the natives have never been outside the little valley in which they were born; while the Government has done little to invite immigration and encourage development. There are two railroads, both unfinished, and the money that was borrowed to build them was wasted in the most ludicrous way.

In 1872 it was decided that the future prosperity of the country demanded the construction of railways connecting the one inhabited valley with the two oceans, and the Congress ordered a survey. It was made by English engineers, who submitted profiles of the most practicable routes and estimates of the cost of construction. There being no wealth in the country, a loan was necessary, and the two banking houses, both operated by Englishmen upon English capital, sought the privilege of negotiating it. The President made his selection. The disappointed banker decided to overthrow the Government and set up a new one that would cancel the contract and recognize his claims. Down on the plains of Guanacasta was a cow-boy, Tomas Guardia by name, who had won reputation as the commander of a squad of cavalry in a war with Nicaragua, and was known over all Central America for his native ability, soldierly qualities, and desperate valor.

The banker who had failed to get his spoon into the pudding called into the conspiracy a number of disappointed politicians and discontented adherents of the existing Government, and it was decided to send for Guardia to come to the capital and lead the revolution. By offering him pecuniary inducements and a promise of being made commander-in-chief of the Federal army if the revolution was a success, the services of the cow-boy were secured. He called together about one hundred men of his own class, made a rendezvous at a plantation just outside of the city limits, and one moonlight

A BANANA PLANTATION.

night rode into town, surprised the guard at the military garrison, captured the commander of the army and all his troops, took possession of the Government offices, and proclaimed martial law. As the Costa-Rican army consisted of but two hundred and fifty men, accustomed only to police duty and parades, this was not a difficult or a daring undertaking. Those of the officials who were captured were locked up, and those who escaped fled to the woods and then left the country. Among the latter class was the "Constitutional President," as the regularly elected rulers in Spanish America are always called, to distinguish them from the frequent "Pronunciamento Presidents" and "Jefes de Militar," or military dictators.

Having thus dethroned the legitimate ruler, Guardia proclaimed himself Military Dictator, and called a Junta, composed of the men who had employed him to overthrow the Government. They met, with great formality, and solemnly issued a proclamation, reciting that the Constitutional President having absented himself from the country without designating any one to act in his place, it became necessary to choose a new Chief Magistrate. In the mean time the Junta declared Guardia Provisional President until an election could be held. The latter took possession of the Executive Mansion, called all the people into the plaza, swore them to support him, reorganized the bureaus of the Government and the army, placing the cow-boys who had come up from Guanacasta with him in charge. The father-in-law of the English banker who suggested the revolution was announced as the candidate for the Presidency, and it was expected that he would be chosen without opposition. But General Guardia, having had a taste of power, thought more of the same would be agreeable, and passed the word quietly around among his officers that he was a candidate himself. As they constituted the judges of election and the returning board, this hint was sufficient, and when the returns began to come in after ejection day, the banker and his co-conspirators found, to their surprise and chagrin, that their tool had become their master, and General Guardia was declared Constitutional President by a unanimous vote, only two thousand ballots having been cast by a population of two hundred thousand.

This cow-boy, when he took his seat, could neither read nor write. He was, however, a man of extraordinary natural ability, gifted with brains and a laudable ambition. He sprang from a mixture of the Spanish and native races, had energy, shrewdness, a cool head, and a fair idea of government: in all respects the most remarkable, and in many respects the greatest man the little republic ever produced. He learned rapidly, and selected the wisest and ablest men in the country for his advisers. Under his administration the nation showed greater development than it has enjoyed before or since, and, so far as lay in his power, he introduced and encouraged a spirit of moral, intellectual, and commercial advancement, established free schools and a university, overthrew the domination of the priests, sent young men abroad to study the science of government, and preserved the peace as he aided the progress of the people. If he had been as wise as he was progressive, Costa Rica would have made rapid strides towards the standard of modern civilization, but in his mistaken zeal for the development of the country he left it bankrupt.

The two railroads were commenced by him. Under the estimates of the engineers the cost of construction and equipment for two narrow-gauge lines, from San José to Port Limon, on the Atlantic coast, and Punta Arenas, on the Pacific, a total distance of one hundred and sixty miles, was placed at $6,000,000—$37,500 per mile. The line from Port Limon was constructed under the direction of a brother of Henry Meiggs, the famous fugitive from

California (who fled to Peru, and lived there like a second Monte Cristo), but the shorter line, from San José to Punta Arenas, was attempted under the personal supervision of the President himself, who went at it in a very queer way.

All the necessary material and supplies to build and equip the road were purchased in England, sent by sailing-vessels around the Horn, and landed at Punta Arenas. But instead of commencing work there, the President, who had never seen a locomotive in his life, repudiated all advice, rejected all suggestions, and ordered the whole outfit to be carried seventy-five miles over the mountains on carts and mule-back, so as to begin at the other end. This undertaking was more difficult and expensive than the construction of the road. But

PICKING COFFEE.

Guardia's extraordinary departure from the conventional was not without reason. It was based upon a mixture of motives, not only ignorance and inexperience, but pride and precaution. The conservative element of the population, the Bourbon hidalgos, and the ignorant and the superstitious peons, were opposed to all departures from the past, and saw in every improvement and innovation a dangerous disturbance of existing conditions. The methods their fathers used were good enough for them. There was also a large amount of capital and labor engaged in transporting freight by ox-carts, which had always been the "common carriers" of the republic, and those interested recognized that the construction of the railway would make their cattle useless, and leave the peon carters unemployed. To resist the construction of the railroad they organized a revolution, threatening to tear up the tracks and destroy the machinery. To mollify this sentiment, and furnish employment for the cartmen to keep them out of mischief, was the controlling idea in Guardia's mind, so with great labor and difficulty, and at an enormous expense, the locomotives and cars were taken to pieces and hauled over the mountains to San José. The first rails were laid at the capital by the President himself, with a great demonstration, and the work continued until the money was exhausted; and the Government, having destroyed its credit by this remarkable proceeding, was unable to borrow more. The loan, which under ordinary circumstances would have been sufficient to complete the enterprise, was all expended before forty miles of track were laid, ten miles of which extend between Punta Arenas, the Pacific seaport, and Esparza, the next town, and thirty miles between San José and Alajuela, at the western end of the valley. This road is now operated by the Government, under the direction of a native engineer, who was never outside the boundaries of the republic, and never saw any railway but this. He is, however, a man of genius and practical ability, and if he were allowed to have his way the road might be a paying enterprise. But the Government uses it as a political machine, employs a great many superfluous and incompetent men—mostly the relatives and dependents of influential politicians—carries freight and passengers on credit, and does many other foolish things that make profits impossible, and cause a large deficiency to be made up by taxation each year. On every train of three cars—one for baggage and two for passengers—are thirteen men. First a manager or conductor who has general supervision, a locomotive engineer and stoker, two ticket takers, two brakemen for each car, and two men to handle baggage and express packages—all of them being arrayed in the most resplendent uniforms, the conductor having the appearance of a major-general on dress parade. Freight trains are run upon the same system and at a similar expense. Shippers are allowed thirty and sixty days after the goods are delivered to pay their freight charges, and passengers who are known to the station agents can get tickets on credit and have the bill sent them upon their return—a concession to a public sentiment that justifies the postponement of everything until tomorrow—the mañana policy that keeps the nation poor.

Thousands of ox-carts are still employed between the towns of Esparza and Alajuela, the termini of the railway, carrying freight over the mountains; and it usually takes a week for them to make the journey of thirty-five miles, often longer, for on religious festivals, which occur with surprising frequency, all the transportation business is suspended. A traveller who intends to take a steamer at Punta Arenas must send his baggage on a week in advance. He leaves the train at Alajuela, mounts a mule, rides over the mountain to the town of Atenas, where he spends the night. The next morning at daybreak he resumes his journey, and rides fifteen miles to San Mateo, breakfasts at eleven, takes his siesta in a hammock until four or five in the afternoon, then mounting his mule again, covers the ten miles to Esparza by sunset, where he dines and spends the night, usually remaining there, to avoid the heat of Punta Arenas, until a few hours before the steamer leaves; and then, if the ox-carts have come with his baggage, makes the rest of his trip by rail.

The journey is not an unpleasant one. The scenery is wild and picturesque. The roads are usually good, except in the dry season, when they become very dusty, and after heavy rains, when the mud is deep. But under the tropic sun and in the dry air moisture evaporates rapidly, and in six hours after a rainfall the roads are hard and good. The uncertainty as to whether his trunks will arrive in time makes the inexperienced traveller nervous.

The Costa-Rican cartmen are the most irresponsible and indifferent beings on earth. They travel in long caravans or processions, often with two or three hundred teams in a line. When one chooses to stop, or meets with an accident, all the rest wait for him if it wastes a week. None will start until each of his companions is ready, and sometimes the road is blocked for miles, awaiting the repair of some damage. The oxen are large white patient beasts, and are yoked by the horns, and not by the neck, as in modern style, lashings of raw cowhide being used to make them fast. They wear the yokes continually. The union is as permanent as matrimony in a land where divorce laws are unknown. The cartmen are as courteous as they are indifferent. They always lift their hats to a *caballero* as he passes them, and say, "May the Virgin guard you on your journey!" Thousands of dollars in gold are often intrusted to them, and never was a penny lost. A banker of San José told me that he usually received thirty thousand dollars in coin each week during coffee season by these ox-carts, and considered it safer than if he carried it himself, although the caravan stands in the open air by the roadside every night. Highway robbery is unknown, and the cartmen, with their wages of thirty cents a day, would not know what use to make of the money if they should steal it. Nevertheless they always feel at liberty to rob the traveller of the straps on his trunks, and no piece of baggage ever arrives at its destination so protected unless the strap is securely nailed, and then it is usually cut to pieces by the cartmen as revenge for being deprived of what they consider their perquisite.

At sunset the oxen are released from their burdens at the nearest *tambo*, or resting-place, upon the way, and are kept overnight in sheds provided for them. At these places are drinking and gambling booths, with usually a number of dissolute women to tempt and entertain the cartmen. The evenings are spent in carousal, in dancing, and singing the peculiar native songs to the accompaniment of the "marimba," the national instrument, which is, I believe, found in no other land.

The marimba is constructed of twenty-one pieces of split bamboo of graded lengths, strung upon two bars of the same wood according to harmonic sequence, thus furnishing three octaves. Underneath each strip of bamboo is a gourd, strung upon a wire, which takes the place of a sounding-board, and adds strength and sweetness to the tones. The performer takes the instrument upon his knees and strikes the bamboo strips with little hammers of padded leather, usually taking two between the fingers of each hand, so as to strike a chord of four notes, which he does with great dexterity. I have seen men play with three hammers in each hand, and use them as rapidly and skilfully as a pianist touches his keys. The tones of the marimba resemble those of the xylophone, which has recently become so popular, except that they are louder and more resonant. The instrument is peculiarly adapted to the native airs, which are plaintive but melodious. At all of the tambos where the cartmen stop marimbas are kept, and in every caravan are those who can handle them skilfully. Tourists generally travel in the cool hours of the morning and evening to avoid the blistering sun, and it is a welcome diversion to stop at the *bodegas* to listen to the songs of the cartmen, and watch them dancing with darkeyed, barefooted señoritas.

The women of the lower classes do not wear either shoes or sandals, but go barefooted from infancy to old age; yet their feet are always small and shapely, and look very pretty under the short skirts that reach just below the knees. The native girls are comely and coquettish in the national dress,

THE MARIMBA.

which consists of nothing but a skirt and a chemise of white cotton, with a brilliantly colored scarf, or "reboza," as they call it, thrown over their heads and shoulders, and serving the double purpose of a shawl and bonnet. The features of the women are small and even, and their teeth are perfect. Their forms, untrammelled by skirts and corsets, are slender and supple in girlhood, and the scanty garments, sleeveless, and reaching only from the shoulders to the knees, disclose every outline of their figures, and are worn without a suggestion of immodesty. Such a costume in the United States would call for police interference; but one soon becomes accustomed to bare arms and necks and legs, and learns that these innocent creatures are quite as jealous of their chastity as their sisters in the land where the standard of civilization forbids the disclosure of personal charms outside the ball-room or the bathing beach. The ladies of the aristocracy imitate the Parisian fashions, except that hats and bonnets are almost unknown. They seldom leave their homes except to go to mass, and at the entrance of a church every head must be uncovered.

There is not a millinery store in the land. Every woman wears a "reboza" of a texture suitable to her rank and wealth, and as it is not considered proper to expose their faces in public, the scarf is generally drawn over the features so as to conceal all but their ravishing eyes. And it is well that this is so, for they plaster their faces with a composition of magnesia and the whites of eggs that gives them a ghastly appearance, and effectually conceals, as it ultimately destroys, the freshness and purity of their complexions. This stuff is renewed at frequent intervals, and is never washed off.

There is a popular prejudice against bathing. A man who has been on a journey will not wash the dust off his face for several days after arrival, particularly if he has come from a lower to a higher altitude, as it is believed that the opening of the pores of the skin is certain to bring on a fever.

While passing over a dusty road upon a hot, sultry day I dismounted at a foaming brook, rolled up my sleeves, and commenced to bathe my head and face and arms. The guide who was with me cried "Caramba!" in astonishment, and tried to pull me away. When I demanded an explanation of his extraordinary behavior he begged me for the love of the Virgin not to wash my face, for I would certainly come down with the fever the next day. I smiled at this remonstrance, and gave myself a refreshing bath, while he looked on as solemnly as if I intended to commit suicide. For an hour after, as we travelled on, he muttered prayers to the Virgin and his patron saint to protect me from the fever, and to-day no doubt believes that I was saved by the interposition of Divine power in answer to his petitions. He afterwards reproached me for not having made a vow because of my remarkable deliverance.

COFFEE-DRYING.

However, if anybody supposes that the inhabitants of the little republic are uncouth, unmannerly, or uneducated, he makes a great mistake. They are quite up to our standard of intelligence, and although education is not so universal as in this country, the leading families of Costa Rica are as cultivated as our own. They surpass us in social graces, in conversational powers, in linguistic and other accomplishments. They have keener perceptions than we, are more carefully observant of the nicer proprieties, can usually speak one or two languages besides their own fluently, and have a cultivated taste for music and the arts. No Costa-Rican lady or gentleman is ever embarrassed; they always know how to do and say the proper thing, and while in many cases their sympathetic interest in your welfare may be only skin-deep, and their affectionate phrases insincere, they are nevertheless the most hospitable of hosts and the most charming of companions. In commerce as well as in society this deportment is universal; in their stores and offices they are as polite as in their parlors, and the same manners are found in every caste. No laborer ever passes a lady in the street without lifting his hat; every gentleman is respectfully saluted, whether he be a stranger or an acquaintance, and in the rural districts whoever you meet says, "May the Virgin prosper you!" or "May Heaven smile upon your errand!" or "May your patron saint protect you from all harm!" He may not care a straw whether you reach the end of your journey or not, and may not have any more regard for your welfare than the fleas on his coat, and if you ask him how far it is to the next place he will tell you a falsehood, but he recognizes and practises the beautiful custom of the country, and says, "God be with you!" as if he intended it as a blessing.

The Government supports a good university at San José, under the direction of Dr. Juan F. Ferras, and a system of free graded schools, managed by the Minister of Education, who is a member of the cabinet. Education is compulsory, the law requiring the attendance of all children between the ages of eight and fourteen; and it is enforced, except in the sparsely settled districts where the schools are infrequent. Those who send their children to private schools, or do not send them at all, are subject to a heavy fine, which goes into the school fund. There is also a poll-tax for the support of the educational system. The schools are entirely free from sectarian influences. In fact, both the Minister of Education and the Director of the University belong to the German school of materialists, towards which all men of education in these countries drift when they leave the Mother Church. There is no other place for them to go. The Protestants in San José have a little chapel where the Church of England service is recited, hymns are sung, and usually Sabbath mornings a selected sermon from some published volume is read by a lay member; but the flock is too small to support a pastor, and none of the missionary societies in England or America appear to care to enter the field. During the administration of President Guardia there was a constitutional amendment adopted separating the Church and the State. The monks and nuns were expelled from the country, the monasteries and nunneries confiscated, and by legislation the priests were deprived of much of their power and perquisites. In 1884, a few months before his death, the late President Fernandez expelled the archbishop from the country. The latter went to him demanding a voice in the management of the university, and a share of the public funds for the use of the Catholic Theological Seminary. The controversy was heated, and when the archbishop departed from the Presidential mansion he left the curse of Rome behind him. Fernandez, hearing that his Grace was talking about a revolution, sent him a passport and a file of soldiers to escort him out of the country, to which he has not been allowed to return.

The confessional is open and public by law, and the priests are forbidden to wear their vestments in the streets. But these statutes are not enforced, and, regardless of the offensive attitude of the Government, the devotion of the masses to the Church is quite as marked as in any of the Catholic countries. The intelligent families, however, are gradually growing unmindful of their ancestral religion, and the next generation will see a more rapid decline of the power of the priests. Business and professional men never attend mass, leaving that duty to their wives and daughters and servants. They are seldom seen inside a church, except upon occasions of ceremony or at funerals. But the women invariably attend mass each morning.

A familiar sight in Costa Rica is a death procession. When some one is dying the friends send for a priest to shrive him. The latter comes, not silently and solemnly, a minister of grace and consolation, but accompanied by a brass band, if the family are rich enough to pay for it (the priest receiving a liberal commission on the business), or, if they are poor, by a number of boys ringing bells and chanting hymns. Behind the band or bell-boys are two acolytes, one bearing a crucifix and the other swinging an incense urn. Then follows the priest in a wooden box or chair, covered by a canopy, and carried by four men wearing the sacramental vestments, and holding in his hand, covered with a napkin, the Host—the emblem of the body of Christ. People upon the streets kneel as the procession passes, and then follow it. Reaching the house of the dying, the band or bell-ringers stand outside, making all the disturbance they can, while the priest, followed by a motley rabble, enters the death-chamber, administers the sacrament, and confesses the dying soul. Then the procession returns to the church as it came. Going and coming, and while at the house, the band plays or the bells are rung constantly, and all the men, women, and children within hearing fall upon their knees, whether in the street or at their labor, and pray for the repose of the departing spirit.

Funerals are occasions of great ceremony. Notices, or *avisos*, as they are called, are printed and posted upon all of the dead-walls, like announcements of an auction or an opera, and printed invitations are sent to all the acquaintances of the deceased. The priests charge a large fee for attendance, proportionate to the means of the family, and when they are poor it is common for some one to solicit contributions to pay it. The spectacle of a beggar sitting at a street corner asking alms to pay the burial fee of his wife or child is a very common one, and quite as often one can see a father carrying in his arms to the cemetery the coffin of a little one, not being able to pay for a priest and a carriage too.

The number of illegitimate births in the country is accounted for, not so much by a low state of morals; as by the enormous fees exacted by the priests for performing marriage ceremonies. Unfortunately the Government has not yet established the civil rite, as is the case in several of the Spanish-American States. It takes all a peon can earn in three months to pay the priest that officiates at his nuptials.

The Government of Costa Rica consists of a President, two Vice-Presidents, who are named by the President, and are called Designado Primero and Designado Segundo (the first and second designated). They have authority to act in the place of the President in case of his absence from the seat of government, or in the event of his death or disability, and he is responsible for their official conduct.

There is a Congress, consisting of a Senate of twelve members and a Chamber of Deputies of twenty-four, elected biennially, as in the United States. Also a Council of six men, selected from the Congress by the President, who act as a sort of cabinet and Supreme Court combined. They are continually in session, have power to review the decisions of the courts, to reverse or affirm them, to issue decrees which have the force of law until the next session of the Congress, to audit the accounts of the Treasury, and perform various other acts. This Council is confirmed by the Congress, and is supposed to act as a check upon the President and the judiciary. The President has a cabinet of two members, appointed by himself, and they are usually the two Vice-Presidents, or Designados. To one he will assign the duty of looking after foreign affairs and the finances of the Government, while the other will have the army, the educational system, and other internal affairs to manage.

The successor of the famous cow-boy President, Guardia, was his brother-in-law, General Prospero Fernandez, one of his lieutenants in the revolution by which he came into power,

DON BERNARDO DE SOTO, PRESIDENT OF COSTA RICA.

and who was made commander-in-chief of the army of two hundred and fifty men when Guardia took the Executive chair. He was a man of fine appearance, but of dull and slow mental powers, spending most of his time upon his hacienda, or plantation, and leaving the affairs of the State to his secretaries, Don Jesus Maria Castro and Don Bernardo de Soto. Fernandez died before the expiration of his term, in the spring of 1885, and was succeeded by De Soto, a young man of whom much is expected. He was a pet and protégé of the great Guardia, and after graduating at the University of San José was sent to Europe to complete his education, and by a study of the world as well as books to qualify himself to succeed his patron in the Presidential chair. Guardia died, however, before De Soto had reached the age that made him eligible to the Presidency, and Fernandez stepped in to fill the interim. He conscientiously acted as a sort of trustee or executor of Guardia's will, and made the young man, then only twenty-seven, his Minister of War, Education, and Public Works. When Fernandez died De Soto assumed the Presidency, just as if he had inherited a crown, there being no other candidate. The President has just passed his thirtieth birthday, and commands the respect and confidence of the people.

Costa Rica was the first discovered of all the countries on this Continent, but of its resources the least is known. The Cordilleras of the Andes pass through the republic from the south-east to the north-west. South of Cartago they divide into two ranges, one running up the Pacific coast, and the other tending towards the Atlantic until it is broken off at Lake Nicaragua. These ranges not only enclose rich valleys, in the chief of which is San José, but along their slopes on either side are extensive tracts of land already cleared and abounding in fertility. Along the coast are large areas of jungle and plains of more or less extent, only slightly developed because of the malarious atmosphere. The Pacific coast is healthier and more thickly settled. A large prairie covers the northern part of the republic, upon which many cattle are grazed, and it extends over the Nicaragua boundary. In the north-eastern corner is an extensive forest, inhabited by bands of roaming Indians, and full of the most valuable timber.

What the country needs is enterprise and capital, and these it must secure by immigration. The population has increased somewhat during the last half century, but entirely from natural causes, as more people have moved away than have come in to settle. No attempt has been made by the Government to attract immigrants until recently, for years ago the conservative element of the population were opposed to inviting strangers into their midst. This sentiment has, however, died out, and there is an increasing desire to do something to call in capital and labor.

The staple products of the country are coffee, corn, sugar, cocoa, bananas, and other tropical fruits, but only coffee and bananas are exported in any quantity. The increase in the coffee crop has been very large, the product in 1850 being fourteen million pounds, while in 1884 it was over forty million. The quality is said to be superior to that grown elsewhere, and the yield greater in proportion to the number of trees. England and France take the greater share of the crop, the exports to the United States reaching only eight million five hundred thousand pounds in 1884. The land is practically free, for the Government sells it at a nominal price per acre, and allows long time for payment. Quite a number of settlers from the United States and the West Indies have come in recently and located on the line of the eastern road, which is to connect Port Limon, on the Atlantic, with the interior.

NOTE TO SECOND EDITION.—On the 29th and 30th of December, 1888, Costa Rica was visited by the most destructive earthquake ever known there. Nearly all the cities and settlements suffered more or less, but San José was almost entirely destroyed. Three-fourths of the buildings were either shaken down or shattered beyond repair, including all the official structures, the Capitol, the President's residence, and the Cathedral. The loss to the Government alone is estimated at $2,000,000, while that suffered by private individuals was several times that amount. No official report upon the loss of life has been made, and the estimates vary from three hundred to seven hundred and fifty.

BOGOTA.

THE CAPITAL OF COLOMBIA.

ALTHOUGH geographically one of our nearest neighbors, Bogota, the capital of the United States of Colombia, is almost as far distant by days, if not by miles, from New York as the interior of India, and quite as difficult to reach. Until recently there has been no direct communication by steam between the ports of Colombia and those of our own country. Within the last three years an English company has established a line of steamships between New York and the mouth of the Magdalena River. Two trips a month are made, the vessels touching at several of the West India ports en route, and making the voyage to Barranquilla in fifteen days. Three times a month the Pacific Mail steamers leave New York for Aspinwall, where a steamer for the Colombian ports and Europe sails almost every day, under the flag of England, Germany, France, Spain, Italy, or the Netherlands. The voyage *via* Aspinwall requires about the same time as the other, fifteen days. There ought to be direct communication not only from New York, but from the Gulf ports, as the demands of commerce require it; and a much larger trade might be obtained if conveniences of transportation existed. But the policy of the United Stated Congress in refusing to aid steamship lines, even by the payment of reasonable compensation for the carriage of mails, prohibits capitalists from investing money in such enterprises, as they would be compelled to compete with the subsidized companies of Europe.

Excepting Aspinwall, which is a cosmopolitan place, the city of Barranquilla is the principal port of Colombia, and to it all merchandise and passengers bound for Bogota and the interior of the country must go. In the old Spanish colony times Carthagena was the greatest commercial metropolis of Colombia, or New Granada, as it was then called; and it is one of the quaintest, as it is one of the oldest, cities in South America. In the time of Philip the Second it was the most strongly fortified place on the continent, and the headquarters of the Spanish naval forces in the New World. It was the rendezvous of the Spanish galleons which came to South America for treasure. There are many rich mines in the mountains back of the city, which have produced millions in silver and gold. Here came the pirates to plunder. They committed so much damage that the King of Spain thought it worth his while to build a wall around the entire city, on the top of which forty horses can walk abreast, and which is said to have cost ninety million dollars.

BARRANQUILLA.

Carthagena was the seat of the Inquisition, and in Charles Kingsley's novel, "Westward Ho!" its readers will find a charming description of the place. It was here that Frank and the Rose of Devon were imprisoned by the priests, and the old Inquisition building in which they were tortured and burned is still standing. But it is no longer used for the confinement and crucifixion of heretics. For nearly sixty years after the overthrow of the Catholic Church it stood empty, but it is now occupied as a tobacco factory. There is an underground passage between the old Inquisition building and an ancient fortress upon a hill overlooking Carthagena, through which prisoners used to be conducted, and communication maintained in time of siege; but, like everything else about the place, it has long been in a state of decay. Some years ago a party of American naval officers attempted to explore the passage, but found it filled with obstructions, and were compelled to abandon the enterprise. The old castle is obsolete now, and in a state of ruin, being used only as a signal station. When a vessel enters the harbor a flag is run up by a man on guard to notify the Captain of the Port and the merchants of its arrival.

CARTHAGENA.

There are some fine old churches and palaces in Carthagena constructed of stone, which show the magnificence in which the old grandees lived when the city was a commercial metropolis. Many of them are empty now, and others are used as tenement-houses. In the cathedral, which is one of the largest and most elaborate to be found on the hemisphere, is a curious object of interest. It is a magnificent marble pulpit covered with exquisite carvings. It ranks among the most beautiful specimens of the sculptor's art in the world. The people of Carthagena think there is nothing under the sun to equal it, and the story of its origin adds greatly to its value and interest. Two or three hundred years ago the Pope, wishing to show a mark of favor to the devout people of Colombia, ordered the construction of a marble pulpit for the decoration of the grand cathedral at Carthagena. It was designed and carved by the foremost artists of the day at Rome, and when completed was with great ceremony placed on board a Spanish galley bound for the New World. While en route the vessel was captured by pirates, and when the boxes containing the pulpit were broken open, and their contents found to be of no value as plunder, they were tipped overboard. But by the interposition of the Virgin, none of the pieces sank; and the English pirates, becoming alarmed at the miracle of the heavy marble floating on the water, fled from the ship, leaving their booty. The Spanish sailors got the precious cargo aboard their vessel again with great difficulty, and started on their way; but before they reached Carthagena they encountered a second lot of pirates, who plundered them of all the valuables they had aboard, and burned their ship. But the saints still preserved the pulpit; for, as the vessel and the remainder of the cargo were destroyed, the carved marble floated away upon the surface of the water, and, being guided by an invisible hand, went ashore on the beach outside the city to which it was destined.

There it lay for many years, unknown and unnoticed. Finally, however, it was discovered by a party of explorers, who recognized the value of the carvings and took it aboard their ship en route for Spain, intending to sell it when they reached home. But the saints still kept their eyes upon the Pope's offering, and sent the vessel such bad weather that the captain was compelled to put into the port of Carthagena for repairs. There he told the story of the marble pulpit found upon the beach, and it reached the ears of the Archbishop. His Grace sent for the captain, informed him that the pulpit was intended for the decoration of the cathedral, and related the story of its construction and disappearance. The captain was an ungodly man, and intimated that the Archbishop was attempting to humbug him. He offered to sell the marble, and would not leave it otherwise. Having repaired the damage of the storm, the captain started for Europe, but he was scarcely out of the harbor when a most frightful gale struck him and wrecked his vessel, which went to the bottom with all on board; but the pulpit, the subject of so many divine interpositions, rose from the wreck, and one morning came floating into the harbor of Carthagena, where it was taken in charge by the Archbishop and placed in the cathedral for which it was intended, and where it now stands.

Near the miraculous pulpit, in the same church, is the preserved body of a famous saint. I forget what his name was, but he is in an excellent state of preservation—a skeleton with dried flesh and skin hanging to the bones. He did something hundreds of years ago which made him very sacred to the people of Carthagena, and by the special permission of the Pope his body was disinterred, placed in a glass case, and shipped from Rome to ornament the cathedral of the former city, along with the miraculous pulpit. The body is usually covered with a black pall, and is exposed only upon occasions of great ceremony, but any one can see the preserved saint by paying a fee to the priests. I purchased that privilege, and was shown the glass coffin standing upon a marble pedestal. The bones are bare, except where the brown skin, looking like jerked beef, covers them, and are a ghastly spectacle. During a revolution at Carthagena some impious soldiers upset the coffin and destroyed it. In the *melée* one of the saint's legs was lost, or at least the lower half of it from the knee down; but the priests replaced it with a wax leg, plump and pink, which, lying beside the original, gives the saint a very comical appearance.

ENTRANCE TO THE OLD FORTRESS, CARTHAGENA.

There is much of interest to see at Carthagena, and the place has had a most romantic and exciting history, being described at length in "Thomson's Seasons." Again and again has it been sacked by the pirates, as it was formerly the shipping-point for the product of the gold and silver mines for which the mountains south of it have been so famous. Tons and tons of gold and silver have been sent thence to Spain. In the times of the viceroys the mines were worked under the direction of the Government. One-fifth of the net product went to the King, another fifth to the Church, while the miner was permitted to keep the remainder. The old records show that the share of the King was several millions a year for two hundred years or more, and that indicates how enormous the profit must have been; for the miners and officials were no more honest in those days than now, and it is not entirely certain that the share to which his Majesty was entitled always reached him.

The fortifications of Carthagena surpass in extent and solidity those of any city in the New World, and are still in good condition, although not occupied, having been constructed without regard to expense and for all time. The massive walls of the city are to all appearance impregnable, and the ancient subterranean passages leading outward to the foot of the adjacent mountains are still visible. The entrance to the magnificent harbor is studded with ancient fortifications, which, though now unused for more than half a century, seem almost as good as new. Formerly the city was connected by ship-channel with the river Magdalena, at a point many leagues above the delta, and was, therefore, in easy communication with the fertile valleys and plateaux of the interior—the gate of commerce in time of peace, and secure alike from protracted siege or successful assault in time of war.

The decline of Carthagena seems to have commenced with the present century, and to have steadily continued to within the past fifteen years, when the commerce of the country began to revive. In the mean time the ship-canal connecting the port with the great fluvial highway of the interior having fallen into disuse, became filled up and overgrown with tropical jungle; so that the few foreign trading-vessels visiting the coast sought harborage farther up, at a place called Barranquilla, near the mouth of the Magdalena. Barranquilla has become the chief city of commercial importance within the United States of Colombia, and is the residence of many of the principal merchants of the republic. It is a growing city, and from a few houses twenty years ago it now has a population of upwards of twenty-five thousand. Situated as it is, so near the outlet of the Magdalena River, it is destined to increase in size and commerce, and to become to Colombia what New York is to the United States—the great commercial emporium of the republic; Aspinwall and Panama, free ports, being more a highway of nations than a part of this country. To this end Barranquilla has many things in its favor. The custom-house is located there. All the river steamers and sailing-vessels on the Magdalena, conveying from the vast back-lying interior to the coast the multitudinous products of the country, start from and return to this place.

But Barranquilla has its drawbacks. As soon as it secured a little commerce a large bar began to form at the mouth of the river, and has grown until it has become a sand-spit which prevents the entrance of steamers. Then a new town, called Sabanilla, was started on the spit, which is connected with Barranquilla by a railway fourteen miles long, owned and operated by a German company. But the harbor of Sabanilla, though now the principal one of the republic, is neither convenient nor safe. It is shallow, full of shifting sand-bars, and exposed to furious wind-storms; while the new port of Barranquilla is quite inaccessible from the delta, by reason of its treacherous sand-bars. So with the opening of the ancient *dique*, or ship-channel, between Carthagena and Calamar, or the construction of a railway between the first-named point and Barranquilla (both of which enterprises are being agitated), Carthagena may regain her ancient prestige and become the chief port of the republic.

Sabanilla is a most desolate place, nothing but sand, filth, and poverty; and were it not for the sea-breeze that constantly sweeps across the barren peninsula upon which it stands, the inhabitants could not survive. No one lives there except a colony of *cargadors*, boatmen, and roustabouts, who swarm, like so many animals, in filthy huts built of palm-leaves, and a few saloon-keepers, who give them wine in exchange for the money they earn. The men and women are almost naked, and the children entirely so. Perhaps the reason for the nastiness of the place is because there is no fresh water; but the inhabitants ought not to be excused on this account, as the beach furnishes as fine bathing as can be found in the world, and is at their very doors. All the fresh water used has to be brought in canoes from a point eight miles up the river, and is sold by the dipperful: but only a moderate quantity is necessary for consumption. Most of the inhabitants are Canary Islanders, who monopolize the boating business along this coast; but sprinkled among them are many Italians, and nearly every nation on earth is represented, even China. The only laundry is run by a Chinaman, and another is cook at a place that is used as a substitute for a hotel. The boatmen are drunken, quarrelsome, desperate wretches; murder is frequent among them, and fighting the chief amusement.

COLOMBIAN MILITARY MEN.

Barranquilla is the most modern town in Colombia except Aspinwall, which it resembles somewhat. It has some fine houses and quite a large foreign colony, many of its merchants being Germans, who live in good style, and enjoy many comforts at an enormous cost; for flour is twenty-five dollars a barrel and meat twenty-five cents a pound, beer twenty-five cents a glass, and everything else in proportion. There is nothing in plenty but fruits and flies. The town is the capital of the State of Sabanilla, and has a considerable military garrison, which is important in keeping down insurrections. During the revolution of 1885 Barranquilla was the headquarters of the insurrectionary army, and, commanding the only outlet from the interior, is naturally a place of consequence, from a military as well as from a commercial standpoint.

The great valley of the Magdalena, extending from the Caribbean coast to the equatorial line, is one of inexhaustible resources. Its width varies from one hundred to one hundred and fifty miles before gradually sloping to a point in the northern borders of the equator. At the mouth of the river Cauca this valley branches off into another of less general width but of greater elevation, and consequently possesses a more equable and temperate climate. The river Cauca is itself navigable by a light-draught steamer as far as Cali, a point less than eighty miles from the port of Buenaventura on the Pacific coast. The lower valley of the Magdalena is one vast alluvial plain, a large portion of which is subject to periodical overflow. In fact, during the rainy season the greater portion of it is usually under water. This, however, might be prevented, and the fertile lands reclaimed, by a system of dikes far less expensive than those of the lower Mississippi. But in a country where population is sparse, and Nature lavish in her bounties, such enterprises are not usually undertaken.

The distance from Barranquilla to Honda, the head of navigation on the Magdalena, is seven hundred and eighty miles, following the course of the river, but in a direct line is only about one-third of that distance. The journey by boat requires from ten to thirty days, according to the condition of the river. In the rainy season the banks are full, and the current so strong that the little steamers cannot make much progress; but if the moon is bright enough to show the course, they are kept in motion night and day. In the dry season the river is shallow, and the boats have to tie up at dark, and remain so till daylight. Then, on nearly every voyage they run aground, and often stick for a day or two, sometimes a week, before they can be got off.

The boats are similar to those used upon the Ohio and other rivers, with a paddle-wheel behind, and draw only a foot or two of water even when heavily laden, so that they can go over the bars. There are two steamboat companies, both with United States capital; one is managed by a Mr. Joy, and the other by a Mr. Cisneros, a naturalized Italian. During the revolution all the boats were seized by the insurgents. Their sides were covered with corrugated iron, so as to make them bullet-proof, a small cannon or two mounted upon the decks, and the cabins filled with sharp-shooters. So prepared, they were used as gun-boats, and were quite effective. Many of them were destroyed, so that transportation facilities upon the Magdalena are not so good as they were.

ON THE MAGDALENA.

The first two hundred miles is a continuous swamp; the next three hundred miles is a vast plain, which is under water about two months in the year, during the floods that follow the rainy season, but at other times is covered with cattle, which are driven into the mountains before the floods come.

The banks along the river were formerly occupied with profitable plantations, which were worked by negro slaves, as neither the Spaniards nor the native Indians could endure the climate and the mosquitoes. But when the emancipation of the slaves took place, in 1824, the plantations were abandoned, and have since been so overgrown with tropical vegetation that no traces of their former cultivation exist. The negroes, who have descended from the former slaves, have relapsed into a condition of semi-barbarism, and while they still occupy the old estancias, lead a lazy, shiftless, degraded life, subsisting upon fish and the fruits which grow everywhere in wonderful profusion. Nature provides for them, and no amount of wages can tempt them to work. A few small villages have sprung up along the river, which are trading stations, and furnish some freight for the steamers in the shape of fruit, poultry, eggs, cocoa-nuts, and similar articles, which are attended to by the women of the country.

The river itself is a great natural curiosity. It flows almost directly northward, and drains an enormous area of mountains which are constantly covered with snow. The current is as swift as that of the Mississippi, which it resembles, and the water, always muddy, is so full of sediment that one can hear it striking the sides of the boat. The water will not mix with that of the sea, and for fifty miles into the ocean it can be distinguished. In some places it is seven or eight miles wide, at others it is scarcely more than a hundred yards, where it has cut its way through the rolling earth. The channel, which has never been cleared, is full of treacherous bars and snags, which are continually shifting, and make it necessary to tie up the steamer every night, except in times of high water during the rainy season. The mosquitoes are monumental in size, and at some seasons of the year, when the winds are strong and blow them from the jungles, it is almost impossible to endure them. The officers and deck hands of the boat all wear thick veils over their faces, and heavy buckskin gloves, awake or asleep; and the passengers, unless similarly protected, are subject to the most intense torment. Often the swarms are so thick that they obscure the sky, and the sound of humming is so loud that it resembles the murmur of an approaching storm.

COLOMBIAN 'GATORS.

Some ludicrous stories are told about adventures with the mosquitoes. I have been solemnly assured that oftentimes when they have attacked a boat and driven its captain and crew below, they have broken the windows of the cabin by plunging in swarms against them, and have attempted to burst in the doors. Although this may be somewhat of an exaggeration, it is nevertheless true that frequently horses and cattle, after the most frightful sufferings, have died from mosquito bites on board the vessels. Not long ago a herd of valuable cattle were being taken from the United States to a ranch up the Magdalena River, and became so desperate under the attacks of the mosquitoes that they broke from their stalls, jumped into the water, and were all drowned. Passengers intending to make the voyage always provide themselves with protection in the shape of mosquito-bars, head-nets, and thick gloves, and when on deck are compelled to tie their sleeves around their wrists and their pantaloons around their ankles.

The alligators are so numerous along the banks that the same story-tellers assert that you could step from the back of one to another, and thus walk for miles without touching ground. They are playful creatures, and not at all timid, but bask quietly in the sun until disturbed, when they plunge into the river. The steamboats are always followed by schools of them, and the passengers amuse themselves by firing at them from the deck. No attempt has been made to kill them for profit, but if some enterprising hunters should go to the Magdalena country and make a business of curing and shipping alligator hides, they would find it a profitable venture.

Once or twice a day the steamboats stop for freight or fuel, which is supplied them by the settlers, and brought on board by naked negroes.

The town of Honda, at the head of navigation, is a place of considerable importance, and at intervals for the last quarter of a century American companies have undertaken the construction of a railroad from it to Bogota—a distance of seventy miles through mountains. About ten leagues of track have been built, but those in charge have been compelled again and again to abandon it because of the revolutions and the impossibility of securing labor. The natives cannot be induced to work, and no wages that the company can pay will induce immigration. But the enterprise is being slowly extended, with the encouragement of the Government in the shape of a concession of money and lands, and ultimately the perseverance which conquers all things will succeed. There is also a liberal concession from the Government to another syndicate of New York capitalists for the construction of a railway into the Cauca valley, where are supposed to be the richest goldmines in the world, from which the hundreds of millions taken away by the Spaniards came.

From Honda to Bogota the journey must be made on mule-back, and it requires four days to cover the seventy miles. Recently there has been a line of stagecoaches established between Bogota and the town of Agrialarge, which shortens the time a day, and the distance by saddle thirty miles. In describing the journey Mr. Scruggs, recently United States Minister to Colombia, says:

VEGETABLE IVORY PLANT.

"After perfecting all necessary arrangements the day previous, the traveller rises at six, takes a light breakfast of chocolate and bread, and hopes to be on the way by seven. But people here take life easily. Servants and guides and muleteers make no note of time, and it is quite useless to try to hurry them, so that if he gets fairly under way by noon he is fortunate. Just beyond the deep, broad valley of the Magdalena are the snow-capped mountains of Tolima. They seem marvellously near, and yet they are more than one hundred miles distant, so very clear and transparent is the pure ethereal atmosphere of this elevated region. In the opposite direction is the dish-shaped valley of Guaduas, fringed with luxuriant foliage of the coffee plantations and the virgin forests of emerald green. In the centre of this valley reposes the parochial village, with its church steeples reaching upward as if in feeble imitation of the adjacent mountain-peaks.

"The valley is watered by the Rio Negro; justly so named, for its waters are as black as ink, so rendered by their passage through the coal and mineral deposits along the foothills of the Sierra. Near by are a noted sulphur spring and the extinct volcano which Humboldt describes as likely, one day, to break out afresh and destroy this beautiful valley. Though quite hot, the atmosphere is singularly dry and sanitary, and the place is often resorted to by invalids from Bogota and the more elevated regions.

"Up to this point our journey has been alternating between deep valleys and dizzy mountain-peaks. We cross one only to encounter another. Such is the Camino Real, or 'Royal Highway,' the only available route between the Colombian capital and the outside world. Within the past few years it has been much improved, it is true, and at great expense to the Government; but it is still little else than a mere mule trail, not wide enough in many places for two mules to walk abreast, and so tortuous and precipitous as to be impassable except on the backs of animals trained to the road. When we reflect that this is the overland highway of an immense commerce, and that it has been in constant use since the Spanish conquest, we naturally marvel that it is no better. It seems to have been constructed without any previous survey whatever, and without the least regard for

EN ROUTE TO BOGOTA.

comfort or convenience, making short curves where curves are quite unnecessary, or going straight over some mountain spur or peak, when the ascent might have been rendered less difficult by easy curves. But, to the observant traveller, the inconveniences and hardships of the journey are, in some measure, compensated by the varied and captivating scenery. He passes through a variety of climates within a few hours' ride. At one time he is ascending a dizzy steep by a sort of rustic stairway hewn into the rock-ribbed mountain, where the air reminds him of a chilly November morning; a few hours later he is descending to the region of the plantain and the banana, where the summer never ends, and the rank crops of fruits and flowers chase each other in unbroken circle from January to December. On the bleak crests of the paramos he encounters neither tree nor shrub, where a few blades of sedge and the flitting of a few sparrows give the only evidences of vegetable or animal life; while in the deep valley just below, the dense groves of palm and cottonwood are alive with birds of rich and varied plumage, and the air seems loaded with floral perfumes until the senses fairly ache with their sweetness.

"This plain is the traditional elysium of the ancient Chibchas, and their imperial capital was near the site of the present capital of Colombia; and perhaps around no one spot on the American continent cluster so many legends of the aborigines, or quite so many improbable stories illustrative of the ancient civilization. Here one can almost imagine himself in the north temperate zone, and in a country inhabited by a race wholly different from the people heretofore seen in the republic. Agriculture and the useful arts seem at least a century ahead of those on the coast and in the torrid valleys of the great rivers. The ox-cart and plantation-wagon have supplanted the traditional pack-mule and ground-sled; the neat iron spade and patent plough have taken the place of wooden shovels and clumsy forked sticks; the enclosures are of substantial stone or adobe, and the spacious farmhouse, or quinta, has an air of palatial elegance compared with the mud and bamboo hut of the Magdalena. The people have a clear, ruddy complexion, at least compared with those heretofore seen in the country, and their dialect is a near approach to the rich and sonorous Castilian, once so liquid and harmonious in poetry and song, so majestic and persuasive on the forum. None of these agricultural implements, and none of these commodious coaches and omnibuses, were manufactured here nor elsewhere in Colombia. They have all been imported from the United States or England. They were brought to Honda by the river steamers, packed in small sections, and thence lugged over the mountains piece by piece.

"One peon will carry a wheel, another an axle, a third a coupling-pole or single-tree, and the screws and bolts are packed in small boxes on cargo mules. The upper part or body of the vehicle is likewise taken to pieces and packed in sections. One man will sometimes be a month in carrying a wagon-wheel from Honda to the plain. His method is to carry it some fifty or a hundred paces and then rest, making sometimes less than two miles a day.

SABANA OF BOGOTA.

"When the vehicle finally reaches the plain, the pieces are collected and put together by some smithy who may have learned the art from an American or English mechanic. One scarcely knows which ought to be the greatest marvel, the failure to manufacture all these things in a country where woods and coal and iron ore are so abundant, or the obstacles that are overcome in their successful importation from foreign countries.

"At the time of the Spanish conquest, in 1537, the inhabitants of this region were the Chibchas, who, according to Quesada, numbered about three-quarters of a million. Their form of government was essentially patriarchal, and their habits were those of an agricultural people given to the arts of peaceful industry. Their religion contained much to remind us of the ancient Buddhists. It imposed none of those revolting sacrifices of human victims which marked the rituals of the Aztecs. They had their divine Mediata in Bohica, or Deity of Mercy. Their Chibchacum corresponded to the Buddhist god of Agriculture. Their god of Science, as represented by earthen images which I have examined, was almost identical with the Buddhist god of Wisdom, as represented by the images in some of the Chinese temples. They had also a traditional Spirit of Evil, corresponding to Neawatha of the ancient Mexicans and to the Satan of the Hebrews. And connected with their flood myth was a character corresponding to the Hebrew Noah, the Greek Ducalaine, and the Mexican Cojcoj.

"The capital of the Chibchan empire was Bocata, of which Bogota is manifestly a mere corruption. It was situated near the site of the present Colombian capital. But their most ancient political capital was Mangueta, near the site of the present village of Funza, on the opposite side of the plain. Near the site of the present grand cathedral, in the heart of the present city of Bogota, was a temple consecrated to the god of Agriculture. Here the Emperor and his cacique, accompanied by the chief men of the country, were wont to assemble twice a year and offer oblations to the deity who was supposed to preside over the harvests—a ceremony not unlike the 'moon feasts' celebrated to-day in many of the interior districts of China.

"The altitude of the plain above the sea-level is 8750 feet, and its mean temperature is about 59° Fahrenheit. The atmosphere is thin, pure, and exhilarating, but it is perhaps not conducive either to longevity or great mental activity. A man, for instance, accustomed to eight hours' daily mental labor in New York or Washington will here find it impossible to apply himself closely for more than five hours each day. If he exceeds that limit ominous symptoms of nervous prostration will be almost sure to follow."

SANTA FÉ DE BOGOTA.

Bogota has a population of one hundred thousand, and is in some respects quite modern, but in others two centuries behind the times. It is built chiefly with adobe houses that have a very unprepossessing appearance on the exterior. But the interiors of many of the houses are elegantly furnished. It costs one thousand dollars to pay the freight on a piano to the city, yet nearly all the well-to-do people have them. From Honda to Bogota they have to be carried on the backs of mules. There are few carriages, because the roads will not allow of them; but there is an extensive system of street-car lines, every bit of material used in their construction being brought in the same manner over the mountains. The cars were shipped in sections not too heavy for a man to carry, and the rails were borne upon the shoulders of a dozen persons. Yet, notwithstanding this enormous expense, the roads, which are owned by New York capitalists, are very profitable investments, the fare charged being twelve and a half cents in Colombian coin, which is equivalent to ten cents in our currency. The street-car drivers carry horns, which they blow constantly, so as to notify the people in the houses of their approach. The streets are narrow, paved with stone, and in the centre of each is a gutter, through which a stream of water is constantly flowing.

MONUMENT IN THE PLAZA OF LOS MARTIRS.

The streets, as in other Spanish-American cities, are named after the saints, battle-fields, and famous generals; but the houses are not numbered, and it is difficult for a stranger to find one that he happens to want to visit.

PLAZA, AND STATUE OF BOLIVAR.

The police do duty only at night. During the day the citizens take care of themselves. Four policemen are stationed at the four corners of a plaza. Every fifteen minutes a bell rings, which causes the guardians of the city to blow their whistles and change posts. By this system it is impossible for them to sleep on their beats. They are armed with lassos, and by the dexterous use of this formidable weapon they pinion the prowling thief when he is trying to escape. They also have a short bayonet as an additional weapon. Petty thefts are the thief crimes. The natives are not quarrelsome nor dishonest.

They will steal a little thing; but as messengers you can easily trust them with three thousand or twenty thousand dollars. When they work they go at it in earnest, but they are not fond of exertion. It is a curious sight to see cargadors going about with loads. They generally go in pairs, one behind the other, with a stretcher. The natives of the lower class are fond of drinking and gambling. They have a beverage called chica, which has a vile smell. It does not intoxicate as quickly as whiskey, but it stupefies.

Society is very exclusive, and strangers call first. If the visit is returned the doors of society are opened. The predominating language is Spanish, but all the upper classes speak French. They get everything from France, too, in the way of dress and luxuries. It is absolutely necessary to speak French to get along. The city is a city of paradoxes—of great wealth, of great poverty, and a peculiar mixture of customs that often puzzle the stranger. The foremost men in the mercantile, political, and literary circles are from the old Castilian families, but so changed by intermarriage that all bloods run in their veins.

The ruling class are the politicians, but they are more under the control of the military than is generally the case elsewhere. Out of thirty-three Presidents that have ruled the republic seventeen have been generals in the army. Among the leading minds are highly educated men who can converse and write fluently in several languages, who can demonstrate the most difficult problems in astronomical or mathematical formulas, who can dictate a learned philosophical discourse, or dispute with any the influence of intricate history. Their constitution, laws, and government are modelled after those of the United States; their financial policies after England; their fashions, manners, and customs after the French; their literature, verbosity, and suavity after the Spaniards. Patriotic eloquence is their ideal, and well it is realized in some of their orators.

Until the ratification of the "concordat" with the Pope, in 1888, education was free and compulsory, sectarian schools were prohibited, and all orders of religious seclusion suppressed; but under that document the ancient relations between the Church and State were restored, the school laws

GOING TO THE MARKET.

were repealed, the education of the children was intrusted again to the priests, and the monks and nuns were permitted to return to the country and reoccupy the cloisters from which they were expelled by the Liberal party several years before. The monasteries, convents, and valuable productive estates which had been confiscated by the Government from time to time since 1825 were restored to the religious orders; and all the educational institutions, including the university, the medical, law, and other scientific schools, the learned societies, the observatory, the libraries, and museums, were removed from the charge of the civil minister of education, placed under the care of the archbishop, with a liberal subsidy from the public treasury for their maintenance, and by the terms of the "concordat" devoted forever "to the glorification and advancement of the Holy Catholic Church." In one or two of the seaports Protestant missionaries are getting a foothold, but very slowly, as everything is against them. The unconquered Indian tribes retain their peculiar religious rites.

A CABALLERO.

Lately banks and bankers have multiplied to a great extent. Paper-money, heretofore almost unknown, is fast supplanting the coin of the country. This places a great power in the hands of the bankers. They are allowed to issue bills far above their specie reserve, charging from three-fourths to one and a half per cent. a month for loans. The profits are very large, some banks paying dividends as high as thirty per cent. per annum. The wholesale and commission merchants comprise a large class. They buy from the lowest-selling market giving the largest credits, and sell to the small tradesmen of their individual section, often supplying these individuals with goods in advance on the coming crop. This gives them control of the produce a long time ahead.

The non-producers are the gamblers and beggars. The people are given to games of chance. Lotteries and raffles find many devotees. Beggars are very plentiful, owing to the peculiar diseases that scourge the country. Saturday is their day; then every merchant places on his table a quantity of small change, and delivers it as the mendicants call. There are a number of hospitals, cared for by the Sisters of Charity.

AN ORCHID.

The Colombians are musicians, and spend a great amount of time and money in gaining this accomplishment. The German piano is found in almost every house, and many young people gain their living teaching this art, while extravagant figures are paid to foreign professors. There are few actors or actresses. The taste of the people is favorable to the growth of this art, and when a really good artist passes through the country he reaps a rich harvest.

Collectors of orchids are often sent out by European houses. They establish themselves at the most convenient place, and send out native runners, paying them from one to thirty cents a plant, according to the kind and condition of the parasites. They are worth from £5 to £100 in Europe. All the lower classes work indiscriminately. Indeed, the women do the heaviest part of the work, carrying over the mountains burdens equal to those of the men, and one or two children besides. Travellers are carried over the mountain-passes in "sillas" upon the backs of natives. These carriers are sure-footed, and capable of great endurance, usually making better time than mules. The sillas are nothing more than rude bamboo chairs, fastened to the backs of the silleros by two belts crossing over the chest and a third passing over the forehead. On a level road these silleros have a gentle trot that does not jar the rider, keeping a pace of four miles an hour for half a day. When they are climbing in the mountains they seldom slip or fall, and very few accidents ever occur unless they happen to get too much agendiente (rum). But it requires time and patience to accustom one to human-back riding, although the natives of the country prefer the silla to the saddle.

Bogota is half a mile nearer the stars than the summit of Mount Washington and at this elevation the climate is delightful, although it is only a few degrees from the equator. The tropical fruits are here found in abundance, as well as the products of the temperate zones.

The streams are full of fish, and the mountains are full of game; but nevertheless the people prefer bacon and codfish to the natural luxuries of their country, and even these cannot be found cooked in any palatable way. Indians will walk for three days—men and women together, and each woman usually carrying a child besides—having heavy loads of produce or long strings of fish upon their backs. The woman will sit all day in the marketplace peddling off her stuff to customers, while the man is patronizing the gambling booths; and at night, if there is any money left, they will both get drunk together, and then spend two or three more days on the road, walking home with empty pockets.

OVER THE MOUNTAINS IN A "SILLA."

There are no hotels worth mentioning in Bogota, only a few *fondas* (or restaurants) and *tambos*, at which the peons stop. There are very few strangers travelling in the country, and they generally carry letters of introduction, and usually packages, to the acquaintances of their friends, who entertain them hospitably. The few who visit the county from the United States stop at a boarding-house kept by a lady from New Hampshire, whose late husband was engaged in business at Bogota. There are probably half a dozen other citizens of the United States at the capital.

The original name of the city was Santa Fé de Bogota (Bogota of the Holy Faith). The plan of the city is irregular, and it lies upon sloping ground, with three or four streams running through it. The houses are never more than two stories in height, built of adobe and whitewashed. The ground-floor has no windows, and the rooms fronting the streets are usually occupied as shops, the proprietors living up-stairs. There is never more than one entrance, which is through a passage into the patio, or court, upon which all the rooms open. The second story is furnished with balconies, upon which the women spend most of their lives.

The cathedral stands, as in all Spanish-American cities, upon the main plaza, and is quite large and imposing as to its exterior; but the interior is bare, damp, and cold, and barren of decoration, except a few tawdry wax or wooden images of the saints. The pulpit is quite an elegant affair, being handsomely inlaid with tortoise-shell and embossed silver. There are two rows of seats, one on either side, which are occupied exclusively by men. The women all kneel through the entire service, or squat upon little pieces of carpet which they bring with them.

A half-century or more ago the erection of a very beautiful capitol of white marble, and of the pure Grecian order of architecture, was commenced, but the building still stands unfinished and unoccupied, a monument to procrastination. There have been several spasmodic attempts to complete it, but they have been interrupted by revolutions, and the money diverted or stolen. The President resides in a dilapidated structure, and the several executive departments of the Government occupy confiscated monasteries and convents, which, under the recent "concordat" with Rome, must be restored to the monks and nuns. There is a fine university, a museum containing many valuable and venerated historical relics, a national library which is composed mostly of ancient tomes, eighty or ninety thousand in number, an observatory, said to be nearer the stars than any other in the world, and a military academy, organized by Lieutenant Lemly, of the United States army, and considered the best on the Southern Continent.

NATURAL BRIDGE OF PANDI, COLOMBIA.

Bogota was once a city famous for its learned societies and literary culture, but during the last decade the entire population have been devoting themselves to politics and war. The revolution of 1884-5 was prolonged and disastrous, and there has been little, if any, improvement in political or commercial conditions since. The Liberal party, representing the young and progressive element, elected as President in 1884 Dr. Rafael Nuñez, and then attempted to overthrow him because of his reactionary tendencies. Nuñez was sustained by the clerical, or Bourbon clement; and having a well-organized army behind him, succeeded not only in maintaining his power, but in re-electing himself for a second term with a Congress unanimously in sympathy with his policy. The Constitution was so amended as to transform the Federation into an inseparable union of States like our own, the name was changed from "The United States of Colombia" to "The Republic of Colombia," and the President was endowed with most extraordinary powers, little short of those exercised by the Shah of Persia or the Czar of Russia. Then a treaty, or "concordat," was entered into with the Vatican, under which the civil as well as the ecclesiastical authority of the Pope is recognized, and all that the Liberal party had accomplished during its struggles for thirty years was wiped out by a single stroke of the pen.

DON RAFAEL NUÑEZ, EX-PRESIDENT.

The extreme ultramontanism of Dr. Nuñez awakened a series of revolutions, and resulted in his abdication of the Presidency; his successor being Dr. Holguin, one of the most prominent and learned leaders of the Clerical party, who has spent his life in Congress, in the executive departments of the Government, and in the diplomatic service.

CARACAS.

THE CAPITAL OF VENEZUELA.

THE voyage from New York to Venezuela is one of the most delightful in the world, and gives the traveller not only a nine days' taste of the sea, but shows him a glimpse of tropical America, and affords him an opportunity to study the peculiar life and customs of our Spanish-American neighbors. A splendid fleet of steamers—the "Red D" line, owned by Messrs. Boulton, Bliss & Dallett, of New York, and sailing under the American flag—furnish as comfortable transportation facilities as can be found on any ocean, and the journey can be made in thirty days, eighteen of which will be spent at sea and at the ports of the Antilles, and the remainder at the capital and chief cities of Venezuela.

If the whole coast of South America had been explored for the worst place in twenty thousand miles to build a city, there could not have been found one with greater natural disadvantages, which human ingenuity cannot overcome, than La Guayra, the seaport of Caracas, capital of Venezuela. It is a town of about six thousand inhabitants, stretched along a rocky beach for about two miles. Five hundred feet from the water the Venezuelan range of the Andes Mountains begins, and rises almost perpendicularly to the height of five and six thousand feet. One hundred feet from the houses the bottom of the sea slopes off into a hundred fathoms of water, and a mile out it is said to be two thousand feet deep. There is not the slightest excuse for a harbor, nor the slightest protection for vessels, which always lift their anchors and get out of the way when indications of a storm are seen. The anchor lies on the sloping rock at the bottom of the sea, but it has to be lifted every few hours, or the shifting sand will bury it beyond recovery. The surf always runs very high when a strong breeze is blowing, and under these circumstances vessels are expected to load and unload. Two wharves, or moles, have been built at an acute angle, with the narrow point open, and into this the lighters are steered, where they are comparatively easy while shifting cargoes. The vessels always stay out far enough to avoid the surf, but rise and fall, tip and rock with the swells that go under them with the motion that the billows of the ocean give.

Clinging to the little ledge between the surf and the foot of the rocks the town stands. There is only one street along which the warehouses are situated, with a rather imposing custom-house and the invariable plaza, or park, in which stands an equestrian statue of Guzman Blanco, the "boss" of Venezuela. There is said to be a statue of Guzman in every town in the republic, erected by his orders, but at the expense of the Government, while he was President. There are three of them at the capital.

The guide-books and geographies say that La Guayra is the hottest and most unhealthy place in the world; that it is hotter than Cairo, or Madras, or Abushar, or Aden, or Yuma; but the United States consul says that this is an absurd and inexcusable falsehood, and represents the city as being a most attractive summer resort. Humboldt says yellow-fever is born there, and that it is the chief distributing point for the plague; the consul says that there is only occasionally a case of fever of a mild type, which is often mistaken for genuine yellow-jack, and people ordinarily recover from it. Humboldt says, too, that in his time this was a famous place for tidal waves; that a lookout was always stationed at the fort, which sits in a crevice in the mountains above the town, to watch for them, and when one was seen coming a gun was fired to warn the vessels, which pulled in their anchors and put out to sea to escape being dashed against the mountains. He also says that it was the worst place for barnacles (*teredo navalis*) in the world, and that vessels were totally ruined by lying at anchor there; but Mr. Bird says these stories are all humbug, and while it might have been so in Humboldt's time, the conditions are totally different now.

WAITING FOR THE NEW YORK STEAMER.

Above the city, among the rocks, are the ruins of old Spanish forts which have been the scenes of the most terrific conflicts, and the ravines have run with blood from the carnage until the sea has been as red as a sunset. In the days of the buccaneers La Guayra was a favorite place for fighting, and there being no harbor, the pirate kings were always cruising after the galleons which came there to load with treasures for the King of Spain. Upon the top of a high bluff overlooking the town is an immense castle, which was at one time the residence of the Captain-general of the Spanish colonies, and is haunted by all sorts of legends and romantic traditions. It is now in ruins, and the underground tunnel which formerly connected it with the Military Barracks, four miles away, has caved in at many places.

To readers of that remarkable novel, "Westward, Ho!" by Charles Kingsley, this castle has a romantic interest, as it was here where the Rose of Devon was carried by her Spanish lover, and where she was sought and found by Aymas and Frank Leigh. But things are different nowadays. The great American house of Boulton, Bliss & Dallett have their headquarters there, control the trade, send vessels to New York every ten days without molestation laden with coffee, and the only blood that flows is shed by the fleas.

I have thus far neglected to give due credit to the tropical flea, to whose industry, enterprise, and assiduous solicitude all travellers in Spanish-America are indebted for a great deal of diversion. At first his attentions are somewhat annoying, and there is a general disposition to conceal acquaintance with him; but when every man, woman, and child in a company is constantly scratching, it becomes difficult to ignore conditions that are common and conspicuous, and everybody admits, first with blushes and then with brazen shamelessness, that he's got 'em. There is no use of trying to conceal the fact. They are as common and as plenty as flies in the basement kitchen of a city boarding-house, and the Venezuela coat-of-arms would more truly represent the condition of the country if it showed a man vainly trying to scratch in seven places at once instead of a wild horse dashing over the pampas. They are little black insects, which will get into your clothing in the most unaccountable manner. You find them in your shoes and under your shirt-collar; you wake up in the night and think you have somehow wandered into a plantation of nettles; or, when you become a little more accustomed to it, dream regularly that you are lying on the prickly side of a cactus. To rub the flesh with brandy does some good, but the better way is to grin and bear it. The pests are bad enough in Mexico; they are worse in the West Indies; but in Venezuela—the less said the better.

IN THE SUBURBS OF LA GUAYRA.

Between La Guayra and Caracas rises a mountain called La Silla (The Saddle), from the shape of its summit, eight thousand six hundred feet above the sea, and there are three roads between the two cities. The shortest is a trail nine miles long, through a ravine, which was used by the Indians at the time of the discovery by Columbus, but it is impassable for quadrupeds, and dangerous for any but expert and experienced mountaineers. Then there is an old wagon-road, steep and rough, for twenty-two miles, which was constructed by the Spaniards after the Conquest. The third is a tramway, narrow gauge, built along shelves which have been excavated in the side of the mountains by English engineers and English capital. The train goes slowly, and there is almost always a track-walker with a spade upon his shoulder in sight. It would not do to run up or down the grades in the night, or at a speed greater than ten miles an hour; hence it requires two hours and a half to make the journey, than which there is no more interesting in the world. The grade averages one hundred and ninety-seven feet to the mile, the highest altitude passed being four thousand six hundred feet; and one does not know which to admire the most—the difficulties nature has placed in the way of man, or the manner in which man has overcome them.

Humboldt, who came up the wagon-road, which runs almost parallel with the tramway for most of the distance, said that the only mountain scenery which equals it is that of the Island of Teneriffe, where a fragment of the alpine grandeur rises from the bosom of the sea. But one can scarcely imagine a picture more imposing or impressive than is represented here. Almost under the equator, with the ocean continually in view, and the mountains rising into the clouds all around you, the little engine puffs and pants like a restless stallion as it climbs around in the crevice that has been dug for the track. The road is solidly constructed, as English railways always are, has all the modern appliances for safety, and has been running so far without an accident; but if anything should break, if the engineer should lose control of the train for an instant, there would be no need of an inquest—there would be nothing for a coroner's jury to sit upon.

Two hundred and fifty years ago that king of buccaneers, Sir Francis Drake, paid a visit to Caracas under circumstances worthy of notice. It was before the forts had been built around La Guayra; in fact, it was owing to the adventure of Sir Francis that the Spaniards put them there. This Mr. Drake, as all know who are familiar with the doings of Queen Elizabeth's time, was a Britain bold, and had a little affair with the Spanish Armada. Having disposed of the enemies of the virgin Queen in the waters around home, he started

STILL MORE SUBURBAN.

out on a cruise for gold and glory, with "Westward, Ho!" inscribed upon the pennant that flew at the royal top-gallant of his main-mast. Mr. Drake was a gentleman of great valor, and his antipathy to the Spaniards and Catholics was pronounced. He started out from Plymouth with a gallant fleet, and when he came across a Spanish galleon or a Spanish town in the colonies he "went for it then and there." The Rev. Charles Kingsley has described the voyage, which continued around the globe, in a most fascinating manner. He followed in the wake of Sir Francis two hundred years after, and his descriptions of South American scenes and scenery are unsurpassed.

Drake's capture of Caracas was considered the boldest of all his achievements. It was in 1595 that he stood in with his squadron at La Guayra, and the inhabitants, when they realized the presence of the man who had devastated the West Indies, abandoned their homes and fled to the mountains, carrying the news of the arrival of the terrible Englishman. The

Alcaldes of Caracas assembled all the men in the country who could carry arms, from the ages of sixteen to seventy, and marched down the wagon-road along which the railway runs, to stay the invader. Half way down they prepared an ambush and lay in wait to annihilate him. Drake landed at La Guayra with seventy men, captured a fellow named Villalpando, who, by gifts of treasure, agreed to guide him up the old, dangerous, and abandoned Indian trail. So, while the gallant Alcaldes with all the men of Caracas were marching down one road Sir Francis was marching up another, which they thought he would not dare to climb. Neither met an enemy, and while the Spaniards were lying in ambush Sir Francis was hanging the traitorous Villalpando in what is now the Plaza Bolivar, drinking the wine from the Spanish cellars, ravishing the women, and plundering the houses of the citizens. But one old hidalgo, named Alonzo de Ledeoma, who remained behind, denounced the invaders from the threshold of his plundered house, declared them to be cravens, and dared the bravest of the Englishmen to meet him in single combat. Sir Francis and his crew jeered at the brave old man, and told him to send for his fellow-citizens who had gone down the mountain-road; but he insisted on fighting them alone, and was accommodated. They killed him as tenderly as they could, set fire to the city, and then, laden with all the portable property of value in Caracas, marched down the ravine to La Guayra again, and sailed away with a million dollars' worth of treasure, captured without the loss of a single man.

The city of Caracas, the capital of Venezuela, as well as its metropolis, and according to geographies one of the most delightful places of residence in the world, lies in a narrow valley between two high ranges of mountains, which lift their heads nearly nine thousand feet on one side, and something over six thousand on the other. To one standing in the centre of the city it seems to be entirely surrounded by peaks, to lie in a pocket or deep depression; but from the top of "Calvary," a hill which used to be a cemetery, but is now a park, one can see two roads that lead out, two passes through the mountains whence the river comes and whither it flows. The natural beauties of the place are very marked, and make it plain why Venezuelans are proud of their chief city. There is an old gentleman at Caracas, Mr. Middleton by name, who for over fifty years has been in the diplomatic service of Great Britain. He has served at Paris, at Madrid, at Mexico, at Buenos Ayres, at Brazil, and his last station was as Minister to Venezuela. When the age came which required him to be placed upon the retired list he would not go back to England, but wished to remain there, where, he says, it is but a step to Paradise. "I have been here since 1869," he remarked; "I have seen this country in war and in peace, and have experienced two earthquakes, the last of which killed three hundred people, but there is no place on earth possessing so many natural and climatic attractions. All I ask is to end my days in this eternal spring."

But, speaking of earthquakes, Caracas is a favorite place for them. The town was entirely destroyed in 1812, and more or less of it has been shaken down at intervals since. The residents are quite sensitive on the subject, and insist that more lives are lost in the United States by fires and cyclones and railroad accidents than in Venezuela by earthquakes. They talk of the great fires in Boston and Chicago as being infinitely more to be dreaded than the earthquake of 1812, which shook every building from its foundation, and buried twenty thousand people in the ruins. There is no doubt a constant danger from volcanic fires, but the people are not subjected to some of the ills we are heir to.

The present Government, under the inspiration of Guzman Blanco, is making earnest efforts to secure immigrants, and is offering the most alluring inducements to settlers upon the public lands. Venezuela is not thickly populated. It has more territory than France, Spain, and Portugal together, and is about one-seventh as large as the United States. The population in 1884 was 2,121,000, with only a slight increase for ten years. The country could sustain a population of 100,000,000, for the soil is exceedingly rich, and produces two crops a year without fertilization or irrigation.

There are three zones, three climates within the limits of Venezuela—from cold too intense to be endured by man to the greatest degree of heat known to the earth's surface. Although the capital is only ten degrees north of the equator, the temperature is delightful, and it is easy to realize the truth of the statement that Caracas enjoys a perpetual spring. The thermometer, which stands about sixty degrees at midnight, rises to seventy-five or eighty at noon, but there is always a fresh breeze blowing either from the ocean or from the snow-capped Andes to the south-west.

There was no printing-press in Venezuela until after the triumph of Bolivar, and the colonies were not encouraged in the arts or the sciences or any form of industry. The most profitable crops of sugar and coffee were kept a monopoly for the crown of Spain, and the people found it to their advantage to produce no more than they needed for their own sustenance, as every ounce of surplus was seized by the Government. Then, after independence was established, the rulers of the country imitated their former oppressors and kept the people down, robbing them in every possible way, until revolution after revolution was the result, and local wars followed each other so rapidly that the country was deluged with blood. Discontent was universal, and discontent always results in conspiracies and revolutions. Bolivar the Liberator (pronounced Bo-leè-var), the Washington of the country, was driven into exile, and died in poverty in a neighboring country. But Bolivar is honored there now, and the public

ON A COFFEE PLANTATION.

veneration is even greater, if possible, than that shown for Washington and Lincoln in the United States. He died of a broken heart in Santa Marta, Colombia, and was originally buried there, but ten years after his death Paez, the man who overthrew the Liberator and drove him into exile, thought it would be a popular thing to bring his bones home. This was done with great ceremony, and they were buried in the cathedral fronting Plaza Bolivar, upon which his equestrian statue stands. But his heart is in Colombia still. It was removed from the body, and remains in an urn in the Santa Marta cathedral.

In the museum of the University, in a beautiful room kept as sacred as the Holiest of Holies, is a collection of relics as precious to the people as fragments of the true cross. There are Bolivar's clothing, his saddle, his spurs, his boots, and books, and every little memento of him that could be gathered up, including the coffin in which his remains were originally buried. There are paintings representing his past achievements on earth and his present glory in heaven, where he is surrounded by cherubim and seraphim covering his head with laurels. The most precious of all the relics is a portrait of Washington, sent to Bolivar in 1828 by George Washington Parke Custis, with this inscription: "This picture of the Liberator of North America is sent by his adopted son to him who acquired equal glory in South America."

When Guzman Blanco turned an old cathedral into a pantheon for the burial of distinguished dead, the remains of Bolivar were for a third time removed, and finally deposited in a beautiful marble tomb. Upon it is a statue of the hero, represented as standing with a military cloak around him—a noble and dignified face. On one side is a statue of "Plenty," scattering corn from a tray; on the other a representation of "Justice." The inscription on the monument is:

SIMON BOLIVAR.

Cineres hic condit; honorat grata et memor patria.

1852.

There is another, an equestrian statue to Bolivar, in the centre of the city, surrounded by a park called by his name, upon which fronts "The Yellow House," as the residence of the President is called, and several of the Federal palaces. The standard coin of the country is called by his name, and is of a value equal to the franc of France. The coins and paper-money bear his portrait as well as his name, and a pathetic attempt is made by the people to show after his death the gratitude they should have paid to the starving exile.

Not far from the statue of Bolivar stands a heroic figure in bronze, with no inscription upon its pedestal but the name "Washington." It was erected to celebrate the centenary of Bolivar's birth, and its dedication was accompanied by a ceremony which has never been equalled in magnificence on the southern continent—a tribute to the man who "filled one world with his benefits and all worlds with his name." There are shops and stores, hotels and streets named after Washington, and his memory is revered as much as at home. But this people, so instinctively republican, so patriotic and appreciative of freedom, never knew what liberty was until within the last ten years. Since then the priests have been dethroned and the schools have been made free.

ON A BACK STREET.

Guzman Blanco may be a tyrant, but he has produced results which are blessing the people. Until he became President the Church ruled the people as it formerly ruled Mexico, but, like Juarez in the latter country, he went to radical and excessive measures to overthrow its tyranny. He confiscated Church property, drove out the nuns and Jesuits, seized the convents, turned them into hospitals and schools, and made the most venerable monastery a pest-house for lepers and small-pox. He deprived the Church of the right to hold or acquire property, seized the cemeteries, and opened them to the burial of the dead of whatever faith. He even went so far as to expel the archbishop because the latter refused to sing a Te Deum when a monument to the man who did all this was erected. With such audacity and by such means has Guzman Blanco deprived the Church of its former power and prestige. His opponents, like those of Juarez and Diaz in Mexico, are chiefly Churchmen (Bourbons), but as he exercises no mercy when his will is violated, they are in a state of the most abject submission.

The schools of Venezuela are supported by the Federal Government from the revenues of the Post-office and a trade license system. Formerly the mails now handled by the railroads were carried by Indian runners over the mountains from the coast, and so from Caracas inland still farther, as is the case yet where there are no railroads. A runner carries a package weighing about sixteen pounds strapped upon his back. His clothing is sufficient, as he leaves a city, to preserve the last requirement of decency. When he gets alone, however, he deposits his fig-leaf in some convenient place, and rapidly "walks in maiden meditation, garment free," until he approaches his destination, when he finds the uniform belonging to that end of the post-route, and dons it for remaining courtesies. These runners are faithful, prompt, serviceable, and of great endurance.

At the post-office you can get two sorts of stamps. The proceeds from foreign postage go into the general treasury. Another stamp is used for local postage, for letters addressed to persons within the town or State, and is required upon commercial paper, upon all deeds, mortgages, leases, contracts, notes, receipts, certificates, etc. The proceeds of its sale are devoted to the support of the schools, which are free to all, but are usually attended by the children of the lower classes. The negroes are particularly eager to learn, and the average attendance of the blacks is very much greater than that of white children, and out of proportion of the population. The ratio of illiteracy is greater among the whites than among the negroes, and people are beginning to complain that servants and laborers are being spoiled by education.

There is a Telephone Exchange, with four hundred and seventy-five subscribers, with branch lines to La Guayra and other cities. The instrument is very popular in all the tropical countries, where any method by which physical exertion may be avoided receives both public and private approbation. The Spaniard shouts "*Oyez, oyez!*" (Hear ye, hear ye!) when he goes to the telephone, the same words that are used by bailiffs to open courts of law in the United States, and it sounds quite odd not to hear the familiar "Holloa!" after the bell jingles. The telephone is extensively used in private houses; and as the etiquette of the country prohibits ladies from shopping or going upon the streets without an escort, they find Mr. Bell's invention a great convenience. They visit with their friends and gossip over the wire, order their meats and groceries from the market, and direct the storekeepers to send up samples of the goods they want to buy. The electric light is quite common also, the Opera-house being illuminated by it, as well as the President's palace, or "Yellow House," as it is called, in imitation of our

President's mansion at Washington, and other public buildings. The Opera-house is subsidized by the Government during the season. There is always a good company here. Performances are given twice a week, and the subsidy received by the present management is forty thousand dollars for the season, with free use of the house and scenery, which belongs to the Government. We attended a presentation of "Robert le Diable," and it was as well rendered as the average operatic performance in the United States. The theatre is a magnificent building of stone, standing in a plaza or park; and although the interior is rather bare of decorations, and the attempt to secure the greatest amount of coolness gives it a barn-like air, in its equipments and arrangement the house is equal to any in New York. The attendance was rather small, or looked so in the great auditorium, which seats two thousand five hundred people, and the President, who is said to be a constant devotee of the opera, was absent.

When Guzman Blanco drove out the nuns and monks he made good use of their property. One monstrous Carmelite monastery, covering an entire block, was confiscated, remodelled, and turned into a university, which is supported by the Government and attended by the youth of Venezuela professionally inclined. Science, law, medicine, and all the ologies but theology are taught here, and the schools are well managed and of a high grade. Attached to the university is a public library and museum, under the care of Professor Ernst, a distinguished German scientist. This institution is supported by the revenues of a coffee plantation confiscated from the monks and now belonging to the Government.

Across a small park from the university, in which stands the inevitable statue of Guzman Blanco, is what is known as the "Palacio Federal," bearing the inevitable marble tablet to keep before the minds of the people that it was erected by that "illustrious American." It is the largest, handsomest, and most useless building in Caracas, and one of the finest in South America. Like all the rest of the improvements it stands upon confiscated ground, where once was a convent, the oldest and largest in the country, whose massive walls were stanch enough to endure the great earthquake of 1812. Guzman had a great time pulling it down, but he is a man of enormous will and energy, and when he resolves upon anything it is as good as done.

The Palacio Federal is the Capitol of Venezuela. It covers an entire square of about two acres, built around a circular park in which are fountains, statuary, and beautiful flowers, and which is reached by grand archways on either side. Owing to an earthquake tendency in these parts the buildings in Caracas are never more than two stories high, and

INTERIOR COURT OF A CARACAS HOUSE.

seldom more that one. This is the tallest structure in the city, having two full stories, with a wide balcony stretching around the interior walls. At one end is a lofty elliptical-shaped room, two hundred feet long, and from forty to one hundred in width, without a pillar. This is the place where official balls and receptions are held, and the Venezuelans are much given to that sort of thing. There is no carpet, the floor being of inlaid woods of different colors, and there has been no attempt at frescoing, and the walls and ceilings are of the most ghastly white, so that the furniture of gilt, and upholstered in the most gorgeous brocades and satins, has a somewhat startling effect. It is arranged, as all Venezuelan furniture is, in rows along the walls. This room is used as a national portrait-gallery also, and there is a collection of about sixty pieces, as good as one often finds and better than we have at Washington, representing the notable men in the history of the republic. On one side is a heroic portrait of Bolivar, and on the other one of Guzman Blanco, looking as grand and proud as if he had made the world. Guzman was the author and creator of this gorgeousness, and the people are not apt to forget it; but he was strictly impartial in making the collection of portraits, and if the men whose faces look down upon us were to meet in the room where their portraits face each other with fraternal cordiality, there would be such a carnival of blood and bruises as has never been seen since the celebrated encounter of the Kilkenny cats.

In one of the wings of the Palacio Federal sits the Supreme Court of the country, and in the other are the offices of the Interior and War Departments, while at the opposite end of the building are the halls of the National Legislature, the Senate and the Chamber of Deputies—two lofty, barn-like rooms, each about sixty feet square, and entirely destitute of decoration, except the never-ending portraits of Bolivar and Guzman. The members sit in ordinary cane-seated office-chairs, without desks or tables, the presiding officers being placed in little coops perched very high up on the walls, with a shelf for the tribune on one side, and another for the clerk on the other.

Congress meets on the 20th of February of each year. The Upper House is composed of two senators from each State, elected by a direct vote of the people, and serving for four years. The Lower House has one representative for each twenty-five thousand population, elected for two years, also by a direct vote of the people. The first duty of Congress when it assembles is to elect from its own members a council of sixteen, and this council selects a President of the republic, with two Vice-Presidents from its members, by ballot. The Council is perpetual, and supposed to be always in session, their constitutional duty being to serve as a check upon the President. They can veto his acts, but he cannot veto theirs. They have power to enact legislation during the Congressional recess, which is known as Decrees of the Council, and is supposed to be reviewed by Congress at the following session. The Council elects the Federal judiciary and confirms the appointments of the President, thus sharing in the executive as well as the legislative power of the Government, and, to a certain extent, in the judicial, as they have the authority to remove as well as appoint judges.

Such is the constitutional form of government in Venezuela; but if common rumor is worthy of belief, its exercise is somewhat mythical. Guzman Blanco is supposed to carry Congress, Council, President, and courts all under his own hat. He nominates senators and members of Congress, and his candidates are invariably elected. He makes out a list of candidates for the Council, and they are chosen. Then the man whom he names is made President. There is a constitutional provision prohibiting the re-election of a President, so that Guzman can serve in that capacity every alternate two years, the intervening time being filled by some friend of his choice, who is said to be entirely subject to his will.

The official residence of the President faces the central plaza, or Plaza Bolivar, and is known as the Yellow House, but is not at present occupied, being too small to contain the family of General Crespo, who has seven children. Guzman Blanco never occupied it, for the same reason, as he has nine children. The Yellow House is a gaudy affair of two stories, with only twelve rooms, including four official parlors, a magnificent state dining-room, servants' quarters, and all that sort of thing. Official dinners are given there nowadays, and occasionally the President receives foreign ambassadors in the parlors.

The city of Caracas is a Federal district, like the city of Washington, with a governor appointed by the President. His office is in a memorable room, corresponding to Independence Hall in Philadelphia. It was formerly the chapel of an old convent, confiscated like the rest, and the remainder of the building is used for the police headquarters, the municipal court, and other local authorities.

SPANISH MISSIONARY WORK.

This narrow little room which the Governor occupies is the same in which the Declaration of Venezuelan Independence was signed, and upon its walls hangs a picture commemorating the event. Strangely enough, beside this painting of the decree of Liberty hangs a heavy gilt frame containing the banner Pizarro carried in the conquest of Peru—the rarest and most interesting relic in all South America. It is about four feet square, of heavy pink silk, faded almost to white, embroidered with gold by the fair hands of

Queen Isabella herself, the design being the combined escutcheons of Aragon and Castile, and it is still in an excellent state of preservation. It is with the keenest irony of contrast that this age-begrimed banner should hang in the room where the first voice was raised against the tyranny it represented; here, beside the voice, scarcely legible now to the eye, but to the mind speaking with mighty force the long story of Spanish oppression, and illustrating the first feeble and unsuccessful protest. This banner was the emblem of cruelty, avarice, and lust, and under its dainty folds more crimes were committed in the name of Christ and civilization than an eternity of perdition could adequately punish.

WOMAN'S CHIEF OCCUPATION.

Of equally striking significance in the room where this banner hangs exists a permanent rebuke and protest against the religion in whose name these crimes were committed. The Government refuses to recognize the authority of the Romish Church even in the sanctity of marriage, and a civil ceremony is essential to legitimate wedlock. The bride and groom may go to the church afterwards, but they must come here first, and in the presence of the civil magistrate make the vows to love, honor, and obey until death do them part, or their issue will have no right of inheritance. The Church has threatened to excommunicate, but the decree of Congress is inexorable, and the archbishop has finally yielded submission. When a couple want to be married, the groom goes to the Governor or his deputy and secures a license, notice of which is given for two weeks in a printed form, which is tacked upon a bulletin-board beside the entrance to the office. Banns are also required to be published for the same period in the official newspaper. Then, if no one appears with cause by which the two should not be united, the bridal-party comes to the office of the Governor, and there make their vows and sign the contract which makes them man and wife.

The following is the form of marriage contract:

"PARISH TRIBUNAL, Caracas, Ja. 18th, 1885.

"This day have appeared before me, presiding over this tribunal, Serapio Antonio Gutierez and Felipa Rivas, and declared that they are unmarried: that he is twenty-five years of age and that she is fifteen; that she is a resident of this parish, and that he is a resident also; that his occupation is that of a merchant, and that her occupation is that peculiar to the home. They declare that they have not changed their places of residence during the last six months, and that they desire to enter into marriage.

"In performance of the foregoing announcement, which has been advertised for fifteen days, as the law directs, in the most public places of this city, and no one having appeared to deny their right to become husband and wife, they therefore on this day agree to become such, and have taken upon them the vows required and recognized by the law. Therefore, this day, at seven o'clock in the evening, assembled with them in the municipal palace, I, General Basidio Gabante, President of the Eastern Federal District, by order of the Governor and President of the Municipal Council, in the presence of Felipe Aguerra, an engineer, citizen of this Republic, and Luis R. Tores, merchant and citizen of the Republic, have declared the evidence of their free will and right to matrimony sufficient under the law.

"Then was read to them, as above named, section thirteen of the law of the Republic, which explains and sets forth the reciprocal rights and duties of the husband and wife. Immediately thereafter I asked Serapio Antonio Gutierez the question, 'Do you wish to take Felipa Rivas as your wife?' who then answered in a distinct voice, 'Yes; I want her, and take her thus.' Then I asked Felipa Rivas, 'Do you take Serapio Antonio Gutierez to be your husband?' who in the same manner answered, 'Yes; I want him, and take him thus.'

"Addressing myself to both, I said, 'You are now joined in matrimony, perpetual and indissoluble, and you are required to support and assist each other, and provide each other, and the children that may be born to you, with the necessaries of the home, and be to each other a comfort and a blessing.

"The above, having been properly witnessed, was signed by the married couple in my presence, and immediately entered in the book of civil registry.

"SERAPIO ANTONIO GUTIEREZ.
"FELIPA RIVAS.

"FELIPE AGUERRA, *Engineer.* } *Witnesses.*
"LUIS R. TORES. }

"JULIO BAEZ PUMAR, *Clerk.* BASIDIO GABANTE, *Prefect.*"

A BODEGA.

Under a glass cylinder, on a stand beneath the banner of Pizarro, is a large book bound in scarlet plush, with heavy gold clasps and hinges, in which the contracts are kept and the record of Venezuelan wedlock preserved. All the Catholics go at once to the church from the municipal palace, and repeat their vows, with the benediction of the priest, but this is not essential. At this same office the record of births and deaths is also kept in the strictest manner. Formerly, as in Cuba, the legitimacy of a child and permission to bury the dead could be acknowledged by the Church alone, but the republic has confiscated all the cemeteries, and opened the gates to those of every faith, Jew or Gentile, Protestant or Catholic.

The Government is very exacting in many respects. One day a little boy was stolen. The only clew was given by some children, who saw their playmate seized by a man who drove away with him in a hack. Every hackman in the city was arrested and thrown into prison; every coach was seized, with its horses and harness, and notice given by the police authorities that not a wheel should be turned in the streets until the child was found. These summary measures made every coach-owner a detective, and finally the hackman who was engaged in the abduction confessed, and the child was recovered without the payment of the ransom demanded.

The police arrangements in Caracas are excellent; there are no robberies or murders, and one seldom sees an intoxicated man upon the streets. Liquor is sold at nearly all the groceries, or bodegas, as they are called, and the *aguardiente* which the common people use is the most vicious sort of fire-water; but the punishment of offenders is extreme, and those who have not sufficient self-control to drink moderately are taken in charge by their friends at the first sign of intoxication. There are several street-car lines in Caracas, and the conductors carry a horn, which they blow upon approaching a street-crossing, as is the practice in Mexico. The cars are all open, and are small, being capable of holding not more than twelve or fourteen people.

The burial of prominent men is attended with great pomp and ceremony, and it is customary to have those who are present at the funeral sign a testimonial to the worth of the dead, or pass a series of resolutions setting forth their merits and distinguished traits. These tributes are placed in the coffin, in order that in case the remains should ever be disinterred, posterity would know the character of him whose bones they handled. When a member of the family dies, it is customary to drape the furniture and pictures of the parlor in mourning, and to let it remain so for a full year.

A GLASS OF AGUARDIENTE.

The etiquette governing the habits of the ladies is the same that exists in Mexico and other Spanish-American countries, it not being proper for them to appear alone upon the streetsor in public places. They go to mass accompanied by a colored woman as a duenna, who carries a chair for her mistress to sit upon during service, there being no seats or pews in the churches. In the evening women are seen in large numbers upon the streets, and at the plaza where the band plays they swarm in gayly dressed crowds. The ladies of Venezuela are said by travellers to rank next to those of Peru for beauty, although it would be as much as a man's life is worth to intimate such a thing to the brothers and lovers of Caracas, who very naturally and properly concede nothing in this respect to "the daughters of the sun," as the Peruvians are called. The Venezuela girl has more animation, more vivacity than her sister across the Cordilleras, and perhaps more intelligence, for she possesses more liberty of thought and action than the ladies in other countries of Spanish America, and more attention is paid to her education. The climate of Caracas is similar to that of Lima, and although the city is almost under the equator, it has an altitude of eight thousand feet, and is surrounded by snow-clad mountains which temper the heat of the tropics and make a temperature like that of June the whole year round. The ladies have therefore the same clear, rich complexion of an olive tint, and the same great "melting eyes." Their features are usually of artistic perfection and their figures Venus-like. They have no national costume, but dress in the latest Paris styles. The milliners and modistes of Caracas go to Paris twice a year, and the wives and daughters of the rich men of the country order their dresses there. There is more society than in Peru, and during the winter season Caracas is very gay. At the opera the boxes are invariably filled with ladies as handsomely dressed and as highly bejewelled as can be seen at the Metropolitan Opera House or the Academy of Music in New York.

There are a large number of American families in Caracas, and several Venezuelan gentlemen have married in the United States. One of the loveliest girls in Venezuela is the granddaughter of "Josh Billings"—the late Henry W. Shaw. Twenty years ago or more a merchant at Caracas named Señor Don Santana sent his son to Poughkeepsie to be educated, and while he was there he met and married the daughter of Mr. Shaw. The young man has succeeded to the business of his father, and is now at the head of one of the largest mercantile houses in the republic.

Mrs. Guzman Blanco is the handsomest woman in the

A VENEZUELA BELLE.

country. She is a tall, slender brunette, with brilliant eyes and complexion and a sylph-like figure. Her husband worships her, and she is said to be the only person in the land to whom the Dictator's iron will has ever yielded. She is quite as famous for her loveliness of disposition as for her personal attractions, and her charity and generosity are proverbial. Every artist in Venezuela has painted her portrait a number of times, and in the room which Guzman Blanco uses as an office there are seven pictures of her, in various costumes and attitudes, and two busts in marble. Mrs. Guzman Blanco is the leader in fashion as well as society, and all her dresses are made by Worth. Each spring and fall, when they are received from Paris, the ladies of Caracas are invited to examine them. In a room adjoining the chamber are a number of large glass-cases, like those in a modiste's shop, in which her treasures always hang; and whenever a reception is given by the Dictator this wardrobe is open to visitors—a new and novel idea, but one which gives the ladies of Venezuela great pleasure. Mrs. Guzman Blanco was in New York with her husband a couple of years ago, where her beauty attracted much attention.

The Venezuelans are the most courteous people that can be imagined. Impoliteness is unpardonable. The clerk with whom you deal over his counter expresses his wish that you may live long and prosper, and thanks you gratefully for giving him the pleasure of showing his goods, whether you purchase anything or not. When a gentleman meets a lady, be she his sweetheart or his grandmother, he always says he "is lying at her feet," and he would rather be shot than pass before her. They are not the semi-barbarians some people in the northern continent suppose. They have accomplishments which ought to make the rest of America ashamed. Usually they are able to speak three or four different languages, have refined tastes in art and music, and, while they lack ingenuity, and usually do things in the hardest way, are nevertheless possessed of the keenest perceptive faculties, and seem almost to read your thoughts. It is not difficult to make known your wants, even if you cannot understand a word of their language. They do not allow smoking in the street-cars and public places, as in Mexico and Havana, and although it is the privilege of the masculine gender to stare at the feminine with all the eyes they have, the men are never rude, and ask the pardon of a beggar when they refuse to give him alms.

But the people always put the locks upon the wrong door, and wrong side up. When they build a house, it seems as if they studied the most difficult mode of construction. They erect solid walls first, and then chisel out cavities for the timbers to rest in. There are no stoves or chimneys, and charcoal is the only fuel. Gas is produced at four dollars and a half per thousand feet, from American coal which costs twenty dollars a ton. There is no glass in the windows, but a grating of iron bars keeps out intruders, and heavy wooden shutters shut out the air and light. Such blinds as are common in North

America would be the most admirable protection, but no one has ever introduced them, and the people will continue to swelter behind solid shutters until the end of time.

THE LOWER FLOOR OF THE HOUSE.

The rooms of houses are not plastered, but the joists are all exposed. The floors are of tile, and paper is pasted upon the walls, which are of cement and stone. In the court of every house are the most beautiful flowers. Tuberoses grow on great trees, and the oleander is as common as the lilac in New England. The parks look like the botanical gardens of the North, and in the evening are always thronged with gentlemen and ladies until a late hour.

Guzman Blanco, the uncrowned king of Venezuela, the man whose authority is more absolute in this republic than is that of any king in Europe in his own dominions, is a native of Caracas, where he was born fifty-five years ago. His father was the private secretary of Bolivar, and at one time a member of his cabinet. He died only a short time since, and his funeral was a pageant which was surpassed in the history of the country only by the demonstration at the removal of Bolivar's remains. He was active in the affairs of State almost until his death; now an exile, now a minister, vibrating between the extremes of power and poverty, as the party to which he was attached was up or down; and under this confusion, in the atmosphere of revolution, young Guzman was educated. He added the name of Blanco—that of his mother—to his baptismal name, to distinguish him from his father, and became Guzman Blanco; but he is more often called General Guzman by the people nowadays. When a mere boy he became a soldier, and had his ups and downs until the year 1874, when he led a successful revolution against the existing authority and became President. Since that year several attempts have been made to overturn him, but none has succeeded, and being a man to win friends as well as to acquire power, his political strength has grown with years until his authority is now absolute.

There is, and always will be, a difference in opinion as to his personal character and motives. That he is vain and imperious is admitted, and that many of his acts would not be tolerated by such a people as those who live in the United States cannot be questioned; but, conceding everything his enemies may say as true, it is nevertheless a fact that since Guzman Blanco has been ruler over this republic it has prospered and had peace—something it never had before. There have been varied and extensive improvements; the people have made rapid strides in progress; they have been given free schools and released from the bondage of the Church; the credit of the Government has been improved, its debts reduced, and the interest to its creditors is for the first time in history paid promptly, in full and in advance. The moral as well as the mental and commercial improvement of the people has been the result of his acts, and as long as he lives their lives and property will be safe.

A man under whose influence such progress has been made can be pardoned for the delinquencies of which Guzman Blanco is accused; and while his vanity is amusing, it nevertheless, in the forms it takes, illustrates the pride he feels in his achievements, and the realization of the importance of his career in the history of his republic.

Upon the pedestal of one of the five statues he has erected to his own memory appear the words:

TO THAT ILLUSTRIOUS AMERICAN,

THE PACIFICATOR AND REGENERATOR OF THE UNITED STATES OF VENEZUELA,

GENERAL ANTONIO GUZMAN BLANCO.

In these words the purpose and ambition of the man appear. To be the "Pacificator and Regenerator" where Bolivar was the Liberator is worthy the ambition of any man; and he who will erect a statue of Washington as the ideal his people should carry in their minds cannot be without a good motive somewhere in his consciousness. Future historians, when they look back upon the career of Guzman Blanco, will be more generous than contemporaneous critics, and will forget that he erected these statues to himself.

There are three statues to Guzman now standing in Caracas, but nobody would believe it if the number of tablets erected in his honor were told. You can scarcely look in any direction without being officially informed in letters carved in enduring marble that this, that, or the other thing was done by the order of, or under the administration of, that illustrious American, etc.

One night all these statues and many of the tablets were pulled down. It is a curious story, and the United States has what the play-bills call a contemporaneous human interest in the affair, for the *casus belli* was a Boston girl.

Guzman, when he was President, had a nephew of whom he was very fond, and who was made by him the commander-in-chief of the Venezuelan army. He was engaged to an American girl, whose parents lived in Caracas then, but now in Boston. For some reason the girl's father and the President had a violent quarrel, and the former was notified that it would be to his welfare to leave the country. In these Spanish-American countries a man who values his life never awaits a second invitation of this sort, and the Boston gentleman, with his family, took the next steamer. They were accompanied to La Guayra by the young general, who made no secret of his sympathy with the father of his *fiancée*, and expressed his views of the President's tyranny in a very emphatic manner. Guzman sent for the young man, and advised him to hold his tongue and let the girl go. The passionate lover gave his uncle some very plain words, which ended in his being offered a choice between his commission in the army and his North American sweetheart. He broke his sword over his knees, threw the severed blade at Guzman's feet, and tore off his epaulettes. That night all the statues of Guzman fell down. It was discovered that the bronze had been sawed where the feet met the pedestals, and a rope used to tumble them over. Of course the young general was suspected, and he followed his girl to Boston to escape his uncle's wrath. The romance ended in a marriage, as all good love stories do, and after residing in Boston the couple returned to Caracas, where they now live—she one of the most attractive and accomplished ladies in the city, and he an exporter of coffee and chocolate. Guzman has never forgiven him, and some of his friends think his life is not safe there, but he laughs at their timidity.

AN OLD PATIO.

Guzman's private residence is the finest in Venezuela, and a full-length portrait of James G. Blaine adorns his parlor. That apartment is very handsomely decorated and upholstered, the work having been done by artists imported from Paris; but there is such a vivid brilliancy in the frescoing, the fabrics, and the furniture that one wishes these tropical people who have so much money had a little more refinement of taste.

One of the most striking incidents in the career of this extraordinary man was his defiance of the Pope. To realize its full significance, it must be understood that Venezuela has always been a Catholic country; that there was not a Protestant church in the whole country; that Guzman was himself born and baptized a Catholic, and that under the Constitution the archbishop was a member of the National Council. Guzman first suppressed all the monasteries and nunneries of the country, and confiscated their property, which was converted into houses of useful education. Then, in 1876, he sent to Congress a message, in which he said:

"I have taken upon myself the responsibility of declaring the Church of Venezuela independent of the Roman Episcopate, and ask that you further order that parish priests shall be elected by the people, the bishop by the rector of the parish, and the archbishops by Congress, returning to the uses of the primitive Church founded by Jesus Christ and His apostles. Such a law will not only resolve the clerical question, but will be besides a grand example for the Christian Church of republican America, hindered in her march towards liberty, order, and progress by the policy, always retrograde, of the Roman Church, and the civilized world will see in this act the most characteristic and palpable sign of advance in the regeneration of Venezuela.

"GUZMAN BLANCO."

To this the Congress replied:

"Faithful to our duties, faithful to our convictions, and faithful to the holy dogmas of the religion of Jesus Christ, of that great Being who conserved the world's freedom with His blood, we do not hesitate to emancipate the Church of Venezuela from that Episcopacy which pretends, as an infallible and omnipotent power, to absorb from Rome the vitality of a free people, the beliefs of our consciences, and the noble aspirations and destinies which pertain to us as component parts of the great human family. Congress offers to your Excellency and will give you all the aid you seek to preserve the honor and the right of our nation, and announces now with patriotic pleasure that it has already begun to elaborate the law which your Excellency asks it to frame."

This declaration of independence caused a great sensation in the Catholic Church, and excommunication was threatened to all who failed in their allegiance to the Vatican; but neither the Government nor the people were to be intimidated, and the Pope has since tried diplomatic measures to restore union with the Mother Church. There has been a nuncio there for several years, and he resides there still, but is making no progress.

Macuto is the Newport of Venezuela—the summer, or rather the winter resort of the wealthy and aristocratic, who find the temperature of Caracas trying upon their constitutions, and seek sea-air, sea-bathing, and flirtations under the palms. It is six miles from La Guayra, and is reached by a tramway, over which a little dummy engine goes shrieking every half hour, and by a broad boulevard which would furnish as delightful a drive as that upon the beach at Long Branch were it not for the dust, which is almost hub-deep, and nearly suffocates one. La Guayra, as I have stated, has the blissful reputation of being the hottest place on earth, shut in as it is by mountains on all sides but the west, and blistering not only in the direct heat but in that reflected from the rocks, which is a great deal more oppressive—a pocket which no air except the west wind, the hottest of all, can reach. But Macuto is around the corner, one might say—around a point of rocks, and upon a little peninsula that stretches out from the beach, where it can catch not only all the breezes that ruffle the sea, but the winds that come from the mountains, down a ravine through which flows a beautiful stream as cool as one in the Adirondacks.

It was Guzman Blanco, of course, who found out this little settlement of fishermen, built the seawall to protect the peninsula, made the boulevard from the city, built the railroad, brought plenty of fresh water from the mountains, and built bath-houses there; so that the people of La Guayra can in twelve minutes leave the hottest place on earth for one where the air is always fresh and cool, where yellow-fever never comes, and where a good salt-water bath can be had for the sum of six cents in Venezuela money.

The bathing arrangements are quite odd. The sharks are so numerous that it is dangerous to bathe in the surf, and nobody cares to have his legs bitten off; so a semicircular pen of piling has been erected, at government expense, reaching about a hundred feet into the sea. Through this piling the surf beats fiercely. The pen is divided in the centre by a high wall, one side being for the ladies and the other for the gentlemen. At the shore end is a miniature castle of stone, likewise divided into two rooms, with a row of benches around the wall, and hooks over them on which to hang clothes. Everybody bathes *au naturel*; bathing-dresses are unknown. You pay five cents for a ticket, and ten cents for a sheet, which is used as drapery and as a towel, and then undress. The attendant hands you the sheet when you are stripped, and, concealing your nakedness with that protection, you climb down the stone stair-way, hang your sheet over the railing, and plunge in. The water is glorious, warm and salty, so dense that it will almost bear you on the surface, and deep enough to swim and dive. When you have had enough of it, you climb up the stairs, seize your sheet and throw it around you, and sit on the bench until you are dry enough to resume your clothes. Some of the more modest ladies, or, they say, those who have no charms to display, wear in the water a sort of night-dress made of towelling, but the pretty ones wear nothing but smiles—not even a blush.

During the day everybody stays in-doors after the bathing-hour, which is about nine o'clock in the morning. The fashionable get up about eight o'clock, drink a cup of coffee, eat a roll, go to mass, saunter down to the bath, and return in time to dress for breakfast, the most elaborate meal of the day, which is served about eleven o'clock. The menu offers soup, fish, game, steaks, sweetmeats, and wine. Then the people loll around till dinner, which comes after five o'clock in the afternoon, and is a repetition of the breakfast, except that roasts are served instead of steaks. After dinner everybody goes to the grand promenade along the beach. The band plays, the ladies are gayly dressed, the gentlemen twirl their canes, admire their small feet in the moonlight, and chatter like a lot of magpies. The promenading and gossiping are kept up until midnight, except twice a week, on Thursdays and Sundays, when there is dancing at the hotel or at some one of the private residences. The season lasts from October, when the rainy period ends, until April, when it begins; but families from Caracas and other cities seldom remain at Macuto more than three or four weeks. The charge at the hotel is four dollars per day—about three dollars and a quarter in American money. If some one would build a first-class American hotel here, and provide the comforts that are found in the States, it would be a paying investment; and I would not wonder if a subsidy would be paid by the Government.

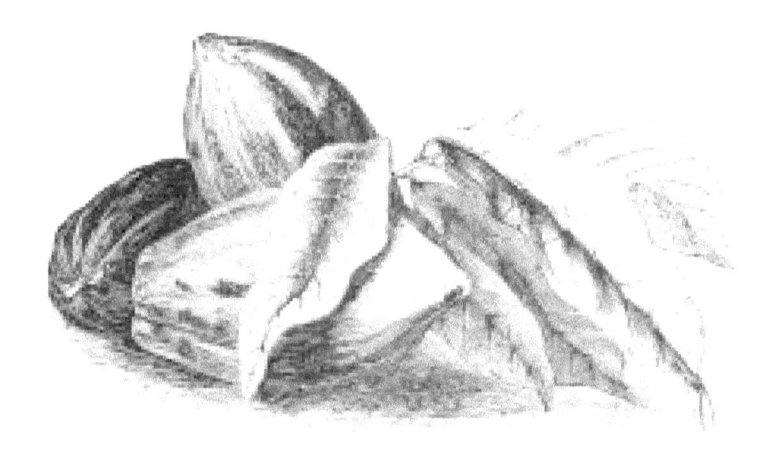

CHOCOLATE IN THE ROUGH.

The coffee plantations, or *quintas*, as they are called, extend from the coast far up into the mountains, and are very prolific. The people here claim to raise the best coffee in the world; and it is a singular fact asserted by the exporters that only the poorer grades go to the United States, while all of the better quality is sent to France and Germany. Just why this is so no one explains, further than repeating the remark so often made that the Americans do not like good coffee.

SEPARATING THE COCOA-BEANS.

Another curious fact is that chocolate costs more here than it does in New York—here where it is grown and manufactured, for very little of the genuine article is sold in our market. When the cocoa-beans are thoroughly dried in the sun they are shipped in gunny sacks to market, where the chocolate manufacturer gets hold of them. He grinds them into a fine powder of a gray color that looks like Graham flour, mixes it with the pure juice of the sugar-cane, called *papillon*, and flavors the mixture with the juice of the vanilla-bean. After being boiled for a certain length of time, this is poured into moulds and allowed to harden, when it becomes the chocolate of commerce. The Caracas chocolate, as all the product of Venezuela is termed, is considered the best in the world. It costs sixty-five cents per pound at the factories there, but can be purchased for forty-five or fifty cents a pound in New York. The best cocoa-beans are forty cents a pound here, but the Yankee manufacturer has a way of increasing their weight and reducing their value by adulteration. Pipe-clay is cheap and heavy, and it is supposed to be harmless. It weighs five times as much as cocoa, and as the profit in lager-beer is in the foam, so is the profit in chocolate in the pipe-clay, or whatever substance it may be mixed with.

Puerto Cabello and Maracaibo are the two great exporting markets of Venezuela, from which the greater part of the coffee and chocolate is shipped. The former place is famous for being one of the most unhealthful in the world, and the bay upon which it is situated is called Golfe Triste (the gulf of tears), because of the terrible scourges which are born in its miasmas. The bottom of the bay is said to be literally covered with the bones of those who have been heaved overboard for the lack of a better place to bury them. The ghost of that most famous of all freebooters, Sir Francis Drake, haunts the place, for he died here of yellow-fever, and his body lies in a leaden coffin thirty fathoms deep in the sea. The place is called Puerto Cabello (the port of the hair), on the pretence that ships are so safe in its harbors that they might be tied to their moorings with a single hair. This is something of an exaggeration, but nevertheless the harbor is the best on the Spanish Main, and has such abrupt banks that a vessel can be run up against the shore anywhere to take her cargo.

Off the coast of Puerto Cabello lies the island of Curaçoa, the quaintest, most novel, and altogether most interesting place on the Spanish Main. It is a fragment of Amsterdam, set upon a coral rock in the middle of the sea. It has always been a colony of Holland, with all the picturesque quaintness, stupidity, and wooden-shoe-oddity of the fatherland. Leaving the tropic scenes of Spanish America at bedtime and waking up in Holland in the morning makes you feel like one of Plato's troglodytes, who were raised in a cavern and then suddenly dropped into the world. You cannot quite allay the feeling that something has been done to you; the appearance of things has changed so suddenly and completely that you do not feel quite right about it.

PUERTO CABELLO.

Curaçoa looks like a toy town built by a child of uncommonly incoherent mind, by taking blocks out of a box and setting them up in irregular rows regardless of size, shape, or color. The general effect is a nightmare of gable-ends and dormer-windows painted a bright yellow. Immense warehouses with great gaping doors and windows stand beside quaint little Dutch cottages surrounded by beautiful gardens, and stores several stories high, of the most elaborate architecture, rise beside low structures as flat fronted and as square cornered as a dry-goods box with a Dutch oven on top of it. Quaint dormer-windows stare at you from the most unexpected places; hideous yellow towers, like the legs of some petrified monster sticking up into the air, meet your view in all directions; and great prison-like fortresses, with portholes like the eyes of needles, and ponderous doors lapping over like the covers of a banker's ledger, appear with surprising frequency. The streets are narrow, crooked, and rough. They begin in the most unreasonable places and go nowhere. Some of them start broadly, but wind around like the track of a serpent, growing narrower and narrower until they suddenly end, like the edge of a wedge, against a stone wall.

Curaçoa is a great place for business, although it is so quiet and sleepy that one might think the whole town had taken a dose of laudanum. It is the distributing point of a large amount of commerce, a harbor of refuge for vessels in distress, the haven of political exiles from South America, and the hotbed of conspiracies and revolutions against neighboring republics.

South of Curaçoa is Maracaibo, with its curious lake, in which are towns built upon stilts, that give the name of Venezuela, or Little Venice, to this land. The explorers, like tourists of modern times, were given to tracing resemblances in America to what they were familiar with in Europe, and they imagined these huts rising on piles above the water looked like the city of canals and gondolas. But there is no more resemblance to Venice than to Chicago, and the name of Venezuela, like that of the continent, is a falsehood which the world has allowed to stand uncontradicted.

QUITO.

THE CAPITAL OF ECUADOR.

ON the west coast of South America is found the perfection of sea-travel—fine ships, fair weather, and a still sea. Although one floats under, or rather over, the equator, the atmosphere is cool, the breezes delicious, and the water as smooth as a duck-pond. The Pacific Navigation Company is a British institution, founded by an American, Mr. William Wheelwright, of New York, which has been sending vessels from Panama to Liverpool, through the Straits of Magellan, for over forty years, and has not only a monopoly of transportation on the coast, but subsidies from the British Government and the various South American States whose ports it enters. It charges enormous rates for freight and passengers, the tariff from Valparaiso being forty dollars per ton for freight and two hundred and ninety-seven dollars per head for passengers for a distance about as great as from New York to Liverpool; but the company gives its patrons the best the country affords, and until the recent steam greyhounds were turned out to race across the ocean, had the finest and largest ships afloat. One set of vessels run from Panama to Valparaiso, where a change is made to another set, built for heavy seas, which go through the Straits of Magellan, via Rio de Janeiro, to Liverpool.

Those which ply along the west coast from Panama southward are built for fair weather and tropical seas, with open decks and airy state-rooms, through which the breezes bring refreshing coolness. Such vessels would not live long in the Atlantic nor in the Caribbean Sea, but find no heavy weather

ALONG THE COAST.

on the Pacific, where the wind is "never strong enough to ruffle the fur on a cat's back," as the sailors say, and ships sail in a perpetual calm. The trip to Chili, however, is long and tiresome, lasting twenty-five days. Less than half the time is spent at sea, as there are thirty-eight ports at which the vessels, under the company's contracts, are obliged to call. Guayaquil, the commercial metropolis of Ecuador, and next to Callao, Peru, and Valparaiso, Chili, the most important place on the coast, is the first stopping-place, four days from Panama. Although the westernmost city of South America, Guayaquil has about the same longitude as Washington, and is only two degrees south of the equator. It is sixty miles from the sea, on a river which looks like the Mississippi at New Orleans, and stretches along the low banks for more than two miles.

One's first impression, if he arrives at night, is that the ship has anchored in front of a South American Paris, so brilliant are the terraces of gas-lamps, rising one after the other, as the town slopes up towards the mountains. When morning dawns the deception is renewed, and one has a picture of Venice before him, with long lines of white buildings, whose curtained balconies look down upon gayly clad men and women floating upon the river in quaint-looking, narrow gondolas and broad-bosomed rafts. Unless he is warned in time, the traveller meets with a sudden and disgusting surprise upon disembarking, for the gondolas are nothing but "dug-outs" bringing pineapples and bananas from up the river; the rafts are balsam-logs lashed together with vines, and the houses are dilapidated skeletons of bamboo, whitewashed, which look as if they had been erected by an architectural lunatic, and would tumble into the river with the first gust of wind. The streets are dirty and have a repulsive smell, and the half-naked Indians which throng them are continually scratching their bodies for fleas and their heads for lice. Half the filth that festers under the tropic sun in Guayaquil would breed a sudden pestilence in New York or Chicago, yet the inhabitants say it is a healthy city, where yellow-fever or cholera never comes.

A narrow-gauge street railway, or *tramvia*, as they call it, reaches from the docks a couple of miles to the edge of the city, and upon its cars the products of the plantations are brought to the docks and loaded by lighters upon outgoing vessels. Like all Spanish ports, this one has no wharfage, but ships of whatever tonnage have to anchor in the river a mile or so from shore, and release or receive freight upon barges, which are towed, not by tugs, for there is not such a thing in all that region, but by oarsmen in a row-boat. Passengers have to reach the steamers in a similar way.

When we arrived there we were immediately surrounded by a crowd of boatmen, who clambered up the sides of the vessel, screaming with all the strength of their lungs the merits of their boats. Their vociferousness and persistency would make the Niagara Falls hackmen green with jealousy; and the fact that most of them were bare up to their thighs, and entirely shirtless, made the scene picturesque, although somewhat alarming to a timid person. The costume of the Ecuador boatmen is equivalent to a pair of cotton bathing-trunks, and they are as much at home in the water as in their canoes.

THE RIVER AT GUAYAQUIL.

With twenty-five or thirty of these naked black men surrounding him, shoving and pushing one another, screaming, gesticulating, and performing a war-dance of the most extraordinary description, a timid man is apt to be deceived by appearances, and imagine that he has fallen into the hands of a tribe of hungry cannibals, instead of a party of innocent Sambos who wish to promote his welfare. As soon as these maniacs discovered we were Americans, they were smart enough to introduce into the bedlam as much of our mother-tongue as they could command, making the scene all the more amusing. One big fellow, black as midnight, with only about half a yard of muslin and a dilapidated panama hat to protect his person from the elements, jumped up and down, yelling at the top of his lungs, "Me Americano! me Americano! Me been to Baltimoore!" Becoming interested in the fellow, we learned that he had been a sailor on a Spanish man-of-war which several years ago visited that city.

Among the crowd of howling dervises was a pleasant-looking fellow with a whole pair of pantaloons and a linen duster on. He was not so noisy as the rest, and could speak a little English. Taking him aside, I told him how large our party was, and where we wanted to go. He agreed to take us and our luggage ashore for two dollars, and was at once engaged; whereupon, instead of going off and minding their own business, the crowd began to abuse Pepe—for that, he said, was his name—and the rest of us in the most violent manner; and when the baggage was brought up they seized upon it, and each man attempted to carry a piece into his own boat. But the mate of the steamer was equal to the occasion, and laid about him with so much energy that the deck was soon cleared.

The street railway only extends to the limits of the city, but a short walk beyond it gives one a glimpse of the rural tropics. At one end of the main street, which runs along the river front, is a fortress-crowned hill, from the summit of which a charming view of the surrounding country can be obtained, but the better plan is to take a carriage and drive out a few miles. The road is rough and dusty, but passes among cocoa-nut groves and sugar plantations, through forests fairly blazing with the wondrous passion-flower, so scarlet as to make the trees look like living fire; with pineapple-plants and banana-trees bending under the enormous loads of fruit they carry. The rickety old carriage passed along until our senses were almost bewildered by visions none of us had ever seen. Nowhere can one find a more beautiful scene of tropical vegetation in its full glory, and no artist ever mingled colors that could convey an adequate idea of nature's gorgeousness here.

The most beautiful thing in the tropics is a young palm-tree. The old ones are more graceful than any of our foliage plants, but they all show signs of decay. The young ones, so supple as to bend before the winds, are the ideal of grace and loveliness, as picturesque in repose as they are in motion. The long, spreading leaves, of a vivid green, bend and sway with the breeze, and nod in the sunlight with a beauty which cannot be described.

THE RIVER ABOVE GUAYAQUIL.

There is considerable business done in Guayaquil, and some of the merchants carry stocks of imported goods valued at half a million dollars, with an annual trade of double that amount. It is the only town in Ecuador worth speaking of in a commercial point of view, and its tradesmen do the entire wholesale business of that republic. The shipments of cocoa, rubber, hides, coffee, ivory, nuts, and cinchona (quinine) bark amount to about $6,000,000 a year, and the imports, the President of Ecuador told us, amount annually to $10,000,000. There is no way to ascertain the truth of his Excellency's statements, as the Government keeps no statistics of its commerce, and he admitted that it was only an estimate based upon the amount of duties collected; but one may be allowed to doubt that a country like Ecuador, the most backward, ignorant, and impoverished in all America, can purchase for many years in succession twice as much as it sells.

AN AVERAGE DWELLING.

Founded in 1535 by one of the lieutenants of Pizarro, Guayaquil has been the market for five hundred miles of coast ever since, but now it is almost destitute of native capital, nearly all the merchants being foreigners, mostly English and German, with one or two from the United States. It is the only place in Ecuador in which modern civilization exists; the rest of the country is a century behind the times. Since its foundation Guayaquil has been burned several times, and often plundered by pirates; now its commercial condition seems secure from all dangers except revolutions, which are epidemic in Ecuador. In fact, the country would feel queer without one. Earthquakes are frequent, but the elastic bamboo houses only shiver—they never fall. To the torch of the revolutionist, however, they are like tinder, and the blocks that have been burned over testify to its effectiveness as a weapon of destruction.

GUAYAQUIL.

Over the entrances to the houses are tin signs, each of which represents the flag of the country of which the dweller within is a citizen; and upon these signs are painted warnings to revolutionary looters or incendiaries—"This is the property of a citizen of Great Britain;" or, "This is the property of a citizen of Germany;" or, "This is the property of a citizen of the United States"—and the robber and torch-bearer are expected to respect them as such, but seldom do.

Bolivar freed Ecuador from the Spanish yoke, as he did Colombia, Venezuela, Bolivia, and Peru, and it was one of the five States which formed the United States of Colombia under his presidency; but the priests had such a hold upon the people that liberty could not live in an atmosphere they polluted, and the country lapsed into a state of anarchy which has continued ever since. The struggle has been between the progressive element and the priests, and the latter have usually triumphed. It is the only country in America in which the Romish Church survives as the Spaniards left it. In other countries popish influence has been destroyed, and the rule which prevails everywhere—that the less a people are under the control of that Church the greater their prosperity, enlightenment, and progress—is illustrated in Ecuador with striking force.

A PERSON OF INFLUENCE.

One-fourth of all the property in Ecuador belongs to the bishop. There is a Catholic church for every one hundred and fifty inhabitants: of the population of the country ten per cent. are priests, monks, or nuns; and two hundred and seventy-two of the three hundred and sixty-five days of the year are observed as feast or fast days.

The priests control the Government in all its branches, dictate its laws and govern their enforcement, and rule the country as absolutely as if the Pope were its king. As a result seventy-five per cent. of the children born are illegitimate. There is not a penitentiary, house of correction, reformatory, or benevolent institution outside of Quito and Guayaquil; there is not a railroad or stage-coach in the entire country, and until recently there was not a telegraph wire. Laborers get from two to ten dollars a month, and men are paid two dollars and a quarter for carrying one hundred pounds of merchandise on their backs two hundred and eighty-five miles. There is not a wagon in the republic outside of Guayaquil, and not a road over which a wagon could pass. The people know nothing but what the priests tell them; they have no amusements but cock-fights and bullfights; no literature; no mail-routes, except from Guayaquil to the capital (Quito), and nothing is common among the masses that was not in use by them two hundred years ago. If one-tenth of the money that has been expended in building monasteries had been devoted to the construction of cartroads, Ecuador, which is naturally rich, would be one of the most wealthy nations, in proportion to its area, on the globe.

A FAMILY CIRCLE.

There once was a steam railroad in Ecuador. During the time when Henry Meiggs was creating such an excitement by the improvements he was making in the transportation facilities of Peru, the contagion spread to Ecuador, and some ambitious English capitalists attempted to lay a road from Guayaquil to the interior. A track seventeen miles long was built, which represents the railway system of Ecuador in all the geographies, gazetteers, and books of statistics; but no wheels ever passed over this track, and the tropical vegetation has grown so luxuriantly about the place where it lies that it would now be difficult to find it. Last year a telegraph line was built connecting Guayaquil with Quito, the highest city in the world; but there is only one wire, and this is practically useless, as not more than seven days out of the month can a message be sent over it. The people chop down the poles for firewood, and cut out pieces of the wire to repair broken harness whenever they feel so disposed. Then it often takes a week for the line-man to find the break, and another week to repair it. In the Government telegraph office I saw an operator with a ball and chain attached to his leg—a convict who had been sent back to his post because no one else could be found to work the instrument. A young lady took the message and the money. There is a cable belonging to a New York company connecting Guayaquil with the outside world, but rates are extremely high, the tariff to the United States being three dollars a word, and to other places in proportion.

CATHEDRAL AT GUAYAQUIL, BUILT OF BAMBOO.

Although almost directly under the equator, the temperature of Guayaquil seldom rises above ninety, and after two o'clock in the day it is always as cool as a pleasant summer morning in New England. A fresh breeze called the *chandny* blows over the ice-capped mountains, and brings health to a city which would otherwise be uninhabitable. On clear afternoons Mount Chimborazo, or "Chimbo" as they call it for short, until recently supposed to be the highest in the hemisphere, can be seen—white, jagged, and silently impressive—against the clear sky.

A COMMERCIAL THOROUGHFARE.

The road to Quito is a mountain-path around the base of Chimbo, traversed only on foot or mule-back, and then only during six months of the year; for in the rainy season it is impassable, except to experienced mountaineers.

During the rainy seasons the recent President, Don Jesus

THE PRESIDENT'S PALACE.

Maria Caamaño, resided in Guayaquil, in a barracks guarded by soldiers, where he could watch the collection of customs and see to the suppression of revolutions. He was the representative of the Church party, and the people of the interior were loyal to him; but the liberal element, which mostly exists on the coast, where a knowledge of the world has come, was in a perpetual state of revolt, and required constant attention. A fortress overlooking the town of Guayaquil, and a gun-boat in the harbor, keep the people in subjection. We called upon the President at his headquarters, and found him swinging in a hammock and smoking a cigarette. He is a man of slight frame, with noticeably small hands and feet, which he appeared quite anxious should not escape our observation. He has a pleasant and intelligent face, but seemed to be bewildered when we drew him into conversation about the commerce of his country. He was educated in Europe, and has the reputation of being a man of culture, although the abject tool of the priests.

THE OUTSKIRTS OF GUAYAQUIL.

Notwithstanding the rest of the country is still in the middle ages, Guayaquil shows symptoms of becoming a modern town. It has gas, street-cars, ice-factories, and other improvements, all introduced by citizens of the United States. The custom-house is built of pine from Maine and corrugated iron from Pennsylvania, and a citizen of New York erected it. An American company has a line of paddle-wheel steamers, constructed in Baltimore, on the river, and the only gun-boat the Government owns is a discarded merchant-ship which plied between New York and Norfolk. Some of the houses, although built of split bamboo and plaster, are very elegantly furnished, and the stores show fine stocks of goods. But the rear portion of the city is so filthy that one has to hold his nose as he passes through it. The people live in miserable dirt hovels, and the buzzard is the only industrious biped to be seen.

A BUSINESS OF IMPORTANCE.

There is no fresh water in town, but all that the people use is brought on rafts from twenty miles up the river, and is peddled about the place in casks carried upon the backs of donkeys or men. It looks very funny to see the donkeys all wearing pantalettes—not, however, from motives of modesty, as the native children go entirely naked, and the men and women nearly so, but to protect their legs and bellies from the gadfly, which bites fiercely here. Bread as well as water is peddled about the town in the same way, and vegetables are brought down the river on rafts and in dug-outs, which are hauled upon the beach in long rows, and present a busy and interesting scene. Guayaquil is famous for the finest pineapples in the world—great juicy fruits, as white as snow and as sweet as honey. It is also famous for its hats and hammocks made of the pita fibre from a sort of cactus. The well-known Panama hats are all made in Guayaquil and the towns along that coast, but get their name because Panama merchants formerly controlled the trade.

A PINEAPPLE FARM.

One afternoon, at Guayaquil, I witnessed a singular ceremony, which is, however, very common there. One of the churches had been destroyed by an earthquake, and funds were needed to repair it. So the priest took the image of the Virgin from the altar, and the holy sacrament, and carried them about the city under a canopy, clad in his sacerdotal vestments. He was preceded by a brass band, a number of boys carrying lighted candles and swinging incense urns, and followed by a long procession of men, women, and children. The assemblage passed up and down the principal street, stopping in front of each house. While the band played, priests with contribution plates entered the houses, soliciting subscriptions, and the people in the procession kneeled in the dust and prayed that the same might be given with liberality. Where money was obtained a blessing was bestowed; where none was offered a curse was pronounced, with a notice that a contribution was expected at once, or the curse would be daily repeated.

A WATER MERCHANT.

All imported goods are first brought to Guayaquil, and from that point distributed. Those destined for Quito are conveyed by steamboat up the rivers for a distance of sixty miles. From the termination of the steamboat route the distance to Quito is two hundred and sixty miles, making the

A FREIGHT TRAIN ON THE WAY.

total distance from Guayaquil three hundred and twenty miles. Between the upper end of the steamboat route and Quito all packages of merchandise that do not weigh more than two hundred pounds are conveyed on the backs of horses, mules, or donkeys. The average cost in United States currency—in which all values are stated—is four dollars per one hundred pounds between Guayaquil and Quito. Pianos, organs, safes, carriage-bodies, large mirrors, and some other articles too heavy or too bulky to be carried on a single horse are placed on a frame of bamboo poles and carried on the shoulders of men the entire land portion of the journey. A piano weighing about six hundred pounds can be carried by twenty-four men in two divisions, one half serving as a relay to the other half. Although labor is very low-priced, the man-carriage is quite expensive. A cart-road, or railroad, both of which are feasible and practicable, would greatly reduce the expense of transportation, and would materially influence domestic manufactures, as well as the introduction of foreign manufactured products. It seems almost impossible that any American goods could, after undergoing such a tremendous carriage, compete with native manufactures, however crude, in Quito, and yet they do. Nearly all the furniture in use in that city is brought from the United States in separate parts and put together on arrival; and in that, the highest and oldest city in America, many people sleep on Grand Rapids beds. The twelve breweries running in Quito import their hops from the United States and Europe, and with railroad facilities American beer, as well as hops, could be liberally sold in Quito. American refined sugars are largely consumed, although the native products are very good.

A PASSENGER TRAIN.

Ecuador, with about one million inhabitants, has only forty-seven post-offices, but they are so widely distributed that it requires a mail carriage of 5389 miles to reach them all; seventy-two miles by canoes and 5317 by horses and mules. About five hundred miles of the seaboard service is also covered by foreign steamship mail service. Between Quito and Guayaquil there are two mails each way per week by couriers—the usual time one way, travelling day and night, being six days. Other sections of the country are less favored by mail service, the receipt and departure of mails ranging from once a week to once a month, as people happen to be going.

During the year 1885 there were carried within the country 2,989,885 letters, and 50,700 letters were sent to foreign countries, eighty per cent. of them being between Guayaquil and the neighboring towns. No interior postage is charged on newspapers, whether of domestic or foreign publication. Interior letter postage is five cents each one-fourth ounce. The postage on letters to foreign countries is twelve cents each half ounce and one cent per ounce on newspapers.

THE COMMON CARRIER.

The social and political condition of Ecuador presents a picture of the dark ages. There is not a newspaper printed outside of the city of Guayaquil, and the only information the people have of what is going on in the world is gained from the strangers who now and then visit the country, and from a class of peddlers who make periodical trips, traversing the whole hemisphere from Guatemala to Patagonia. These peddlers are curious fellows, and there seems to be a regular organization of them. They are like the old minstrels that we read of in the novels of Sir Walter Scott. They practise medicine, sing songs, cure diseased cattle, mend clocks, carry letters and messages from place to place, and peddle such little articles as are used in the households of the natives. It often takes them three or four years to make a round trip, going invariably on foot, and carrying packs upon their backs. When their stock is exhausted they replenish it at the nearest source of supply, and are ever welcome visitors at the homes of the natives. This internal trade does not amount to much in dollars and cents, but supplies the lack of retail establishments and newspapers.

HOTEL ON THE ROUTE TO QUITO.

The capital and the productive regions of Ecuador are accessible only by a mule-path, which is impassable for six months in the year during the rainy season, and in the dry season it requires eight or nine days to traverse it, with no resting-places where a man can find a decent bed, or food fit for human consumption. This is the only means of communication between Quito and the outside world, except along the mountains southward into Bolivia and Peru, where the Incas constructed beautiful highways which the Spaniards have permitted to decay until they are now practically useless. They were so well built, however, as to stand the wear and tear of three centuries, and the slightest attempt at repair would have kept them in order.

Although the journey from Guayaquil to Quito takes nine days, Garcia Moreno, a former President of Ecuador, once made it in thirty-six hours. He heard of a revolution, and springing upon his horse went to the capital, had twenty-two conspirators shot, and was back at Guayaquil in less than a week. Moreno was President for twelve years, and was one of the fiercest and most cruel rulers South America has ever seen. He shot men who would not take off their hats to him in the streets, and had a drunken priest impaled in the principal plaza of Quito, as a warning to the clergy to observe habits of sobriety or conceal their intemperance. There was nothing too brutal for this man to do, and nothing too sacred to escape his grasp. Yet he compelled Congress to pass an act declaring that the republic of Ecuador "existed wholly and alone devoted to the services of the Holy Church," and forbidding the importation of books and periodicals which did not receive the sanction of the Jesuits. He divided his army into four divisions, called respectively "The Division of the Blessed Virgin," "The Division of the Son of God," "The Division of the Holy Ghost," and "The Division of the Body and Blood of Christ." He made the "Sacred Heart of Jesus" the national emblem, and called his bodyguard the "Holy Lancers of Santa Maria." He died in 1875 by assassination, and the country has been in a state of political eruption ever since.

WAITING FOR THE MULES TO FEED.

Although the road to Quito is over an almost untrodden wilderness, it presents the grandest scenic panorama in the world. Directly beneath the equator, surrounding the city whose origin is lost in the mist of centuries, rise twenty volcanoes, presided over by the princely Chimborazo, the lowest being 15,922 feet in height, and the highest reaching an altitude of 22,500 feet. Three of these volcanoes are active, five are dormant, and twelve extinct. Nowhere else on the earth's surface is such a cluster of peaks, such a grand assemblage of giants. Eighteen of the twenty are covered with perpetual snow, and the summits of eleven have never been reached by a living creature except the condor, whose flight surpasses that of any other bird. At noon the vertical sun throws a profusion of light upon the snow-crowned summits, when they appear like a group of pyramids cut in spotless marble.

EN ROUTE TO THE SEA.

Cotopaxi is the loftiest of active volcanoes, but it is slumbering now. The only evidence of action is the frequent rumblings, which can be heard for a hundred miles, and the cloud of smoke by day and the pillar of fire by night, which constantly arises from a crater that is more than three thousand feet beyond the reach of man. Many have attempted to scale it, but the walls are so steep and the snow is so deep that ascent is impossible even with scaling-ladders. On the south side of Cotopaxi is a great rock, more than two

SOMEWHERE NEAR THE SUMMIT.

thousand feet high, called the "Inca's Head." Tradition says that it was once the summit of the volcano, and fell on the day when Atahaulpa was strangled by the Spaniards. Those who have seen Vesuvius can judge of the grandeur of Cotopaxi if they can imagine a volcano fifteen thousand feet higher shooting forth its fire from a crest covered by three thousand feet of snow, with a voice that has been heard six hundred miles. And one can judge of the grandeur of the road to Quito if he can imagine twenty of the highest mountains in America, three of them active volcanoes, standing along the road from Washington to New York.

THE ALTAR.

The city of Quito lies upon the breast of a very uncertain and treacherous mother, the volcano Pichincha, which rises to an altitude of sixteen thousand feet, or about four thousand five hundred feet above the plaza. Since the Conquest the volcano has had three notable eruptions—in 1575, 1587, and 1660, when the city was almost entirely destroyed. In 1859 there was a severe earthquake followed by an eruption, which, while it did not do much damage in the city itself, caused great destruction and loss of life in the surrounding towns and villages. In 1868 the great convulsion which extended along the entire South Pacific coast was severely felt in Ecuador, where, it is stated, seventy-two towns were destroyed and thirty thousand people killed.

A STREET IN QUITO.

There was a great scare in Ecuador in the summer of 1868 because of the violent eruption of the volcano Tunguragua, one of the largest in the group, rising nearly two thousand feet above the line of perpetual snow; but after a few days of agitation, in which immense masses of lava and ashes were thrown out of the crater, the eruption subsided without doing much damage.

WHERE PIZARRO FIRST LANDED.

Here in these mountains, until the Spaniards came, in 1534, existed a civilization that was old when Christ was crucified; a civilization whose arts were equal to those of Egypt; which had temples four times the size of the Capitol at Washington, from a single one of which the Spaniards drew twenty-two thousand ounces of solid silver nails; whose rulers had palaces from which the Spaniards gathered ninety thousand ounces of gold and an unmeasured quantity of silver. Here was an empire stretching from the equator to the antarctic circle, walled in by the grandest groups of mountains in the world; whose people knew all the arts of their time but those of war, and were conquered by two hundred and thirteen men under the leadership of a Spanish swineherd who could neither read nor write.

The age of Quito is unknown. The present city was built by the Spaniards after the Conquest, but it stands upon the foundations of a city they destroyed, which was older than the knowledge of men. The history of the ancient place dates back only a few years before the arrival of the Spaniards in the country; for they, ignorant men, interested in nothing but plunder, destroyed every means by which its antiquity could have been traced.

Ecuador was the scene of the first conquest. The Spaniards, under Pizarro, landed first on the island of Puna, at the mouth of the harbor of Guayaquil, and first stepped upon the main coast at Tumbez, in Peru, a few miles southward. Here they found that the Incas, for the first time in the history of that remarkable race, were at war. Huayna-Capac, the greatest of the Incas, made Quito his capital, and there lived in a splendor unsurpassed in ancient or modern times. At his death he divided his kingdom into two parts, giving Atahualpa the northern half, and Huscar what is now Bolivia and the southern part of Peru. The two brothers went to war, and while they were engaged in it Pizarro came. Everybody who has read Prescott's fascinating volumes knows what followed. With the aid of the Spaniards Atahualpa conquered his brother, and then the Spaniards conquered him. When he lay a prisoner in the hands of the guests he had treated so hospitably, he offered to fill his prison with gold if they would release him. They agreed, and his willing subjects brought the treasure; but the greedy Spaniards, always treacherous, demanded more, and Atahualpa sent for it. Runners were hurried all over the country, and the simple, unselfish people surrendered all their wealth to save their king. But Pizarro became tired of waiting for the treasure to come, and the men in charge of it, being met by the news that Atahualpa had been strangled, buried the gold and silver in the Llanganati, where the Spaniards have been searching for it ever since.

No amount of persuasion, temptation, or torture could wring from the Indians the secret of the buried gold. Two men of modern times are supposed to have known its hidingplace. One of them, an Indian, became mysteriously rich, and built the Church of San Francisco, in Quito. On his deathbed he is said to have revealed to the priest who confessed him that his wealth came from the hidden Inca treasure, but he died without imparting the knowledge of its location.

EQUIPPED FOR THE ANDES.

Another man, Valverde by name, a Spaniard, married an Inca woman, and is supposed to have learned the secret from her, for he sprang from abject poverty to the summit of wealth almost in a single night, "without visible means of support." Valverde, when he died, left as a legacy to the King of Spain a guide to the buried treasure. Hundreds of fortunes have been wasted, and hundreds of lives have been lost, in vain attempts to follow Valverde's directions. They are perfectly plain to a certain point, where the trail ends, and cannot be followed farther because of a deep ravine, which the credulous assert has been opened by an earthquake since Valverde died. These searches have been prosecuted by the Government as well as by private individuals; and if all the money that has been spent in the search for Atahualpa's ransom had been expended on roads and other internal improvements, the country would be much richer, and the people much more prosperous than they are.

The devotion of the Indians to the memory of their king, who was strangled three hundred and fifty years ago, is very touching. When "the last of the Incas" fell, he left his people in perpetual mourning, and the women wear nothing but black to-day. It is a pathetic custom of the race not to show upon their costumes the slightest hint of color. Over a short black skirt they wear a sort of mantle, which resembles in its appearance, as well as in its use, the *manta* that is worn by the ladies of Peru, and the *mantilla* of Spain. It is drawn over their foreheads and across their chins, and pinned between the shoulders. This sombre costume gives them a nun-like appearance, which is heightened by the stealthy, silent way in which they dart through the streets. The cloth is woven on their own native looms, of the wool of the llama and the vicuna, and is a soft, fine fabric.

While the Indians are under the despotic rule of the priests, and have accepted the Catholic religion, three hundred and fifty years of submission have not entirely divorced them from the ancient rites they practised under their original civilization. Several times a year they have feasts or celebrations to commemorate some event in the Inca history. They never laugh, and scarcely ever smile; they have no songs and no amusements; their only semblance to music is a mournful chant which they give in unison at the feasts which are intended to keep alive the memories of the Incas. They cling to the traditions and the customs of their ancestors. They remember the ancient glory of their race, and look to its restoration as the Aztecs of Mexico look for the coming of Montezuma. They have relics which they guard with the most sacred care, and two great secrets which no tortures at the hands of the Spaniards have been able to wring from them. These are the art of tempering copper so as to give it as keen and enduring an edge as steel, and the burial-place of the Incarial treasures.

THE OLD INCA TRAIL.

THE OLD INCA TRAIL.

The Spaniards are the aristocracy, poor but proud—very proud. The mixed race furnishes the mechanics and artisans; while the Indians till the soil and do the drudgery. A cook gets two dollars a month in a depreciated currency, but the employer is expected to board her entire family. A laborer gets four or six dollars a month and boards himself, except when he is fortunate to have a wife out at service. The Indians never marry, because they cannot afford to do so. The law compels them to pay the priest a fee of six dollars—more money than most of them can ever accumulate. When a Spaniard marries, the fee is paid by contributions from his relatives.

It is a peculiarity of the Indian that he will sell nothing at wholesale, nor will he trade anywhere but in the marketplace, on the spot where he and his forefathers have sold garden-truck for three centuries. Although travellers on the highways meet whole armies of Indians bearing upon their backs heavy burdens of vegetables and other supplies, they can purchase nothing from them, as the native will not sell his goods until he gets to the place where he is in the habit of selling them. He will carry them ten miles, and dispose of them for less than he was offered at home. An old woman was trudging along one day with a heavy basket of pineapples and other fruits, and we tried to relieve her of part of her load, offering ten cents for pineapples which could be had for a quartillo, or two and a half cents, in market. She was polite but firm, and declined to sell anything until she got to town, although there was a weary, dusty journey of two leagues ahead of her. The guide explained that she was suspicious of the high price we offered, and imagined that pineapples must be very scarce in market, or we would not pay so much on the road; but it is a common rule for them to refuse to sell except at their regular stand. A gentleman who lives some distance from town said that for the last four years he had been trying to get the Indians, who passed every morning with packs of alfalfa (the tropical clover), to sell him some at his gate, but they invariably refused to do so; consequently he was compelled to go into town to buy what was carried past his own door. Nor will the natives sell at wholesale. They will give you a gourdful of potatoes for a penny as often as you like, but will not sell their stock in a lump. They will give you a dozen eggs for a real (ten cents), but will not sell you five dozen for a dollar. This dogged adherence to custom cannot be accounted for, except on the supposition that their suspicions are excited by an attempt to depart from it.

In Ecuador there are no smaller coins than the quartillo, and change is therefore made by the use of bread. On his way to market the purchaser stops at the bakery and gets a dozen or twenty breakfast-rolls, which cost about one cent each, and the market-women receive them and give them as change for small purchases. If you buy a cent's worth of anything and offer a quartillo in payment, you get a breakfast-roll for the balance due you. The landlord at the hotel requires you to pay your board in advance, because he has no money to buy food and no credit with the market-men; the muleteers ask for their fees before starting, because their experience teaches them wisdom. There is scarcely a building in the whole republic in process of construction or even undergoing repairs. Death seems to have settled upon everything artificial, but Nature is in her grandest glory.

A TYPICAL COUNTRY MANSION.

Architecturally, Quito is not unlike other Spanish-American towns, except that it is dirtier and a little more dilapidated. There is not even an excuse for a hotel, and private hospitality is restricted by the poverty of the people. Few people ever go there—only those who are compelled—and the demand for a hotel is not sufficient to justify the establishment of one. One-fourth of the entire city is covered with convents, and every fourth person you meet is a priest, or a monk, or a nun. There are monks in gray, monks in blue, monks in white, monks in black, and orders that no one ever heard of before. There are all sorts of priests, also, in all sorts of rigs, wearing the outlandish hats which are seen elsewhere only upon the theatrical stage. Some of the holy fathers look as if they had just been "making up" for a comic opera, and the jolly or grim old fellows one sees in Vibert's pictures are found on almost every corner in Quito.

A WAYSIDE SHRINE.

At the entrance to many dwellings may be seen the figure of a saint with candles burning around it, and the people appear to be continually coming from or going to church. The bells are constantly clanging, and it seems to a stranger as if the entire city were given up to perpetual devotions. The next most noticeable thing is the filthiness. The streets are used as water-closets, in daylight as well as in the dark, and are never cleaned from one year's end to another. There are no wagons or carriages, and only seldom can a cart be seen, the backs of mules, men, and women being the only vehicles of transportation. There is an unaccountable prejudice against water in every form, the natives believing that its frequent use will cause fevers and other diseases. When they have returned from a journey they never think of washing their faces for several days, for fear of taking a fever, but wipe off the flesh with a dry towel. I do not believe a Quito woman ever washes her face. She keeps it constantly covered with chalk, and looks as if some one had been trying to whitewash her. I do not know how she would look *al fresco*, but she has beautiful eyes, lips, and teeth, and a perfect figure till she reaches the age of thirty-five or thereabouts, after which she becomes either very fat or very lean.

CHARCOAL PEDDLER.

If it were not for the climate, Quito would be in the midst of a perpetual pestilence; but notwithstanding the prevailing filthiness, there is very little sickness, and pulmonary diseases are unknown. Mountain fever, produced by cold and a torpid liver, is the commonest type of disease. The population of the city, however, is gradually decreasing, and is said to be now about sixty thousand. There were five hundred thousand people at Quito when the Spaniards came, and a hundred years ago the population was reckoned at double what it now is. Half the houses in the town are empty, and to see a new family moving in would be the sensation of the decade. Most of the finest residences are locked and barred, and have remained so for years. The owners are usually political exiles, who are living elsewhere, and can neither sell or rent their property. Political revolutions are so common, and the results are always so disastrous to the unsuccessful, that there is a constant stream of fugitives leaving the State.

Although Ecuador is set down in the geographies as a republic, it is simply a popish colony, and the power of the Vatican is nowhere felt so completely as here. The return of a priest from a visit to Rome is as great an event as the declaration of independence; and so subordinated is the State to the Church that the latter elects the President, the Congress, and the judges. Not long ago a law was in force prohibiting the importation of any books, periodicals, or newspapers without the sanction of the Jesuits. A crucifix sits in the audience-chamber of the President and on the desk of the presiding officer of Congress. All the schools are controlled by the Church, and the children know more about the lives of the saints than about the geography of their own country. There is not even a good map of Ecuador.

No lady ever goes to mass (and all go once a day) without a small Indian boy or a maid-servant following her with a strip of carpet or hassock, upon which she kneels during service. There are no pews in the churches, but the floors are marked off like a chess-board, and each square numbered. These squares, about two or three feet in dimensions, are rented to those who belong to the parish, and when a man goes to church he hunts for his place on the floor and kneels down within the narrow space.

As in Mexico, servants go in droves. Families seldom have less than four or five, and each adult brings along all his or her kin, who are expected to lodge and feed with the father's or mother's employer. But it does not cost much to keep them, and the wages of my lady's maid in New York or Chicago would support a whole village. They want nothing but black beans, called frijoles, and tortillas. Meat and bread are unknown luxuries.

GOVERNMENT BUILDING AT QUITO.

The Spaniards are famous for their politeness, and in Ecuador, as in all other parts of South America, courtesy is a part of their religion. The lowest, meanest man in Quito is politeness personified, but it is all on the surface. He will stab you or rob you as soon as your back is turned. The Ecuadorian gentleman will promise you the earth, but will not give you even a pebble. This hypocrisy results in mutual distrust. No one ever believes what is said to him; partnerships in business are seldom formed, and corporations are unknown. If a man gets a little cash he never invests it in public enterprises, but keeps it in a stocking for fear he may be swindled—and the fear is well founded. Only the Indians keep faith, and that exclusively among themselves. To steal from a Spaniard they consider not only proper but justifiable. The Spaniards stole all they have from them. They never rob, swindle, or betray one another. They are as faithful as death to their own race.

COURT OF A QUITO DWELLING.

Once upon a time there was a revolutionary conspiracy among the Indians. An uprising was to occur simultaneously all over the republic. As the natives could neither read nor write, they were given bundles of sticks, each bundle containing the same number. One was to be burned each day, and the night after the last was burned was to see the uprising. None betrayed the secret. Of the many thousands who were admitted to the conspiracy not one violated faith.

All sorts of labor are done in the most primitive manner. The agriculturists do not plough, but plant the seed by poking a hole in the ground with a stick. Threshing and corn-shelling are done by driving horses over the grain. The hair is removed from hogs, not by hot water and scraping, but by burning. Everything is done in the slowest and most difficult way. For that reason, and because the interior is so isolated from the rest of mankind, the country does not know the meaning of the words progress and prosperity. Until the influence of the Romish Church is destroyed, until immigration is invited and secured, Ecuador will be a desert rich in undeveloped resources. With plenty of natural wealth, it has neither peace nor industry, and such a thing as a surplus of any character is unknown. One of the richest of the South American republics, and the oldest of them all, it is the poorest and most backward.

On the south-west side of Quito, within half a mile of the city's centre, flows the Machangari River, a small, rapid, and never-failing stream. The rapid fall of the water provides mill-sites every few rods, which are utilized by six small flour-mills and a small manufactory of woollen blankets. The six flour-mills, having a total of eighteen run of stone, give employment to twenty-four men, whose daily wages range from twelve to twenty-five cents. In the whole woollen blanket manufactory forty persons are employed, at average daily wages of twelve cents. Aside from the water-motors mentioned, the only motor in use is a small steam-engine in a suburban village, used in a sugar refinery where twelve persons work for wages ranging from twelve to twenty cents per day. The manufacture of adobe, hard brick, and roofing-tile is carried on more or less in conjunction, and gives employment to about three hundred men and women, the women exercising the right of doing any kind of work

WHAT THE EARTHQUAKES LEFT

performed by the men. No machinery is used, the brick and tile being moulded by hand in a box. These workers receive each twelve cents a day. The making of pottery is carried on in a small way at about fifty places, furnishing work for about one hundred persons, who when hired earn twelve cents a day. There is one manufactory of silk and high hats at which twelve men are employed, at twenty-five cents a day. There are also about fifty places at which Indian felt hats are made, a total of one hundred persons being employed, with wages at twelve cents a day. Matting manufacturing is carried on at three places, at which hand-looms only are used. The material employed is the fibre of the cactus, which is very serviceable. Thirty persons at this pursuit earn from eighteen to twenty cents per day wages. There is no foundery in Quito, and all of the iron-working is restricted to what is done in a few blacksmith shops. There is one combined cart and blacksmith shop, at which carts are made and general repairing is done, employing ten men at twenty-five cents a day. The industries mentioned have long been established. There are also numerous tailor shops, shoe-shops, tin-shops, and carpenter shops. At the latter are made sofas, bureaus, tables, and all other articles of furniture difficult of transportation by pack-animals. Nearly all the chairs in use were brought from the United States, packed in parts, and were put together when sold. Coffins also are made at the carpenter shops. All of the work done at these shops is done by hand.

A PROFESSIONAL BEGGAR.

The only industry that has sprung up in recent years is that of beer-making, which has been inspired and promoted by the German element. There have been established twelve breweries, which employ a total of one hundred and twenty men, at average daily wages of twenty cents. The barley used is of native growth, and is bought at a low price. The hops are imported from the United States and Europe, and by reason of expensive transportation are very costly.

AN ECUADOR BELLE.

Though Quito has a population of about sixty thousand, it has had for a long period considerable note as a place of art in sculpture and painting, and has several public-schools of ordinary grade, and three universities, in charge of the priests, yet it has never been a field in which literature thrived, or the business of printing flourished. It contains no newspaper, and but one weekly journal is issued. This is the oficial paper, and is devoted solely to the publication of official documents. Its circulation is about one thousand copies, exclusively among government and foreign officials, and is gratuitous. The principal printing establishment is owned and managed by the Government, in which twenty persons are employed. Among its material are one rotary press (on which the official paper is printed), five hand-lever presses, and a good assortment of type. No work is done except for government use. There are five other small printing concerns, each employing from two to six persons, at which is done the miscellaneous printing of the public. They use nothing but hand-lever presses. The presses and type were purchased, in the United States.

Revolutions in Ecuador are frequent, and they usually begin by an attempt to assassinate the President. The plan of procedure is usually for the discontented political faction to create a mutiny in the army, either by bribes to the officers or promises of promotion. As the private soldiers always obey their officers, like so many automatons, and are as willing to fight on one side as the other, to secure the officers is to secure the army. The next step is to seize the barracks and arsenal, put the President to death, proclaim some one else provisional dictator, and then call a junta, or convention, to nominate "a constitutional Executive." Señor Caamaño seems to bear a charmed life, for during his term of four years as President he had numerous remarkable escapes. The last attempt to assassinate him was in January, 1886, while he was journeying from Guayaquil to Quito. He was riding, as travellers usually do, by night, to escape the heat of the sun, when his small escort was attacked by a band of mountaineers, and fled, leaving the President to look out for himself. He jumped from his horse, ran into the forest which lines the road, and creeping through the trees to the river, swam to the other side, and made his way, thirty miles on foot, to the hacienda of a friend, where he knew he would find refuge. For two days and nights he was in the forest without food, and when he finally reached a safe haven was totally exhausted. For a week or ten days he lay ill with a fever, but couriers were sent to Guayaquil and Quito who arrived there before the reports of his assassination, and assured the officials of the Government of his safety. At the same time a mutiny broke out at the military garrisons in both cities, but was quelled, and the leaders summarily shot.

Since the inauguration of Don Antonio Flores as President, in 1888, Ecuador has been at peace, and shows bright promises for the future. He is the foremost statesman of the republic; has ability, wealth, knowledge, and experience surpassing most of his fellow-citizens, and, what is equally effectual among the Spanish-American people, the prestige of a venerated name. His father was a Venezuelan, and at one time represented New Grenada in the Cortes at Madrid. General Flores stood with Bolivar at the head of the Revolution for Independence, organized the Republic of Ecuador, and was its first President. The son has inherited his father's ability, his patriotism and zeal, and has spent his life in the civil, diplomatic, judicial, and military service. He did not seek the presidency, and therefore entered upon the duties of his office free of all entanglements, and with the one purpose, to modernize this Hermit of Republics, and bring its people to the standard of nineteenth century civilization.

From Guayaquil to Callao, and in fact to the end of the continent, the western coast of South America presents an unbroken line of mountains, with a strip of desert between them and the sea. Occasionally some stream from the mountains brings down the melted snow and opens an oasis. These oases have been utilized by the planters as far back as the Conquest, when the industrious Jesuits made as vigorous a war upon the desert as upon the Incas, and conquered one as easily as they conquered the other. Wherever this barren strip has been irrigated it produces enormous crops of sugar, coffee, and other tropical products, and the whole of it might be redeemed by the introduction of a little capital and industry. If the money that has been wasted in revolutions had been expended in the development of its mines, and the soldiers had dug irrigating ditches with as much ardor as they have fought each other, there would be no richer country on the globe. Wherever the Incas touched the earth it produced in profusion, and their wealth was fabulous. Their empire extended three thousand miles north and south, and about four hundred miles east and west, from the Pacific to the great forests of the Amazon, which their simple tools were unable to subdue.

In no part of the world does nature assume more imposing forms. Deserts as repulsive as Sahara alternate with valleys as rich and luxuriant as those of Italy. Eternal summer smiles under the frown of eternal snow. The rainless region—this desert strip which lies between the Andes and the sea—is

A HOTEL ON THE COAST.

about forty miles in width, and the panorama presented to the voyager is a constant succession of bare and repulsive wastes of sand and rocks, uninhabited, whose silence is broken only by the incessant surf, the bark of the sea-lions, and the screams of the water-birds which haunt its wave-worn and forbidding shore. The coast is dotted with small rocky islands, which have been the roost of myriads of birds for ages, and furnish guano for commerce. The steamers seem to furnish them their only entertainment, and they surround every vessel which passes, soaring about and above the masts, screaming defiance to the invaders of their resorts. The water, too, is full of animal life. Nowhere does the sea offer science so many curious forms of animate nature; monsters unknown to northern waters can be seen from the decks of the steamers, and at night their movements about the vessel are shown by a line of fire which always follows their fins. The water is so strongly impregnated with phosphorus that every wave is tipped with silver, and every fish that darts about leaves a brilliant trail like that of a comet. The larger fishes, the sharks and porpoises, find great sport in swimming races with the ship, and under the bowsprit a small army of them are to be seen every evening, sailing along beside the vessel, darting back and forth before its bows, leaping and plunging over one another. Their every motion is apparent, and the outlines of their bodies are as distinct as if drawn with a pencil of fire. Nowhere is this phenomenon so conspicuous.

The first point beyond Guayaquil is the island of Puna, where Pizarro first landed, and where he waited with a squad of thirteen men while the deserters from his expedition went back to Panama in his ships, promising to send reinforcements, which afterwards came. Beside Puna is the famous Isle del Muerto (dead man's island), which looks like a corpse floating in the water. Just below, and the northernmost town of Peru, is Tumbez, where Pizarro met the messengers from Atahualpa's army who came to ask the object of his visit.

Behind Tumbez are the petroleum deposits of Peru, which have been known to the natives ever since the times of the Incas, but they were ignorant of the character or the value of the oil. A Yankee by the name of Larkin, from Western New York, came down here to sell kerosene, and recognized the material which the Indians used for lubricating and coloring purposes as the same stuff he was peddling. An attempt has been made to utilize the deposits, which are very extensive, but so far they have not been successful in producing a burning fluid that is either safe or agreeable.

At each of the little ports on the Peruvian coast the steamer stops and takes on produce for shipment to Liverpool or Germany. These towns are simply collections of mud huts, inhabited by fishermen or the employés of the steamship company, dreary, dusty, and dirty. Back in the country, along the streams which bring fertility and water down from the mountains, are places of commercial importance, the residences of rich hacienda owners, and the scenes of historic events as well as prehistoric civilization. The products of the country are sugar, coffee, cocoa, and cotton, while those of the town are

"Panama" hats and fleas. In each one of the ports the natives are busy braiding hats from vegetable fibres, and the results of their labor find a market at Panama and in the cities of the coast, where, as in Mexico, a man's character is judged by what he wears on his head. The hats are usually made of *toquilla*, or *pita*, an arborescent plant of the cactus family, the leaves of which are often several yards long. When cut, the leaf is dried, and then whipped into shreds almost as fine and tough as silk. Some of these hats are made of single fibres, with not a splice or an end from the centre of the crown to the rim. It often requires two or three months to make them, and the best ones are braided under water, so as to make the fibre more pliable. They sometimes cost as much as two hundred and fifty dollars, but last a lifetime, and can be packed away in a vest-pocket, turned inside out, and worn that way, the inside being as smooth and well finished as the other. The natives make beautiful cigar-cases too; but it is difficult for a stranger to purchase either them or their hats, because they have an idea that all strangers are rich, and will pay any price that is asked. One old lady offered me a cigar-case of straw, such as is sold in Japanese stores for one or two dollars, and politely agreed to sell it for twenty dollars. When I told her I could get a silver one for that price, she came down to eighteen dollars, then to twelve dollars, and finally to one dollar. They have no idea of the value of money, and are habitually imposed upon by local traders, who exchange food for their straw-work at merely nominal rates, and then sell the hats at enormous figures.

At each of the ports where the steamer stops an army of officials come aboard to get a good dinner or breakfast and a cocktail or two at the expense of the steamship company. They wear gay uniforms and swords, and there is usually one inspector, or official, for every ten packages of merchandise. First, there is the "captain of the port," with his retinue; then the governor of the district, with his staff; then the collector of customs, with a battalion of inspectors; and, finally, the commandante of the military garrison and all his subordinates. The deck of the vessel fairly swarms with them, and as the steamer's arrival is the only event to give variety to the monotony of their lives, they celebrate it for all it is worth. It is little wonder that the governments of these South American countries are poor, with all these tax-eaters at every little town of four or five hundred inhabitants.

CUSTOMS OFFICERS.

There are a great many more railroads in Peru than is generally supposed. Nearly all of the coast towns have a line connecting them with the plantations of the interior; and as there are no harbors, but only open roadsteads, expensive iron piers have been constructed through the surf from which merchandise is lifted into barges or lighters and taken to the ships, which anchor a mile or so from the shore. Where there are no piers the lighters are run through the surf when the tide is high, are loaded at low tide, and then floated off to buoys to await the arrival of vessels.

A HOME ON THE COAST.

All along the coast there is a system of "deck trading" carried on by the people of the country. Men and women come on board with market produce, fruits, and other articles, which are strewn about the deck, and are sold to people who visit the vessel at each port for the purpose of buying. These traders are charged passage-money and freight by the steamship companies, but are a nuisance to the other passengers. Each female trader brings a mattress to sleep upon, a chair to use during the day, her own cooking and chamber utensils, and spends a greater part of her life abroad, sailing from one port to another.

At Payta we took on a battalion of Peruvian soldiers, with one brass-mounted officer to every seven men. The Peruvian soldier always has his wife with him; at least there is a woman who maintains such a relation. The ceremony of marriage is not observed, nor is it to any great extent in civil life, for the expense of matrimony is so great that among the *cholos*, as the peasants are called, men and women live their lives together without any formality, and with the sanction of public sentiment, even if they lack the sanction of the law. For this the Catholic Church is responsible, and to it can be traced the cause of the illegitimacy of more than half of the population. The fee charged by the priests for performing the ceremony of marriage is so excessive that the poor cannot pay it; hence marriage is practically placed under what may be called a prohibitory tariff. This prevails in all of the South American countries where the Church still holds its power, but in those which are now under the control of the Liberal party the rite of civil marriage has been established by law, and the ceremony now costs from twenty-five cents to a dollar.

With each company of Peruvian troops is a squad of women called *rabonas*, generally one to every three or four men, volunteers who serve without pay but receive rations, and are given transportation by the Government. They are always with the men—in camp, on the march, and in battle. In camp they do the cooking and other necessary work; on the march they share the exposure and fatigue, being treated exactly as the men are, and do most of the foraging for the messes to which they belong. In battle they nurse their own wounded, rob the dead, cut the throats of enemies whom they find lying alive on the field, carry water and ammunition, and perform other brutal or useful services. They are always enumerated in the rosters of troops and in the reports of casualties, which read: so many men and so many rabonas killed and wounded; for they share the soldier's death as well as his privations.

Some of these wives of the regiment have children with them, and there is scarcely a company without a dozen or so little youngsters, without any clew to their paternity, following their mothers' heels. They are poor, miserable, degraded creatures, just one degree above the dogs with which

PERUVIAN SOLDIER AND RABONA.

they sleep. Their powers of endurance are extraordinary. Often it is the case that they will march twenty or thirty miles over a dusty road, carrying a child on their back, without water or food. When the latter is scarce they eat leaves of the coca-tree, which when mixed with lime are said to be very palatable and nourishing. Each woman carries a little bag of lime round her neck, into which she dips her fingers and draws out a few grains of powder to leaven a lump of leaves she is constantly chewing. The poor children have the hardest time, for they are always without rest or shelter, and often without food. But it is the experience they are born into, and they know nothing of a better life. The officers told me that the children often die on the march, when their mothers strip the clothes from them, and throw the bodies into the sand or woods, without even a burial or a tear, glad to be relieved of an encumbrance by death.

With the battalion which boarded our steamer at Payta were two women and thirty children. They were quartered upon the hurricane-deck, without any shelter but the starlit tropic sky, and were packed in, men and women together, like steers in a cattle-car. Water and food were furnished them, the latter consisting only of frijoles and tortillas. Instead of complaining of their beds upon the surface of the shelterless deck, the soldiers told me that it was the most comfortable place they had found for months, and would be glad to stay there always; but the passengers and officers of the ship would have objected, as the stench that came from them was something horrible, resembling that which is usually noticed in a crowded emigrant-car.

One night, on the unsheltered deck of the vessel, without surgical assistance or even the knowledge of the officers or crew, a child was born. The mother wrapped it in an old blanket and laid it down upon the boards. Thirty-six hours afterwards she, with the rest of the party, climbed down th ship's side on a ladder, got into a launch in which there was scarcely standing-room, and was towed to shore, where a long and tiresome march into the mountains was to be begun the same night. On her arms was the baby, and on her back was a bag which looked as if it weighed fifty or sixty pounds. She was a mere girl, perhaps sixteen or seventeen years of age, and they said it was her first baby, of which she, like all young mothers, was uncommonly proud. This appeared to be a commonplace occurrence, for it was scarcely noticed by the other women or men of the crowd, and when I asked an officer which of his company was the father of the child, he replied, "*Dios sabe*" (God knows). He said there had been four similar accouchements in his company within six months, and that he thought the mothers and babies were all doing well.

"Will the child live?" I asked the surgeon.

"Live? yes; you couldn't drown it."

The custom of having rabonas with the army grew out of the habit the Indians had of taking their wives to war, and the marital ties became slackened by common consent. The Government not only licenses but encourages the practice, as it makes the men more contented, and, as a sanitary measure, the surgeons say, is beneficial. The ratio of disease is very small in the armies where the rabonas are allowed, as compared with that in others, and any experienced surgeon can see why this is so.

All the private soldiers in South America, at least upon the west coast, are Indians or negroes, and all the officers white. A white man, a Spaniard, whatever be his station in life, cannot be forced or persuaded to carry a musket. During the defence of Lima against the army of Chili, however, lawyers, merchants, clerks, and everybody, regardless of caste or condition, served in the ranks as they did during our war, but without uniform. They would fight in defence of their homes, but were too proud to wear the uniform of a common soldier. Hence the rank and file is composed chiefly of Indians, or *cholos*, a term which is used to designate the mixed race descended from the ancient and aboriginal Inca and his conqueror the Spaniard. There are very few full-blooded Indians in the country, for during the three hundred and fifty years of Spanish supremacy the original inhabitants were almost entirely exterminated. There are a good many negroes and Chinamen in Peru who are mixed with the natives indiscriminately, and they all go to compose the cholos.

There are military schools for the education of officers, and the line and staff of the armies are made up of the sons of the aristocracy, as in Germany and England. They wear a very gaudy uniform, and always appear in it, whether on duty or not. Officers are never seen in anything but full military dress, with plenty of gold lace and "flubdubs."

The soldiers are all "volunteers." Conscription is forbidden by the constitution of most of the republics, and a "volunteer" is an Indian who is captured on the highway, or in a saloon, or at his home, and locked up until there are enough to send to headquarters, where he is taken before a recruiting-officer, and made to sign a statement setting forth that he "volunteered" to serve his country as long as his services are needed. Then his hands are tied behind him, and he is lashed to a dozen or more other "volunteers," who are driven down to the garrison, where uniforms are put on them, muskets furnished, and they are turned over to a drill-sergeant, who puts them through the simple tactics until they know how to carry a gun and fire it. I saw a drove of about one hundred and fifty of these "volunteers" come into Lima one day, tied up like chickens or turkeys in bunches of ten each, with an escort of twenty men, who had probably gone through the same process of "volunteering" a year or so before, and rather enjoyed the remonstrances of the conscripts. Behind the column came seventy-five or so women, weeping and chattering, and some of them had children tugging at their hands and skirts. The women could stay with their husbands if they liked, and become rabonas, and probably most of them did. With such material composing its army did Peru attempt to defend its coast and cities, with their enormous wealth, against assault by Chili.

LOOKING SEAWARD.

The soldiers of Chili are of an entirely different sort. They are naturally belligerent, and in the late war with Peru were promised free license to plunder. The soldiers of Peru were peaceable, quiet, inoffensive cholos, a silent, suffering race of people who had served under a system of peonage all their lives, had no idea what they were fighting for, and made as weak a defence as possible. Whenever they met the Chillanos in battle they always fled, even when they outnumbered the enemy; for the Chillano, reckless, daring, and combative, never remained in line of battle, but always fought with a charge and a whoop, carrying everything before him, taking no prisoners, but cutting the throat of every man he could reach.

The battle of Arica is a good example of all the engagements of the war between Chili and Peru. South of that town, which lies upon the Pacific coast, rises a great hill or promontory twelve hundred feet, and almost perpendicular, out of the sea, and then slopes off at a steep grade to the plain behind it. Upon the peak of this precipice the Peruvians placed a heavy battery for the protection of the city, manned by about twelve hundred soldiers. The Chillano men-of-war came in one day and engaged this fort in an artillery duel at long range which lasted until nightfall. During the darkness about two thousand soldiers were landed above the town; they flanked it, and creeping carefully to the foot of the hill, lay until daylight, when they dashed up the slope with a fearful charge. The cannon were all turned seaward, and were useless; the men were surprised in their sleep, and the demoralization among the Peruvians was so great that scarcely a shot was fired. Being shut off from escape, they jumped over the precipices into the sea, preferring drowning to having their throats cut with the knives of the Chillanos, who always carry them for that purpose. This was known, and always will be known, as the Arica massacre, for nearly three-fourths of the Peruvians were slaughtered.

The island of San Lorenzo, which was once the seat of a powerful fortress, protects the harbor of Callao, the second port on the Pacific coast of South America in population and commercial importance. It is the headquarters of the steamship lines and of the great mercantile houses, and the population is about one-half of foreign birth. One can hear all the languages of the earth spoken at Callao, and when we

A BOATMAN ON THE COAST.

arrived upon the dock there was a group to illustrate the cosmopolitan character of the citizens. A Chinaman, an Arab, a negro, and a Frenchman were sitting upon a box, while around them were clustered Spaniards, Englishmen, Irishmen, Germans, and Italians. The city is irregular and shabby-looking, but has been a place of great wealth. Millions after millions of dollars' worth of silver have been shipped from here by the Spaniards—silver stolen from the temples of the Incas, or dug from the mines which they operated before the Spaniards came. It was here that the old buccaneers used to rendezvous and waylay the galleons on their way to Spain. Of recent years the importance of Callao has very much decreased. A constant succession of wars and revolutions in Peru has destroyed its commerce; and although there is usually a great deal of shipping in the harbor, the present amount of trade is below that of the past. There are two lines of railroad to Lima, the capital of the republic, which lies six miles up in the foot-hills of the Andes.

LIMA.

THE CAPITAL OF PERU.

ALTHOUGH the glory of Lima has long since faded, it is easy to see how grand and beautiful the place was in the days of its ancient prosperity, when it was called "The City of the Kings." Few places possess such historical or romantic interest as this old vice-regal, bigoted, corrupt, licentious capital of Peru, the second city founded by the Spaniards in South America, and the seat of Spanish power for more than three centuries. Pizarro selected the location, and founded the city on the 6th of January, 1535, that being the anniversary of the manifestation of the Saviour to the wise men, the Magi. The pious old cutthroat called it "The City of the Kings"—*Ciudad de los Reyes*. The Emperor gave the infant capital a coat of arms of his own design, being three golden crowns upon an azure field, with a star above them. But the name Lima, which was an Inca term to denote the presence of an oracle near where the city stood, was at once applied to the place by the natives, and being so much easier to pronounce, soon forced itself into common usage in spite of Pizarro and the King, and is now alone recognized.

The population of Lima is about one hundred and twenty-five thousand. It has been much larger, for during the last twelve years war and decay have been the rule, and peace and growth the exception. Before that time there had been quite a "boom," owing to the energy of Henry Meiggs, the California fugitive, and to the introduction of railroads; but the devastation of foreign invaders and the havoc of domestic revolutionists have made Lima only a pitiful shadow of its former greatness.

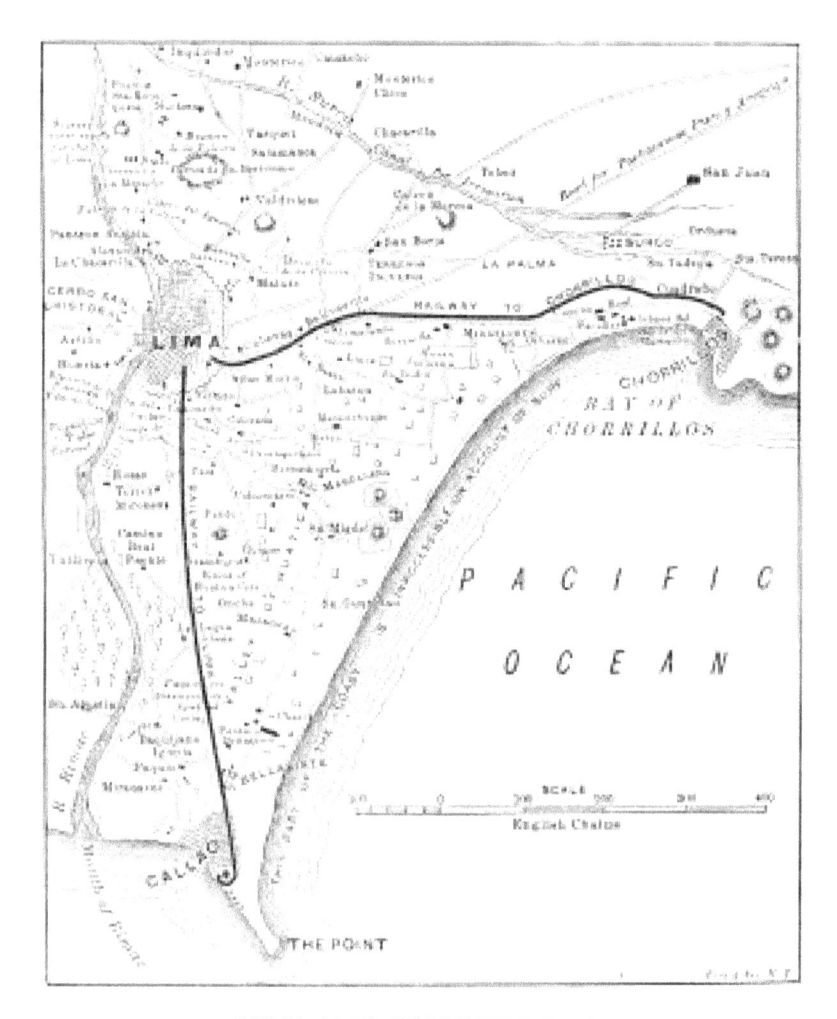

LIMA AND ITS ENVIRONS.

The churches and convents and monasteries of Lima are the finest and most expensive in America, while the architecture of private structures surpasses that of any other Spanish-American city except Santiago. The old palace of Pizarro, which was erected by him when the city was founded, and in which he was assassinated, is still used for the offices of the Government; while the Senate occupies the council-chamber of the old Inquisition building, which is famous for its ceiling of carved work, and infamous for the cruel and bloody work that has been done within its walls. This ceiling was imported from Spain in the year 1560, and was carved by the monks of the mother-country as a gift to the Inquisition council of the new. Here sat the most extensive and important dependency of the Church of Rome, extending its jurisdiction over the whole of the New World, roasting heretics upon live coals or stretching them upon the rack, long after the Inquisition in Europe had ceased to exist. The torture-room, which adjoined the council-chamber, is now a retiring-room for the Senate, while the dark pockets in the walls, in which heretics were sealed up until they were smothered, are used as closets and wardrobes.

The Chamber of Deputies occupies the ancient home of the College of St. Marcas, the oldest institution of learning in America, founded by the Society of Jesus in 1551, sixty-nine years before the Pilgrims landed at Plymouth.

The San Franciscan convent and church are two of the most extensive structures in the whole of America, and cost as much as the Capitol at Washington, if not more. The whole interior is covered with the most beautiful tiles, which have stood the test of three centuries, and still surpass the best that modern genius can produce. These tiles are celebrated all over Europe, not only for the enormous quantity of them—for they cover many acres of surface—but for the beauty of their design and perfect finish. In this convent is shown the bed on which St. Francis died, the sack-cloth robe that he wore, his sandals, his rosary, and the coffin in which his body was taken to Rome. The monk who acted as our cicerone insisted that the founder of his order died in the room in which these relics were, and pointed out the exact spot where he breathed his last; but a brief cross-examination brought him up to an explanation that he meant that this room was modelled upon the one in which St. Francis died.

Lima did produce a saint, however—Santa Rosa, a woman who was famous for her wealth, her beauty, her self-abnegation, and her devotion to the Church, and was canonized by Pope Clement X. in 1671. Her remains lie in the Church of Santo Domingo, and an extensive convent has been erected in her honor. She was the only American ever canonized, and the fact that a Peruvian received this exclusive honor has made her not only the patron saint, but one of the great figures in the history of the Catholic Church on this continent. The anniversary of her birth is always celebrated throughout South America, and the third centennial, which occurred in April, 1886, was the occasion of one of the grandest demonstrations ever seen on the coast of the South Pacific.

A PERUVIAN INTERIOR.

Six months before, the most reverend archbishop at Lima, the dean of the Catholic hierarchy in Spanish America, issued an eloquent pastoral, calling upon his flock to unite with him in honoring the memory of Santa Rosa, the only American saint and the patroness of two continents. The invitation was generously responded to. The Government immediately made as liberal an appropriation of money as was possible in the depleted condition of the treasury; private citizens and corporations contributed to the funds, and a commission of distinguished persons was appointed to form a programme of the festivities. A cordial invitation was sent by the archbishop to the principal religious dignitaries in South and Central America and Mexico to visit Lima on this memorable occasion, and to accept the national hospitality.

On the 20th the ceremonies were commenced. The body of Santa Rosa was taken from its resting-place in the Church of Santo Domingo, and borne in solemn procession to the church erected in her honor. The day was declared a holiday. From every housetop flags and streamers were floating; the different legations and consulates hoisted their national emblems; flowers were strewn in the streets through which the cortege was to pass; and from the windows and balconies hung superb drapery of silk and velvet. The remains of the saint, deposited in a beautifully ornamented urn, were carried on the shoulders of the Dominican monks, and the mayor and municipality of the city, with the few remaining survivors of the War of Independence, acted as the guard of honor. The municipal and private schools of both sexes followed, the little girls charmingly dressed in white and blue, the favorite colors of Santa Rosa, and with garlands of roses in their hands. Along the route the different fire brigades had erected artistic arches from their ladders and apparatus, and as the procession passed, white doves were loosened from their fastenings, and flew gracefully amid the banners and canopies overhanging the streets. In some of the streets traversed carpets were laid down and covered with roses. Arriving at the Church of Santa Rosa of the Fathers, the precious urn was deposited on the altar, surrounded by a dazzling blaze of light, and was watched over during the night by a special guard of honor.

The next day the same ceremony was repeated, the object being to carry the remains of the saint to those places with which her life was most intimately associated. Thus the Convent of Santa Catalina, the Church of Santa Rosa of the Mine—establishments founded by the intercession of the Rose of Peru—were visited, and the final ceremonies were performed at the cathedral. The interior of the cathedral, larger than the cathedral in New York, was handsomely decorated with hangings of scarlet velvet bound with gold; the superb altar, with its pillars cased in silver, covered with lights and flowers; and the venerable archbishop, with his numerous retinue of monsignori, canons, and friars, officiated at the solemn high-mass, with the votive offering especially permitted by the Holy Father, in reply to a request from the Lima ecclesiastics.

The square without was filled by troops from the citadel of Santa Catalina, national salutes were fired, and all Lima in gala dress was in the streets. The Ministers of State, the Justices of the Supreme and Superior courts, and all of the principal authorities, joined in the procession, which, after the conclusion of the ceremony at the cathedral, proceeded to Santo Domingo to deposit the remains underneath the grand altar, where for nearly three centuries they have rested.

Santa Rosa was born at Lima in the year 1586. She was of humble parents, her father being a matchlock man in the escort of the viceroy, and her mother a woman of the lower class. She was christened under the name of Isabel, but while yet an infant the beautiful color appearing on her cheeks caused her to be called Rosa. From her earliest years she manifested a deep religious spirit, and although poor in the world's goods, her extraordinary charity and self-sacrifice for the poor and sick brought her into the notice of the people. Refusing all the inducements and invitations to enter upon a monastic life, she steadily dedicated her efforts towards doing good. Many miraculous cures are attributed to her. She died in 1617. Shortly after her death the authorities of Lima petitioned the archbishop that the necessary investigation be initiated to establish her sanctity, and when the proofs were obtained they were laid before Pope Urban VIII. at Rome, who in 1625 sent a commission to Lima to conclude the investigation. After due consideration of the facts presented to the Holy College at Rome, Pope Clement IX., in 1668, ordered the canonization of Rosa under the title of St. Rosa of Lima.

In Lima, for a population of about one hundred and twenty thousand, there are one hundred and twenty-six Catholic churches and twelve monasteries and convents; and the same religious privileges extend all over Peru. There are two Protestant churches in the republic. One of them is in Lima, and is usually without a pastor, being of the Church of England school, and supported by the English-speaking residents; the other is at Callao, and an active young Protestant, Rev. Mr. Thompson, formerly of Philadelphia, is its pastor. The church is unsectarian, and is largely sustained by the Pacific Steam Navigation Company, a British corporation which has a monopoly of commerce on the west coast, and keeps its headquarters at Callao. No attempt at Protestant missionary work has ever been made in Peru, although Mr. Thompson says the field is very inviting. His time is spent mostly among the sailors who haunt Callao by the hundreds, and in looking after the English-speaking congregation under his charge. There is no Sunday in Peru. The shops are open on that day as usual, and in the afternoon bull-fights, cock-fights, and similar entertainments are always held. The women invariably go to mass in the morning, and represent the entire family, as very few men are ever seen in the churches. Under President Prado, from 1869 to 1876, the Catholic Church was subjected to the same sort of treatment it has received in the other republics, but his successors were more hospitable towards the priests, and the Church is regaining much of its ancient influence. Some of the confiscated monasteries have been restored, and a bishop presides over the lower branch of the national legislature, having been elected by a popular vote in one of the interior cities. He is a jolly-looking old padre, rosy and rotund, and has not the appearance of suffering much mortification of the flesh.

The bones of Pizarro, the Indian butcher, lie in the crypt of the grand cathedral which he built in 1540, and which is still the most imposing ecclesiastical edifice in all America. It is said to have cost nine million dollars; and that amount may have been spent upon it, but the money came from the old Inca temples, which were robbed of their gold and silver ornaments and stripped of their carved timbers by the Spaniards. The latter never produced anything in Peru by their own efforts. They simply expended their plunder for the benefit of themselves and the Church. Of the ninety millions of dollars in silver and gold which Pizarro is said to have realized from his evangelical work among the Indians, the King of Spain got one-fifth and the Church even a larger share, so that it could afford to build cathedrals and convents as fine as those of Europe, and endow them with fabulous wealth.

Prescott says that from a single Inca temple Pizarro took 24,800 pounds of gold and 82,000 pounds of silver. One of his lieutenants asked for the nails which supported the ornaments in this temple, and got 22,000 ounces of silver. It was this money that erected the magnificent churches which Lima has to-day, and which made the capital of the New World the most luxurious and profligate known to history.

Later, the marvellous products of the mines of Potosi and Cerro de Pasco added to the fabulous wealth of Peru. In 1661 La Palata, the viceroy, rode from the palace to the cathedral on a horse every hair of whose mane and tail was strung with pearls, whose hoofs were shod with shoes of solid gold, and whose path was paved with ingots of solid silver. It was during this time that the galleons from the East, "from far Cathay," laden with gems and silks and spices, went to Callao to exchange them for the products of Potosi and Pasco; while, out of sight, on the verge of the horizon, Sir Francis Drake and the bold John Hawkins and other buccaneers lay-to in their swift-sailing cruisers to snatch the

GRAND PLAZA, LIMA.

treasure-ships as they came around the island of San Lorenzo, and carry home the booty to lay it at the feet of Elizabeth, the virgin queen of England.

But all this grandeur is gone, and the last traces of it are now to be found in the pawn-shops of Lima, which are full of rare old silver, paintings, china, and lace. The people are so poor that they are compelled to sell their jewels to get bread and meat. The stagnation of business has deprived them of their ordinary incomes from real estate, and the war has taken off the laborers, so that the sugar haciendas and the mills are idle. I met people whose incomes were formerly hundreds of thousands of dollars, from rentals and interest on investments, who are now compelled to patronize the pawn-shops, because their tenants cannot pay rent and their investments no longer produce a profit. The paper-money of the country is as valueless as the Confederate bills were during our civil war. One issue, the Incas, is entirely worthless. The Government tried to enforce its circulation by locking up men who refused to accept it as legal tender; but the merchants marked up the prices of their goods, and charged two thousand dollars a yard for calico, when the Treasury surrendered, and issued another loan which is almost as bad as the first. You give a twenty-dollar bill to your bootblack and two hundred and fifty dollars an hour for a hack. It costs about six hundred dollars a day for board at the hotel, and fifty dollars for a bunch of cigarettes.

House-owners who have leased their property for a term of years without specifying in what sort of money the rent shall be paid are compelled to accept this worthless paper at par. I met a lady whose income from rents ten years ago was more than a thousand dollars a week in gold, but now it is only the same amount in paper—scarcely enough to pay the servants—and she is selling her bric-à-brac to live. The haciendas and farms are no longer tilled, because for several years past all the laborers have been pressed into the army; and the sugar plantations are useless, for the machinery by which they were operated was destroyed by the Chilians during the recent war.

A PERUVIAN CHAMBER.

The devastation which the Chilian army created was almost equal to that caused by Pizarro when he invaded the homes of the peaceful Incas. The lines of march of the Chilians are shown by the complete destruction of everything they could break down or burn. Whole cities, villages, farms, factories, were swept away by a malicious desire to do as much injury as possible, regardless of the rights of non-combatants, and in violation of all the laws of civilized war. The beautiful winter resorts of Peru, Milleflores (its Newport) and Chorillos (its Long Branch), the residence-places of the wealthy people and the haunts of those who sought rest—where there were palaces as beautiful as those of Paris, and parks like the legendary gardens of Babylon—were entirely destroyed, not by accident, but by dynamite and other explosives. Exquisite marble statues now lie in fragments upon the ground, artistic fountains were shattered, trees were girdled, irrigating ditches destroyed, and every possible vandalism was committed, not only on the property of Peruvians, but upon that of foreigners, whose claims for damages will amount to more than Chili can ever pay.

The magnificent trees in the parks, along the boulevards, and even in the botanical garden, were cut down for fuel by the soldiers of Chili; the entire museum of Peruvian curiosities, one of the largest and finest in the world, was packed up and shipped to Santiago; the books in the National Library were thrown into sacks and sent after the museum, and historical paintings were cut from their frames as private plunder. The greatest painting of Peru—Marini's "Burial of Atahualpa, the last of the Incas"—was stolen from the wall where it hung, but the protests of the diplomatic corps induced the Chilians to return it. The churches and private houses were stripped in a similar manner, and what could not be stolen was burned. Nothing was sacred in the eyes of these modern vandals, whose purpose was to deprive the Peruvians of everything they prized.

The evidence of a refined taste in art and music is everywhere apparent in Peru. There is scarcely a home without a piano, and the city of Lima once rivalled Madrid in its treasures of art. There remain but two notable statues—that of Columbus, in marble, representing him in the act of handing a crucifix to an Indian girl; and that of Bolivar the Liberator, upon a rearing horse, in bronze (like the statue of Jackson in Washington), which stands in front of the old Inquisition building, on the spot where heretics were burned two hundred years ago. The famous arch over the old bridge, which was erected in 1610, has been destroyed, and many other artistic ornaments of the city which have been written of again and again are gone.

INTERIOR OF A LIMA DWELLING.

The President occupies the former residence of Henry Meiggs, the Californian, who did so much for Peru. It is a magnificent structure, erected and furnished when money had no value to the owner; but, like everything else in Lima, it is only a relic of its original beauty, and as a measure of economy a corner of the lower floor is rented for a grocery.

Those who have travelled everywhere say that the women of Lima are the most beautiful in the world. There is something about the climate of the country, where rain never falls,

A PERUVIAN PALACE.

and where decay is almost unknown, that gives them a brilliancy of complexion that women of other lands do not possess. Perhaps their national costume does much to heighten their beauty, for any woman not positively ugly would look well in the embroidered manta that the ladies of Lima always wear. This manta is a shawl of black China crape, and the amount of silk embroidery upon it indicates the wealth of the wearer. Some of them are extremely beautiful and cost as much as five hundred dollars; but ordinary mantas, such as the majority wear, can be bought for fifteen or twenty dollars in Peruvian money, which is worth twenty-five per cent. less than American gold. A very common article of dyed cotton is imported from England at a cost of three or four dollars, for the use of the negro and Indian women. The manta is worn by every woman, regardless of her rank or wealth, whenever she appears on the street; but in their homes, at the opera, and when they go out to afternoon receptions or evening balls, the ladies adopt the Parisian styles, and dress with a great deal of taste.

A PERUVIAN BELLE.

The manta is square in shape and about two yards in size. It is folded so as to be triangular, and the centre of the fold is placed upon the forehead, where there is usually a bit of lace that hangs down to the eyes. One end of the manta falls down the front of the dress as far as the knee, while the other is thrown around the shoulders and fastened at the breast with an ornamental pin. Thus, usually only the face is shown; and when a maiden or a matron wishes to disguise herself, she draws the shawl up so as to cover her mouth and nose, and permit only her great black, roguish eyes to be seen. And such eyes! Always large, age never seems to dim them, and no degree of self-discipline can rob them of or subdue their coquettish appearance. The poet who wrote

"Of that dark queen
For whose mere smile a world was bartered,"

described a Lima lady. The manta is usually drawn so closely about the figure as to show its outlines with the most conspicuous distinctness, and the young women of Lima are as famous for their beauty of form as for their beauty of face.

WATCHING THE PROCESSION.

They are always slender, generally short of stature, and as graceful as sylphs; but they lose their beauty of figure with maternity, and one seldom finds a married woman more than thirty or thirty-five years of age, if she is the mother of children, who retains the statuesque grace of maidenhood. They ripen early, reach their prime at sixteen or seventeen, and generally marry at that age. At twenty-five they are fat, but they never lose the radiance of their eyes or their complexion. Their stoutness comes from the lack of exercise and the excessive use of sweetmeats, for they spend their lives in rocking-chairs, munching *dulces*, as they call confectionery.

There is a romantic story about the manta which explains the reason that it is always black. The Peruvian women never wear colors in the street, and this custom is observed by the aristocracy as well as by the peasantry; nor do they ever wear bonnets except at an opera, and there very seldom. The same is true of the women of Ecuador and Chili, although in the city of Valparaiso, which is the most modern in its customs and in the style of living of any place on the west coast, the use of the manta is gradually dying out, and it is worn only at church. No woman with a bonnet on will be admitted to any Catholic church on the west coast. Sometimes strangers wear them in, but the sextons and ushers invariably ask that they be removed. Mrs. Admiral Dahlgren, of Washington, in her book called "South Sea Sketches," relates that she was ordered out of a church because she was wearing a bonnet, and misunderstanding what was said to her, took no notice of the command until quite a commotion was raised, when some lady explained its cause. A bonnet is called a *gorra* in Spanish, and Mrs. Dahlgren was very much amused at its similarity to the familiar Irish ejaculation.

It is said that the custom of wearing the manta originated among the Incas, but that they wore colors until the assassination of Atahualpa, their king, by the Spaniards under Pizarro. Then every woman in the great empire, which stretched from the Isthmus of Panama to the Strait of Magellan, abandoned colors and put on a black manta, and it has since been worn as perpetual mourning for "the last of the Incas." There is probably some truth in this story, for in the graves of the Incas that have been destroyed by scientific resurrectionists, have been found female mummies with mantas of brilliant colors wrapped around them, and fastened

THE DAUGHTER OF THE INCAS.

with pins very much like those worn at the present day. It is also true that the natives, the peons of Peru and Ecuador, the descendants of the Incas, never wear anything except black, and still celebrate with impressive and appropriate ceremonies the anniversary of the day on which Atahualpa was strangled. In Chili the custom has died out, for the Inca empire was never able to sustain itself there against the savage Araucanian tribes of Indians who inhabited the southern range of the Andes.

The Inca women in Peru and Ecuador are not at all pretty. They are dwarfish in stature, broad across the shoulders, and resemble in feature the squaws of the North American tribes, except that they have the almond-shaped eyes of the Mongolians; and it is probably true, as urged by the antiquarians, that the Incas were of the same origin as the Chinese, for their customs, their adeptness at all sorts of ingenious work, and their manner of living bear a striking resemblance to those of the interior provinces of the Chinese empire. The Incas have had their blood diluted by intermarriage with the lower grades of the Spanish race, and it is very difficult to find pure natives now. The people of the mixed race are called cholos.

It is the transplanted Spanish rose, the pure Castilian type, that blooms with the greatest beauty in the gardens of Peru. The climate has refined it, and has clarified the dark olive tint that is found in Castile. The greatest beauties in Lima are the descendants of the oldest families—those of the longest residence in the country—and their loveliness appears not only to have been transmitted from generation to generation, but to have been enhanced thereby. This is true not alone of the aristocrats, for some of the loveliest girls belong to the humbler families, and are found in the tenement-houses, clothed in the shabbiest garments, which serve only to heighten their loveliness, and to make them fair prey for the wolves that prowl around in Lima as they do everywhere else. The fate of these girls, if described, would make a chapter more horrible to contemplate than the disclosures recently made in London. Their beauty is a fatal gift, and their poverty and ignorance make them an easy prey to the tempter. Seldom are they allowed to remain at home after the age of fourteen or fifteen, when they become the mistresses of the haughty dons. But the social laws of Spanish America are so liberal that these women are treated much better than in lands of higher civilization, for it is not only expected that every

RUINS OF THE WAR.

man who can support a mistress will do so, but his reputation will suffer among his fellows if he does not.

Just now the country is prostrated, the effect of a long series of wars during which it was robbed of everything that the army of Chili could carry away; so that there is very little gayety and not much display of dress. But the people retain the relics of their former prosperity, and the ladies of the present generation have inherited the treasures their mothers bought and wore at the time when money was so plenty. Much of this finery—the jewels and laces—has gone to the pawnbrokers, and many of the most aristocratic families in the republic are now living upon its proceeds. The women are, like the French, very skilful in dress-making, and everything they wear is becoming. They imitate the Parisian styles with the greatest ingenuity, and have remarkable taste in making over old clothes.

The pawnshops are full of beautiful things. Here are toilet sets of solid silver, beautifully chased, including the meaner vessels of the bedroom, which betoken the luxury and extravagance of an age when the mines of the Andes were pouring out silver, and the guano-beds of the sea were being turned into gold. Similar reminiscences of ancient glory can be seen to-day in the toilets of the ladies, in the heirlooms which they wear on their wrists, on their breasts, and in their ears, as well as in the rich, old-fashioned fabrics which their grandmothers wore before them, made in the days when people did not intend things to wear out.

It is very difficult to secure admission to the aristocratic circles of Peru. They are as exclusive as any such circle in the world, and social laws are rigid. But an American who goes to Lima with good letters of introduction will be received with cordial hospitality, and be admitted to circles which the resident, however rich and respectable, can never enter. American naval officers are especially welcome, and the Peruvian belles are as strongly attracted by the glitter of brass buttons as are their sisters in the United States. Since the war there have been few public balls and few receptions, as the people are living from hand to mouth, with little hope to brighten the commercial horizon; but when you bring a letter to a Peruvian gentleman, his house and all his belongings "are at your disposition, señor," and he is offended unless you accept his hospitality, although you may be aware that he has to pawn some heirloom to pay for the dinner he gives you.

INTERIOR OF THE ORDINARY SORT OF HOUSE.

The ancient social restrictions which make it a breach of decorum for a gentleman to meet a lady alone until after marriage, still exist in Peru. If you call at the residence of Señor Bustamente you must ask for him, and if he is not at home you may leave your compliments for the ladies of the family, but under no circumstances ask to see them. If he is

A VERY COMMON SPECTACLE.

at home your welcome will be cordial, and you will be asked to a seat upon the sofa, which is always reserved for guests, and is the place of honor. You will be entertained by him until the ladies appear one by one, for they always stop to dress. No Spanish-American lady is ever ready to receive a caller. The lady of the house and her daughters will chat with you about the opera and the bull-fight and the latest scandal, and will perform brilliantly upon the piano, but beyond that her powers of entertainment do not go. If you can get Señorita Dolores over in the corner—and she will be delighted with a *tête-à-tête*—you will find that she knows nothing whatever about the world beyond her own limited circle of acquaintance. She has not the vaguest idea of the United States, and does not know whether Paris is in America, or New York in England. She will look at you with her great eyes with the most childish innocence, and ask if the bullfights in New York are as exciting as those of Lima, and if there is as agile a picador in the States as Señor Rubio. When you tell her that bull-fighting is not recognized as a legitimate amusement in New York, she will exclaim "Santa Maria!" and ask what entertainment you have when the opera-house is closed. Then, when you say that eight or ten theatres are always open, she will cry out to papa across the room to take her to New York by the next steamer.

The señorita got her education at a convent, has learned to embroider, to play the piano, to dance, and has committed to memory the lives of the saints; and there her accomplishments end. She is so beautiful that you are sorry you explored her mind; you feel guilty of having exposed her ignorance; you wish that you could simply sit and look at her, a picture of loveliness, forever; but when you ask her to dance, and she moves away with you in a waltz or mazourka, you discover that however empty her head may be, the education of her feet has not been neglected. No one who has ever waltzed with a Peruvian girl will wish for another partner. She is simply animated gracefulness, and her endurance is remarkable. She clings a little closer than our girls would consider consistent with propriety, and dances with an abandon that would call out a remonstrance from a watchful mamma in the States. She gives her whole mind and soul to it, regardless of consequences, and sighs when the music ceases, as if there were nothing more in life to enjoy.

A PERUVIAN MILK-PEDDLER.

The air and light of Lima are very favorable for photography, and the city has galleries as fine as any in New York. The reception-rooms, corridors, show-windows, and even the ceilings, are lined with portraits of belles of the town, which are on sale not only there but at the news-stands and printshops. In Havana and Venezuela, to have the photograph of a young lady is equivalent to the announcement of an engagement, but in Peru it signifies nothing. You can buy the portraits of your neighbors' daughters anywhere in town, and their popularity is estimated by the number sold. Lima girls, with their great black eyes and shapely figures, make fine subjects for a photographer, and strangers usually take home collections of the pictures of beauties. The photograph dealers have their portraits put up in covers ready for the market, like views of Niagara Falls or Coney Island.

Milk is peddled about Lima by women, who sit astride a horse or a mule, with a big can hanging on either side of the saddle. When they ride up to a door-way they give a peculiar shrill scream, which the servants within recognize.

Most of the embroidery and other similar work in Lima is done by the nuns, who are very expert at it. They make the finest sort of lace, embroider towels, napkins, handkerchiefs, and skirt-fronts for dresses on silk and velvet. At some of the shops you can buy dress patterns; that is, skirt-fronts, sleeves, collar, cuffs, belt, etc., embroidered in the finest possible style, and ready to make up. It is one of the ancient customs handed down from the days of the viceroys. The nuns make most of the confectionery sold in the city, moulding the unrefined sugar into artistic shapes, coloring it to imitate nature, and flavoring it to suit the palate.

The fashionable entertainment in Peru is bull-baiting. The bull is not killed, as in Spain and Mexico and other countries, and no horses are slaughtered in the ring. The animal is simply teased and tortured to make a Liman holiday. The young men of the city do the baiting, and it is regarded as a very high-toned sort of athletic sport, like polo at Newport. The young ladies take darts made of tin, decorate them with ribboned lace and rosettes, and give them to their lovers to stick into the hide of the bull. The great feat is to cast these darts so as to strike the bull in the fore-shoulder or in the face, and in order to do it he who throws them must stand before the animal's horns. Active young fellows perform very dexterously, but it takes nerve and agility, and at times fair señoritas have seen their lovers badly gored.

Another form of entertainment is what is called *Buena Noche*, or "Good Night." Then the band plays in the principal plaza, fireworks are exploded at the expense of the shopkeepers and saloon-men, whose profits are increased,

MINDLESS OF CARE.

hucksters surround the place with tables, selling cakes, candies, ice-cream, and peanuts, and all the populace come out to gossip and flirt. These festivals furnish about the only opportunity for Vilkins to get a word alone with his Dinah, for on a "Buena Noche" he can offer her his arm, and promenade up and down the plaza, murmuring soft nothings in her ear as long as she will hear them, or until the great bell of San Pedro strikes midnight, when there are a hustle and a bustle, and everybody goes home.

Some of the largest and finest stores in Lima are owned and managed by Chinese merchants, who have the monopoly of the trade in mantas and silk dress-goods. Italians usually keep the bodegas and eating-houses. There are half a dozen large American mercantile establishments, and the house of Grace Brothers, of which Mr. William R. Grace, ex-mayor of New York, is the head, practically monopolizes the foreign trade of Peru. Much of the business in the interior is done by itinerant peddlers, who carry their wares on their backs, and tramp over the whole continent from the Isthmus to Patagonia. There is also a class of itinerant doctors of Indian blood, called *collahuayas*, who travel on foot from Bogota, in Colombia, to Buenos Ayres, carrying the news from place to place, and practising a sort of voodoo system over the sick. They are well known throughout the country, and exercise a remarkable influence among the natives, who entertain them as guests of distinction wherever they go.

All the benevolent institutions of Lima are supported by a "Sociedad de Beneficencia," an organization of citizens who raise money by private subscriptions, and by bull-fights, cock-fights, and lotteries. The Penitentiary is a noble building, erected on the plan of the Philadelphia House of Correction, by a Philadelphia architect, the prisoners in which are engaged in making uniforms, shoes, and other equipments for the army. Capital punishment is abolished in Peru, but political offenders are tried by military courts, and shot when found guilty of conspiracy or treason. There are in the prison one hundred and thirty-five unhanged murderers serving out life sentences.

There are four daily newspapers in Lima, in which are published cablegrams from all parts of the world. They are edited with ability, but their writers indulge in the grandiose, florid style that sounds very funny to the plain-spoken American. One of the editors was sent to jail and fined five hundred dollars, besides having his paper suppressed, for making some reflections upon the acts of Congress; but as soon as he got out of prison he started another paper, and he is now blazing away in the most fearless manner, just as if the penitentiary were not half empty and the Government in need of convict labor. The papers make their appearance on the street about ten o'clock at night, and are cried by newsboys, who make as much racket as our own. In the morning carriers deliver copies to regular subscribers. Advertising patronage seems to be pretty good in Lima, for the newspapers have about two pages of display "ads." to every one of reading matter; but they do not get good rates, and times are so hard that the merchants give very little cash, but require the editors to "trade it out" in the country fashion. Advertising is always an index to commerce, and the condition of Peru is illustrated by the fact that almost every merchant in Lima is selling out at cost—*gran realization*, they call it. Credit is not given at the stores except to the Government, and that is compulsory. The foreign merchants will not sell to the authorities except for cash, and the native merchants do not want to, for only in one instance in a hundred are they ever paid.

All the houses in Lima are built on the earthquake plan—either of great thick walls of adobe, or mere shacks of bamboo reeds, lashed together by thongs of rawhide, and plastered within and without with thick layers of mud. This style of architecture will answer in a country where it never rains, and where cyclones never come, but if a good pour should fall in Lima, much of the town would be washed into the river Rimac and carried out to sea. There is never more than one entrance to a house, and that is protected first by a great iron grating, and then by solid doors. The windows are covered with bars. This was done as a precaution against bandits in early times, and against revolutionists in later days; and a very essential precaution it has been, for during the time of the viceroy bands of robbers came down from the mountains, and hordes of pirates from the sea. Through the single entrance passes every one who comes and goes—the butcher, the baker, the priest who comes to shrive the dying, and the young man to whom Mercedes is engaged.

The roofs of the dwellings are always perfectly flat, and among the common people are used as barn-yards and henneries. In many cases a cow spends all her days on the roof of her owner's residence, being taken up when a calf, and taken down at the end of life as fresh beef. In the mean time she is fed on alfalfa, and the slops from the kitchen. Chicken-coops are still more common on the roofs of dwellings, and in the thickly populated portions of the town your neighbors' cocks waken you at daylight with reminders of St. Peter.

Lima is a poor place to sell umbrellas, for along the coast from the northern boundary of Peru, far south-west to the end of the Chilian desert, rain never falls. There is a disagreeable, dismal, sticky, rheumatic dew, however, which is worse than a shower; for during the winter season, beginning in April and ending in October, it penetrates the thickest clothing, and gives one the sensation described by Mantilini as "demnition moist." The thermometer is pretty regular, however, and ranges from sixty to eighty degrees Fahrenheit during the year, January being the hottest month, and July the coolest. Pulmonary complaints are unknown, but fevers are very common, and the mortality among infants is pitiable. At Callao yellow-fever is usually endemic, and there are three or four deaths every week among the marine population, as the sanitary regulations are not well enforced, and the city is dirty.

The chamber occupied by the Peruvian House of Deputies is a long, narrow apartment in what was formerly the University of St. Mark, the oldest institution of learning in America, having been founded in 1551, and confiscated by the Government from the Church in 1869. The spectators sit in a very high, narrow gallery over the heads of the representatives, who are arranged in two rows of chairs, without desks, around the three walls of the chamber, the presiding officer and clerks having the fourth wall at their back. The centre of the room is occupied by a long table, at one end of which sits the presiding officer, who is a priest (with an appearance of having lived on the fat of the land), and at the other end a crucifix is placed, upon which the members of Congress are sworn to support the Constitution. When a formal speech is made, the orator stands upon a platform, with a desk or table before him, and a running debate is participated in by members from their chairs.

The Senate Chamber is in the old Inquisition building, just across the Plaza de Bolivar, in which one hundred heretics are said to have been burned to death, and thousands publicly scourged.

The people of Peru entertain the most cordial sentiments towards the United States, which is the more remarkable because of the feeling prevalent in all classes that the administration of President Garfield was the cause of many of the losses and much of the misery which they suffered during the war with Chili. They cannot be convinced that they were not trifled with and betrayed at the most critical period of their history, and that Mr. Blaine was not responsible. Without entering into the controversy as to whether Mr. Blaine authorized General Hurlbut to interfere, or whether General Hurlbut's action was voluntary, it is nevertheless true that the moment he stepped in Chili held back, and the moment he withdrew she renewed the devastation of her sister republic with a hundred-fold more energy than before. If our Government had taken the same stand in the war between Chili and Peru that she occupied regarding the troubles in the Central American States, thousands of lives, property worth millions of dollars, and the richest resources of Peru might have been saved. Mr. Blaine's original attitude was that the

VIEW OF CUZCO AND THE NEVADO ASUNGATA FROM THE BROW OF THE SACSAHUAMAN.

United States would not tolerate the dismemberment of Peru, and that was clearly and plainly announced, with a wholesome effect. All at once the protest was withdrawn, without warning, without any premonition, and then, with a knife at her throat and a revolver at her heart, Peru consented to surrender the coveted provinces.

General Hurlbut had been condemned for acting imprudently, for getting our Government into a scrape without excuse, for committing it to a policy that was not tenable; but no one can visit Peru and see the results of the war without respecting the memory of General Hurlbut. He acted from the noblest impulses, in behalf of humanity, in defence of civilization. Whether he tried to put a stop to the war with or without authority, he was justified in doing so—justified in trying to prevent the burning of defenceless cities, the murder of non-combatants, the robbery of homes, and the despoliation of everything that was sacred.

Peru was overcome, conquered, and resistless. Her army was destroyed, and her citizens, who had attempted to defend her capital with what weapons they could gather, were smitten down like grass before the scythe. There was scarcely a voice to be raised in defence of the women and children. Then the pillage commenced. Dynamite and petroleum were the weapons of Chili, and millions of dollars' worth of private property was swept away daily, until the Chilians got tired of murder, of rapine, of pillage and devastation. It was these which General Hurlbut tried to prevent, and had our Government supported him, or at least had not interfered, he would have been successful. As it is, the Chilians laugh and the Peruvians mutter curses, when "the foreign policy of the United States" is mentioned. It is said that Hurlbut exceeded his instructions, and much of the blame of failure was thrown upon him. He was a proud and sensitive man, and felt censure keenly. His disgrace, and the neglect of his Government to sustain him in the attitude he had taken, not only shortened but ended his life, and he died in Lima a broken-hearted man. But he has been canonized by the people of Peru as a political saint, and they worship his memory as they do that of Bolivar—the Washington of South America, the man who gave liberty to five republics. They regard Hurlbut as the noblest of all Americans. His portrait hangs in their parlors, and is still for sale at the photograph galleries and picture stores. His funeral was attended by the greatest demonstration Peru has ever witnessed, and the grateful people would erect a statue to him if they had money enough left to pay the expense.

When Chili conquered Peru, Admiral Lynch, the Irishman who commanded the Chilian army, set up General Iglesias as "provisional President until the pacification of the country." General Caceres, who commanded a division of *montañes*, or mountaineers, refused to surrender, and rejected the terms of peace dictated by Chili. He retired to the Andes, and carried on a guerilla warfare as long as the Chilian army was in Peru. When Lynch and his legions retired, Caceres turned his attention to the government with the alliterative title which the Chilians left in Lima, and for three years kept Iglesias busy defending the coast and the capital from his assaults. Business was almost entirely suspended; commerce was stagnant, because Peruvians were producing nothing, and had no money to pay for imported goods. The people lived on the pawn-shops, and the Government, deprived of its revenues, resorted to extreme conscription and confiscation measures. Caceres hovered around Lima for three years with his army of Indian guerillas, doing little fighting, but producing terror everywhere. Iglesias had no force to suppress his rival, and could only defend the capital and chief seaports against attack.

In the centre of Lima, as in all Spanish-American towns, is a plaza, or public square, with a fountain and statuary in the centre, and the palace, the cathedral, the archbishop's residence, the municipal offices, and other public institutions facing it on the four sides. Into this plaza, the very heart of the city, in August, 1885, the Government troops permitted Caceres and his mountaineers to come; but they had

BETWEEN BATTLES, BALLS.

sufficient notice of his approach to enable them to place sharp-shooters in the towers of the churches, cannon on the roof of the palace, and musketeers on the roofs of all the buildings around it. The buildings are two stories high, with the front walls reaching two or three feet above the roof, so that those who participated in this novel defence of the city had good breastworks to protect them. When Caceres came into the plaza he was met with volleys from all sides, and the pavements were strewn with the dead. He made a desperate struggle, but his Indians, few of whom had ever been in a city before, and none of whom had ever been under fire, scattered and were lost in the labyrinth of narrow streets, where they were pursued and killed by cavalrymen, who plunged out of the palace at full gallop when it was seen that the forces of Caceres were wavering. Of the three thousand men who came with the mountain general, two thousand lay dead or wounded upon the pavements of Lima before the battle was two hours old, and with the rest, who were called together by trumpeters, Caceres retired to Arequipa to prepare for another campaign.

On the last day of December, 1885, he repeated the attack with better success, and captured the city, ending a seven years' war in Peru. A provisional government was organized until April, when Caceres was elected constitutional President, and has since, in a thorough, wise, and patriotic way, been trying to restore a crushed and devastated nation.

General Andres Caceres, the successful leader, the chosen President of Peru for a term ending April, 1890, is a man about fifty years of age, a native of the ancient town of Ayacucho, and the son of a colonel of the army of Chili. His mother was a Peruvian, and his father spent the later years of his life in Peru. The mother had Indian blood in her veins, and from her Caceres has inherited much of the Indian disposition and character which have given him his popularity among the montañes who followed his standard in the struggle. At an early age Caceres entered the army, and having by his daring energy and military skill won the confidence and admiration of President Castilla, was sent to Europe to learn the art of war in the French and German military schools. Upon his return he was detailed for duty as an engineer, but when the war with Chili broke out he was made a general of division, and was perhaps the most successful officer in the Peruvian army.

Don Miguel Iglesias, the head of the government which Caceres tried so long to overthrow, is a descendant of one of the oldest and most aristocratic families of Peru, and before the war with Chili he occupied several posts of eminence and honor, having been Secretary of the Treasury, and afterwards Secretary of War. He is a *plantador*, or planter, and lives at the old town of Caxamarca, which the readers of Prescott's story of the Conquest will remember as the seat of Atahualpa. During the war with Chili General Iglesias also took a prominent part, but was not considered a successful military leader, having no taste or inclination in that direction. After the downfall of the Calderon government Iglesias was made provisional President, and continued to exercise power for four years, but lacked the energy and ability necessary to meet the crisis; and although the people generally regarded him as an honest and patriotic man, he lost their confidence, and the victory of Caceres was welcomed.

Another of the leading men of Peru is Don Nicolas Pierola, who has been a conspicuous figure in the political dramas and military tragedies that have been enacted during the last ten years, and will continue to be heard from in the future. He has had a most remarkable career, having been four times banished from the republic. Pierola is a son-in-law of the ill-starred Emperor Iturbide of Mexico, whose daughter he met while a student in Paris. His life has been a romantic one, and illustrates the ups and downs of South American politics. Pierola *père* was a famous scientist and *littérateur*, and was the intimate friend and co-worker of Humboldt, Sir Humphry Davy, Doctor Von Tschudi, the Austrian philosopher, and other men of that age. He was for a long time a professor of natural sciences at the University of Madrid, and returned to Peru, his native country, to pursue his inquiries into the traditions of the Incas, and to preside over the university at Arequipa, the second city in Peru. He had something to do with politics too, and was the Peruvian Minister of Finance for several years.

A WARRIOR AT REST.

Pierola the younger, who was educated in Europe, is one of the most accomplished and able men in South America. He commenced life as an editor, and in 1864 became the manager of *El Tiempo*, the organ of President Pezot, who was overthrown by a revolutionary army under General Prado. The latter banished the young and ardent editor until he was himself overthrown. Then Pierola returned to Peru, and became the Minister of Finance under President Balta, being the ruling spirit of the administration, and inaugurating the vast system of public improvements under Henry Meiggs. Prado again led a successful revolution, and in 1878 Pierola was banished for the second time. When the war with Chili broke out he returned to Peru, and tendered his allegiance and his sword to the man who had driven him into exile. His services were accepted, and he became the commander of a regiment, and afterwards a general of division.

In December, 1879, President Prado deserted his post and secretly fled from the country, leaving a proclamation on his desk which authorized the Vice-

President to exercise the duties of the office "until he had returned from the transaction of some very urgent and important business which demanded his presence abroad." The army of Chili had been successful in several battles, and was marching upon the capital. The army of Peru had been practically destroyed; its ports were blockaded, its treasury was empty, and the President, Prado, had fled from the results of his blundering imbecility. He has never returned, and is understood to be in Europe.

There was a mere gleam of hope left for Peru, and the people called on Pierola to become their leader. A junta or convention of leading men was quickly called, and the power of military and political chief, which is the polite way of describing a dictator, was conferred upon Pierola. He had no money, no ammunition, and only the frightened remnants of a demoralized army; but he made the best fight he could, and compelled the Chilian army to stop the carnival of devastation they had begun. When Peru was conquered the Chilian Government would not recognize Pierola as dictator, and in the absence of Prado, the constitutional President, set up a dummy administration of their own choice, with which terms of peace were made, forfeiting the strip of territory containing the deposits of guano and nitrate of soda. This was what

GATE-WAY TO THE ANDES.

Chili desired, and for this she made the war. Her Government knew that Pierola would never consent to sacrifice the richest portion of the republic, hence it refused to treat with him, and caused his banishment for the third time.

Pierola went to France again, and remained in exile until May, 1885, when he was sent for by the business men of Lima, who endeavored to secure a suspension of hostilities between Caceres and Iglesias, the leaders of the rival factions of Peru, and to place Pierola in power, in order to restore peace to the country and revive its paralyzed trade and industries. He returned reluctantly, and his friends arranged to have him proclaimed President, but the Iglesias Government hearing of the plot, banished him for a fourth time, shortly before Caceres captured the city. Pierola is now in France, but expects to return to Peru, and do his share towards restoring the country. This can be done only by the introduction of foreign capital and labor, as the landowners and merchants of Peru are bankrupt, and the native laboring element largely reduced by the casualties of almost thirteen years of constant warfare. A large amount of English and American capital is already going into the country, and will tempt labor to follow. The most important act of the Government has been to contract with Mr. Michael P. Grace, of New York, recently, for the completion of the famous Oroya railroad, and the development of the Cerro del Pasco mines.

A quarter of a century ago an unknown man, a fugitive from justice, arrived at the port of Callao, and appeared among the Spaniards, as Manco Capac, at once the Adam and the Christ of the Incas, appeared to the Indians two thousand years before. As the mysterious and deified Manco Capac taught the Indians a knowledge of the agricultural and mechanical arts, this unknown man taught their successors to build railroads, and stands to-day as the ideal of Yankee enterprise and engineering genius. He plunged the Government of Peru into a debt that will never be paid, but laid the foundations for a system of internal development that would bring the republic great wealth if peace could be only secured.

HENRY MEIGGS.

Everybody has heard of Henry Meiggs, the partner of Ralston, the California banker, who drowned himself in the Golden Gate, the friend of Flood, O'Brien, Mackey, Sharon, and one of the princes of the golden era of '49. Bret Harte has written of him, and Mark Twain has used him as a text. He committed forgeries in San Francisco years ago, and when his crime was discovered he took a boat and rowed out into the bay; but instead of jumping overboard, as Ralston did twenty years afterwards, he climbed upon the deck of a schooner, purchased her, and sailed away from the scene of his remarkable career. He went to Peru, bringing much of his wealth and all of his irresistible energy with him. These he applied to the difficulties that had staggered that country, and overcame them. He sent back money to California to reimburse with good interest those who lost by his forgeries, but remained away till he died, one of the richest, most influential, and famous men on the coast. From Ecuador to Patagonia, through Peru, Bolivia, and Chili, Meiggs's enterprises extended, and the result is a series of railroads at right angles with the coast, connecting the interior of the country with the seaports, and giving the estates, and the mines in the mountains, the sugar haciendas, and the nitrate beds, easy outlets to the ocean. Nearly every port on the west coast has its little railroad, from twenty to two hundred and fifty miles in length, some of them reaching into the very heart of the Andes, the arteries of the continent's commerce, and intended to make profitable possessions which would otherwise have no worth.

The Oroya road, which Meiggs left incomplete, has been counted as the eighth wonder of the world, for there is nothing in the Rocky Mountains or the Alps which compares with it as an example of engineering science, or presents more sublime scenery. But neither scenic grandeur nor engineering genius can alone make a railroad pay, particularly if it goes nowhere. In this instance the money gave out, and Meiggs died when the road was only partially completed, there remaining fifty miles between the present terminus (Chicla) and the point which was aimed at—the mines of Cerro del Pasco, one of the richest and most extensive silver deposits in the world. Most of the grading and tunnelling between Chicla and the mines has been completed, and it only remains to lay the ties and rails and put in the bridges to send a locomotive over the Andes into the great valley which stretches north and south between the two Cordilleras. This Mr. Grace has agreed to do. The completion of the line to the mining regions will cost ten million dollars, but that portion already constructed and in operation, with all its rolling stock, station-houses, and equipments of every sort, he gets for practically nothing, as under the conditions of a ninety-nine years' lease he has the use of the railroad and all that belongs with

THE HEART OF THE ANDES.

it free for the first seven years, and pays but twenty-five thousand dollars per year rental for the property during the remainder of the term. In other words, Mr. Grace gets a property which cost twenty-seven million six hundred thousand dollars, eighty-six miles of railroad already equipped and in operation, fifty miles of the most expensive tunnelling and grading in the world for nothing, provided he will complete the line. And more than this, he gets the Cerro del Pasco silver mines, which were worked for centuries by the Jesuits, and have yielded hundreds of millions of dollars even under the primitive system of working which was applied to them by the monks and the native Indians. They were discovered by a native, who while watching sheep on the hills was overtaken by night. He piled together a few stones, under the lee of which he built a fire. In the morning he noticed that the heat had split some of the stones, and he was attracted by something shining from what had been the interior of one of them. He picked up the stone, and took it home to show to his friends. The bright substance was found to be silver, and the great mines of the Cerro del Pasco were discovered.

From 1630 to 1824 the mines of the Cerro del Pasco are said to have produced nearly twenty-seven thousand two hundred tons of pure silver. The ore is not in fissure veins, but in an enormous mass, similar to the carbonates of Leadville, and yields from forty to one hundred dollars per ton. It is worked at a cost of three dollars per ton. Even the tailings, which the priests and Indians have left during the two and a half centuries they have been digging away in their rude manner, can be shipped to New York at a profit, and they amount to millions of tons, with silver enough in them, it is estimated, to pay the cost of constructing the road, and to afford it a business that will pay the expense of operating.

AN INCA REMINISCENCE.

About ten per cent. of the Cerro del Pasco district is now occupied by native miners, who are pegging along in the old-fashioned way, losing more silver than they gain in their operations, and securing about one-quarter of the profit they could obtain by the use of improved machinery. Their mines are constantly flooded with water, and have to be abandoned for the greater part of the year. There are also a number of old mines, which were worked first by the Jesuits and then by the Government, but which have been given up long since and allowed to fill with water. These abandoned mines Mr. Grace agrees to pump and place in working order, and when they are cleared he has the privilege of working them to his own profit for ninety-nine years. The local miners have agreed to give him twenty per cent. of their gross product for introducing pumping machinery and operating it. The same set of pumps will serve the whole district, and the revenue which will be derived from the native miners will pay the expense of keeping in order the mines which Mr.

Grace will operate. It is estimated that seven hundred and fifty thousand dollars will clean up the property and pay for the necessary machinery to do thorough work, and the profits cannot be overestimated if all that is told of the mines is true.

I will not repeat the fables and tradition about these mines, of which the air is full. The El Dorado for which the world was hunting two centuries ago was but a shadow of the substance said to have been found here. Away in the heart of the Andes, almost beyond the reach of men, involving an enormous cost for transportation, and an expense of operation which miners of modern times would consider unprofitable, the priests and monks in past centuries found untold tons of treasure. The one-fifth which was always set apart for the King of Spain, and of which a record was scrupulously kept by the viceroys, reached into the millions, and the tithes which were paid to the Church amounted to millions more. During the last few decades the mines have scarcely been worked, for as large a product of silver as Peru could consume was found in more convenient localities.

COWHIDE BRIDGE OVER THE RIMAC.

The railroad was begun by Mr. Meiggs in 1870. Starting from the sea, it ascends the narrow valley of the once sacred Rimac, rising five thousand feet in the first forty-six miles to a beautiful valley, where the people of Lima have found an attractive summer resort; then it follows a winding, giddy pathway along the edge of precipices and over bridges that seem suspended in the air, tunnels the Andes at an altitude of fifteen thousand six hundred and forty-five feet—the most elevated spot in the world where a piston-rod is moved by steam—and ends at Oroya, twelve thousand one hundred and seventy-eight feet above the sea. Between the coast and the summit there is not an inch of down grade, and the track has been forced through the mountains by a series of sixty-three tunnels, whose aggregate length is twenty-one thousand feet. The great tunnel of Galera, by which the pinnacle of the Andes is pierced, will be, when completed, three thousand eight hundred feet long, and will be the highest elevation on the earth's surface where any such work has been undertaken. Besides boring the mountains of granite and blasting clefts along their sides to rest the track upon, deep cuttings and superb bridges, the system of reverse tangents had to be adopted in cañons that were too narrow for a curve. So the track zigzags up the mountain side on the switch and back-up principle, the trains taking one leap forward, and after being switched on to another track, another leap backward, until the summit is won; so that often there are four or five lines of track parallel to each other, one above another, on the mountain side. Almost the entire length of the road was made by blasting. There is no earth in sight except what was carted for use in ballasting, and the work of grading was done, not by the pick and shovel, but with the drill and hundreds of thousands of pounds of powder.

INCA RUINS OF UNKNOWN AGE.

It is estimated that the construction of this road cost Peru seven thousand lives. Pestilence and accident, landslides, falling boulders, premature explosions, *sirroche*—a disease which attacks those who are not accustomed to the rare air of the high latitudes—fevers due to the deposits of rotten granite, and other causes resulted in a frightful mortality during the seven years the road was under construction; but the project was pushed on until the funds gave out. The cost in human life was no obstacle. At several points it was necessary to lower men by ropes over the edges of precipices to drill holes in rocks and put in charges of blasting-powder, and this reckless mode of construction was attended by frequent fatalities. A curious accident occurred at one point on the line, where a plumber was soldering a leak in a water-pipe. A train of mules, loaded with cans of powder, was being driven up the trail. One of them rubbed against the plumber, who struck at the animal with his red-hot soldering-iron, which in some way came in contact with the powder, and caused an explosion that blew the whole train of mules, the gang of workmen, the plumber, and everybody who was by, over the precipices, the sides and bottom of which were strewn with fragments of men and mules for a mile.

A SETTLEMENT OF THIS CENTURY.

The scenic grandeur of the Andes is presented nowhere more impressively than along the cañon of the Rimac River, which this railroad follows. The mountains are entirely bare of vegetation, and are monster masses of rock, torn and twisted, rent and shattered by tremendous volcanic upheavals. At

A CITY OF FOUR CENTURIES AGO.

the bottom of the cañon, and where it occasionally spreads out into a valley of minute dimensions, are the remains of towns and cities, whose origin is hidden in the mists of fable, and whose history is unknown. This region bears no resemblance to any other picture of nature—lifted above the rest of the world, as coldly and calmly silent, as impenetrable, as the arctic stars. Here was developed a civilization which left memorials of its advancement, genius, and industry carved in massive stone, and written upon the everlasting hills in symbols which even the earthquakes have been unable to erase. Here are the ruins of cities which were more populous than any that have existed in Peru since—evidences of industry which their destroyers were too indolent to imitate, and of a skill which could cope with everything but the destructive weapons of the invaders. A survey of their remains justifies the estimates given of their enormous population, which are that the people once herded in these narrow valleys were as numerous as those now spread over the United States. The struggle which they had to sustain themselves is shown in the traces of their industry and patience. They built their dwellings upon rocks, and buried their dead in caves, in order to utilize what soil there was for agriculture. They excavated great areas in the desert until they reached moisture enough for vegetation, and then brought guano from the islands of the sea to fill these sunken gardens. They terraced every hill and mountain side, and placed soil in the crevices of the rocks, until not an inch of surface that could grow a stalk of maize was left unproductive.

The steep mountains along the Rimac are terraced up to the very summit, these terraces being often as narrow as the steps of a stairway, and many of them are walled up with stone. They are veritable hanging-gardens, and lie on such slopes that they look as if it were impossible for any one to get foothold to cultivate them, or even for the roots of what was planted there to sustain the mighty winds which sometimes sweep down the valley.

A BIT OF INCA ARCHITECTURE.

The irrigation system of the Incas was perfect, their ditches extending for hundreds of miles, and curving around the hills, here sustained by high walls of masonry, and there cut through the living rock. They were carried over narrow valleys upon enormous embankments, and show evidence of engineering skill as great as that which lifted the Meiggs railroad above

RELIC OF A PAST CIVILIZATION.

the clouds into the mountains. Massive dams and reservoirs were erected to collect the floods that came from the melting snows, and the water was taken to localities which were rainless. Under these conditions, in this great struggle for existence, the Incas established and sustained a Government—the first in which the equal rights of every human being were recognized—and worshipped a being whose attributes were similar to those of the Christian God. The great sea, breaking with ceaseless thunder upon the rocky coast, impressed the dweller in the desert with reverence and awe, and he recognized by an equally natural logic that the sun was the source of light and happiness. Hence these two objects, the sun and the sea, were personified, and were seated upon the thrones in the magnificent pantheons of the Incas. The race which conquered them came with dripping swords and lust for plunder. Skilled in the arts of peace, but powerless in war, there was no adequate resistance, and the blood-and-gold-thirsty Pizarro rode up this valley on a mission of murder, rapine, and destruction. The towns stand as he left them, with not even an echo to break the silence. Occasionally the Spaniards built new places of residence to utilize the improvements of the Incas, but in 1882 the Chilian army came down the valley, and treated the Peruvians as Pizarro had treated the race which he found here.

RUINS OF THE TEMPLE OF THE SUN.

A visit to the Incas' cemeteries, where millions of bodies are buried in the drifting sand, gives a clew to the extent of the original population, as well as to their arts, religion, and customs. The dead were preserved after the custom of ancient Egypt, and a few moments' toil with a shovel will disclose mummies whose features are perfectly preserved, whose eyes are petrified, whose fingers are clasped with rings, and who are surrounded with such implements and utensils as those who buried them thought they would need in the other world. As the soldier takes his blanket and the cooking-kit, his food and his portable treasures, so did the doctrine of future life cause the dead Incas to be equipped for their departure from one world to another. In this rainless region, protected by the magnetic sand, nothing can decay, and the contents of the Inca graves are as well preserved as if their age were counted by days instead of centuries. Wood, vegetable, and flesh petrify, fabrics and articles of stone and clay are preserved. There is no moisture to produce decay of the bodies, and there are no insects to consume them. The contents of the sand-hills are protected from every form of destruction, and their extent has never been measured.

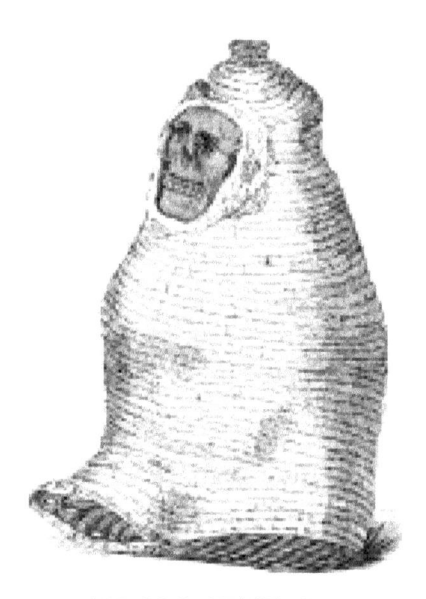

AN OLD SETTLER.

FRESH FROM THE TOMB.

It is still fashionable to go on resurrection expeditions to the Inca burying-grounds for mummies, and for the articles that were placed in their graves. In each grave are found articles of decoration, as well as the utensils required by the spirits to set up house-keeping in the happy land—rings and other ornaments of gold and silver, cups and platters of both metals made in quaint designs, copper articles, strings of beads, weaving and cooking apparatus, water-jugs, weapons of war, and other curiosities that interest antiquarians nowadays. Professor Ramondi, a distinguished French scientist in Lima, has a collection of Inca relics for which he was offered two hundred thousand dollars in gold by the British Museum. Under the patronage of the Government he is writing a voluminous work on the antiquities of Peru, three volumes of which have been published, and five more are yet to come.

The most curious things in Peru are the mummies' eyes—petrified eyeballs—which are usually to be found in the graves, if one is careful in digging. The Incas had a way of preserving the eyes of the dead from decay, some process which modern science cannot comprehend, and the eyeballs make very pretty settings for pins. They are yellow, and hold light like an opal. It is an accepted theory among scientists, however, that before the burial of their mummies the Incas replaced the natural eye with that of the squid, or cuttle-fish, and that these beautiful things are shams.

LA PAZ DE AYACUCHO.

THE CAPITAL OF BOLIVIA.

"The Callao painter" is something that skippers dread. Its brush is the breeze, and its pigments are in the air. It comes and goes without premonition, and its work is usually done in the night. A vessel will enter the harbor of Callao with its timbers as white as the virgin snow, and its planking as clean as holy-stone and elbow-grease can make them. The disgusted sailors may awaken in the morning and find everything covered with a brown, nasty film, which penetrates the cabin, and even the battened hatchways of the vessel, filling the air with a repulsive odor, and clinging to the wood-work until it is scraped off. It looks like a chocolate-colored frost, but does not melt in the sun. When it is damp one can remove it easily, but if it once dries it sticks like paint, and its tenacity is not easily overcome. The origin and source of this mysterious and aggravating artist is unknown, but it is peculiar to that harbor. Nowhere else is the phenomenon noticed, or at least ship-masters who have sailed the world over say that Callao is the only place where a ship can be painted inside and outside in a single night. Of course there are theories about it which may or may not hold good, and over them scientific minds have argued, and will argue interminably. Some say that the guano is forced up by vapors into the atmosphere, while others assert that it is a species of volcanic dust driven through the water by subterranean forces. However, the only point on which all agree is that it is a repulsive phenomenon, and has been the cause of more profanity than anything else which seamen encounter on the west coast. It is never noticed on land, but only in the harbor, and for a few miles up and down the shore.

The glory of Callao as a shipping centre has departed. Where formerly there were a hundred vessels in the harbor, there are only half a dozen now. The lack of trade in Peru, the poverty of the people, the enormous tariffs imposed by the Government, and the exorbitant port dues charged, have driven commerce away. Two years ago the Government in its poverty and need of funds was willing to dispose of everything it could control for spot cash, and practically sold the harbor at Callao to a French company, to whom the docks and anchorage have been leased for a term of years at two hundred thousand dollars a year. This company has the right to tax shipping to any extent it pleases, and has established a system of rules so oppressive as to drive most of the vessels away.

WHERE PERU'S WEALTH CAME FROM.

From Callao to Valparaiso the coast is a panorama of desolation—a constant succession of bleak and barren cliffs, with not a green or lovely thing for fifteen hundred miles. On one side is the Pacific Ocean, with its great swells sweeping almost around the globe, as regular and constant as the throbbings of the human pulse. On the other side rise the impenetrable Andes in a range whose altitude averages fifteen thousand feet, and whose peaks tower twenty and twenty-two thousand feet above the sea. Between the ocean and the mountains for a thousand miles, with a varying width from twenty to fifty miles, lies a strip of drifting sand, which no rivers water, and where rain never falls. All the water used by the inhabitants is taken from the ocean, that for mechanical purposes being used in its natural condition, and that for food being condensed into steam, and purged of its salt by machinery. There is not a well or a spring along the coast, and drinking-water is an article of merchandise, like ice or flour, costing about seven cents a gallon to the consumers.

Some distance below Callao, upon a great rock which rises from the sea, and shows an unbroken surface to the western sun, is carved the image of a candelabra—an eight-horned candlestick—about one hundred feet long and fifty feet across from end to end of the lower arms. The execution is perfect, and it is said to be carved in lines about a foot deep and a yard wide. When and how the picture came there no one can tell. The oldest sailor on the coast says that the oldest man he knew when a boy could tell nothing of its origin. They call it "The Miraculous Candlestick," and pious Catholics say that St. James dropped it when he came to Peru and placed himself at the head of the Spaniards, at the time they were driving the Incas out of their ancient homes.

In the interior of Peru, upon a similar rock, is the imprint of a human foot as long as a pikestaff, which is supposed to mark where the Apostle alighted when he dropped down from heaven to aid in the subjugation of the heathen and the triumph of the Cross. At any rate, like the foot of St. James, this image of the Holy Candlestick, if made by human labor, must have cost months and months of toil at a time when such things were needed to impress the Indians with a reverence for the Church of Rome and the doctrines it taught. Sometimes, if the wind blows seaward, the carving is covered by the drifting sand, when the padre of the nearest village goes down with a lot of Indians to dig it out.

A PERUVIAN PORT.

The first port of importance on the coast south of Callao is the town of Mollendo (pronounced *Molyendo*), the western terminus of the railway that furnishes means of communication for Bolivia and the interior of Peru to the sea. It was built in 1876 by Henry Meiggs for the Peruvian Government, at a cost of forty-four million dollars—an enormous average of one hundred and thirty-five thousand dollars per mile; for it is only three hundred and twenty-five miles long. Its western terminus is the highest point now reached by steam, being something over fourteen thousand five hundred feet above the sea, although the Oroya road will be higher when it reaches the Cerro del Pasco mines. No other railway in the world can show an equal amount of excavation or such massive embankments, but the Oroya road has more tunnels. The line is now under the management of a Boston man, Mr.

Thorndike, and everything is conducted upon the United States plan. Along the side of the track, for a distance of eighty-five miles, is an eight-inch iron pipe, for the purpose of supplying the stations with water, as there is none on the coast; and it is the longest aqueduct in the world, coming from springs in the mountains, seven thousand feet above the sea, to the port of Mollendo.

THE OLD TRAIL.

Across a hot, lifeless, desolate desert the railway runs one hundred and seven miles to the city of Arequipa—the name appropriately signifying "a place of rest;" and it is one of the oldest, most celebrated, and beautiful towns in Peru, situated in a small oasis in the desert, rich in its agricultural resources, and surrounded by valuable mines. Just behind the city is as magnificent and imposing a mountain as can be found anywhere in the world—the volcano Misti, 18,538 feet high, and covered with eternal snow. The city was founded by Pizarro in 1540, and has always been second to Lima in size and importance, being the political as well as the commercial capital of the Southern provinces, and the seat of a university which for nearly three hundred years has been the most famous upon the west coast in South America, and has

AREQUIPA.

graduated the most eminent scholars and statesmen in the history of Peru.

Crossing the Paso de Arricroo between the greatest cluster of peaks in the Andes, south of Quito, the railway reaches Vuicarrago, one hundred miles from Arequipa, the highest town in the world, where the barometer in the plaza shows an elevation of 14,443 feet. The ascent to it is usually made by stages, the traveller taking two or three days for it, so as to accustom himself gradually to the altitude; for the sudden change from tide-water to this enormous elevation—a distance of only two hundred and seven miles—generally brings on that distressing disease sirroche. It is always painful, and often dangerous. The first symptom is numbness of the limbs, then dizziness and nausea; the blood bursts from the ears and nose, the lips crack and bleed, a feeling of faintness makes it impossible to stand, and there is no cure but absolute quiet or a return to a lower altitude. During the construction of the railway a great many men died from the effects of the dreaded sirroche, which is often followed by a sudden and quickly fatal mountain fever. Few people escape the ailment, and no animal but the llama and others of that species native to the mountain regions can survive. At every town along the road droves of llamas can be seen which have been driven in from the mountain settlements laden with furs and skins, or with ore from the mines. The llama is the only beast of burden in the Upper Andes, and is docile, patient, sure-footed, and speedy. It can carry a burden of one hundred pounds, which is fastened to a pack-saddle, and when that weight is exceeded will lie down and refuse to move until the surplus is removed. The llama is about as large as a one-year-old colt or a good-sized black-tail buck. It has a heavy coat of wool; but those that are used for transportation purposes are seldom sheared.

The vicuña, a sort of gazelle, a gentle, timid animal, is found in large numbers in the interior of the Andes, particularly in Bolivia. It is fawn-colored, has long, soft, silken hair, with a peculiar gloss that resembles what are known as "changeable

THE VICUÑA.

silks," and changes color in different lights. In the old Inca days, before the Spanish invasion, centuries ago, the vicuña was the royal ermine of the Inca kings, and no one but the Imperial family and nobles of a certain rank was allowed to wear it. The animal was also protected by some sacred tradition, and was allowed to go unharmed in the forests, where it accumulated in great numbers; but the Spanish invaders, regardless of all rights, human and divine, hunted it down, and slaughtered it for food. The Indians expected that some severe penalty would be visited upon the invaders for destroying and eating the sacred animal, and lost faith when they escaped divine retribution. Now vicuña skins are very scarce and are expensive, and the natives attempt to

LAKE TITICACA.

LAKE TITICACA.

impose upon strangers who seek them robes made of the skins of guanaco kids, killed and skinned the moment they are born.

The guanaco is supposed to be a cross of the vicuña and the llama, and is next in value and beauty to the vicuña. If the kid is killed the moment it is born the hair has the same color, and is about as fine as the genuine vicuña, but is not so long or so luscious. This animal is numerous, easily domesticated, and breeds rapidly. It is almost as plentiful in South America as the goat, and is valuable for its skin and flesh. The body is deep at the breast, but narrow at the loins, and is covered with long, soft, very fine hair, which is usually a pale yellow, except under the belly, where it is a beautiful snowy white. It has many of the characteristics of the North American deer, being very swift-footed and graceful, combined with the strength and endurance of the llama, being able to carry a load of from seventy-five to one hundred and twenty-five pounds for a long distance. The flesh resembles that of the antelope, but is not as juicy as venison. The skin is invaluable to the Indians, as it furnishes the material of which their garments are made. Occasionally in the stomach of a guanaco is found what is called a "bezoar" stone, a magical sort of affair, which will cure any kind of disease if carried in the pocket. Large numbers of guanaco skins are sent to Europe, where they are used for carriage robes, for lining coats and cloaks, for trimming, and for other purposes to which fine fur is adapted. Large quantities of alpaca and also llama wool are exported from Chili and Peru; some of it comes to the United States.

The alpaca is a sort of cross between the llama and the sheep. The llamas, alpacas, and guanacos have a peculiar way of defending themselves. If abused or made angry by teasing, they will turn upon their assailants, and squirt a pint or so of saliva, like a shower-bath, from between their teeth, being able to throw it with great force five or six feet. If this saliva gets into the mouth or eyes, or upon any place on the flesh where the skin is broken, it is poisonous, and inflammation sets in at once. It is said that men frequently die of blood-poisoning from this cause, and a native will keep clear of the nose of a vicious guanaco as a colored person will avoid the heels of an Irish mule.

A STREET IN CUZCO.

Traversing the pass of Alto del Crucero, 14,660 feet above the level of the sea, and the highest altitude reached by any railway in the world, the road descends into the great basin of Titicaca, the heart of the Andes, stretching northward and southward between the two great chains of the Cordilleras for fifteen hundred miles, almost level, and twelve thousand feet above the ocean. Here in majestic splendor lies Lake Titicaca, one of whose islands was the Eden of the Incas, the birthplace of that prehistoric empire whose civilization has been the wonder and mystery of centuries. Here Manco

RUINS OF AN INCA TEMPLE.

Capac (the Adam) and Mama Ocllo (the Eve) of Inca tradition, the Children of the Sun, arose like Aphrodite, and bearing a golden rod, marched down the valley until they reached the place where Cuzco now stands, and there commanded the Indians to erect a city, the seat of an Imperial dynasty which lasted a thousand years, and possessed a wealth and an industry that had no measure. Around the lake stand the mighty temples and palaces, erected of blocks of stone as large as those of the Pyramids, quarried and conveyed by means that still remain a mystery, and will never be known. These monuments of an extinct civilization, these evidences of art and industry that surpass any prehistoric architecture on the earth, are standing now in mute impressiveness, mocking decay, as they taunted the conquistadors who tried to overthrow them. But the Spaniards stripped them of their treasures, murdered their inmates, and destroyed everything that could not withstand their power.

CONVENT OF SANTA DOMINGO, CUZCO.

The riches of Peru and Bolivia have been their curse from the time when Pizarro invaded the continent to the plunder of their nitrate deposits by Chili. It is true that few countries have suffered from such an evil, but it is nevertheless a fact that the wealth of these republics has been the cause of their disasters. For three hundred years the people sat with folded hands, and enjoyed the profits of the development of their natural resources by foreigners, and now, stripped of them, sit impoverished, mourning the departure of their prosperity.

Just how much plunder Pizarro got in his raids upon the Incas is not known, and cannot be estimated, but millions went to the King of Spain as his twenty per cent.; the Catholic Church got millions more as her share; Sir Francis Drake, John Hawkins, and other pirates got away with an immense amount of gold and silver; and the quantity expended in the erection of churches, convents, monasteries, and palaces by the viceroys is incalculable. History asserts that ninety millions of dollars' worth of precious metals was torn from the Inca temples, and the faithful subjects of Atahualpa filled the room in which he was imprisoned with gold, in their endeavor to satisfy the avarice of the invaders. Prescott and Robertson and other historians tell fabulous stories of the wealth of the Incas, and we know it was enough to restore financial prosperity to Spain, and to give every cutthroat who came to the coast a fortune.

WHAT THE SPANIARDS LEFT.

The amount of money made by Peru from her guano deposits cannot be estimated any more accurately than by the plunder stolen from the Incas. The exports have continued from 1846 to the present day, and the annual shipments have amounted to millions of tons, valued between twenty and thirty million dollars, and this to the benefit of a State whose population has never reached two millions, and three-fourths of which were Indians who had no share in its profits. The exhausted lands of the Old World required this manure to revive them, and their owners paid high prices for what cost Peru nothing. The result of this revenue was the continuation of the extravagance among the people which was practised by their forefathers when the mountains poured out streams of silver. It was an epidemic of riches, and the Government of Peru, instead of wisely hoarding its source of wealth and protecting it, plunged into a system of reckless expenditure, until the end of the war found its revenues cut off and the country burdened with a debt of two hundred and fifty million dollars which it never can pay.

WHERE THE GUANO LIES.

But even if Peru and Bolivia have been robbed of all their guano, the deposits of nitrate of soda in the deserts along their coasts would have made them rich again; but Chili has stolen these also. The whole coast, from the twenty-third to the twenty-fifth parallel of latitude, appears to be one solid mass of this valuable mineral, fit for a hundred different uses, and worth in the market from forty to sixty dollars a ton. It was discovered in 1833 by an accident, the hero of the discovery being a forlorn old Englishman by the name of George Smith. There is no telling how much lies in the mines, but it is the opinion of those who have explored the country that at the present rate of excavation it will take eight or ten centuries to dig it away.

A NITRATE MINING TOWN.

Under the sand of this desert, which drifts before the wind like snow, nature has laid the bed of nitrate. No one knows how it was formed, and man has not attempted to measure its extent. The sand is first shovelled off, and then a crust of sun-baked clay from four to twelve inches thick is removed. This discloses a bed of white material that looks like melting marble, full of moisture, and is as soft as cheese. The strata is often four or five feet thick, and averages two or three feet. It is broken up by crow-bars and shovelled into carts, then taken to crushers, which grind it up into particles as large as pebbles. These are lifted by elevators into great vats, where it is boiled until dissolved in ordinary sea-water. Then the solution is run off into a series of shallow iron vats exposed to the air, which, being moistureless, and heated by constant sunshine, causes rapid evaporation. The salt from the water mixed with the nitrate causes crystallization, and after a certain period of exposure to the air and sun the vats are found to be covered upon the bottom and sides with white sparkling crystals, like alabaster, under a yellowish liquor. This liquor is carefully drawn off, for it is even more valuable than the saltpetre, and is conducted by pipes to another crucible, where it is boiled and chemically treated until it produces the iodine of commerce, useful for a hundred medical and chemical purposes, and costing as much per ounce as the saltpetre brings per hundred-weight. The liquor having been withdrawn, the saltpetre is shovelled upon drying-boards, where it is exposed to the sun for a while, then put into bags and shipped to Europe and America. It is graded like wheat and corn, according to quality. The highest grade goes to the powder-mills, the next to the chemical works, and the third to the fertilizer factories, where it is made into manure. The iodine is packed in little casks, and covered with green hides, which shrink with drying until they are as tight as a drum-head, and keep out moisture. It was these nitrate of soda deposits that caused the late war between Chili and Peru.

After the independence of South America, when the several republics were being divided, Bolivia was given a little strip of land between Peru and Chili in order that she might have a pathway to the sea. It lay between the twenty-third and the twenty-fifth parallels, and was so recognized on all the maps of Chili, as well as those of other nations. It was a barren, waterless desert, worthless in every respect, as was originally supposed, but some years ago the rich deposits of silver and nitrate of soda were discovered. When their value became known, Chili suddenly ascertained that under some ancient right this strip of territory belonged to her, and kindly offered to divide it with Bolivia in such a way as to leave the silver and soda on the Chilian side. Bolivia of course resisted, and having a treaty of offence and defence with Peru, called upon the latter nation to assist in the defence of her rights. This was the real cause of the war. The ostensible excuse for it was that Bolivia charged an export duty of ten cents a hundred-weight on nitrate exported. This the Chilians deemed excessive, and sent a fleet to defend her citizens in refusing to pay it. Now that she has secured the territory and the mines, she charges one dollar and twenty-five cents a hundred-weight export duty on the same article at the same place, and thinks people impertinent when they complain. The results of the war are that Bolivia has not only lost her seaports and her nitrate, but Peru has lost all her guano and a large portion of her richest territory, while Chili is so much the richer.

GUANO ISLANDS.

At one time Peru might have prevented the invasion of her territory, and caused the entire army of Chili to perish, but the instincts of noble generosity and the unwritten law of common humanity were observed. If Peru had been as merciless as Chili the struggle would have been shortened and the result would have been different. Along the coast from Guayaquil, Ecuador, to Coquimbo, Chili, a distance of more than two thousand miles, stretches a desert on which a drop of rain never fell. Occasionally a stream, born of a union between the burning sun and the eternal snows of the Andes, finds its way to the sea, bringing nourishment to the soil and making a little oasis where men can live. But unless the water-supply is very great—and it is only so occasionally—the stream is swallowed by the thirsty sands and absorbed by the atmosphere, which is so dry that nothing ever decays, and causes more rapid evaporation than is known elsewhere. In this desert lie the nitrate mines, and towns have sprung up around them the inhabitants of which are supplied with water by artificial means. Salt water is turned into fresh by means of enormous condensers, and a supply is kept in vast iron reservoirs, from which it is sold to the people at a price about the same as we pay for beer. At the saloons one can get a glass of filtered ice-water for five cents; at the reservoirs a bucket of warm, nasty stuff is sold for ten.

If you ask a learned man why it never rains there, he will say that the clouds are deprived of all their moisture when they cross the mountains from the eastward, and when they come up from the westward ocean are at once sucked dry by the heat that radiates from the sun-baked sands. Occasionally along the coast are found immense cemeteries in which the Incas buried their dead; and the contents of the graves are as well preserved as if their age were counted by weeks instead of centuries. The most interesting and extensive of the burial grounds is at Pachacamac, south of Lima, in Peru, where millions of bodies lie, often in three stratas, and very generally in two. Near this place was the famous temple dedicated to Pachacamac, the chief divinity of the Incas, and whom they acknowledged as the creator of the world. It was the Mecca of that day, and each believer was expected to visit it at least once in his life. The pilgrims came from all parts of the empire, bringing votive-offerings, which made the temple very rich; and Pizarro is said to have obtained a vast quantity of plunder from it. Around the temple arose a large city of monasteries to accommodate the priests and devotees, and inns to shelter the pilgrims; but the place is in ruins now.

ACROSS THE CONTINENT.

At one of these towns the whole army of Chili was concentrated—forty thousand men—preparing for the invasion of Peru. The Peruvian gun-boat *Huascar* (pronounced *Wascar*) came into the harbor, and with a few shots might have destroyed the reservoirs and the condensing establishments, and left these forty thousand men to die of thirst, for there was no fresh water within two hundred and fifty miles of them. But the commander of the *Huascar* had a heart. He was a noble, generous German—Admiral Grau—and he sent word to the Chillano commander that he presented his army with their lives. He said he would not attack defenceless men, and sailed off in pursuit of some Chillano gun-boats which had run away when they saw the *Huascar* coming.

A STATION ON THE ROAD.

The present terminus of the Bolivia railroad is at Puno, a little town of five thousand inhabitants, at an elevation of twelve thousand five hundred feet; but it is proposed to extend it farther up the valley, through another pass of the Andes, and then down the eastern slopes to the head of navigation on the Amazon—neither a difficult nor an expensive undertaking. An expedition has recently started from Buenos Ayres to make an exploration from the head of navigation on the Paraguay River into the mountains of Bolivia, for the purpose of constructing a cart-road, and ultimately a railroad to connect the mining regions of the latter republic with the Atlantic ports of the continent, and great hopes are entertained of its success. The little town of Puno owes its origin to the rich mines that surround it, and some of them are producing generously. It has a small amount of other commerce in hides and wool, coca-leaves, and cinchona. It is the centre of the alpaca wool trade, and considerable is exported.

To reach La Paz, the capital of Bolivia, from Puno one must cross Lake Titicaca, sailing its full length, and, reaching its southern shores, mount a mule and ride twenty-five miles along the ancient highway of the Incas, a wonderful road, nearly four thousand miles long, built eight hundred years or more ago, and still in a good state of preservation, notwithstanding the neglect of the Spaniards to keep it in repair.

Perhaps the most glorious monuments of the civilization of the Incas were the public or royal roads, extending from the capital to the remotest parts of the empire. Their remains are still most impressive, both from their extent and the amount of labor necessarily involved in their construction, and in contemplating them we know not which to admire most—the scope of their projectors, the power and constancy of the Incas who carried them to a completion, or the patience of the people who constructed them under all the obstacles resulting from the topography of the country and from imperfect means of execution. They built these roads in deserts, among moving sands reflecting the fierce rays of a tropical sun; they broke down rocks, graded precipices, levelled hills, and filled up valleys without the assistance of powder or of instruments of iron; they crossed lakes, marshes, and rivers, and without the aid of the compass followed direct courses in forests of eternal shade. They did, in short, what even now, with all of modern knowledge and means of action, would be worthy of the most powerful nations of the globe. One of the principal of these roads extended from Cuzco to the sea, and the other, which is followed to La Paz, ran along the crest of the Cordilleras from one end of the empire to the other, their aggregate lengths, with their branches, being about four thousand miles. Modern travellers compare them, in respect of structure, to the best works of the kind in any part of the world. In ascending mountains too steep to admit of grading, broad steps were cut in the solid rocks, while the ravines and hollows were filled with heavy embankments, flanked with parapets, and planted with shade-trees and fragrant shrubs. They were from eighteen to twenty-five Castilian feet broad, and were paved with immense blocks of

CHASQUIS AT REST.

stone. At regular distances on these roads tambos—buildings for the accommodation of travellers—were erected. To these conveniences were added the establishment of a system of posts, by which messages could be transmitted from one extremity of the Incas' dominions to the other in an incredibly short time. The service of the posts was performed by runners—for the Peruvians possessed no domestic animals swifter of foot than man—stationed in small buildings, likewise erected at easy distances from each other all along the principal roads. These messengers, or *chasquis*, as they were termed, wore a peculiar uniform, and were trained to their particular vocation. Each had his allotted station, between which and the next it was his duty to speed along at a certain pace with the message, dispatch, or parcel intrusted to his care. On drawing near to the station at which he had to transmit the message to the next courier, who was then to carry it farther, he was to give a signal of his approach, in order that the other might be in readiness to receive the missive and no time be lost; and thus it is said that messages were forwarded at the rate of one hundred and fifty miles a day.

CHASQUIS ASLEEP IN THE MOUNTAINS.

The bridges constructed by the Peruvians were exceedingly simple, but were well adapted for crossing those rapid streams which rush down from the Andes and defy the skill of the modern engineer. They consisted of strong cables of the cabuya, or of twisted rawhide stretched from one bank to the other, something after the style of the suspension-bridges of our times. Poles were lashed across transversely, covered with branches, and these were again covered with earth and stones, so as to form a solid floor. Other cables extended along the sides, which were interwoven with limbs of trees, forming a kind of wicker balustrade. In some cases the mode of transit was in a species of basket or car, suspended on a single cable, and drawn from side to side with ropes. It would appear at first glance that bridges of this description could not be very lasting, yet a few still exist which are said to have been constructed by the Incas more than four hundred years ago. The modern inhabitants of some parts of Peru, Bolivia, and Chili still use the same means of crossing their torrent rivers.

A BIT OF LA PAZ.

The city of La Paz has about seventy thousand inhabitants, mostly Aymara Indians, poor, degraded, and ignorant. The full name of the place is La Paz de Ayacucho, and it means "the peace of Ayacucho," being so christened in 1825, to commemorate the victory which established the independence of Bolivia from the hated crown of Spain. At that time the republic was a part of the old Province of Peru, and a separate State was founded by Bolivar, the Venezuelan Liberator of the Continent, who gave freedom to these people as he did

THE CATHEDRAL AT LA PAZ.

to his own countrymen, and the new republic was christened in his honor. La Paz was originally called Nuestra Señora de la Paz—"the peace of the Virgin"—by Alonzo de Mendoza, who founded it in 1548. It is thirteen thousand feet above tide-water, and is surrounded by a group of gigantic mountains, the most notable of which is the volcano Illiniani, twenty-one thousand three hundred feet high. Through the city runs the river Chiquiapo, a noble mountain-stream, which is crossed by a number of fine old bridges. The streets are narrow, irregular, and uneven, being paved with stone, and having narrow sidewalks, scarcely broad enough for two people to pass. The town resembles all others of Spanish construction, except that the houses are mostly built of stone instead of adobe, the walls being massive and enduring, and in some instances ornamented with carved stone or stucco-work. The cathedral is large and grand, the front being handsomely carved, and in a niche over the entrance stands a marble image of the Virgin, which was presented to the city by Charles of Spain, and transported from the seaboard at an enormous cost. The cathedral is built entirely of stone, and was over forty years in course of erection, hundreds of men being constantly employed. No derricks or other machinery were used in its construction, but the walls were built in a curious way. As fast as a tier of stone was laid, the earth was banked up against it inside and outside, and upon this inclined plane the stones for the next tier were rolled into their places. Then more earth was thrown on, and the process repeated until, when the walls were finished, the whole building was immersed in a mountain of dirt. This was allowed to remain until the roof was laid, when the earth was carried away upon the backs of llamas and men. It is said to have taken thirteen years to clear out the inside of the building, as the earth could only be taken away through the narrow windows and doors. There are fourteen other churches of considerable size, and several large monasteries, which are now used for military barracks and schools. A university is sustained by the Government, and there is a nominal free-school system, but education is at a low ebb.

In the centre of the city runs the Alameda, a public promenade which is frequented by all classes of citizens, and during the twilight hours is quite gay. The cemetery is very extensive, and one of the finest in South America. There are few stores or shops, most of the trading being done in the market-places, where all things are sold, and by peddlers who go through the city with baskets of provisions and notions upon their heads, crying their wares. The way customers call street-venders is worth noticing and imitating. They step to the door or open a window, and give utterance to a short sound resembling shir-r-r-r-r—something between a hiss and the exclamation used to chase away fowls—and it is singular what a distance it can be heard. If the peddler is in sight, his attention is at once arrested; he turns, and comes direct to the caller, now guided by a signal addressed to his eyes—closing the fingers of the right hand two or three times, with the palm downward, as if grasping something—a sign in universal use, and signifying "Come." There is here no bawling after people in the streets, for in this quiet and ingenious way all classes communicate with passing friends or others with whom they wish to speak. The practice dates, I believe, from classical times. A curious custom is the peddling of fuel through the streets. Llamas are loaded with their own excrement, which when dried in the sun is called *taquia*, and sold by the basketful. It is used by all classes for cooking.

AN ANCIENT BRIDGE IN LA PAZ.

The mineral wealth of Bolivia has been proverbial almost from time immemorial. The silver-mines of Potosi have long been celebrated as perhaps the richest deposit of silver ore in the world. From the year 1545, when they were discovered, to the year 1864, these mines, according to official data, produced the enormous sum of $2,904,902,690 of our money. Besides Potosi there are other rich silver-mines, and many large deposits of gold. The great want of these mines is skilled labor and improved modern machinery. In early days the Indians were forced to work them against their will, and were treated with great harshness and cruelty. The historical student will call to mind the efforts of philanthropists to mitigate their sufferings. When their labor could no longer be controlled, the mines fell into comparative decay. The Indians will not work them with energy and industry to-day. They doubtless hold in memory through their traditions the wrongs inflicted on their ancestors by merciless taskmasters. If worked by experienced miners, with all the improved modern machinery, the gold and silver deposits would yield as abundant returns, perhaps, as in the days of their early history. Recently a party of Californians have gone into the country and taken charge of a gold-mine. If a good many others would follow them, mining in Bolivia would experience a renaissance that would remind the Bolivians of the El Dorado of the olden time.

A BOLIVIAN ELEVATOR.

The most useful to mankind of all the natural products of South America was quinine, the drug made from the bark of the cinchona-tree, which was discovered in Bolivia by a Franciscan friar in the early days of the Conquest, and was called cinchona in honor of the Countess of Conchona, whose husband was the Viceroy of Peru. She introduced it into Spain as a remedy for fevers, and there is no drug in the catalogue that has been used in such quantities or with such success by suffering mankind. The entire supply formerly came from Peru and Bolivia, and it was known as Peruvian bark, but afterwards the forests along the entire chain of the Andes were found to contain it, and it furnished one of the chief articles of export from South America for three centuries. The supply has been greatly diminished by the destruction of the trees, as it was the habit formerly to cut down the trunk, and strip it as well as the branches of the bark. Nowadays the forests are protected by law, and the trees are allowed to stand, a portion of the bark being stripped off each year, which nature replaces again.

A BOLIVIAN CAVALRYMAN.

England, with that provident foresight which characterizes much of her political economy, several years ago sent agents into Ecuador, Peru, and Bolivia, under the direction of the celebrated botanist Mr. Spruce, and made a collection of cinchona plants, which were taken to Java, Ceylon, and India, and there have been transplanted and cultivated with great success and profit. It is found that under proper treatment the tree produces a very much greater amount of quinine, of a much superior quality, and at less cost than the bark can be gathered in the mountains of South America, so that shipments have almost entirely ceased, and the market receives its supply from the British possessions.

A HOME IN THE ANDES.

Another plant is coming into prominence, and its export has very largely increased within the last few years. This is the coca, from which cocoaine and other medicinal and nerve stimulants are made. In the valleys of the Andes there are, and have been from time immemorial, extensive plantations of the coca shrub. It is indigenous in these regions, but the natives of Peru and Bolivia cultivate the plant in terraces which are likened to the vineyards of Tuscany and the Holy Land. *Erythroxylon coca* is allied to the common flax, and forms, says Dr. Johnston, a shrub of six or eight feet, resembling our blackthorn, with small white flowers and bright green leaves. The leaves, of which there may be three or four crops in the year, are collected by the women and children, and dried in the sun, after which they are ready for use, and form the usual money exchange in some districts, the workmen being paid in coca-leaves. Among the Peruvians and Bolivians the coca-leaves are rolled with a little unslaked lime into a ball (*acullico*) and chewed in the mouth. Coca-chewing resembles in some respects the smoking of opium. Both must be taken apart, and with deliberation. The coca chewer, three or four times in the day, retires to a secluded spot, lays down his burden, and stretches himself perhaps beneath a tree. Slowly from the *chuspa*, or little pouch, which is ever at his girdle, the leaves and the lime are brought forth. The ball is formed and chewed for perhaps fifteen or thirty minutes, and then the toiler rises refreshed as quietly as he lay down, and returns to that monotonous round of labor in which the coca is his only and much-prized distraction. Some take it to excess, and to these the name of *coquero* is given. This is particularly common among white Peruvians of good family, and hence the name "Blanco Coquero" in that country is a term of reproach equivalent to our "habitual drunkard." The Indians regard the coca with extreme reverence. Von Tschudi, the Austrian scientist, who made the most thorough study of the ancient customs of the Incas, says, "During divine worship the priests chewed coca-leaves, and unless they were supplied with them it was believed that the favor of the gods could not be propitiated. It was also deemed necessary that the supplicator for Divine grace should approach the priests with an acullico in his mouth. It is believed that any business undertaken without the benediction of coca-leaves could not prosper, and to the shrub itself worship was rendered. During an interval of more than three hundred years Christianity has not been able to subdue this deep-rooted idolatry, for everywhere we find traces of belief in the mysterious powers of this plant. The excavators in the mines of Cerro del Pasco throw chewed coca upon hard veins of metal, in the belief that it softens the ore and renders it more easy to work. The Indians even at the present time put coca-leaves into the mouths of dead persons, in order to secure them a favorable reception on their entrance into another world, and when a Peruvian on a journey falls in with a mummy, he, with timid reverence, presents to it some coca-leaves as his pious offering."

JUAN FERNANDEZ.

The coca-plant resembles tea and hops in the nature of its active principles, although differing entirely from them in its effects. In the coqueros the latter are not inviting. "They are," says Dr. Von Tschudi, "a bad breath, pale lips and gums, greenish and stumpy teeth, and an ugly black mark at the angles of the mouth. The inveterate coquero is known at the first glance; his unsteady gait, his yellow skin, his dim and sunken eyes encircled by a purple ring, his quivering lips, and his general apathy all bear evidence of the baneful effect of the coca-juice when taken in excess." The general influence of moderate doses is gently soothing and stimulating; but coca has in addition a special and remarkable power in enabling those who consume it to endure sustained labor in the absence of other food.

CUMBERLAND BAY.

Down the coast, just before reaching the city of Valparaiso, is an island which possesses an interest for every one who has been a boy. Occasionally an excursion visits the place, and the Englishmen, who constitute a large fraction of the population of Valparaiso, with what few Americans there are, go over to spend a day or two, and renew their youth. It is the island of Juan Fernandez, where Robinson Crusoe and his man Friday, "who kept things tidy," had the experience that has given the world of boys as much enjoyment as any that ever came from a book. There was a Robinson Crusoe—there is not a doubt of it—and there was a man Friday too, and the island stands to-day exactly as it is described in the narrative; but the surprising adventures of

Mr. Crusoe as therein related do not correspond exactly with the local traditions of the story. The island was a favorite stopping-place for vessels in the South Seas, as it has good ship-timber, plenty of excellent water, abounds in fruits, goats, rabbits, and other flesh for food, and the rocks on the coast are covered with lobsters, shrimps, and crayfish. It was a popular resort for buccaneers also, who ran into a well-protected harbor to repair damages and get provisions. Juan Fernandez, a famous Spanish navigator, discovered it in 1563, and the King of Spain gave him a patent to the island, but as he never occupied it his title lapsed. In 1709 the Scotchman Selkirk, or Selcraig, became mutinous on board the ship *Cinque Ports*, and had to choose between being hung at the yard-arm or put ashore at Juan Fernandez alone. He took the latter alternative, and was left on the rocks with his sailor's kit and a small supply of provisions. To his surprise, after he had been on the island a few days, he found a companion in an Indian from the Mosquito Coast of Central America, who some years before had come down on the pirate *Damphier*, and going ashore on a hunting expedition, was lost and abandoned by his comrades. This was the man Friday. Some years after, Selkirk and the Indian were rescued by Captain Rogers, of an English merchant-ship, and taken to Southampton, where the Scotchman told his story to Daniel Defoe, and it got into print, with some romantic exaggeration.

The island is accurately described in the story, and the visitor who is familiar with "Robinson Crusoe" can find the cave, the mountain-paths, and other haunts of the hero without difficulty; but Defoe has located it in the wrong geographical position, having placed it on the other side of the continent, and mixed up Montevideo with Valparaiso. It is about twenty-three miles long and ten miles wide in the broadest part, and is covered with beautiful hills and lovely valleys, the highest peak reaching an elevation of nearly three thousand feet. A hundred years ago the Spaniards introduced blood-hounds to kill off the goats and rabbits, and to keep the pirates away, but the scheme did not work. Upon her independence, in 1821, Chili made Juan Fernandez a penal colony, but thirty years after the prisoners mutinied, slaughtered the guards, and escaped. Then it was leased to a cattle company, which has now thirty thousand head of horned cattle and as many sheep grazing upon the hills. There are fifty or sixty inhabitants, mostly ranchmen and their families, who tend the herds and raise vegetables for the Valparaiso market.

Great care has been taken to preserve the relics of Alexander Selkirk's stay upon the island, and his cave and huts remain just as he left them. In 1868 the officers of the British man-of-war *Topaz* erected a marble tablet to mark the famous lookout from which Mr. Crusoe, like the Ancient Mariner, used to watch for a sail, "and yet no sail from day to day." The inscription reads: "In memory of Alexander Selkirk, mariner, a native of Largo, county of Fife, Scotland; who lived upon this island in complete solitude for four years and four months. He was landed from the *Cinque Ports* galley, 96 tons, 16 guns, A.D. 1704, and was taken off in the *Duke*, privateer, on February 12th, 1709. He died Lieutenant of H.B.M.S. *Weymouth*: 47 years. This tablet is erected upon Selkirk's lookout by Commodore Powell and the officers of H.B.M.S. *Topaz*, A.D. 1868."

TABLET TO ALEXANDER SELKIRK.

No one ever goes to Juan Fernandez without bringing away rocks and sticks as relics of the place. There is a very fine sort of wood peculiar to the island which makes beautiful canes, as it has a rare grain and polishes well.

SANTIAGO.

THE CAPITAL OF CHILI.

NATURE never intended there should be a city where Valparaiso stands, but the enterprise of the Chillanos, aided by English and German capital, has built there the finest port on the west coast of South America, and the only one with all the modern improvements. The harbor is spacious and beautiful, and ten months in the year it is perfectly safe for shipping, but during the remaining two months, when northern gales are frequent, vessels are often driven from their anchorage, and compelled to cruise about to avoid being dashed upon the rocks on which the city is built. The harbor is circular in form, with an entrance a mile or so wide facing the north. A breakwater built across the entrance would give the shipping perfect protection, but the sea is so deep—more than a hundred fathoms—that such a work is considered impracticable. In this harbor, drawn up in lines like men-of-war ready for review, are hundreds of vessels, bearing the flags of almost every nation on the earth except that of our own. Occasionally the Stars and Stripes are seen, but so seldom that, as an American resident expressed it, "they cure all the sore eyes in town." Trade is practically controlled by Englishmen, all commercial transactions are calculated in pounds sterling, and the English language is almost exclusively spoken upon the street and in the shops. An English paper is printed there, English goods are almost exclusively sold, and this city is nothing more than an English colony.

In Valparaiso, as everywhere else in Chili, there is an intense prejudice against the United States, growing out of the attitude assumed by our Government during the late war with Peru. The prejudice has been aggravated and stimulated by the English residents. This, with the natural arrogance of the Chillanos, who think they have the finest country on earth, and that the United States is their only rival, makes it rather disagreeable sometimes for Americans who go there to reside. For this and other reasons our commerce with Chili has fallen off from millions to hundreds of thousands, and it will be difficult to increase it as long as the prejudice of the people exists, and lines of English, French, German, and Italian vessels connect Valparaiso with the markets of Europe.

THE HARBOR OF VALPARAISO.

There is no steam communication with the United States, and all freight is sent in sailing-vessels around the Horn or by way of Hamburg or Havre. The freight charges from Valparaiso to New York by way of the Isthmus are more than double those to the European ports, and it is about thirty per cent. cheaper to ship goods from New York to Europe, and from there to South America, than by way of Aspinwall and Panama. Passenger fares as well as freight are subject to this discrimination. One can go from Valparaiso to Europe *via* the Strait of Magellan—a voyage of forty-one days—cheaper than to Panama—a voyage of twenty days, which ought to be made in ten. It costs about ten cents per mile on a steamer from Valparaiso to the Isthmus, to California, or to New York, and about two cents a mile to Europe. As if this were not enough, the steamship company, a British corporation which controls navigation on the west coast, arranges its time-tables so as not to connect with the New York steamers at the Isthmus, and its steamers usually arrive at Panama the day after the Pacific Mail ship leaves Aspinwall, so as to subject the traveller to the expense and annoyance of ten days' delay on the fever-haunted Chagres. Freight and mails receive the same treatment, and every possible obstacle is raised to divert trade from the United States to Europe.

Valparaiso means "the Vale of Paradise," but somehow or other there was a misconception in this particular, for there is no vale and no symptoms of Paradise. An almost perpendicular mountain ridge forms a crescent around the bay, towards the shores of which descend steep, rocky escarpments. Here and there watercourses have furrowed ravines, or barancas, as they are called, which offer the only means of reaching the outer world. Along the narrow strip of sand which lies between the sea and the cliffs the town stretches three or four miles. In some places there is width enough for only a single street, at others for three or four running parallel to each other, but they only extend a few blocks. The one street, the only artery of commerce in Valparaiso, is "the Calle Victoria," stretching around the entire harbor, and skirted by all the banks and hotels, the counting-houses of the wholesale firms, the shops of the retailers, the Government buildings, and the fine private residences. The rocky cliffs have been terraced as the town has grown, and the city now extends back upon the hills a long distance, one man's house being above another's, and reached by stairways, winding roads, and steam "lifts," which carry passengers up inclined planes, like those at Niagara and Pittsburg. What roads there are were laid out by the goats that formerly fed upon the mountain side, and these twist about in the most confusing and circuitous fashion. One has to stop and pant for breath as he climbs them, and an alpenstock is needed in coming down. The hacks in Valparaiso have three horses attached to them, and the teaming is done in carts drawn by four oxen.

An evening view of Valparaiso from a steamer in the bay is quite novel, as the lines of lights, one above the other, give the appearance of a city turned up on end. Electric lamps are placed upon the crests of the cliffs, throwing their rays over into the streets and upon the terraces below with the effect of moonlight. During the day, however, the irregular rows of houses, of different shapes and elevations, clinging to the precipices, look as if a strong wind might blow them overboard, or an earthquake shake them off into the bay.

The business portion of Valparaiso along the beach shows some fine architecture, more elaborate than is to be seen elsewhere in Central and South America, there being a rivalry in handsomely carved façades and other adornments. The shops and stores are as large, and contain as complete an assortment of goods, as those in any city in the world. There is no city in the United States having the population of Valparaiso (125,000) with so many fine shops, and such a display of costly and luxurious articles. The people are wealthy and prosperous, the foreign element is large and rich, and the place is famous, as is Santiago, the capital, for the extravagance of its citizens. Some of the private residences are palatial in their proportions and equipments, and millions of dollars are represented under the roofs of bankers and merchants. There are clubs as fine as the average in New York or London, public reading-rooms, libraries, picture-galleries, and all the elements which go to make up modern civilization. The parks and plazas are filled with beautiful fountains, and with statuary of bronze and marble, much of which, to the shame of Chili, was stolen from the public and private gardens of Peru during the late war. The Custom-house is being torn away to give place to a magnificent monument to Arthur Pratt, an Irish hero of that struggle. Pratt's reckless courage made him the ideal of all that is great and noble in the mind of the Chillanos, who have erected a monument to his memory in nearly every town. Streets and shops, saloons, mines, opera-houses, and even lotteries are named in his honor, and the greatest national tribute is to destroy the old custom-house in order to erect his monument in the most conspicuous place in the principal city.

The oddest thing to be seen in Valparaiso is the female street-car conductors. The street-car managers of Chili have added another occupation to the list of those in which women may engage. The experiment was first tried during the war with Peru, when all the able-bodied men were sent to the army, and proved so successful that their employment has become permanent, to the advantage, it is said, of the companies, the women, and the public. The first impression one forms of a woman with a bell-punch taking up fares is not favorable, but the stranger soon becomes accustomed to this as to all other novelties, and concludes that it is not such a bad idea after all. The street-cars are double-deckers, with seats upon the roof as well as within, and the driver occupies a perch on the rear platform, taking the fare as the passenger enters. The Chillano is a rough individual; he is haughty, arrogant, impertinent, and abusive. There is more intemperance in Chili than in any other of the South American States, and consequently more quarrels and murders, but the female conductors are seldom disturbed in the discharge of their duties, and when they are, the rule is to call upon the policemen,

VICTORIA STREET, VALPARAISO.

who stand at every corner, to eject the obstreperous passenger.

Street-car riding is a popular amusement with the young men about town. Those who make a business of flirting with the conductors are called "mosquitoes" in local parlance, because they swarm so thickly around the cars, and are so great a nuisance. Not long ago a comic paper printed a cartoon in which some of the best-known faces of the swells of Valparaiso appeared on the bodies of mosquitoes swarming around the car of "Conductor 97," who had the reputation of being the prettiest girl on the line. This put a stop to the practice for a while, and caused some of the fashionable young men to retire to the country, but it was soon resumed again. The conductors, or conductresses, are usually young, and sometimes quite pretty, being commonly of the mixed race—of Spanish and Indian blood. They wear a neat uniform of blue flannel, with a jaunty Panama hat, and a many-pocketed white pinafore, reaching from the breast to the ankles, and trimmed with dainty frills. In these pockets they carry small change and tickets, while hanging to a strap over their shoulders is a little shopping-bag, in which is a lunch, a pocket-handkerchief, and surplus money and tickets. Each passenger, when paying his fare, receives a yellow paper ticket, numbered, which he is expected to destroy. The girls are charged with so many tickets, and when they report at headquarters are expected to return money for all that are missing, any deficit being deducted from their wages, which are twenty-five dollars per month.

The women of Chili are not so pretty as their sisters in Peru. They are generally larger in feature and figure, have not the dainty feet and supple grace of the Lima belles, and lack their voluptuous languor. In Valparaiso half the ladies are of the Saxon type, and blonde hair looks grateful when one has seen nothing but midnight tresses for months. Here, too, modern costumes are worn more generally than in other South American countries, and the shops are full of Paris bonnets. But the black manta, with its fringe of lace, is still common enough to be considered the costume of the country, and is always worn to mass in the morning. The manta is becoming to almost everybody. It hides the defects of homely forms and figures, and heightens grace and beauty. It makes an old woman look young, a stout woman appears more slender under its graceful folds, and even a skeleton would look coquettish when wrapped in the rich embroidery which some bear.

In Chili mantas and skirts of white flannel are worn by *penitentas*—women who have committed sin, and thus advertise their penitence, or those who have taken some holy vow to get a measure nearer heaven, and who go about the street with downcast eyes, looking at nothing and recognizing no one. They hover around the churches, and sit for hours crouched before some saint or crucifix. In the great cathedral at Santiago and in the smaller churches everywhere these penitentas, in their snow-white garments, are always to be seen on their knees, or posing in other uncomfortable postures, looking like statues. They cluster in groups around the confessionals, waiting to receive absolution from some fat and burly father, that they may rid their bodies of the mark of penitence they carry, and their souls of sin. Ladies of high social position and great wealth are commonly found among the penitentas, as well as young girls of beauty and winning grace. The women of Chili are as pious as the men are proud, and this method of securing absolution is quite fashionable. Souls that cannot be purged by this penitential dress retire to a convent in the outskirts of the city, called the Convent of the Penitentes, where they scourge themselves with whips, mortify the flesh with sackcloth, sleep in ashes and upon stone floors, and feed themselves on mouldy crusts, until the priests by whose advice they go give them absolution. They are usually women who have been unfaithful to their marriage vows, or girls who have yielded to temptation. After the society season and the carnivals, at the end of the summer, when people return from the fashionable resorts, and at the beginning of Lent, these places are full. For those whose sins have been too great to be washed out by this process, whose shame has been published to the world, and who are unfitted under social laws to associate with the pure, other convents are open as a refuge. Young mothers without husbands are here cared for, and their babes are taken to an orphan asylum in the neighborhood, to be reared by the nuns for the priesthood and other religious orders.

It was from one of these places that the famous Henry Meiggs got his second wife, and the adventure is still related with great gusto by the gossips of Chili. An American dentist named Robinson lived in the same block on which the convent was situated, and from the roof of his house the garden of the nuns was plainly visible. Boccaccio never told a more romantic tale, for it involved notes tied to stones and thrown into the garden, rope-ladders, excited nuns, infuriated parents, and an outraged Church. But the adventure was followed by forgiveness and marriage, and the widow now lives in Santiago, in the luxury which her legacy from the great railroad contractor provides.

In the orphan asylum at Santiago there are said to be two thousand children of unknown parentage, supported by the Church, and this in a city of two hundred thousand people. There is a very convenient mode for the disposition of foundlings. In the rear wall surrounding the place is an aperture, with a wooden box or cradle which swings out and in. A mother who has no use for her baby goes there at night, places the little one in the cradle, swings it inside, and the nuns on guard hearing a bell that rings automatically, take the infant to the nursery. The next morning the mother, if she has no occupation to detain her, applies for employment as a wetnurse. However this plan may be regarded by stern moralists, it is certainly an improvement on infanticide, a crime almost unknown in Chili. But one may hunt the country over to find a house of correction for men. Sin, shame, and penitence appear to be the exclusive attributes of the weaker sex. Men are never seen at the confessional; they never wear white wrappings to advertise their guilt; and at mass in the morning the average attendance is about one man to every hundred women.

Santiago is reached from Valparaiso by a railway which is run on the English plan, and is similar in its equipment and system of management to those of Europe. The scenery along the line is picturesque, the snow-caps of the Andean peaks being constantly in view, and Aconcagua, the highest mountain on this hemisphere, can be seen nearly the entire distance. A few miles from Valparaiso, and the first station on the road, is Vin del Mar, the Long Branch of Chili, where many of the wealthy residents of the country have fine establishments, and usually spend the summer. It is by far the most modern and elegant fashionable resort in South America, and reminds one of the popular haunts along the Mediterranean. The journey to Santiago is made in about five hours, and one is agreeably surprised when he arrives to find in the capital of Chili one of the finest cities on the continent.

Although the climate of Santiago is similar to that of Washington or St. Louis, the people have a notion that fires in their houses are unhealthful, and, except in those built by English or American residents, there is nothing like a grate or a stove to be found. Everybody wears the warmest sort of underclothing, and heavy wraps in-doors and out. The people spend six months of the year in a perpetual shiver, and the remainder in a perpetual perspiration. It looks rather odd to see civilized people sitting in a parlor, surrounded by every possible luxury that wealth can bring (except fire) wrapped in furs and rugs, with blue noses and chattering teeth, when coal is cheap, and the mountains are covered with timber. But nothing can convince a Chillano that artificial heat is healthful, and during the winter, which is the rainy season, he has not the wit to warm his chilled body. It is odd, too, to see in the streets men wearing fur caps, and with their throats wrapped in heavy mufflers, while the women who walk beside them have nothing on their heads at all. During the morning, while on the way from mass, or while shopping, the women wear the manta, as they do in Peru, but in the afternoons, on the promenade, or when riding, they go bareheaded. Although the prevailing diseases are pneumonia and other throat and lung complaints, and during the winter the mortality from these causes is immense, the Chillano persists in believing that artificial heat poisons the atmosphere; and when he visits the home of a foreigner, and finds a fire, he will ask that the door be left ajar, so that he may be as chilly as usual. At fashionable gatherings, dinner-parties, and that sort of thing, I have seen women in full evening-dress with bare arms and shoulders, with the temperature of the room between forty and fifty Fahrenheit. They often carry into the *salon* or dining-room their fur wraps, and wear them at the table, while at every chair is a foot-warmer of thick llama wool, into which they poke their dainty slippered toes. These foot-warmers are ornamental as well as useful, have embroidered cases, and are manufactured at home, or can be purchased of the nuns, who spend much of their time in needle-work.

Every lady seen on the street in the morning carries a prayer-rug, often handsomely embroidered, which she kneels upon at mass to protect her limbs from the damp stone floors of the churches, in which there are never any pews. It used to be the proper thing to have a servant follow my lady, bearing her rug and prayer-book, but that fashion has now become obsolete.

The shops do not open until nine or ten o'clock in the morning, close from five to seven to allow the proprietors and clerks to dine, and are then open again until midnight, as between eight and eleven o'clock at night most of the retail trading is done. The finest shops are in the arcades or *portales*, like the Palais Royal in Paris, and are brilliantly lighted with electricity. Here the ladies gather, swarming around the pretty goods like bees around the flowers, and of course the haughty and impertinent dons come also to stare at them. It seems to be considered a compliment, a mark of admiration, to stare at a woman, for she never turns away. To these nightly gatherings come all who have nothing serious to detain them, and the flirtations begun at the portales are the curse of the women of Santiago. It is not rude to address a lady who has returned your glance, and while she may repulse her admirer, she will nevertheless boast of the attention as a pronounced form of flattery.

The shops are full of the prettiest sorts of goods, the most expensive diamonds, jewellery, and laces. The Santiagoans boast that everything that can be found in Paris can be purchased there, and one easily believes it to be true. There is plenty of money in Chili; the people have a refined taste and luxurious habits. Many of the private houses are palatial, and the toilets of the women are superb. The equipages to be seen in Santiago are equal to those of New York or London, and the Alameda, on pleasant afternoons, is crowded with handsome carriages, with liveried coachmen and footmen, like Central Park or Rotten Row.

The Alameda is six hundred feet in width, broken by four rows of poplar-trees, and stretches the full length of the city—four miles—from "Santa Lucia" to the Exposition Park and Horticultural Gardens. In the centre is a promenade, while on either side is a drive-way one hundred feet wide. The promenade is dotted with a line of statues representing the famous men or commemorating the famous events in the history of Chili, a country which has assassinated or sent into exile some of her noblest sons, but never fails to perpetuate their memory in bronze or marble. On the Alameda, from three to five o'clock every afternoon during the season, several military bands are placed at intervals of half a mile or so, and the music calls out all the population to walk or drive. During the summer the music is given in the evening instead of the afternoon, when the portales are deserted for the out-door promenade.

Fronting the Alameda are the finest palaces in the city, magnificent dwellings of carved sandstone often one or two hundred feet square, with the invariable patio and its fountains and flowers in the centre. Houses which cost half a million dollars to build and a quarter of a million to furnish

SANTA LUCIA.

are common; and there are some even more expensive. The former residence of the late Henry Meiggs, surrounded by a forest of foliage and a beautiful garden, stands in the centre of a park eight hundred feet square. It is a conspicuous example of extravagance, having cost a mint of money, every timber and brick and tile being imported at enormous expense. It is at present unoccupied, and in a state of decay, there being no one, since the death of Meiggs, with the courage or the means to sustain such grandeur. But though the nabobs seek the boulevard of the city to display their wealth and architectural taste, some of the side streets have residences quite as grand, and even more aristocratic. These more retired quarters have an air of gentility which the Alameda has not acquired—a sort of established aristocratic repose—a riper, richer, and more honorable quiet, that suggests something of social distinction and haughty exclusiveness, venerable solitude and commercial solidity. Another monument to the extravagance of men is known as "O'Brien's Folly." It is a magnificent structure, modelled after a Turkish palace, and its cost was fabulous. The owner was an Irish adventurer, who discovered one of the richest silver mines in Chili, and who lived like a prince until his money was gone. His castle is now unoccupied, and he is again in the mountains prospecting for another fortune.

"Santa Lucia" is the most beautiful place I have seen in South America. It is a pile of rocks six hundred feet high, cast by some volcanic agency into the centre of the great plain on which the city stands. It was here that the United States Astronomical Expedition of 1852, under Lieutenant Gillis, made observations. Before that time, and as far back as the Spanish Invasion, it was a magnificent fortress, commanding the entire valley with its guns. Tradition has it that the King of the Araucanians had a stronghold here before the Spaniards came. After the departure of the United States expedition Vicunæ McCenna, a public-spirited man of wealth in Santiago, undertook the work of beautifying the place. By the aid of private subscriptions, and much of his own means, he sought all the resources that taste could suggest and money reach to improve on nature's grandeur. His success was complete. Winding walks and stairways, parapets and balconies, grottoes and flower-beds, groves of trees and vine-hung arbors, follow one another from the base to the summit; while upon the west, at the edge of a precipice eight hundred feet high, are a miniature castle and a lovely little chapel, in whose crypt Vicunæ McCenna has asked that his bones be laid. Below the chapel, three or four hundred feet on the opposite side of the hill, is a level place on which a restaurant and an out-door theatre have been erected. Here, on summer nights, come the population of the city to eat ices, drink beer, and laugh at the farces played upon the stage, while bands of music and dancing make the people merry. This is the resort of the aristocracy. The poor people go to Cousino Park, at the other end of the Alameda, drink *chicha*, and dance the *cuaca* (pronounced *quaker*), the Chillano national dance.

THE ZAMA-CUACA.

The cuaca is a sort of can-can, except that it is decent, and the men instead of the girls do the high kicking. But when the dancers are under the influence of chicha—that liquor which tastes like hard cider, but is ninety per cent. alcohol—skirts and modesty are no impediments to the success of the dance. The couples pair off and face each other, while on benches near by are women thrumming guitars and singing a wild barbaric air in polka time. Each woman and man has a handkerchief which he or she waves in the air, and they sway around in postures that are intended to show the grace and suppleness of the performer, and often do. The dance usually ends with a wild carousal, in which men and women mingle promiscuously, embrace each other, and then go off to the chicha bars to get stimulants for the next. It is common in fashionable society to end the tertulias with the cuaca, as in the United States with the ancient "Virginia reel;" and if the young people are unusually hilarious, scenes occur which watchful dowagers desire to prevent. School-girls at the convents dance the cuaca when the nuns will allow them; and although in its ordinary form it is not nearly so immodest as some of our dances, license has been taken so often as to bring it into disrepute. One evening at the opera a pretty married woman was pointed out as the most graceful and agile cuaca dancer in Chili, and it was asserted that she could throw her heels higher than her head.

At the other end of the Alameda are the Exposition grounds and Horticultural gardens, laid out in good style, and improved to the highest degree of landscape architecture. There is a fine stone and glass building, a miniature copy of the Crystal Palace in London, used as the National Museum of Chili, whose contents were mostly stolen from Peru during the late war. A zoological garden has been added, to exhibit the animals brought from Peru, like the curiosities of the museum, as contraband of war. The elephant died from the severity of the climate, two of the lions are missing from the same cause, and the rest of the menagerie are suffering from exposure and cold to which they are unaccustomed.

The opera-house at Santiago is owned by the city, and is claimed to be the finest structure of the sort in all America. It certainly surpasses in size, arrangement, and gorgeousness any we have in the United States. It is built upon the European plan, with four balconies, three of which are divided off into boxes upholstered in the most luxurious manner. The balconies are supported by brackets, so that there are no pillars to obstruct the view. Under the direction of the mayor, each year, the boxes are sold at auction for the season, and the receipts given, in whole or in part, as a subsidy to the opera management.

EXPOSITION BUILDING, SANTIAGO.

Everywhere one goes in Santiago and other cities in Chili are to be seen the ornaments of which Peru was so mercilessly plundered—statuary and fountains, ornamental street-lamps, benches of carved stone in the parks and the Alameda, and almost everything that beautifies the streets. Transports that were sent up to Callao with troops brought back cargoes of pianos, pictures, furniture, books, and articles of household decoration stolen from the homes of the Peruvians. Lampposts torn up from their foundations, pretty iron fences and images from the cemeteries, altar equipments of silver from the churches, statuary from the parks and streets, and everything that the hands of thieves and vandals could reach, were stolen. Clocks—one of which now gives time to the marketplace of Santiago—were taken from the steeples of the churches, and even the effigies of saints were lifted from the altars and stripped of the embroideries and jewels they had received from their devotees. In the courtyard of the post-office at Santiago are two statues of marble which cause the American tourist to start in surprise, for George Washington and Abraham Lincoln stand like unexpected ghosts before him. Their presence is not announced in any of the guide-books, which is accounted for by the fact that they, like most everything else of the kind in Chili, were brought from Peru.

The new hotel, in the eyes of foreigners who have been compelled to stop at the old ones, is the finest ornament in Santiago. It is a magnificent structure, with three hundred thousand dollars' worth of furniture from Paris, and a five thousand dollar cook from the same place. All the rooms have grates for fires—which is an innovation—and are furnished as handsomely as any of the hotels in New York, while the restaurant is as good as Delmonico's. Of course there must be some oddity about the place—it would not be suited to the country if there were not—and here it is that the bar is placed in the café where the ladies lunch. It is the only hotel bar in South America; and the proprietor, who wanted to introduce all the modern improvements, was rather bewildered in selecting the location of this one. It is a gorgeous affair of silver and crystal, and the ladies admire it as much as do the men. At first they were disposed to walk up and say, "The same for me, if you please," with their brothers and husbands, but have been convinced that the proper form is to sit at the tables and take their drinks there. To see a lady drinking a cocktail in the bar-room of the Grand Central of Santiago may startle the prohibitionist who goes there, but it is quite as much the fashion as is the sucking of mint-juleps through a straw on the balconies of a Long Branch hotel.

The Chillano is the Yankee of South America—the most active, enterprising, ingenious, and thrifty of the Spanish-American race—aggressive, audacious, and arrogant, quick to perceive, quick to resent, fierce in disposition, cold-blooded, and cruel as a cannibal. He dreams of conquest. He has only a strip of country along the Pacific coast, so narrow that there is scarcely room enough to write its name upon the map, hemmed in on the one side by the eternal snows that crown the Cordilleras, and on the other side by six thousand miles of sea. He has been stretching himself northward until he has stolen all the sea-coast of Bolivia, with her valuable nitrate deposits, all the guano that belonged to Peru, and contemplates soon taking actual possession of both those republics. He has been reaching southward by diplomacy as he did northward by war; and under a recent treaty with the Argentine Republic he has divided Patagonia with that nation, taking to himself the control of that valuable international highway, the Strait of Magellan, and the unexplored country between the Andes and the ocean, with thousands of islands along the Pacific coast whose resources are unknown. By securing the strait, Chili acquired control of steam navigation in the South Pacific, and has established a colony and fortress at Punta Arenas by which all vessels must pass.

Reposing tranquilly now in the enjoyment of the newly acquired territory along the Bolivian and Peruvian border, and deriving an enormous revenue from the export tax upon nitrate, the Chillano contemplates the internal dissensions of Peru, and waits anxiously for the time when he can step in as arbitrator and, like the lawyer, take the estate that the heirs are silly enough to quarrel over. It is but a question of years when not only Peru but Bolivia will become a part of Chili; when the aggressive nation will want to push her eastern boundary back of the Andes, and secure control of the sources of the Amazon, as she has of the navigation of the strait.

On the beautiful Alameda of Santiago stands a marble monument erected several years ago, after the partition of Patagonia, to commemorate the generosity of the Argentine Republic. That statue will some day be pulled down by a mob. The people are already regretting the impulsive cordiality which suggested it, and are looking with jealous eyes at the progress and prosperity of their eastern neighbor. But Chili will find in the Argentines a more formidable foe than the nation has yet met, and her generals will have some of the conceit taken out of them if the armies of the two ever come into collision. Although the Argentine Republic is making more rapid strides towards national greatness, there is no

STATUE OF BERNARD O'HIGGINS, SANTIAGO.

doubt that at present, in all the conditions of modern civilization, Chili leads the Southern Continent, and is the most powerful of all the republics in America except our own. Her statesmen are wise and able, her people are industrious and progressive, and have that strength of mind and muscle which is given only to the men of temperate zones. There is a strong similarity between the Chillanos and the Irish. Both have the same wit and reckless courage, the same love of country and patriotic pride; and wherever a Chillano goes he carries his opinion that there never was and never can be a better land than that in which he was born; and although he may be a refugee or an exile, he will fight in defence of Chili at the drop of the hat. There is something refreshing in his patriotism, even if it be the most arrogant vanity. Our people are becoming ashamed of their Fourth of July, and the Declaration of Independence is the butt of professional jokers. The Chillano will cut the throat of a man who will not celebrate with him the 18th of September, his Independence Day; and there is a law in the country requiring every house to have a flag-staff, and every flag-staff to bear the national colors—a banner by day and a lantern by night—on the anniversaries of the republic. All the schools must use text-books by native authors, all the bands play the compositions of native composers, and visiting opera and concert singers are compelled to vary their performances by introducing the songs of the country. It is said that a Frenchman can never be denationalized. The same is true of the Chillano. There has not been a successful revolution in Chili since 1839; and although there is nowhere a more unruly and discordant people, nowhere so much murder and other serious crimes, in their love of country the haughty don and the patient peon, the hunted bandit and the cruel soldier, are one.

PATRICK LYNCH.

Many of the leading men of Chili are and have been of Irish descent. Barney O'Higgins was the liberator, the George Washington of the republic, and Patrick Lynch was the foremost soldier of Chili in the late war. The O'Learys and McGarrys and other Chillano-Irish families are prominent in politics and war and trade. There is a sympathetic bond between the shamrock and the condor, and nowhere in South America does the Irish emigrant so prosperously thrive. Chillano wit is proverbial. The jolly, care-for-nothing peasant is the same there as upon the old sod, and the turgid, grandiloquent style of literature which prevails in other portions of Spanish-America in Chili finds a substitute in the soul-stirring, fervid oratory which is one of the gifts of the Irish race. A Chillano driver who was beating a mule was remonstrated with. The man looked up and remarked that it was the most obstinate animal he ever drove. "The beast thinks he ought to have been a bishop," he said.

The vanity of the Chillano passes all comprehension. The officers of the army and navy actually offered their services, through the British minister, to England when there was a rumor of war with Russia; and with the slightest encouragement they would be willing to take the domestic as well as the international complications off the hands of the British cabinet. One day the English paper at Valparaiso published a satire, announcing that the Lords of the Admiralty had selected three leading Chillano naval officers to command the Bosporus, the Baltic, and the North Atlantic fleets. The officers as well as the people would not accept the bogus cablegram as a joke until the next issue of the paper, in which it was explained; and the former were actually polishing up their swords and uniforms to take their new commands.

The Chillano is not only vain but cruel—as cruel as death. He carries a long curved knife, called a *curvo*, as the Italian carries a stiletto and the negro a razor, and uses it to cut throats. He never fights with his fists, and knows not the use of the shillalah; he never carries a revolver, and is nothing of a thug; but as a robber or bandit, in a private quarrel or a public mob, he always uses this deadly knife, and springs at the throat of his enemy like a blood-hound. There is scarcely an issue of a daily paper without one or two throat-cutting incidents, and in the publications succeeding feast-days or carnivals their bloody annals fill columns.

PEONS OF CHILI.

As a soldier the Chillano is brave to recklessness, and a sense of fear is unknown to him. He will not endure a siege, nor can he be made to fight at long range; but as soon as he sees the enemy he fires one volley, drops his gun, and rushes in with his curvo. His endurance is as great as his courage, and no North American Indian can travel so far without rest or go so long without food and water as the Chillano peon, or *roto*, as the mixed race is called. As the cholo in Peru is the descendant of the Spaniards and the Incas, so is the roto in Chili the child of the Spaniards and the Araucanian Indians, the race of giants with which the early explorers reported that Patagonia was peopled—"Menne of that bigginess," as Sir Francis Drake reported, "that it seemed the trees of the forests were uprooted and were moving away." They have the Spanish tenacity of purpose, the Indian endurance, and the cruelty of both. Each soldier, in the mountains or the desert, carries on his breast two buckskin bags. In one are the leaves of the coca-plant, in the other powdered lime made of the ashes of potato-skins. The coca is the strongest sort of a tonic, and by chewing it the Chillano soldier can abstain from food or drink for a week or ten days at a stretch. He takes a bunch of leaves as big as a quid of tobacco in his mouth, and occasionally mixes the potato-ashes with the saliva to give the juice a relish. Canon Kingsley, in that remarkable novel, "Westward Ho!" describes two of the band of Amyas Leigh as deserting their companions at the sources of the Amazon, and takes them into a beautiful bower with two Dianas of the Indian type. There they chew coca-leaves with the girls, sink into a voluptuous stupor, and give themselves up to love, like the lotos-eaters, until Amyas comes to remonstrate. The men recommend him to follow their example with the Venus who has been found in an Indian queen and admires the young commander; and the Puritan is on the point of yielding to the fascination of the scene, when a reptile comes, strangles one of the girls, and revives the moral instincts of the men. The reverend word-painter was misinformed as to the peculiar influence of the drug, as it does not produce a stupor in those who use it. It is not a narcotic, but a stimulant.

The Chillano soldier is not easily subjected to discipline, and outvandals the Vandals in the destruction of property, as the present condition of Peru will prove. He burns and destroys everything within his reach that has sheltered an enemy. No authority can restrain his hand. The awful scenes of devastation that took place have nothing to parallel them in the annals of modern warfare. On the battle-fields nine-tenths of the dead were found with their throats cut, and the Chillanos took no prisoners except when a whole army capitulated. They ask no quarter and give none. The knowledge of this characteristic, and the fear of the Chillano knife, were powerful factors in the subjugation of the more humane Peruvians.

The Chillanos are cruel to beasts as well as to men. Horses are very cheap in Chili. A good native broncho can be purchased for five dollars, and his owner knows no mercy. The beasts are driven until they drop, and then new ones are sought and subjected to the same treatment. No care is taken to protect or make the animals comfortable. Although the weather is usually cold, stables for horses or cattle are almost unknown. When their labor is over they are turned into a corral, or a pasture, or the street, to seek their own food.

The Chillanos are also careless of machinery. While they are quick to learn, and have much native mechanical ingenuity, they cannot be trusted as machinists. The magnificent cruiser *Esmeralda*, one of the finest ships-of-war afloat, was built in England for the Chillian Government at a cost of one and a half million dollars, but she had not been in the hands of native engineers six weeks before her engines needed repairs and her boilers were ruined. In 1885, during the troubles between England and Russia, she was chartered by the British Government, but afterwards returned to Chili. The Chillanos have a line of steamers running from Valparaiso up and down the coast. They are the finest ships on the Pacific, built on the Clyde, with all modern improvements, but the engineers and captains are Englishmen or Scotchmen. The Government owns and manages the railroads in the republic, but the locomotive drivers are foreigners. Every three or four years—usually before a Presidential election—these men are discharged and natives employed in their stead; but until election is over, and the old engineers are restored to their places, there is a carnival of accidents, and passenger travel is practically suspended. On all railroads are heavy grades and dangerous curves, requiring the greatest care on the part of locomotive drivers. The reckless Chillano thinks it great fun to run a train down a grade at full speed, and a collision is his delight. He enjoys seeing things smashed up, and knows nothing of the necessity of operating trains on schedule time.

THE "ESMERALDA."

In trade the Chillano is a Yankee. At market or in the native shops the buyer is not expected to pay the price first asked. He is expected to enter into a *negotio*, and the seller is disappointed if he loses an opportunity to show his shrewdness in the barter. There is no regularly established price for any article. A market-woman will ask two dollars for a basket of fruit for which she expects to get fifty cents. She will haggle and chatter, plead and remonstrate, and if you start towards another stall, will abandon half a dozen other customers and follow you around, until she finally "splits the difference," and goes away smiling at her success. The traveller meets with this experience everywhere, particularly at the posadas; and the only safe way to avoid being mercilessly swindled is to make a bargain in writing beforehand.

Most of the hotel-keepers are women, whose husbands are engaged in other occupations; but all the servants, including the cooks and chamber-"maids," are men. There are better cooks and better classes of food than in other South American countries, and one seldom fails to find a good inn even in the country villages. The markets of Chili, too, are better. The beef, mutton, and other meats have the flavor that is found only in temperate climates; the fish are not so rank and coarse as those caught in tropical waters; and while vegetation is not so prolific, the fruits of the earth have a finer taste. There are oysters equal to those of New Orleans or Mobile, clams and lobsters, and plenty of shrimps, called *camarons*.

Another oddity is the milk stations. At distances of a few blocks on all but the principal business streets is a platform where a cow is tied, which is milked to order by a dairy-maid whenever a customer calls. On a table near by are found measures, cans, and glasses, and often a bottle of brandy, so that a thirsty man can mix a glass of punch if he chooses. In the morning these stands are surrounded by servants from the aristocratic houses, women and children, with cups and buckets, awaiting their turn; and as fast as one cow is exhausted another is driven upon the platform.

The scarcity of lumber has caused the poorer classes to use corrugated sheet-iron as a building material, while the rich use stone for exterior walls, and sun-dried brick or adobe for partitions. There are whole blocks in Valparaiso in which nothing but corrugated-iron houses can be seen, both roof and walls being of the same material. It is said to bear the effects of earthquakes well. People expect an earthquake about once in ten days the year round, and more frequently during the changes of season; but great damage is seldom done. There are two kinds of earthquake, the *terremoto* and the *temblor*. The latter is only a quivering or shaking of the ground, and is quite common; the other describes the convulsions of the earth when it cracks and rolls like the swell of the sea, overthrows cities, and buries towns in their own ruins. Valparaiso and Santiago have never known any of the latter sort, which are confined to the mountain districts and the neighborhood of volcanoes.

There are more comforts among the people than elsewhere upon the continent, and a higher degree of taste, as is shown by the articles offered for sale in the shops as well as in the houses of the residents, which is owing in a great degree to the example of the large foreign population. The Rev. Dr. Trumbull, who has been in Chili forty-five years, says that he has noticed a marked change in this respect within the last decade, and has seen a gradual and permanent growth in refinement and honesty.

In Chili, as in all the Spanish-American countries, every man and woman is named after the saint whose anniversary is nearest the day on which he or she was born, and that saint is expected to look after the welfare of those christened in his or her honor. These names sound well in Spanish, but when they come to be translated into unpoetic English there is an oddity, and often something comical, about them. For example, the name of the recent President of Chili is Domingo Santa Maria—which, being interpreted, means Sunday St. Mary. The name of the President of Ecuador is Jesus Mary Caamaño (apple), and that of the Governor of the Province of Valparaiso is Domingo Torres (Sunday Bull). A waiter at the hotel happened to be a Christmas gift to his parents, whose family name was Vaca (cow), and in honor of the day they called him Jesu Christo Vaca. Such blasphemy would not be tolerated in any other country; but the use of the Saviour's name is very common, even upon the signs of stores and saloons in cities, and in the nomenclature of the streets. I met a girl once whose name was Dolores Digerier (sorrowful stomach).

In Chili women are employed not only as street-car conductors, but they do all the street-cleaning, and gangs of them with willow brooms sweeping the dirt into the ditches can be seen by any one who has curiosity enough to get up at daylight. They occupy the markets, too, selling meats as well as vegetables. On the streets they keep fruit-stands, and have canvas awnings under which, if you choose, you can sit and eat watermelons, a fruit much esteemed in Chili. Outside of the cities the women keep the shops and the drinking-places, and do all the garden work. The laundry work is done at public fountains, as in other of the Spanish-American countries; but the washer-women of Chili do not go almost naked, as some of their neighbors do.

The native Peruvian, the descendant of the ancient Incas, has learned nothing since the Conquest, and has forgotten most of the arts his fathers knew, among them being the process by which the ancient race rendered copper as hard as steel. Thousands of dollars have been offered for that secret by modern bidders, but it is lost forever, and the ingenuity and knowledge of modern chemists cannot discover the process. The modern Inca wears the same blanket, or poncho, made of vicuña hair, that his fathers did, and the same shoes made of raw hide. He has rougher roads to travel than has the native of Central America, hence his shoe is made to curl over on the sides and behind, so as to protect the toes and the heel from contact with the rocks. It is cut in a single piece from hide when green, and is made to curl by stretching it over a primitive sort of last and keeping it in position until dry. The shoe is attached to the foot by a thong, which passes along the entire top of the shoe, laced through holes cut in the hide, and ending at the heel in two strips, which are secured around the ankle. The evolution of the native shoe is found in Chili; and although it lacks the maturity and sanctity of age, which the Peruvian article enjoys, is a rather more nobby

INCA QUEEN AND PRINCESS.

affair. The sole is made of wood, rudely cut by hand with a knife, and over the instep passes a piece of patent leather reaching from the toes to the ankle, which is nailed to the sole by rows of brass-headed tacks. The toes and heel are entirely without protection, and it requires a great deal of experience to keep the shoe on. It is worn in the coldest weather, over a very heavy and thick stocking knit of llama wool, and an uglier pair of feet and legs than are shown by the short-skirted peasant women of Chili were never seen. The men wear the same sort of shoe—not quite so fancy in design nor of such fine materials, however; but as they spend most of their time in the saddle it is not so bad.

The Crœsus of South America is a woman, Donna Isadora Cousino, of Santiago, Chili, and there are few men or women in the world richer than she. There is no end to her money and no limit to her extravagance, and the people call her the Countess of Monte Cristo. She traces her ancestry back to the days of the Conquest, and has the record of the first of her fathers who landed early on the shores of the New World. His family was already famous, for his sire fought under the ensign of the Arragons before the alliance with Castile. But the branch of the family that remained in Spain was lost in the world's great shuffle two or three centuries ago, and none of them distinguished themselves sufficiently to get their portraits into the collection which Señora Cousino has made of the lineage she claims.

Like her own, the ancestors of her late husband came over in the early days, and in the partition of the lands and spoils of the Conquest both got a large share, which they kept and increased by adding the portions given to their less thrifty and less enterprising associates, until the two estates became the largest, most productive, and most valuable of all the haciendas of Chili, and were finally united into one by the marriage, twenty-four years ago, of the late Don and his surviving widow. While he lived he was considered the richest man in Chili, and she the richest woman, for their property was kept separate, the husband managing his estate and the wife her own, and the people say that she was altogether the better "administrator" of the two. This fact he acknowledged in his will when he bequeathed all of his possessions to her, and piled his Pelion upon her Ossa; so that she has millions of acres of land, millions of money; flocks and herds that are numbered by the hundreds of thousands; coal, copper, and silver mines; acres of real estate in the cities of Santiago and Valparaiso; a fleet of iron steamships, smelting-works, a railroad, and various other trifles in the way of productive property, which yield her an income of several millions a year that she tries very hard to spend, and under the circumstances succeeds as well as could be expected. From her coal-mines alone Señora Cousino has an income of eighty thousand dollars a month; and there is no reason why this should not be perpetual, as they are the only source in all South America from which fuel can be obtained, and those who do not buy of her have to import their coal from Great Britain. She has a fleet of eight iron steamships, of capacities varying from two thousand to three thousand six hundred tons, which were built in England, and are used to carry the coal up the coast as far as Panama, and around the Strait of Magellan to Buenos Ayres and Montevideo. At Lota she has copper and silver smelting-works, besides coal-mines, and her coaling ships bring ore down the coast as a return cargo from upper Chili, Peru, and

Ecuador; while those that go to Buenos Ayres bring back beef and flour and merchandise for the consumption of her people.

Although Lota is only a mining town, as dirty and smoky as any of its counterparts in Pennsylvania, it is the widow's favorite place of residence, and she is now building a mansion that will cost at least a million dollars. The architect and the chief builder are Frenchmen, whom she imported from Paris, and much of the material is also imported. Not long ago she shipped a cargo of hides and wool in one of her own steamers to Bordeaux, and it is to return laden with building supplies for this mansion. She herself has no time to go across the sea, but the captain of her ship will bring with him decorators and designers and upholstery men, who will finish the interior of her mansion regardless of expense.

The structure stands in the centre of what is undoubtedly the finest private park in the world—an area of two hundred and fifty acres of land laid out in the most elaborate manner, containing statuary, fountains, caves, cascades, and no end of beautiful trees and plants. The improvement of the natural beauty of the place is said to have cost Señora Cousino nearly a million dollars, and she has a force of thirty gardeners constantly at work. The superintendent is a Scotchman, and he informed me that his orders were to make the place a paradise, without regard to cost. In this park there are many wild animals and domesticated pets, some of which are natives of the country, others imported; and the flowers are something wonderful.

Señora Cousino has another park and palace an hour's drive from Santiago, the finest estancia in Chili, perhaps in all South America; nor do I know of one in North America or Europe that will equal it. This is "Macul," and the estate stretches from the boundaries of the city of Santiago far into the Cordilleras, whose glittering caps of everlasting snow mark the limit of her lands. In the valleys are her fields of grain, her orchards, and her vineyards, while in the foot-hills of the mountains her flocks of sheep and herds of cattle feed. Here she gives employment to three or four hundred men, all organized under the direction of superintendents, most of whom are Scotchmen. She has in her employ at "Macul" one American, whose business is that of a general farmer; but his time is mostly occupied in teaching the natives how to operate labor-saving agricultural machinery.

Farming in Chili is conducted very much as it was in Europe in old feudal times, each estate having its retainers, who are given houses or tenements, and are paid for the amount of labor they perform. It is said that Señora Cousino can marshal a thousand men from her two farms if she needs them. The vineyard of "Macul" supplies nearly all the markets of Chili with claret and sherry wines, and the cellar of the place, an enormous building five hundred feet long by one hundred wide, is kept constantly full. Señora

Cousino makes her own bottles, but imports her labels from France. On this farm she has some very valuable imported stock, both cattle and horses, and her racing stable is the most extensive and successful in South America. She takes great interest in the turf, attends every racing meeting in Chili, and always bets very heavily on her own horses. At the last meeting her winnings are reported to have been over one hundred thousand dollars outside of the purses won by her horses, which are always divided among the employés of the stables.

In addition to "Macul" Señora Cousino has another large estate about thirty miles from Santiago; but she gives it very little attention, and has not been there for a number of years. In the city she has two large and fine houses, one of them being the former residence of Henry Meiggs—the finest in Santiago at the time it was built. All the timber and other materials used in its erection was brought from California. It is built mostly of red cedar. The construction and architecture are after the American plan, and in appearance and arrangement it resembles the villas of Newport.

The other city residence of Señora Cousino is a stone mansion erected on the Spanish plan, with a court in the centre, and is ornamented with some very elaborate carving. The interior was decorated and furnished many years ago by Parisian artists at an enormous cost, and the house is fitting for a king. There is no more elaborate or extensive residence in America, and the money expended upon it would build as fine a house as that of W. H. Vanderbilt in New York. The widow, however, spends but very little time within its walls, as she prefers her home at Lota, where most of her business is.

Her ability as a manager is remarkable, and she directs every detail, receiving weekly reports from ten or twelve superintendents who have immediate charge of affairs. While she is generous to profligacy, she requires a strict account of every dollar earned or spent upon her vast estates, and is very sharp at driving a bargain. One of her Scotch superintendents told me that there was no use in trying to get ahead of the señora. "You cannot move a stone or a stick but she knows it," he said. In addition to her landed property and her mines she owns much city real estate, from which her rentals amount to several hundred thousand dollars a year. She is also the principal stockholder in the largest bank in Santiago. Not long ago she presented the people of that city with a park of one hundred acres, and a race-course adjoining it.

SEÑORA COUSINO.

Fabulous stories of the señora's extravagance are told. A million of dollars is a trifle to a woman whose income is so enormous, and there is nothing in the world that she will not buy if she happens to want it. She does not care much for art, but has a collection of diamonds that is very large and valuable, and she sometimes appears loaded down with them. Usually she looks quite shabby, as she has no taste or ambition for dress, and her party toilets, which are ordered from Paris, are seldom worn. Of late she has been a sufferer from sciatica, which has not only destroyed the señora's own pleasure, but has seriously impaired the comfort of those who have relations with her. Although a comparatively young woman, being somewhere between forty-five and fifty years of age, she declares that she will never marry again; and there is not a man in Chili who has the courage to ask her. Not long since she took a fancy to a young German with a very blond beard and hair, and insisted that he should give up his business and make his home with her. The inducements she offered were sufficient, and for several months the young man has been tied to her apron-strings, having the ostensible employment of a private secretary. But the señora is very fickle, and will probably throw him overboard, as she has many others, when the whim seizes her.

Señora Cousino has two daughters and one son. Neither of the girls inherits her mother's business ability, or at least has not developed it; but they are very popular in society. Señorita Isadora, the elder, has a great deal of musical talent, and performs on the violin and piano. Both are bright and pretty. One is about seventeen, and the other nineteen years of age. Their brother, a young man of twenty-three or twenty-four, will share the property with them. It is quite an unusual thing for a youth with so much money to develop the business capacity and industry which he shows. He looks after the estancia at "Macul," and spends from six to eight hours a day in the saddle, riding about the place. He seldom joins in the festivities that his mother enjoys so much, and is quite pronounced in his disapproval of her extravagance. He is to marry a young lady of rather humble station, and it is expected that the Meiggs mansion, which has been previously described, will be presented to the bride by his mother as a wedding-gift.

The struggle between the Catholic Church and the liberal progressive element in Chili, which has been going on for a number of years, is now at its height. In all of the nations of Central and South America a similar struggle has occurred. In Mexico and all Central America, in Colombia, Venezuela, Peru, Chili, the Argentine Republic, and Uruguay the Liberals are uppermost, and have control of the State. Ecuador and Bolivia are still in the hands of the priests, and are ruled at Rome. But even in these republics there is a growing tendency towards liberalism, and the day will soon arrive when the power of the Church in politics will be overcome, and its authority over temporal affairs denied. The Clerical party is growing in Peru. It has revived during the prostration of that republic, and although the liberal element is still in power, the Government is so weak that it cannot defy the Church as it once could. Therefore, the priests and monks and Jesuits, who were driven out years ago, are returning in large numbers to resume their authority over the common people and intrigue for an administration favorable to them.

In Chili there has been no confiscation of church property, as in some of the other States, and at the capital there are still over two thousand monks and as many nuns. The Jesuits have been expelled for engaging in conspiracy against the Government, but the outer orders of friars are permitted to remain. A dispute between the archbishop and the President some years ago caused the former to retire from Chili, and the Pope sent over a nuncio to try and arrange matters; but this legate criticised the Government so severely from the pulpit that he was given a passport and an escort of military, and now there are no relations whatever between the Pope and Chili, although the Catholic faith is still recognized by the Constitution as the established religion of the republic. The radical element of the Liberal party favors extreme measures, but the Conservative faction, of which Ex-President Santa Maria is the leader, wisely prefers to take steps slowly, and avoid revolution.

The Liberal party has a majority in Congress, and has passed several laws by which the authority and influence of the Church has been greatly crippled. The Liberal majority in Congress has placed the appointment of bishops in the hands of the President of the republic instead of the Pope; it has declared civil marriage to be the only legal one; it has opened the cemeteries to Jew and Gentile; taken the registers of births, marriages, and deaths out of the hands of the Church, and given them to civil magistrates; established non-sectarian schools, and passed a compulsory education law, under which all citizens who send their children to the priests and nuns to be taught have to pay a tax or fine to the State. These measures have all been bitterly fought by the clergy, but they have been compelled to yield in every instance. Just now the last act of Congress in this direction, establishing civil marriage, and recognizing the legitimacy of only those children born of parents wedded in this way, is the bone of contention, and has caused the bitterest struggle which the State has seen.

It formerly cost twenty-five dollars to be married by the Church, and a large part of its revenues came from that source. The peons, who scarcely ever are able to accumulate so much money, therefore lived in a state of concubinage, and more than half the children born in Chili were illegitimate. Now a marriage certificate can be secured from a civil magistrate for twenty-five cents, and persons cohabiting without it are subject to fine and imprisonment. The archbishop has issued a decree excommunicating from the Church all persons who are married by the civil right, and the Catholics of the country, comprising ninety-nine per cent. of the population, are in a serious dilemma. They are compelled to choose between excommunication and imprisonment, and therefore in the upper classes weddings are no longer fashionable. Some people go first to the church and then to the magistrate, and run the risk of excommunication; but the more conscientious prefer to remain single.

Just now in Santiago there is a young man of brilliant attainments, a member of Congress and a leader of the Liberal party, who wants to marry the daughter of a prominent merchant. The engagement has been existing for several years, and both parties are willing to fulfil it according to a civil law; but the girl's mother is a devout Catholic, and will not consent to a wedding without the blessing of a priest. The young man is willing to go to the church as well as to the magistrate, but the archbishop has forbidden any priest to marry him without a full retraction by him of his political record. This he refuses to make, and the couple are preparing to go to the United States or some European country to have the ceremony performed.

Not long ago there was a marriage in high life in one of the southern provinces of Chili, which attracted wide attention from the fact that it was the first defiance of the Church in that part of the country. On the Sunday following the wedding the couple were denounced by the bishop from the pulpit of the cathedral, and the Catholic newspaper published some brutal comments to the effect that the young couple had placed themselves on the level of beasts by cohabiting without the blessing of the Church. The bride's brother belabored the editor so that he will be a cripple for life, and would have given the bishop a similar chastisement had not the latter kept out of the way.

At the last Presidential election, which occurred in June, 1886, Señor Balmaceda, the Liberal candidate, was elected to succeed President Santa Maria, who had served his full term of four years. He was bitterly opposed by the priests, who realized that his success would be their permanent discomfiture, and there were several serious riots, in which many were killed and wounded. But Balmaceda was peacefully inaugurated in September, and the Congress which assembled at the same time has an overwhelming majority in sympathy with the Administration. The issue at the election was the enforcement of the civil marriage statute, and some measures will be taken to reduce the Church to subjection. A law to expel from the country priests who intimidate citizens from obeying the civil marriage act has already been proposed. This will be open war; but priests who threaten to excommunicate will be sent into exile, where they will shortly be followed by the monks and nuns, and a general confiscation of church property will be the next step. It is estimated that one-third of the entire property in Chili is owned by the Church. Much of this property is held in trust for certain saints, to whom it has been bequeathed by devout persons, or purchased by the gifts of the people. Saint Dominic, for example, is one of the largest property-holders in South America, and has an income of more than a million dollars a year from his estates, which are ably managed by the Dominican friars. It is proposed to assess a tax upon these estates, which now pay nothing towards the support of the Government; and if the monks refuse to pay, the property will be confiscated.

Protestantism is making rapid progress in Chili. There are several missions under the care of the Presbyterian Board of the United States, and a number of self-supporting churches and schools. There is also a Presbyterian College and Theological Seminary, and a Young Ladies' Seminary with about one hundred and fifty boarding scholars; but the common people still cling to the superstitions and practices of the past. Crucifixes upon which the bodies of bleeding Christs are displayed, with all the symbols of the Crucifixion—the sponge, hammer, nails, spear, and other implements—are erected in the public streets. They are accompanied by an announcement from the archbishop that whoever says a certain number of prayers at these places will receive total absolution for all past sins.

A beautiful marble monument has been erected on the site of the church which was burned about twenty years ago on the Feast of the Virgins. As usual on that day, high mass was celebrated by the bishop, and at this particular church, which was that of the patron saint of maidens, there was a

A BELLE OF CHILI DRESSED FOR MORNING MASS.

very large attendance of girls from all classes of society. The church was handsomely draped, and cords to which candles were hung were stretched between the pillars. Being insecurely placed, these burning candles fell into the crowd below and set the clothing of the girls on fire. There was a panic, and the entire crowd became jammed against the doors, which, folding inward, could not be opened. The roof caught fire and, burning, fell with crushing destruction upon the heads of those below. The priests took no means to rescue the worshippers, but managed to get out unharmed themselves, carrying with them all the plate and other valuable contents of the altar. Their cowardice and neglect were universally condemned, and they were compelled to leave the country.

It is not known how many lives were lost, and the inscription upon the monument—which stands in the centre of a plaza occupying the site of the church—gives no clew; but it is estimated that at least three thousand young ladies perished, and there was mourning in almost every house in Santiago. After the fire the bodies were found packed in a solid mass of flesh, the heads and upper portions of the forms being destroyed, while the limbs and lower portions of the bodies were uninjured. Since that calamity the Feast of the Virgins has been celebrated with mourning in Chili.

It is one of the rules of the Church that no women shall participate in the services except as silent worshippers. All the music and singing is given by men, usually monks, who are well trained. Sometimes, as on Easter or Christmas, when mass is celebrated with more than usual magnificence, opera-singers of both sexes are introduced into the choir to assist in the performance; but the women are compelled to dress in the clothes of men, for fear of offending St. Paul or some other anti-woman's rights potentate by wearing petticoats.

At the beginning of the fishing season at Valparaiso it is customary to take the image of St. Peter, the patron of fishermen, in a boat and row it over the bay, in order to bless the fish; and those who expect to reap the reward of this patronage are highly taxed to pay for this performance. Every method by which money may be extorted from the people, every pretence which their ingenuity can invent, is practised by the priests to enrich the Church, and the funds are wasted by them in riotous living. Their looks are sufficient to convict them of the gluttony and libertinism of which they are accused, and it is a common thing to see them reeling through the streets in a state of intoxication.

In the wall of one of the handsomest residences, by the side of the main entrance, is a niche in which a statue of the Mother of Christ has been placed—a gaudy, tinsel-covered figure, with a halo of gas-jets and a mantle of gilt-embroidered satin. An iron grating protects the image from the street, but through the bars have been thrust garlands of flowers and gifts of various sorts—votive offerings from people in bodily distress or mental disorder. The lady who lives in this house, the wife of a wealthy native merchant, some years ago became very ill, and made a vow to the Virgin that if her health was restored she would show her gratitude in this manner; and there the statue stands to illustrate the woman's piety. Almost daily people who are ill, as its owner was, and others in distress of mind from some cause or another, come to it with such offerings as their condition permits them to make, and trustfully appeal to the Holy Mother for relief. It is said that many miraculous cures have resulted from faith in the power of this image, and people always lift their hats and reverently cross themselves as they pass it by.

The 13th of May is the anniversary of the most destructive earthquake Santiago has ever seen, which occurred about forty years ago. The responsibility for the calamity lay with a woman who had a private saint, a household idol, to whom she offered prayers. This image deemed fit to withhold from her some favor she had asked, and she, angry, cast it violently into the street. This caused the earthquake! and it did not cease until the fear-stricken people took the image to the Church of St. Augustine, near by, where it was placed in a niche of honor, and has since been devoutly worshipped by them as the patron or preventer of earthquakes. For the lack of a better name, and because the image bears no resemblance to any saint that was ever known or told of, the people call him "Señor May." Originally he was "Señor Thirteenth of May," but now plain "Señor May," for short. Each year, as the 13th of May comes round—the anniversary of his "martyrdom," as the people call it—the entire population assemble to pay honor to the saint, and appeal for his intercession in preventing a recurrence of the earthquake, and, as everybody knows, these appeals have never been denied. "Señor May" protects the city at least one day in the year. As the church is not large enough to accommodate the multitude, the saint is taken out into the street and carried at the head of a procession, in which the bishop, the municipal authorities, companies of military, religious orders, and others march. The occasion is recognized by the Government and the municipality, and by commercial circles. Business houses are closed, and factories dismiss their workmen to take part in the ceremonies. The day is celebrated as universally as Thanksgiving Day in the United States, and the saint receives rich gifts from people who are grateful that their houses have not been shaken to pieces.

I was present at the celebration in 1885. First in the procession came a squad of policemen to clear the way, for the entire population was jammed into the streets; and in the windows and upon the roofs of houses the nobility and gentry of the city stood, watching the performance as eagerly as the gamins of the streets, and throwing garlands and bunches of flowers into the path over which "Señor May" was to pass. Men fought and cursed, struck and stabbed each other in the struggle to do homage to the image, and all the police in the city were present to preserve order and arrest disturbers of the solemn scene. The Government offices were closed, and the President himself, the leader of the anti-Church party, did not go to the palace.

Following the policemen came a line of monks in cowls and frocks of all colors. There were monks in white, monks in black, monks in gray, and monks in brown—Carmelites, Capuchins, Franciscans, and every order being represented. Then came a procession of priests in their vestments, with novitiates, each bearing a lighted candle and chanting some monotonous service. Behind them were a dozen altar-boys, some with incense-lamps which perfumed the air, and others with trays of flowers, which were scattered in the street for the bishop, who came next, to tread upon. He walked under a crimson canopy, wearing his most resplendent vestments, and bearing in his hands the Host—the Holy Sacrament—the body and blood of the Redeemer. Behind him were other incense-burners, and more boys with flowers. Then came, borne upon the shoulders of twenty men, the image of "Señor May"—an ugly and repulsive-looking effigy, draped with the most fantastic garments, rich embroideries, and much gold lace. Upon the pedestal were packages and caskets containing the offerings received that day; and as he passed along one and another would be added, handed from the houses or the crowd to the priests of St. Augustine's Church, who surrounded the image to collect them.

The crowd fell upon their knees as this ghastly feature of fanaticism passed by. Every head was uncovered, and every reverent tongue murmured a prayer. Men pushed and struggled, women screamed, and the policemen struck forward and backward with their swords to prevent the people from surging into the streets. Then came more chanting priests, and another battalion of monks, then more incense-bearers, and a spectacle of even greater repulsiveness—an image of a bleeding Christ upon a crucifix, naked, with the drapery of a ballet-dancer about his loins! More priests and more monks, and then a band of music and a regiment of infantry in parade uniforms, followed by a long line of bareheaded men, each with a lighted candle in his hand. This part of the procession received large and continual additions. People from the crowd fell into line at the rear, and were furnished with candles by attendants, who carried boxes of them in a cart, until the line reached out for a mile or more. After the parade the images were returned to the Church of St. Augustine, where high mass was celebrated by the bishop, to which admission was secured only by ticket.

The next morning the newspapers contained long descriptions of the procession. The contest then, as now, going on between the Liberal party and the clerical element for political control gives the utterances of the official organ of the Government (Liberal) peculiar significance. I quote the brief paragraphs in which reference was made to the event of the month:

"The procession of 'Señor May' took place yesterday, accompanied by many religious festivities in the temple of St. Augustine. The people and the municipality joined with the church to give a transcendent recognition in a most solemn and impressive manner of the historic 'Señor May.' From the early hours of the day the surroundings of the temple of St. Augustine were occupied by great throngs of the faithful, who awaited the inauguration of the parade. A little before four o'clock there arrived the forces of the army, with the national band at their head, and took position in front of the church in accordance with the orders from the commander-in-chief of the army.

"Having been put in motion, the procession filed with difficulty through the great number of people who crowded the streets and followed with many prayers and significant rejoicing. The pedestals of the saints were beautifully adorned and covered with many valuable and votive offerings, the tender gifts of piety from the faithful. A committee from the municipal authorities, appointed to contribute to the solemnity of the occasion, participated in the ceremonies. The bands of music played various sentimental airs during the march.

"To resume, the acts of recognition to the most potent 'Señor May,' made in compliance with the vows of the year 1847, after the terrible catastrophe of the 13th of the present month, have been perfectly carried out by the Catholic capital of Chili."

Farming in Chili is conducted on the old feudal system, very much as it is in Ireland. The country is divided into great estates owned by people who live in the cities, and seldom visit the haciendas. There are only two classes of people, the very rich and the very poor, the landlords and the tenants. On each estate are a number of cottages with garden patches around them, which are occupied by the tenants, and in payment for which the landlord is entitled to so many days' labor each year at his option. Should more labor than is due be required of the tenant, he is paid for it, not in money, but in orders upon the supply store or commissary of the estate, where he can get clothing or food or rum—especially rum. Tenants are usually given small credits at these stores, and are kept in debt to the landlords. As the law prohibits them from leaving a landlord to whom they owe money, the poor are kept in perpetual slavery, like the party in mythology who was always rolling a stone uphill. Even under this cruel system of peonage master and slave usually get along pretty well together, but old-fashioned feudal wars are kept up between estates, as was the case in England centuries ago. The peon will always fight for his landlord, and bloody encounters are constantly occurring. There are in Chili to-day the same old family feuds that existed in the Middle Ages of Europe between the Montagues and the Capulets. Somebody stepped upon the coat-tails of somebody else, or kicked his poodle dog, away back in the early history of the country, and the two families have been slashing and hacking at each other ever since, while nobody can explain what it is all about. The tenant will always cut a throat in his master's honor, but he can never get any richer in Chili than he is to-day.

Everybody goes on horseback; even the beggars ride. The gear of the Chili saddle-horse—and horses are seldom broken to harness, all the teaming being done with oxen—is a most curious and complicated affair. The bit is a long, heavy, flat piece of iron, which rests on the horse's tongue, and presses against the roof of his mouth. At each end is a hole, through which is passed a large iron ring about four inches in diameter, which encircles the lower jaw. At each side of the mouth is placed another iron ring to which the reins are fastened. The whole affair weighs about five pounds, and is sufficiently powerful to break a horse's jaw if suddenly jerked. The reins are made of fine-plaited hide or horse-hair, about the thickness of the forefinger, and are joined together when they reach the pommel of the saddle, terminating in a long lash called a *chicote*, at the end of which is either a handsome tassel or a small piece of lead. When not in use the chicote hangs down the flank of the horse, often dragging on the ground. Sometimes the load of lead is heavy, and furnishes a weapon of offence and defence as formidable as a slung-shot, and the poor horse is often beaten with it without mercy. Fancy bits are made of plated or solid silver, and bridles plated with gold, with reins made of golden wire, can be found in the larger cities. I saw a bridle in Chili, belonging to Señora Cousino, that is said to have cost two thousand five hundred dollars; and one often hears of gifts of this sort that are worth one thousand dollars or more.

The Chili saddle is even more queer and complicated than the bridle. First, six or seven sheepskins are placed upon the horse's back, one on top of the other; a leather strap is passed around them and firmly secured; a skeleton saddle, or rather a piece of wood cut in the shape of a saddle-tree, with a cantle at each end, comes next, and on top of this any number of sheepskins; or, if the owner is rich, rare furs furnish a seat, which is called the *montura*. The four corners are fastened down by broad leather straps, ornamented with silver or brass buckles, to enable the rider to wedge himself in, and the whole is bound around the horse's belly with a broad band of leather or canvas. Sometimes aristocratic and wealthy riders have a high pommel like that of the Mexican saddle, which is covered with silver, and stamped on the top with his family coat of arms. The amount of silver on a man's riding equipment is understood to indicate his wealth and station in life, and there is a great deal of competition in this direction among the swell caballeros. The stirrups of the ordinary citizen are made of two huge pieces of wood, with a hole cut through for the foot, while those of the aristocrat are brass or silver slippers. The wooden affair, the poor man's stirrup, is rudely cut out of oak, or other hard wood, by hand, and usually weighs as much as four or five pounds. The brass one is quite as heavy, but much more ornamental.

A SOLID SILVER SPUR.

When the rider is seated in the saddle his legs are entirely concealed by the furs and sheepskins, which add to his warmth, and on his back he wears the *poncho* of the country, which is the most comfortable and convenient garment that human ingenuity has ever produced. It is about the size of the rubber poncho used in the United States, but is woven of vicuña hair or lamb's-wool, and keeps the wearer cool by day, as the rays of the sun cannot penetrate it, and warm by night. It answers as well for an umbrella as for an overcoat, and sheds the rain better than rubber, for the oil is not extracted from the wool of which it is made. The vicuña is the mountain-goat of the Andes, but is becoming scarce, and nowadays a vicuña poncho is as rare and expensive as a camel's-hair shawl, which it very much resembles, being worth from one hundred and fifty to five hundred dollars. A fully equipped saddle-horse of a caballero, or gentleman, with vicuña poncho and spurs of silver, with saddle and bridle mounted with the same metal, often represents an investment of four or five thousand dollars. Very often the stirrup is made of solid silver, beautifully chased, and those used by ladies are generally so. The English manufacturers are able to produce the ornaments and stirrups so much cheaper than the native workmen, who have no labor-saving machinery, that nearly all are now imported, and they have succeeded in imitating the poncho very well too. But among the aristocrats it is considered the height of vulgarity to use modern English saddlery or the imitation poncho, for these articles have been handed down from generation to generation, and the older they are the more valuable, no sort of usage wearing them out.

In Guatemala I was presented with a pair of stirrups which had been worn by the cavalry of Cortez when they made their raid into Central America and conquered that continent in 1535. This pair was handed down from generation to generation, in the family of Mr. Sanchez, the "Minister of Hacienda," or Finance, of the Guatemala Government: they are made of iron, with wide flanges to protect the feet and legs of the cavalier from the high grass and brambles of the country through which he had to ride. This style was long ago abandoned, and is now only seen in museums.

OVER THE ANDES.

He who wishes to make the journey from the Chilian to the Argentine Republic and the east coast of South America has a choice of routes. He may go by sea, around through the Strait of Magellan, which will cost him fifteen days' time and two hundred dollars in money, or he may climb over the Andes on the back of a mule, a journey of five days, three of which only are spent in the saddle amid some

MOUNT ACONCAGUA.

USPALLATA PASS.

of the grandest scenery in the world. The highest mountain in the Western Hemisphere is Aconcagua, which rises 22,415 feet above the sea to the northward from Valparaiso and Santiago, and in plain view from both cities when the weather is clear. Chimborazo was for a long time supposed to be the king of the Andes, and in the geographies published twenty years ago it is described as the highest summit in the world. No one has ever reached the peak of either mountain, owing to the depth of snow and impassable gorges, but recent measurements, taken by means of triangulation, give Aconcagua an excess of about 2000 feet over old "Chimbo." Scientists have reached an altitude higher than the summit of either in the Himalaya Mountains of India, where Mount Everest is claimed to rise between 27,000 and 30,000 feet. Humboldt made Chimborazo famous, and very few travellers have gone beyond the point he reached; but no serious attempt has ever been made to explore the summit of Aconcagua, as the Chillanos do not often go where their horses cannot carry them. In mountain gloom and glory Chimborazo is said to surpass all rivals, standing as it does within sight of the sea, and surrounded by a cluster of twenty peaks, like a king and his counsellors. But Aconcagua is grand enough, and has nothing near it to dwarf its size. The latitude in which it stands brings the snow line much lower than upon Chimborazo and the other peaks of Ecuador, which are almost upon the line of the equator, and the purity of the atmosphere gives the spectator an opportunity to see its picturesqueness at a long distance.

From Santiago, Chili, there is a Government railway as far as the town of Santa Rosa, which passes around the base of Aconcagua, and furnishes the traveller with a most sublime panorama of mountain scenery. There mules and men are hired for the ride over the Cumbre Pass to Mendoza, on the eastern slope of the Andes, to which a railroad has been recently opened by the Argentine Government. Here one can take a Pullman sleeper, and ride to Buenos Ayres as comfortably as he can go from New York to St. Louis, the distance being about the same.

This railroad was opened in May, 1885, with a grand celebration, in which the Presidents of Chili and the Argentine Republic, with retinues of officials, participated. The event was as important to the commercial development of Argentine as was the first Pacific Railway to the United States, as it opened to settlement millions of square miles of the best territory in the republic, and furnished a highway between the two seas.

CAUGHT IN THE SNOW.

The people of the United States have very little conception of what is going on down in that part of the world. They do not realize that there is in Argentine a republic which some day is to rival our own—a country with immense resources, similar to those of the United States, situated in a corresponding latitude, prepared to furnish the world with beef and mutton and bread, and stretching a net-work of railways over its area that will bring the products of the pampas to market. Geographers do not keep pace with the development of this part of South America, and to present accurate accounts of its condition should be rewritten every year. Who knows, for instance, except those who have been there, that a man can ride from Buenos Ayres across the pampas to the foot-hills of the Andes in a Pullman car?

ROAD CUT IN THE ROCKS.

The late war between Peru and Chili robbed Bolivia of all her sea-coast, and the ports from which her produce was shipped, and at which her imports were received, now belong to the Chillanos, who charge heavy export and import duties. The opening of this railroad has caused the trade of Bolivia to be diverted to the Atlantic, and the extension of the line to the northward, which is already in progress, will make Buenos Ayres and other cities on the river La Plata the *entrepots* for Bolivian commerce. It is not much farther now from the centre of Bolivia to the Argentine Railway than to the Pacific coast, and the feeling of resentment towards Chili

A STATION IN THE MOUNTAINS.

makes the difference exceeding small. Long trains of mules are passing up and down the mountains, and their numbers will constantly increase until the Pacific sea-ports will see nothing that is grown or used in the country which Chili so ruthlessly robbed. One great difficulty, however, lies in the fact that from April to November the mountain passes are blockaded with snow, and it is always dangerous, and often impossible, to make the journey. Native couriers, who use snow-shoes, and find refuge in "casuchas," or hollows of the rocks, during storms, cross them the year round, carrying the mails. Sometimes, indeed often, they perish from exposure or starvation, or perhaps are buried under avalanches. The passes are about thirteen thousand feet high, and are swept by winds that human endurance cannot survive. During the summer the journey is delightful, and though attended by many discomforts, has its compensations to those who are willing to rough it, and who are fond of mountain scenery. Ladies often venture, and enjoy it. Not long since a party of thirteen school-ma'ams from the United States, who are teaching under contract with the Argentine Government, crossed the mountains to Chili, and had "a lovely time." Plenty of mules and good guides can be secured at the termini of the railways, but travellers have to carry their own food and bedding. There are no hotels on the way, but only "schacks," or log houses, which furnish nothing but shelter. Very often people who are not accustomed to high altitudes are attacked with sirroche, from which they sometimes suffer severely.

The road over the mountains is always dangerous, clinging as it does to the edge of mighty precipices and upon the sides of mountain cliffs, and only trained mules can be used on the journey. During the winter season the winds are often so strong as to blow the mules with their burdens over the precipices, and leave them as food for the condors that are always soaring around. These birds know the dangerous passes, and keep guard with the expectation of seeing some traveller or mule go tumbling over the cliffs. Cowhide bridges, the construction of which is not satisfactory to nervous men, stretch across the ravines after the manner of modern suspension-bridges, and a floor or path, made of the branches of trees lashed together with hides, and just wide enough for a mule to pass, is laid. Travellers usually dismount and lead their mules when they cross these fragile structures, for the hide ropes which are intended to keep people from stepping off do not look very secure. The oscillation of these bridges is very great, and a man who is accustomed to giddiness will want to lie down before he gets half-way over. It is remarkable that so few accidents happen, and when they do occur it is usually because a traveller is reckless or a mule is green. The foxes sometimes gnaw the hides, but no accidents have occurred from this cause for many years.

THE CONDOR.

The journey on mule-back usually takes five days of travel, at the rate of twenty or thirty miles a day, but good riders, with relays of mules, often make it in three days. The whole route is historical, as it has been in use for centuries. There is scarcely a mile without some romantic association, not a rock without its incident; and tradition, incident, and romance line the path from end to end. The Incas used the path before the Spaniards conquered the country, and Don Diego de Almagro crossed it in 1535 as he passed southward to Chili after the conquest of Peru.

PATAGONIA.

THE spinal column of the hemisphere, extending from the Arctic to the Antarctic Sea, and called the Cordilleras, breaks suddenly at the foot of the Southern continent, and is divided by a narrow and deep ravine called the Strait of Magellan. Before the strait is reached, along the western coast of South America are numberless islands, cast into the sea by some convulsion of nature, like sparks flung from hammered iron. Few of these islands have ever been explored, but they all bear a close resemblance to the main-land in their geological formation, and it is believed that deposits of copper, silver, and other minerals, as well as coal, exist under their surfaces. On Chiloe, the largest of the Chili archipelago, mining companies are already operating to a small extent, but of the resources of the other islands little or nothing is known. They rise in picturesque outlines from the water, some of them to an elevation of several thousand feet, and the panorama presented to voyagers in what is known as Smythe's Channel is beautiful and grand. This is a narrow fiord, named from its first explorer, scooped out, the geologists say, by the action of ice during the glacial epoch, running along the main coast, and protected against the violence of the ocean by the numerous fragmentary formations that line the shore. A glance at the map of Patagonia will show how many of these islands there are, and how slender is the thread of sea which separates them from the continent.

The water in the channel is deep and smooth, but the passage is avoided by navigators because of the powerful currents and the frequency of snow-storms, which prevail at all seasons of the year. Vessels that take this course are compelled to anchor at night, unless there is a very bright moon, and always lie up when the snow falls, because of the circuitous turns, and the danger of collisions with ships and icebergs. Smythe's Channel is so narrow in places that two steamers cannot pass between the mighty rocks which rise on either side. Most of the steamships prefer to risk the storms which rage outside, where they can have plenty of sea-room, and shorten their voyages by sailing at night as well as by day. There is no more dangerous sailing in the world than off the west coast of Patagonia and around the Horn, and vessels bound southward from Valparaiso are very lucky if they enter the Strait of Magellan without catching a gale of wind.

CAPE FROWARD (PATAGONIA), STRAIT OF MAGELLAN.

The glaciers of Switzerland and Norway are insignificant beside those which can be seen from ships passing the Strait of Magellan. Mountains of green and blue ice, with crests of the purest snow, stretch fifteen and twenty miles along the channel in some parts of the strait. They are by no means as lofty as those of Europe, but appear more grand, rising as they do from the surface of the water in a land where winter always lingers, and where the sun sets at three o'clock in the afternoon. The line of perpetual snow begins at an elevation of only two thousand feet, and water always freezes at night, even in the summer-time. The highest mountains in Terra del Fuego are supposed to reach an altitude of seven thousand or eight thousand feet, but the eye of man has seldom seen them, covered as they are with an almost perpetual haze or mist, and presenting difficulties which the most ardent and experienced climber cannot surmount. The highest mountain known in this region is Mount Sarmiento, one of the most imposing of the Andean peaks, which rears a cone of spotless snow nearly seven thousand feet, almost abruptly from the water at its feet. It stands in what is known as Cockburn Channel, not far from the Pacific, and on clear days its summit can be distinguished from the decks of passing ships. The beauty of this peak is much enhanced by numerous blue-tinted glaciers, which descend from the snowy cap to the sea, and look, as Darwin the naturalist, who once saw it, said, "Like a hundred frozen Niagaras." There are other mountains quite as beautiful, but they sit in an atmosphere which is seldom so clear as that which surrounds Sarmiento, and cannot often be seen by voyagers.

The Terra del Fuego Indians, the ugliest mortals that ever breathed, are always on the lookout for passing vessels, and come out in canoes to beg and to trade skins for whiskey and tobacco. The Fuegians, or "Canoe Indians," as they are commonly called, to distinguish them from the Patagonians, who dislike the water, and prefer to navigate on horseback, have no settled habitation. They have a dirty and bloated appearance, and faces that would scare a mule—broad features, low foreheads, over which the hair hangs in tangled lumps, high cheek-bones, flat noses, enormous chins and jaws, and mouths like crocodiles', with teeth that add to their repulsiveness. Their skin is said to be of a copper color, but is seldom seen, as they consider it unhealthy to bathe. They are short in stature, round-shouldered, squatty, and swelled, a physical deformity said to be due to the fact that most of their lives is spent in canoes. The women are even more repulsive in their appearance than the men, and the children, who are uncommonly numerous, look like young baboons. Their intelligence seems to be confined to a knowledge of boating and fishing, and they exercise great skill in both pursuits. Scientists who have investigated them say that they are of the very lowest order of the human kind, many degrees below the Digger Indians.

FUEGIANS VISITING A MAN-OF-WAR.

Although these people are in a perpetual winter, where it freezes every night, and always snows when the clouds shed moisture, they go almost stark naked! The skins of the otter and guanaco are used for blankets, which are worn about the shoulders and afford some protection; but under these neither women nor men wear anything whatever except shoes and leggings made of the same material, which protect the feet from the rocks. There is some little attempt at adornment made by both sexes in the way of necklaces, bracelets, and ear-rings made of fish-bones and sea-shells, which are often ingeniously joined together. The women will sell the skin blankets that cover their backs for tobacco, standing meantime as nude as a statue of Venus!

Their food consists of mussels, fish, sea animals, and similar sorts, which they catch with the rudest kind of implements. Their fishing-lines are made of grass, and their hooks of fish-bones. For weapons they have bows and spears, the former having strings made of the entrails of animals, and the latter being long, slender poles, with tips of sharpened bone. They also use slings with great dexterity, which are made of woven grass, and are said to bring down animals at long range. During the day they are always on the water in canoes or dugouts made of the trunks of trees, the whole family going together, and usually consisting of a man, two or three wives, and as many urchins as can be crowded into the boat. When night falls they go ashore and build a fire upon the rocks, to temper the frigid atmosphere. Around this fire they cuddle in a most affectionate way. The name of the islands upon which they live came from these fires. The early navigators, when passing through the strait, were amazed to see them spring up as if by magic all over the islands every night at sundown, and so they called them Terra del Fuego, or the Land of Fire. The English shorten the appellation, and thus the place is known as "Fireland."

No one has ever been able to ascertain whether these people possess any sort of religious belief or have religious ceremonies. Across the strait the Patagonians, or Horse Indians, are of a higher order of creation, and perform sacred rites to propitiate the evil and good spirits, in which, like the North

A FUEGIAN FEAST.

American savages, they believe; but the Fuegians are too degraded to contemplate anything but the necessity of ministering to their passions and appetites. They eat fish and flesh uncooked, and appreciate as dainties the least attractive morsels. Their language is an irregular and meaningless jargon, apparently derived from the Patagonians, with whom they were, some time in the distant past, connected. Bishop Sterling, of the Church of England, a devoted and energetic man, who has charge of missionary work in South America, with headquarters on the Falkland Islands, has made some attempt to benefit these creatures, but with no great success. He has a little schooner in which he sails around, and has succeeded in ingratiating himself among the Fuegians by giving them presents of beads and twine, blankets and clothing. They use the first for ornaments, the second for fishing gear, but trade off the other things for rum and tobacco the first chance they get. As long as his gifts hold out he will be kindly received, no doubt, and his devotion will meet with encouragement, but if he should land among them without the usual plunder they would probably kill him at breakfasttime and pick his ribs for lunch. Towards the Atlantic coast the savages are of a higher order, and the bishop has established a missionary station in a little town in which they live. His assistants have succeeded in persuading the inhabitants of this village to wear clothing, and they run a primary school from which much good may come.

The Falkland Islands lie off the coast of Terra del Fuego about two hundred and fifty miles, and belong to the British crown. There is a town of about eight hundred inhabitants called St. Louis, where the Governor lives, and a coaling station is maintained for the benefit of English men-of-war. The chief use of the islands otherwise is sheep-raising, and the wool exports are becoming quite large. Nothing else grows there, however, because of the low temperature and the barrenness of the soil. One line of steamers touches at the Falklands once a month or so, carrying provisions to the colony and bringing away the wool.

One of the curious things about the Strait of Magellan is the Post-office. In a sheltered place, easy of access from the channel, but secluded from the Indians, is a tin box, known to every seaman who navigates this part of the world. Every passing skipper places in this box letters and newspapers for other vessels that are expected this way, and takes out whatever is found to belong to him or his men. All the newspapers and books that seamen are done with are deposited here, and are afterwards picked up by the next vessel to arrive, and replaced with a new lot. It is a sort of international postal clearing-house, and sailors say that the advantages it offers have never been abused during the half century the system has existed.

Every time a vessel passes through the strait the Fuegian Indians come out in their canoes to show their sociability,

THE SIGNS OF CIVILIZATION.

and trade what property they are fortunate enough to be possessed of for tobacco and rum. The steamer we were on ran through several fleets of dugouts, greatly to the danger of those who occupied them, as they paddled across our course in the most reckless manner. In each of the frail canoes were three or four people and several children, who screamed and gesticulated in the most violent manner. They came so near the ship that we could distinguish their features and hear their words, which were clamors for *tabac* (tobacco) and *galleta* (food). In one canoe stood an old hag with long gray hair, and a face that reminded me of Meg Merriles. A more weird and witchlike being never presented itself to human eye, and she did not have a thread upon her dirty skin from head to foot. Stark, staring naked she stood in the group around her, with the thermometer about forty degrees above zero, and, as she saw the vessel did not propose to stop, shook her wrinkled arms at us, and uttered curses loud and deep. There was a fire in the boat in which she stood, and around it huddled another woman, naked, but with a guanaco robe over her shoulders, and several children, while the father sat in the stern and paddled his own canoe, leaving the wife or mother, whichever she was, to do all the talking.

In another canoe stood a repulsive-looking man, who had taken off his guanaco robe, and stood naked, flapping it at us, and yelling like a lunatic. His companions were two naked women and several youngsters, and they all joined in the chorus with a vigor that we expected would split their throats, leaving the canoe to drift as it would, finally coming into collision with another, at which there was a good deal of scrambling, and an exchange of Fuegian compliments, the nature of which we could not understand. What they wanted was rum and tobacco, having acquired a taste for this pernicious weed from the sailors. For a plug of "Navy" they would exchange a guanaco blanket that could not be bought in New York for seventy-five dollars, as the guanaco is one of the rarest and finest of skins. The anger and disgust that was pictured upon the faces of these creatures when they found that the vessel was not slackening her speed would have furnished a model for the expressions on the souls that are lost. The passengers were about as much disappointed as the Fuegians, for having all read and heard of them, we anticipated much gusto, as the Spaniards say, in making their acquaintance.

Scientists have long differed as to whether the Firelanders were cannibals, but this point has been recently settled by a practical demonstration, and there is no doubt that they actually eat human flesh when they can get it, and pick the bones very clean. In October, 1884, during a snow-storm, the steamer *Cordillera*, of the Pacific Steam Navigation Company's line, struck a rock in the Strait of Magellan, about forty miles west of Punta Arenas, and to save as much as possible of the ship and cargo the captain drove her upon the beach, where she now lies, almost within a stone's-throw of passing vessels. The wreck was soon after abandoned by all but two men, who were left in charge until wrecking machinery could be brought from Valparaiso. One of these men was William Taylor, a quartermaster or petty officer of the ship, and his companion, an ordinary seaman. They were well armed, and it was supposed were capable of protecting themselves, but it turned out that they were not. One night I was sitting upon the rickety old dock at Punta Arenas, waiting for the purser of our ship to take me on board, when Taylor was introduced to me, and told his story in a most graphic way.

He said that when he and his partner were left in charge of the vessel, it was with the understanding that they were to be relieved on the 21st of December, and they were given food enough to last until that time. After the captain and crew had gone, and the two men were alone on the ship, the Indians made their appearance nearly every day, and bits of food were thrown over the side of the vessel into their canoes. Taylor and his companion each carried two revolvers, and were not at all alarmed, as the vessel lay very high on the sand, and it did not seem possible that the Indians could climb up its iron sides. Although several canoes hovered around the place daily, the savages made no unfriendly demonstrations, and no notice was taken of them further than to exchange salutations, and give them meat and bread now and then. One day the Indians traded them a string of fresh fish for a plug of tobacco, and at other times gave them furs for the same consideration. About noon on the 15th of December, while the sailor was cooking dinner in the galley, Taylor, who was at work below, heard several shots fired from a revolver on deck, with shrieks and other sounds, which proved that a fight was going on there. He drew both of his pistols, and rushing up-stairs, saw the bleeding body of his companion lying upon the deck, and one of the savages hacking at it with the cook's knife. About twenty or twenty-five others were performing a war-dance around one of their number who lay dead, and a single glance at the scene convinced Mr. Taylor that he could find no pleasure in attending the

PORT FAMINE.

circus. The Indians did not see him, and he crept quickly below and stowed himself in a large coil of rope in the forward part of the hold. The space in the centre of the coil was large enough to contain his body in a stooping position, and making the hatchway as fast as he could, he piled bags of beans around the sides and on the top of the rope, so as to entirely conceal it. For two days he hid himself here, feeding upon dry uncooked beans and a box of sea-biscuits, which he fortunately found in the hold; but he was entirely without water. The third day, fearing that he would die of thirst, he crept out and drew a bucket of water from a cask on the second deck, which he carried back to his place of concealment. On this excursion he neither heard nor saw signs of the Indians, and after two days more had passed, screwed his courage up to the point of making an exploration. Arranging everything so that he could make a hasty retreat if necessary, and using bean-bags to make a rifle-pit from which he could defend himself if pursued, he crept quietly into the saloon of the vessel, where he found that the Indians had been indulging in "a high old time." Glasses and crockery were smashed, mattresses were dragged from the cabin, and everything that was movable lay scattered helter-skelter over the dining-tables and floor. It was evident that a search had been made for him, as doors which were locked had been broken open, although no attempt had been made to remove the coverings from the hatchways which led into the hold. Only one deck presented signs of a search, and above all was perfectly quiet. Going up-stairs, Taylor found human bones, picked clean, scattered around the galley. He did not touch them, because to look at them gave him the "shivers," he said, but he saw enough to convince him that not only had the body of his companion been eaten, but also that of the savage who had been killed in the fray. It was evident that the savages had enjoyed a long and lively picnic, for there were several places on the deck where fires had been built. It was a wonder to him that the vessel had not been burned to the water's edge. While hunting around for food, he found the head of his companion with the neck chopped off close to the jaws, the eyes punched out, and the fleshy part of the cheeks cut off. The sight of this was so horrible that he abandoned further exploration, and returned to his place of confinement so faint and bewildered that he could scarcely find his way. That night he crept out again, and finding some canned meat and fruit, lowered himself overboard and swam ashore, concluding that the Indians would return to the vessel, and that he would be safer in the rocks and bushes. Here he concealed himself for several days, awaiting the vessel that was to arrive from Valparaiso on the 21st of the month. The 25th passed without any sign of relief, and on the morning of the 26th he started on foot for Punta Arenas, where he arrived two days after. Here he told his story, and instead of being welcomed with hospitality, was arrested and thrown into jail, charged with the murder of his companion. A boat was sent down to the wreck, and such evidence was found there as to convince every one of the truth of his statement; whereupon he was released, and is now at Punta Arenas, in the employment of the Steamship Company, on an old hulk which lies in the harbor and is used for the storage of coal.

I have not told the story in as graphic a manner as it was related to me by William Taylor that night under the antarctic stars, but have given only the facts of his narrative, without embellishment of sailors' slang and oaths. He lives in the hope of "steering within hailing distance of some of the savages, when he proposes to give them something worse than a rope's-end."

It is believed there is much gold in Terra del Fuego, as nuggets have been discovered by the missionaries in the streams. The Argentine Government proposes to make an exploration soon, and sanguine people think the time is not far distant when the islands of the archipelago will be filled with successful prospectors. Seals and other fur-bearing animals are plenty, but many skins are not sent to market for the reason that supplies can be obtained cheaper elsewhere.

There used to be a State called Patagonia, and one can still find it referred to in old geographies, but by the combined efforts of Chili and the Argentine Republic it has been wiped off the modern maps of the world. The United States ministers at the capitals of the two republics named assisted in dissecting the territory, and were presented with beautiful and costly testimonials as tokens of the artistic manner in which it was done. It was agreed that the boundary-line of Chili should be extended down the coast and then run eastward, just north of the Strait of Magellan, so that the Argentines should have the pampas, or prairies, and Chili the strait and the islands. The map of Chili now looks like the leg of a tall man, long and lean, with a very high instep and several conspicuous bunions.

It was a diplomatic stroke on the part of Chili to get control of the Strait of Magellan, that great international highway through which all steamers must go; and the archipelago along the western coast, comprising thousands of islands which have never been explored, and which are believed to be rich in what the world holds valuable, also fell to her share; but the Argentines got the best of the bargain in broad plains, rich in agricultural resources, rising in regular terraces from the Atlantic seaboard to the summits of the Cordilleras, whose snowy crests stand like an army of silent sentinels, marking the line upon which the two republics divide—plains as broad and useful as those which stretch between the Mississippi River and the ranges of Colorado, and as good for cattle as they are for corn.

STARVATION BEACH.

It was a rather unusual proceeding, this partition of the Patagonian estates. It is commonly the custom to divide property after the owner's death; but in this instance the inheritance was first shared by the heirs, and then the owner was mercilessly slaughtered. They called it a grand triumph of the genius of civilization over the barbarians, and the success of the scheme certainly deserved such a designation; but in this case as in many others the impediment to civilization was swept away in a cataract of blood. General Roca, the recent President of the Argentine Republic, was the author and executor of the plan of civilizing Patagonia, and he did it as the early Spanish Conquistadors introduced Christianity into America, with the keen edge of a sword. His success won him military glory and political honors, and made him what he is to-day, the greatest of the Argentinians.

There were originally two great nations of Indians in what was known as Patagonia, but the Spaniards called them all Patagonians, because of the enormous footprints they found upon the sand. The early explorers reported them to be a race of giants. The first white man that interviewed these people was Magellan, the great navigator who discovered the strait which bears his name, and who was the first to enter the Pacific Ocean. He had with him a romancer by the name of Pigafetta, who gave the world a great amount of interesting information without regard to accuracy. All the navigators who followed Magellan felt in duty bound to see and describe as amazing things as their predecessor had witnessed, and even went much further in their endeavors to keep up the European interest in the New World. Hence, in the sixteenth century, fables which are still repeated, but have no more foundation than the tales of the warrior woman who gave a name to the greatest stream on earth, found their way into history.

This man Pigafetta, for example, says that the Patagonia Indians "were of that biggeness that our menne of meane stature could reach up to their waysts, and they had bigg voyces, so that their talk seemed lyke unto the roar of a beaste." In order to secure credit for courage, the early navigators told astonishing yarns about the fierceness of these Indians, who still have a reputation for fighting which, no doubt, is well founded. Rum and disease have, however, made sad work among the race, which is in its decadence; and the ambition of the Patagonian now is only equal to that of the North American Indian—that is, to get enough to eat with the least possible labor. They hang around the ranches to pick up what is thrown to them in the way of food, stealing and begging, and occasionally they bring in skins to the settlements to exchange for fire-water.

USE OF LASSO AND BOLAS.

Later explorers discovered that there were two distinct races among the aborigines: first, the canoe Indians of the coast; and, second, the hunters of the interior, who are expert horsemen, raise cattle, and resemble the Sioux of the United States or the Apaches of the Mexican border. The two nations spoke languages entirely different, and had no resemblance in their manner or habits of life. Those of the south, who extended over into the curious islands of Terra del Fuego, are uglier in appearance, fiercer in disposition, and are believed to be cannibals. In fact, there is a recent instance of man-eating in the Strait of Magellan which appears to be authentically reported. The canoe Indians are called *Tehueiche*, and the horsemen of the north—the plains or pampa Indians—are called *Chenna*. The latter appear to be closely allied to the Araucanians of Chili, a race which the Spaniards were never able to subdue, but with which they have intermarried extensively, and produced the present peon of Chili, who has all the vivacity and impulsiveness of the Spaniard united with the muscular development, the courage, and the endurance of the Indian. The frontier of the Argentine Republic, until a few years since, was constantly harassed by the Chennas—murder, arson, and pillage were the rule—and the development of the nation was seriously checked, until General Roca was sent out with an army to exterminate them.

IN THEIR OSTRICH ROBES.

The dividing line between the Argentine Republic and what was known as Patagonia was the river Negro, which flows along the forty-first parallel, about nine hundred miles north of the Strait of Magellan. The greater portion of this country is well-watered pampas, or prairies, that extend in plainly marked terraces, rising one after the other from the Atlantic to the Andes; but towards the south the land becomes more bleak and barren, the soil being a bed of shale, with thorny shrubs and tufts of coarse grass, upon which nothing but the ostrich can exist. The winters are very severe, fierce winds sweeping from the mountains to the sea, with nothing to obstruct their course. These winds are called *pamperos*, and are the dread of those who navigate the South Atlantic. During the winter months the Indians were in the habit of driving their cattle northward into the foot-hills of the Andes for protection; and, leaving them there, they made raids upon the settlements on the Argentine frontier, killing, burning, and stealing cattle and horses. Terror-stricken, the ranchmen fled to the cities for protection; so that year by year the frontier line receded towards Buenos Ayres, instead of extending farther upon the plains.

A PATAGONIAN BELLE.

President Roca was then a general of cavalry, and had won renown in the war against Lopez, the tyrant of Paraguay. He was sent with two or three regiments to discipline the Indians, and he did it in a way that was as effective as it was novel. While the Indians were in the mountains with their cattle he set his soldiers at work, several thousands of them, and dug a great ditch, twelve feet wide and fifteen feet deep, from the mountains to the Rio Negro, scattering the earth from the excavation over the ground with such care as to leave nothing to excite the savages' suspicions. Then, when the ditch was completed, he flanked the Indians with his cavalry and drove them southward on the run. Being ignorant of the trap set for them, the savages galloped carelessly along until thousands of them were piled into the ditch, one on top of the other—a maimed, struggling, screaming mass of men, women, children, and horses. Many were killed by the fall, others were crushed by those who fell upon them, while those who crawled out were despatched by the sabres of the cavalrymen.

Those who were not driven into the ditch fled to the eastward hunting for a crossing, which the soldiers allowed them no time to make, even if they had had the tools. Shovels and picks and spades were unknown among the Patagonians, and as they are the wards of no nation, muskets and ammunition had never been furnished them to do their fighting with. It was very much such a chase as Chief Joseph of the Nez Perces gave General

Howard in the North-west a few years ago, and finally ended in General Roca's driving the Indians into a corner, with the impassable Rio Negro behind them, where the slaughter was continued until most of the warriors fell. The remainder were made prisoners and distributed around among the several regiments of the Argentine army, in which they have proven excellent soldiers. The women and children were sent to the Argentine cities, where they have since been held in a state of semi-slavery by families of officials and men of influence. The dead were never counted, but were buried in the ditch which encompassed their destruction.

Northern Patagonia was thus cleared of savages, and civilization stretched out its arms to embrace the pampas, which are now being rapidly populated with ranchmen. The grass is very similar to that of our own great plains, but water is more plentiful and regular than in the South-west Territories of the United States. Towards the Andes there is some timber, and the foot-hills are well wooded. Grazing land in this country is sold at a nominal price by the Argentine Government, or is leased to tenants for a term of eight years, in lots of six thousand acres, at a rental of one hundred dollars per year. Locations nearer the cities, of course, cost more money, and are hard to get, as they are already occupied by people who secured titles to the land years ago by "concessions" from Congress or other means.

Not long ago the United States Consul at Buenos Ayres received a letter from a New York capitalist, in which the latter proposed that they should pool their issues and secure a "concession" from the Argentine Government to gather up the wild cattle on the pampas. The capitalist, who had been overhauling his geography, discovered that "immense herds of wild horses and cattle are roaming ownerless upon the pampas of the Argentine Republic and Patagonia," and thought it would be a good scheme to take a lot of Texas cow-boys down and corral them, if the permission of the Government could be obtained. He proposed that the consul should obtain such permission, while he would furnish the cow-boys and the necessary capital, and the two would become partners in the Patagonia cattle trade on an extensive scale.

The astonished consul did not answer the letter. It was a tempting scheme, but there were several obstacles in the way of its success, the first being that there were no wild cattle on the pampas, and never had been. The Indians had large herds, which were "absorbed" by prominent officials when General Roca concluded his scheme of extermination; but it would be quite as reasonable to make such a proposition to the Governor of Colorado. There are about thirty million cows, five million horses, and one hundred million sheep grazing on the pampas of the Argentine Republic and Patagonia, but they are all properly branded, and valued at something like four hundred millions of dollars. The annual number of beeves slaughtered reaches nearly four millions, and about ten million sheep are turned into mutton each year.

The Argentinians think that their country is to be the greatest of all the world in cattle and wool production, and the figures loom up very much like it, as the increase within the last twenty years has been about four hundred per cent. At present the Argentine Republic has more sheep than any other nation, but the value of the wool product is less by one-third than that of Australia, because the fleece is so much lighter. The clip per animal in Australia is worth about one dollar, while in the Argentine Republic it sells for about fifty cents.

The capital of Patagonia, if the territory of that name may be said to have a capital, as there is only one town within its limits, is Punta Arenas, or Sandy Point, located about one-third of the distance from the Atlantic to the Pacific, in the Strait of Magellan. It belongs to Chili, and was formerly a penal colony; but one look at it is enough to convince the most incredulous that whoever located it did not intend the convict's life to be a happy one. It lies on a long spit which stretches out into the strait, and the English call it Sandy Point, but a better name would be Cape Desolation. Convicts are sent there no longer, but some of those who were sent thither when Chili kept the seeds and harvests of her revolutions still remain there. There used to be a military guard, but that was withdrawn during the war with Peru, and all the prisoners who would consent to enter the army got a ticket of leave. The Governor resides in what was once the barracks, and horses are kept in what was used as a stockade. Hunger, decay, and dreariness are inscribed upon everything—on the faces of the men as well as on the houses they live in—and the people look as discouraging as the mud.

They say it rains in Punta Arenas every day. That is a mistake—sometimes it snows. Another misrepresentation is the published announcement that ships passing the strait always touch there. Doubtless they desire to, and it is one of the delusions of the owners that they do; but as the wind never ceases except for a few hours at a time, and the bay on which the place is located is shallow, it is only about once a week or so that a boat can land, because of the violent surf. Our arrival happened to be opportune, for the water was smooth, and we landed without great difficulty, the only drawbacks being a pouring rain and mud that seemed bottomless.

The town is interesting, because it is the only settlement in Patagonia, and of course the only one in the strait. It is about four thousand miles from the southernmost town on the west coast of South America to the first port on the eastern coast—a voyage which ordinarily requires fifteen days; and as Punta Arenas is in about the middle of the way, it possesses some attractions. Spread out in the mud are two hundred and fifty houses, more or less, which shelter from the ceaseless storms a community of eight hundred or one thousand people, representing all sorts and conditions of men, from the primeval Indian type to the pure Caucasian—convicts, traders, fugitives, wrecked seamen, deserters from all the navies in the world, Chinamen, negroes, Poles, Italians, Sandwich Islanders, wandering Jews, and human drift-wood of every tongue and clime cast up by the sea and absorbed in a community scarcely one of which would be willing to tell why he came there, or would stay if he could get away. It is said that in Punta Arenas an interpreter for every language known to the modern world can be found, but although the place belongs to Chili, English is most generally spoken. There are a few women in the settlement, some of them faithful mothers and wives, no doubt, but the most of them have defective antecedents, and are noted for a disregard of matrimonial obligations.

There are some decent people here—ship agents and traders who came for business reasons, a consul or two, and among others an Irish physician, Dr. Fenton, who is the host and oracle sought for by every stranger who arrives. Occasionally some yachting party stops here on a voyage around the world, or a man-of-war cruising from one ocean to the other, and steamers bound from Europe to the South Pacific ports, or returning thence, pass every day or two; so that communication is kept up with the rest of the universe, and the people who live at this antipodes, where the sun is seen in the north, and the Fourth of July comes in the depth of winter, are pretty well informed as to affairs at the other end of the globe. The latitude corresponds to about that of Greenland, and if you tip the globe over you will see that it is the southernmost town in the world, farther south than the Cape of Good Hope or any of the inhabited islands. The emotions that come with the contemplation of the fact that you are about as far away from anywhere as one can go are quite novel; but in the midst of them you are summoned to confront the fact that the world is not as large as it looks to be, for here is a man who used to live where you came from, and another who once worked in an office where you are employed. There is a news-stand where you can purchase London and New York papers, often three or four months old, but still fresh to the long voyager, and shops at which Paris confectionery and the luxuries of life can be had at Patagonia prices.

There is a curiosity-shop near the landing, which is kept by an old fellow who was once a sailor in the United States navy, and fought under Admiral Farragut at Mobile—at least he says he did, and he speaks like a truthful man. Here are to be purchased many interesting relics; and passengers who are fortunate enough to get ashore, go back to their ship loaded down with Indian trifles, shells and flying fish, tusks of sea-lions, serpent-skins, agates from Cape Horn, turtle-shells, and the curious tails of the armadillo, in which the Indians carry their war-paint. But the prettiest things to be bought at Punta Arenas are the ostrich rugs, which are made of the breasts of the young birds, and are as soft as down and as beautiful as plumage can be.

The plumes of the ostrich are plucked from the wings and tail while the bird is alive, but to make a rug the little ones are killed and skinned, and the soft fluffy breasts are sewed together until they reach the size of a blanket. Those of a brown color and those of the purest white are alternated, and the combination produces a very fine artistic effect. They are too dainty and beautiful to be spread upon the floor, but can be used as carriage robes, or to throw over the back of a couch or chair. Sometimes ladies use them as panels for the front of dress skirts, and thus they are more striking than any fabric a loom can produce. Opera cloaks have been made of them also, to the gratification of the æsthetic. They are too rare to be common, and too beautiful to ever tire the eye.

This town of Sandy Point is quite a market for other sorts of furs, which are brought in by the Indians of Patagonia from the mountains. Several large houses in Valparaiso and Buenos Ayres have agents there, and the shipments to Europe are quite large. The chief articles of export in this line are ostrich feathers and guanaco (pronounced *wanacko*) skins.

THE GUANACO.

The fur-bearing animals of South America are numerous, and some of them are very fine. The mountains of the lower half of the continent abound with vicuñas, guanacos, alpacas, and chinchillas, while the archipelago of Chili and Terra del Fuego, with its thousands of islands, fairly swarm with seals. Very many furs are shipped to Europe, but the seals are seldom touched except by the native Indians, who use their flesh for food and their skins for garments. The supply of seals is practically inexhaustible. They are found in large numbers as far north as Guayaquil, on the west coast, and the passengers on the steamships passing up and down are entertained by their antics. The seals have helped the sea-birds to create the supply of guano upon the Peruvian coast, and this valuable fertilizing material is largely composed of decayed seal flesh and bones, as well as the remnants of the fishes they have dined upon for thousands of years.

The skins of the northern seals are worthless, but farther south, as the archipelago is reached, a colder climate exists, the fur is thicker, and the skins have value. If the reader will take the map of South America, and examine the configuration of the continent south of the fortieth parallel, he will see how numerous these islands are, and every one of them is swarming with seals. There have been some attempts at seal-fishing in Terra del Fuego, but the Indians are so fierce as to make it dangerous for small parties to visit the islands, and only a few skins are shipped from Punta Arenas.

The guanaco skins are considered very fine. These are the wearing apparel of the Indians, and with the ostrich rugs constitute the chief results of their chase. In Patagonia ostriches are not bred, as at the Cape of Good Hope, but run wild, and are getting exterminated rapidly. The Indians chase them on horseback, and catch them with *bolas*—two heavy balls attached to the ends of a rope. Galloping after the ostrich, they grasp one ball in the hand, and whirl the other around their heads like a lasso coil. When near enough to the bird, they let go, and the two balls, still revolving in the air if skilfully directed, will wind around the long legs of the ostrich, and send him turning somersaults upon the sand. The Indians then leap from the saddle, and if scarce of meat they will cut the throat of the bird and carry the carcass to camp. If they have no need of food, they will pull the long plumes from the tail and wings, and let him go again to gather fresh plumage for the coming season.

The bolas are handled very dexterously, and well trained Indians are said to be able to bring down an ostrich at a range of two or three hundred yards. But it is not often necessary to draw at that distance. Horses accustomed to the chase can overtake a bird on an unobstructed plain; but the

PATAGONIAN INDIANS.

birds have the advantage of being "artful dodgers," and as they carry so much less weight, can turn and reverse quite suddenly. The usual mode of hunting them is for a dozen or so Indians to surround a herd and charge upon it suddenly. In this way several are usually brought down before they can scatter, and those that get away are pursued. As they dodge from one hunter they usually run afoul of another, and before they are aware they are tripped by the entangling bolas. People who are passing through the strait often stop over and await another steamer at Punta Arenas to enjoy an ostrich chase. They can secure trained horses and guides at moderate rates. One who has never thrown the bolas will be amazed, the first time he tries it, to find how difficult it is to do a trick that looks so easy.

BUENOS AYRES.

CAPITAL OF THE ARGENTINE REPUBLIC.

THE HARBOR, BUENOS AYRES.

The Chillanos claim to be the Yankees of South America, and it is their proudest boast, but the Argentinians are more entitled to that distinction. Chili, commercially and in her political affinities, is to all intents and purposes an English colony. She reckons her transactions in pounds, shillings, and pence, and her statute-books bear the law of entail. There is no democracy outside her constitution, and a peon can never be anything else. The poor may not acquire land, but must be the retainers of the rich and the tenants of the great estates which are tied up forever from them. In the Argentine Republic, on the contrary, the pampas are divided like the prairies of our own great West. Any man may acquire an estancia by location upon the public lands and the payment of a nominal price per acre; so the country is settling up with those who have fled from the conditions that exist in Chili, free thought, free speech, free air, and free land being their inducement. The city of Buenos Ayres is the only one of the South American capitals in which modern ideas and manners of life prevail. The town is of mushroom growth, like Chicago. There were no old prejudices to uproot, no antiquated bigotry to tear down. It looks less like Spain than any of the other capitals, and more like a modern American community.

The first impressions of the traveller are unfavorable, and you wonder what possessed the Spaniards to locate this capital where it stands. But Buenos Ayres is like Topsy—it simply "growed." The first man who came was Juan Diaz de Solis, in 1515. He discovered the Rio de la Plata, and was murdered by the Indians. Then came the famous Sebastian Cabot, who explored the country as far up the river as Paraguay ten years later, and was followed by Pedro de Mendoza in 1535, who obtained permission from the Spanish

Government to equip an expedition to subdue the country, provided—as was always the rule in the Pickwick Club—he did the same at his own expense. Mendoza came with eleven hundred men, went ashore where he first saw land, established a camp as a basis of operations, and from the purity of the atmosphere called it Buenos Ayres, or "good air." He had no intention of founding a city at this location; his purpose was to rest there a while and keep a base of supplies, until he had found a path to the mythical El Dorado, which was supposed to lie somewhere in the interior of South America.

The approach to Buenos Ayres, which stands about one hundred miles above the mouth of the Rio Plata—or "the river Plate," as it is more commonly called by English writers—is perplexing to navigators, as the mouth of the river is beset with mud-banks and sand-bars—accumulations that come down from the interior of the continent upon the swift waters, and, like the shoals in the Mississippi, are constantly shifting. The voyage from the Strait of Magellan to the place is not a comfortable one, and the captain is always glum and anxious. When it is calm weather he is nervous, and keeps his eye on the barometer for fear of a gale; and when the gale comes, as it does about three or four days in a week, the jokes of the passengers do not appear to entertain him. These gales are called *pamperos*, and sweep across the pampas of Patagonia with the violence of a tornado. Many a brave ship has gone down a victim of their fierceness, and the sailors are as much afraid of them as of the tempests which haunt Cape Horn.

Our captain was unusually anxious, because we had a priest on board. Ever since the days of Jonah there has been a superstition among sailors that clergymen always bring bad luck, particularly a Catholic priest. In trying to discover why the forebodings over a priest should be greater than those over a Protestant parson, the conclusion is reached that it is because the priest wears the sign of his office in his apparel, and is thus more conspicuous. Many captains of sailing-vessels will not take clergymen as passengers under any circumstances, always protesting, of course, that they do not share the common superstition, but basing their objections upon the ground that it would demoralize the sailors. A missionary to one of the South American countries waited in New York for over three months to get passage by a sailing-vessel, and although several started in the mean time for the port he wanted to reach, he was finally obliged to go on a steamer by way of England. The steamer was lost in a storm off the coast of British Guiana. He and other of the passengers were saved in the life-boats, but the chief mate and several of the seamen were drowned. This superstition prevails among sailors of all races, but the Spaniards are the most sensitive to it, as they are to omens of all kinds. The Spanish seamen believe that if the decks are wet by the sea the first day out, they will have fine weather for the rest of the voyage, and for this reason they often leave their moorings in a storm when skippers of other countries would wait for fair weather. There is scarcely a tar in the Spanish service who cannot find some significance in every incident.

Through the Strait of Magellan and up the east coast of

THE CITY OF BUENOS AYRES.

South America vessels are followed by myriads of sea-birds—albatrosses, Mother Carey's chickens, and a beautiful species of the gull variety not found elsewhere, known as the "cape pigeon." Their plumage is beautiful, of the purest white, mixed with the most intense black, and nature has clothed them so warmly for the severe climate in which they live that their skin is as thick as fur, and is used for the manufacture of robes and rugs. More than a hundred breasts of these birds are needed for an ordinary sized robe, however, so that they are a luxury few can afford. I saw in Montevideo a mass of tiny feathers, black and white, as fine and soft as eider-down, that was lined with scarlet silk, and cost two hundred and fifty dollars. Nothing more beautiful could be imagined. Robes made of the breasts of ostriches are lovely enough, but one of cape-pigeons' breasts is passing lovely.

The sailors catch them by throwing overboard a long piece of coarse twine and trailing it in the wake of the ship. As hundreds of the birds are constantly sailing along the surface of the water, they get tangled in the cord and are drawn in, but it requires as much dexterity to get them aboard as to land a lively trout. Sometimes brass or tin tags are tied to their necks, with names and dates scratched upon them, when they are released. The officers of our ship reported that upon a previous voyage they got a bird with one of these tags on, bearing inscriptions showing that it had been caught twice before. They gave the little stranger another indorsement and let him go. The albatrosses of the southern hemisphere are very large, sometimes measuring ten and twelve feet from wing to wing; but they are worthless, and are stupid, awkward birds, that often dash themselves against the side of a ship from pure stupidity.

There is no port of importance between Punta Arenas, in the Strait, and the river Plate except Bahia Blanca (White Bay), near where the United States astronomical expedition made its observations at the last transit of Venus. The entire coast for fifteen hundred miles is barren of civilization, except the cabin of some hardy frontiersman, who has set up a ranch and is waiting for the country to grow down to him.

LOADING CARGO AT BUENOS AYRES.

Montevideo, the capital of Uruguay, lies a few miles below Buenos Ayres, on the other side of the river, and vessels usually touch there, for it is a place of great commercial importance, more accessible to shipping and more favorably located in every respect than the latter city, which lies stretched along a low sandy bank seven or eight miles beyond the anchorage of ships. There is no harbor at Buenos Ayres—not even an excuse for one—and it is beyond the power of human genius to give vessels direct access to the city. The water is so shallow that they anchor seven, eight, and ten miles out, and are loaded and unloaded by means of flat-bottomed lighters, which are towed back and forth. Two or three times a week during the winter, when a pampero is blowing, the water is carried out to sea by force of the wind, and these lighters are left high and dry upon a beach over which they were floating a few hours before. Then they have to be unloaded by means of carts on wheels eight to ten feet in diameter, which are driven into the water until nothing can be seen of the mules that draw them but their indignant noses and nodding ears. It is amusing to see the heads of these mules sticking out of the water at an elevation which must be very uncomfortable, but one they are used to. Passengers who arrive on these occasions are transferred from the ship to a lighter, then to a mule-cart, and sometimes are carried ashore on the back of a stormy Italian, who never fails to swear by all the saints and the Virgin that the man on his back is the heaviest he has ever carried, and demands more than the regular fee for extra baggage, so to speak. Lacking confidence in the sincerity of the cargador, the passenger will promise him heaven and earth and the sea if he will not drop him into the water, and then fights it out when he gets safely ashore.

GOING ASHORE AT BUENOS AYRES.

Notwithstanding the commercial disadvantages of Buenos Ayres, it is the most enterprising, prosperous, and wealthy city in South America—a regular Chicago—the only place on the whole continent where people seem to be in a hurry, and where everybody you meet appears to be trying to overtake the man ahead of him. It is all bustle and life night and day, and is so different from the rest of South America that the traveller is more impressed than he would be if he came direct from the United States. Elsewhere people always put off till to-morrow what they are absolutely not compelled to do to-day.

In the other countries mañana (manyana) is king, and mañana means tomorrow, but in Buenos Ayres the idea seems to be that the liveliest turkey gets the most grasshoppers, and everybody is trying to get as many as he can. Merchants do not shut up shop to go to dinner, as is the rule elsewhere in Spanish-America, and morning newspapers are not printed on the afternoon of the previous day. To do as much as possible this week, and a good deal more, is the motto, and that accounts for the progress of the republic.

And it is a republic, not only in name but in fact. There is no bossism there, as in other Spanish-American countries. Every man is a sovereign, and he will not permit the soldiers to count the votes. There is always a good deal of a rumpus during election times, and the defeated party often raises a revolution, but since the tyrant Rosas was overthrown, no man has attempted to bully or oppress the Argentine people.

Our knowledge of the Argentine Republic amounts to little more than we know of the Congo State, and the man who goes there from the United States is kept in a state of astonishment until he leaves. Then, as he sits on shipboard and reflects over what he has seen, he cannot find an exclamation point big enough to do justice to his description of the country. The Argentinians think it is wicked indifference on our part to know so little about them, for the surprise of the few American visitors wounds their self-esteem. They are a proud people, like all the rest of the Spanish race, and, unlike some nations, have many things to be proud of. They know all about us. There are many men in the Argentine Republic who can tell you the percentage of increase in population, industry, and progress in the United States, as shown by the latest statistics, but how many people in the United States are aware that that country is growing twice as fast as ours? How many members of the Senate or the House of Representatives at Washington, how many members of the Cabinet or Justices of the Supreme Court, know that the increase of population in the Argentine Republic during the last twenty-five years has been one hundred and fifty-four per cent., while in the United States it has been only seventy-nine per cent., and that Buenos Ayres is growing as fast as Denver or Minneapolis?

The people are right when they assert that their country is the United States of South America, and there is nothing else that they are so proud of. They study and imitate our institutions and our methods, and in some cases improve upon them. You can buy the New York dailies and illustrated papers at any of the news-stands in Buenos Ayres, although they are six weeks old, and the people purchase and read them. They understand the significance of the cartoons in *Puck*, and read *Harper's Magazine* and the *Century*. Blaine's book and Grant's Memoirs are on sale, and the issues of our Presidential campaigns are as well understood as their own local squabbles.

The greatest benefit to be derived by a traveller in the countries of South America is to make him think well of his own; but, nevertheless, his vanity receives a severe shock when he comes to the Argentine Republic, and discovers how little he knows of what is going on in the world.

The succession of surprises that greet one on either hand keep him reminded of his own ignorance. It is perfectly natural, however, because we have no communication with the Argentine Republic, and have not had since the day when steam was substituted for canvas as a motive power on the sea. There was a time when we almost monopolized the commerce of that country, but during our civil war the ships were withdrawn, and the sailors went into the navy. Then when peace came all hands were called to the development of our own resources, and we were so busily engaged in building railroads, opening up farms, establishing ranches, working mines, and erecting new towns and cities in the great West, that we forgot that there was anybody to be looked after in South America. Twenty-five years ago our knowledge of the continent was pretty good, but we have learned nothing since. Our geographies read as they did then, our histories have not been rewritten, and our maps remain unaltered. But in the mean time mighty changes have been taking place among our neighbors that have escaped our attention. They have been growing as we have grown, and instead of a few half-civilized, ill-governed people upon the pampas of the Argentine Republic, a great nation has sprung up, as enterprising, progressive, and intelligent as ours, with "all the modern improvements," as house agents say, and an ambition to stand beside the United States in the front rank of modern civilization. While we have been occupied with our own internal development, the European nations have gone in and taken the commerce to which we by the logic of political and geographical considerations are entitled.

Twenty-three lines of steamships connect the Argentine Republic with the markets of Europe, and from forty to sixty vessels are sailing back and forth each month. In the harbor of Buenos Ayres, or in what they call the harbor, are dozens of steamships and scores of sailing-vessels, showing every flag but that of the United States; for an American steamer never goes there, and only occasionally a bark or brigantine, chartered at New York or Philadelphia, with a cargo of lumber or railway supplies. Nearly all the goods these people buy of us are sent by way of Europe, as mails and passengers usually go, and very little is bought in the United States that can be purchased elsewhere. The reason for this is very plain—we have no transportation facilities, while those afforded for trade in Europe are as regular and convenient as exist between Liverpool and New York.

A PRIVATE RESIDENCE IN BUENOS AYRES.

And this trade is worth having. The Argentine Republic imports nearly one hundred million dollars' worth of manufactured merchandise every year, of which about one-third is from England, one-fifth from France, one-fifth from Germany, while the United States comes in at the tail-end of the list, along with Sweden, Denmark, and Chili. While England sent $35,375,628 worth there in 1885, we sent $7,000,000 worth, mostly lumber, railway locomotives and cars, and agricultural implements. While she sent $7,000,000 worth of cotton goods, we sent $600,000 worth; while she sent nearly $7,000,000 worth of hardware and other manufactures of iron and steel, we sent about $500,000 worth; and so on, down through the list of manufactured articles in which we, with equal transportation facilities, can compete with any nation on the globe. Our goods are more popular there, as everywhere in South America, so popular that the manufacturers at Manchester and Birmingham imitate our trade-marks, and send cargoes of merchandise which appears to have been produced in the United States, but never got nearer to Yankeeland than Liverpool.

There is not a country in all the world so deserving of attention as this, and particularly of our attention, for the time is drawing near when we must confront the results of its enterprise in the markets of the world. In its resources as well as in the character of its people it resembles the United States. Here are found pampas like our prairies, rich and fertile in the lowlands, and covered with fine ranges as they rise in mighty terraces from the Atlantic to the Andes; while in the foot-hills of the mountains are deposits of gold and silver similar to those of Colorado, whose wealth is yet untold. In the north is a soil that will produce cotton, rice, and sugar, like Louisiana and Texas; then come tobacco lands, like those of Virginia and Tennessee; then, as the temperature grows colder towards the south, are wheat and corn fields, as yet a tithe of them untilled, but suggesting Iowa, Nebraska, and Kansas. This vast area, as vast as that which lies between Indiana and the Rocky Mountains, is furnished with natural highways even more tempting to navigation than the Mississippi, the Ohio, and the Missouri rivers, and which find their sources in forests as extensive as those that shelter our great lakes.

Already the pampas produce wheat enough for domestic consumption and 9,000,000 bushels for export, and the production is increasing with the greatest rapidity. Nearly 100,000,000 sheep—more than are owned in any country of the world—are grazing on the ranges, and producing 200,000,000 pounds of wool for export; already beef and mutton are sent to England in refrigerator ships at prices cheaper than we can compete with, and few of our people know it.

THE COLON THEATRE, BUENOS AYRES.

A mistaken notion prevails everywhere among the American people about the social and political condition of the Argentine Republic, as well as about its commerce. There are banks at Buenos Ayres with capital greater than any in the United States, and occupying buildings finer than any banking-house in New York, palaces of marble and glass and iron. The Provincial Bank has a capital of $33,000,000, and $67,000,000 of deposits. It does more business than any one of our banks, and more than the Imperial Bank of Germany, being exceeded by but two banks in the world. The National Bank has a capital of $40,000,000, another has $8,000,000, another has $7,000,000, and several have $5,000,000. If we compare the banking capital and deposits of the Argentine Republic with those of the United States we find that they amount to $64 per capita of population there, and only $49 per capita with us. They have a Board of Trade and a Stock Exchange, where business is conducted upon the same plan as in New York or Chicago, and with as great an amount of excitement.

There are more daily papers in Buenos Ayres than in New York or London—twenty-three in all. Two of the dailies are published in the English language, one in French, one in German, and one in Italian; the rest are in Spanish. There are two illustrated weeklies, one of them comic, and three monthly literary magazines. The leading daily, *La Nacion*, is a great blanket-sheet larger than the New York *Evening Post*, and has a circulation of thirty thousand copies. The expression of opinion in the newspapers is as free as with us, and the editors are not under such restrictions as in other of the South American republics. There is a peculiar law of libel, and editors charged with this offence are tried by what is called a jury of honor, a sort of arbitrating committee, who decide upon the justice of the facts stated. Sometimes they compel the publisher to apologize, but more often console the complainant with advice "to grin and bear it." The telephone and electric light are used extensively as in the United States, there being two telephone companies, and the manager of one told me that the number of instruments engaged is larger in proportion to population than any city in the world.

There are nine prominent theatres in Buenos Ayres, giving performances every night in the week, including Sunday, a permanent Italian opera, and a permanent French opera bouffe. One of the theatres is English, with all the plays given in that language, another is French, and a third is Italian; the rest are Spanish. There is a curious innovation in theatre and opera management in Buenos Ayres, which might be imitated by managers in the United States. The first gallery, or what we call the "dress circle," is reserved exclusively for ladies, and no gentlemen are admitted. There is a separate box-office and entrance, and ladies who desire to attend but have no escorts are thus given an opportunity without being subjected to the annoyances suffered if they go in the usual way. They can ride to the private entrance in street-car or cab, and be as safe from the impertinence of loafers as if they had a dozen brothers or husbands around them. These galleries are almost always filled, which is the best evidence of their popularity and the success of the system.

Buenos Ayres has its parks, boulevards, and race-courses, like other modern cities; in fact, there is nothing in the line of civilized amusements that it is without. Everybody keeps a carriage and nearly everybody rides. Nowhere in the world are horses so cheap, and the stock as well as the equipages are very fine. A good pair of carriage-horses, the very best, can be had for one hundred and fifty dollars, and saddle-horses that are equal to any in the world can be purchased for thirty or forty dollars. The Argentine horseman invests his money in silver-mounted saddles and bridles, and a riding-gear with solid-silver stirrups, heavily mounted saddle, etc., is worth between four and five hundred dollars. All the swells have them, and the ladies who ride are similarly mounted, having a beautiful stirrup in the form of a slipper, often of solid silver. The parks and boulevards are crowded with haughty dons and ravishing señoritas during driving hours, and present a very brilliant and attractive scene.

The two Argentine Universities, under the patronage of the Government, are among the best in America, and rank with Yale or Harvard in curriculum and standard of education. They have large and able faculties, many of them Germans, with four branches, namely, law, medicine, engineering, and scientific, and the ordinary classical course. The library has about sixty thousand volumes, representing the literature of all languages, and the museum is quite extensive. The public-school system is also under the patronage of the Government, under a compulsory education law, and includes all grades from the kindergarten to the normal school. The distinguished ex-President of the Republic, Dr. Sarmiento, who was formerly Minister to the United States, is the especial patron of education, and it is his ambition to make the school system of the Argentine Republic the finest in the world. He studied the educational systems of all our States, and finally adopted that of Michigan for his own country.

Ex-President Sarmiento is the leading advocate of the higher education of women in South America, having gained his advanced ideas while Minister to the United States. He was an intimate friend and regular correspondent of Mrs. Horace Mann, Mrs. Julia Ward Howe, Mrs. Elizabeth Cady Stanton, and other prominent women in the United States, and imbibed from them the theories of the equality of the sex which their lives have been spent in demonstrating. Through his instrumentality some forty American girls, graduates of Vassar, Wellesley, Mount Holyoke, and Western institutions, have been employed under liberal contracts by the Argentine Government in the normal schools and female seminaries of the country, and their success has been phenomenal. These teachers receive salaries varying from one hundred to one hundred and sixty dollars per month, and are placed in positions, social as well as professional, which they could not hope to acquire at home. In every instance they have conducted themselves with the most commendable dignity; and although some of the economists in Congress and in the newspapers are grumbling over the large salaries they receive, they are treated with the greatest distinction, and are entertained by the Government in a manner that our own educational authorities might well imitate.

One of them had a misunderstanding with the Papal Nuncio not long ago, which caused an immense amount of excitement. He attempted to interfere with the management of her school, on the ground that she was proselyting the children to Protestantism. She gave the envoy of his Holiness the Pope to understand that she was running that institution, and when he brought the case to the attention of the Government she defended herself with such success that the President of the Argentine Republic sent him his passport and advised him to take the next steamer for Rome. The archbishop interfered, and he was summarily banished also. Since then the Pope has been without an ambassador in the republic, but the Yankee school-ma'am is solid with the Government and the people, and goes on teaching heresy.

A Brazilian who went to Cornell University for an education married an Ithaca girl, and took her back to Brazil, where he is engaged as a civil engineer. There are a good many young Spanish-Americans with English wives. More of the men go to England than to the United States for collegiate training, for the reason that the English universities advertise down there, while the American colleges do not. There is no necessity for the Argentinians to send their sons away for learning, as their educational system is as good as our own, and the most expensive in the world, with the exception of Australia. The amount expended by the Government for educational purposes is $10.20 per pupil annually, while in the United States it averages only $8.70, in Germany $6.00, and in England $9.10. There are thirty colleges and normal schools for the higher education of men and women in the republic, with 430 teachers and 6710 students, and 2726 public schools with 6214 teachers and 201,329 pupils, in a total population of less than 4,000,000.

The Government of Chili, which attempts a close competition with the Argentine Republic in matters of education as well as other modern improvements, has contracted with fifty young ladies from Germany to manage its female seminaries and normal schools at much lower salaries than the Yankee school-ma'ams receive.

The Argentinians have made as rapid advancement in the way of charity and philanthropy as in education, and one finds throughout the country as many benevolent institutions as in New York or other cities of the United States in proportion to the population. There are hospitals, dispensaries, homes for the indigent aged, orphan asylums, blind, and deaf and dumb asylums, insane asylums, public libraries, free art schools, and all sorts of institutions founded by benevolence and liberally endowed. There is a Board of Health enforcing strict sanitary regulations, the streets are swept every night, the police are admirably organized, the public buildings and parks are lighted by electricity, and all the features of modern civilization have been introduced into the political and domestic economy. The plantation owners mostly reside in Buenos Ayres, and have telephonic wires between their offices and estancias. Instead of yelling " Hello!" into a telephone, they say "Oyez, oyez!" as our bailiffs do when they open court.

The post-office of Buenos Ayres handled 20,000,000 packages in 1885, which is pretty good for a city of 434,000 inhabitants, and its progress is no better illustrated than by the increase of mails. In 1865 only 1,000,000 pieces were handled by this office, and in 1875 only 7,000,000, while during the first six months of 1887 over 16,000,000 pieces passed through the office. There is a mail leaving and arriving for and from Europe nearly every day, but all mail for the United States goes and comes by way of Great Britain, because of the lack of direct steamship communication.

There are three gas companies with 240 miles of pipe, lighting 26,000 houses or stores, with 3300 street-lamps. There are 32 miles of paved streets, 40 miles of sewers, some of which are large enough for a railway-train to pass through. There are 1100 licensed hacks, and 2715 licensed express-wagons; five street-railway companies, with 93 miles of track, carrying 1,850,000 passengers monthly. Between tramways and public carriages the inhabitants of Buenos Ayres spent an average of $8.00 per capita for city locomotion in 1885.

Throughout South America all the dentists and many of the photographers are immigrants from the United States, and if there is any one among them who is not getting rich he has nobody but himself to find fault with, because the natives give both professions plenty to do. Nowhere in the world is so large an amount of confectionery consumed in proportion to the population as in Spanish America, and as a natural consequence the teeth of the people require a great deal of attention. As a usual thing Spaniards have good teeth, as they always have beautiful eyes, and are very particular in keeping them in condition. Hence the dentists are kept busy, and as they charge twice as much as they do in the United States, the profits are very large. In these countries it is the custom to serve sweetmeats at every meal—dulces, as they are called—preserved fruits of the richest sort, jellies, and confections of every variety and description. Many of these are made by the nuns in the convents, and are sold to the public either through the confectionery stores or by private application. A South American housewife, instead of ordering jams and preserves and jellies from her grocer, or putting up a supply in her own kitchen during the fruit season, patronizes the nuns, and gets a better article at a lower price. The nuns are very ingenious in this work, and prepare forms of delicacies which are unknown to our table.

At a dinner-party I attended dessert was brought in in a novel form. A tray which appeared to be filled with hard-boiled eggs was placed before the hostess, who gave each guest a couple, and poured over them some sort of a syrup or dressing. In a strange country the tourist is always on the lookout for odd things; but this seemed to cap the climax—hard-boiled eggs for dessert at a swell dinner-party. But it was soon discovered that the white of this bogus egg was *blanc-mange*, and the yolk was made of quince jelly, egg-shells being used for moulds. This was an idea of the nuns, and one of their ingenious fixings.

The atmosphere is so clear as to be admirable for photography. The Spanish-American belle has her photograph taken every time she gets a new dress, and that is very often. The Paris styles reach here as soon as they do the North American cities, and where the national costumes are not still worn there is a great deal of elaborate dressing. The Argentine Republic is one of the few countries in which photographs of ladies are not sold in the shops. Elsewhere there is a craze for portraits of reigning beauties, and the young men have their rooms filled with photographs of the girls they admire taken in all sorts of costumes and attitudes.

There are in South America a great many physicians and surgeons from the United States, and they usually, if worthy, have a more extensive practice than the natives. There is an excellent field for female physicians here, and it is at present unoccupied. In most of the countries of South America a physician is not permitted to see a lady patient except in the presence of her husband, and many women die for lack of attention. The social laws are inflexible in this respect, and many women will suffer torments rather than expose themselves to criticism by receiving treatment from male practitioners. No woman, except she be of the common laboring class, will visit the office of a physician, and as fees for attendance at their homes are very high, many suffer and die from neglect based upon motives of modesty and economy. There is only one lady physician that I know of in South America, and she is practising with great success in Guatemala. Others might secure equal advantages in Venezuela, Colombia, Peru, Chili, the Argentine Republic, Uruguay, and Brazil; but it would be necessary for them to acquire a thorough knowledge of the Spanish language, and secure favorable introductions before hanging out their shingles. These introductions might be obtained through the American consuls and legations, or from merchants of social and commercial standing. There is a strong prejudice against the professional employment of native women, but the American ladies who have come to South America as teachers have not only been cordially received but in many cases have been lionized. In many of the aristocratic families American girls are employed as governesses, and are treated with great deference. Mrs. Barrios, the widow of the late President of Guatemala, had three New York ladies in her family—one as a companion for herself, and the other two employed in the nursery. In Peru, Chili, the Argentine Republic, and other countries French and English governesses are common, and in fact there are few others employed, as the native girls who would accept such positions lack the necessary education.

There are two notable Boston men in Buenos Ayres—notable, however, for different reasons. One is Samuel B. Hale, the most prominent merchant and capitalist in the country; and the other is D. Warren Lowe, *alias* Winslow, editor of the *Buenos Ayres Daily Herald*. There is no man in all South America more respected and beloved, or who possesses the confidence of the people to a greater degree than Samuel B. Hale. He came in 1829 from Boston to do a little trading, and has since remained, amassing an immense fortune, and now, at the age of eighty-two, looks back upon such a career as few men are permitted to contemplate.

Although we of the United States have very little to do with the Argentine Republic nowadays, the pioneers of that country were Americans. In 1826 William Wheelwright, of Pennsylvania, was wrecked upon this coast, and found his way to a small town named Quilmes, barefooted, hatless, and starving. He remained in the country, and forty years later built the first railroad in the Argentine Republic—from Buenos Ayres to Quilmes. But in the mean time he had done still greater service in establishing the first steamship line between Europe and South America—the Pacific Steam Navigation Company—which now has a monopoly of the traffic on the west coast, and sails vessels from Panama through the Strait of Magellan to Liverpool. In 1839 Mr. Wheelwright foresaw the immense trade these countries were capable of developing, and went to New York to present his scheme to Aspinwall, Garrison, Astor, Vanderbilt, and other capitalists, but they rejected it. He then went to England, where he secured the necessary capital, established his line, and turned the whole course of South American commerce from its natural channel. Every one connected with the company has made a fortune, and dividends of fourteen and fifteen per cent. are still paid. In 1852 there were in the harbor of Buenos Ayres six hundred vessels from the United States—more than double the number from all other nations combined. Now only two per cent. of the shipping annually reaching that harbor belongs to the United States. Both Chili and the Argentine Republic have erected fine monuments to Mr. Wheelwright, the father of their foreign commerce and their internal improvements, for he built the first railway in Chili as he did in the Argentine Republic.

Another citizen of the United States, Thomas Lloyd Halsey of New Jersey, introduced sheep and cattle. The Spaniards had a few domestic animals before the independence of the republic, but Mr. Halsey established the first ranch. Now there are over ninety million sheep and thirty million cattle in the country. Both Wheelwright and Halsey are dead; but Mr. Hale, who was contemporary with them, and was the pioneer commission merchant and importer, still lives. His immense business interests are now in the hands of Mr. Pierson, his son-in-law, also a Boston man, who went out as a clerk thirty years ago; and the husband of another daughter represents the London banking-house of Baring Brothers in Buenos Ayres.

In the old days Mr. Hale bought wool and hides and furs in the Argentine Republic and in Uruguay, and shipped them to Boston. The vessels returned loaded with cotton goods and Yankee notions of all sorts, which were exchanged for the produce; and this system of barter went on until the War of the Rebellion, when most of the vessels were withdrawn, and the tariff on wool made it unprofitable to ship the chief product of the republic to the United States. Then Mr. Hale turned his attention to the European trade, and did a very large business in exporting and importing until about 1880, when he sold out to Mr. C. S. Bowers, also a Boston man, and retired from the market. He still purchases large quantities

AN ARGENTINE RANCHMAN.

of wool and hides for shipment to Europe, but does not import any longer, and he devotes most of his attention to loaning money and dealing in standard securities. In addition to his commercial business, Mr. Hale owns and manages some of the largest estancias in the Argentine Republic, having several hundred thousand sheep and sixty thousand cattle. He is famous for his hospitality and generosity, and many of the philanthropic institutions of the country have enjoyed with him the financial results of his successful career. He has also been active in the promotion of public enterprises and in encouraging steamship lines, and is not only the oldest and most prominent merchant, but is regarded as the leading public benefactor.

The social condition of the Argentine Republic is as much advanced as its commerce, and the old customs are rapidly dying out. The education of girls has become popular, and the young ladies are no longer restricted in their association with men, as in other Spanish-American countries. Formerly, if a young man fell in love with a girl, he told her father or grandmother about it, which was about as satisfactory as kissing through a telephone. Under the new regime etiquette gives him the privilege of telling the old, old story into the girl's own ear, and it appears to work just as well for all concerned.

It is the only country in South America in which girls can go out riding with their lovers, or receive them at home as they do in the United States. The supposition that it is unsafe to leave a woman alone with any man but her husband or father does not exist in the Argentine Republic, except among some of the families of the ancient Spanish aristocracy which still adhere to the old tradition.

One finds a good deal of club life in Buenos Ayres, there being as many as seven fine club-houses, most of which have all the modern improvements, with reading-rooms attached, in which are found newspapers from all parts of the world.

Their restaurants and cafés are as good as the average in New York and London, and the people being epicurean in their tastes, caterers import delicacies from all parts of the world. Lobsters and Spanish mackerel are brought in refrigerator ships, and Southdown mutton from England, with all sorts of delicacies from France. One day I saw a negro going through the streets with a large tray on his head, containing a leg of mutton, a haunch of venison, Spanish mackerel, lobsters, shrimps, and oysters, and a printed placard upon his back announcing that dishes of this sort were served daily at the Maison de Paris.

The hotels are not good. They are up to the average in South American cities, but do not correspond with the other evidences of advancement in Buenos Ayres. They have no regular rates, but charge each guest as much as his appearance and manners suggest he can afford to pay. When they get hold of an American, as citizens of the United States are always called, they bleed him to the last drop. "I thought you Americans never disputed a hotel-bill," a Boniface said to me one day, when I had expressed my indignation at his charges. "We always expect Englishmen to, but Americans never," and he shrugged his shoulders as if my conduct was a disgrace to my country.

The steamers which run from Buenos Ayres to Montevideo and up the river to Paraguay are, to the surprise of every traveller, as fine and gorgeous as those on Long Island Sound—great, splendid palaces with no end of gilt and gingerbreadwork, with stewards and cabin-boys in livery, wine-rooms, smoking-rooms, bands of music, and all that sort of thing. There are two lines in active rivalry, and they are trying to see which can set the finer table. The bill of fare is as good as that of a first-class hotel in New York, and two kinds of wine, claret and Rhine wine, are served without extra charge. On each steamer are three or four swell cabins, called bridal chambers, each being fitted up without regard to expense, and containing all the flub-dubs that can be crowded into them, including pianos and sideboards, with well-filled bottles of wine and brandy in the rack, all included in the price of passage, which is double that of the ordinary cabin. The swells always take these cabins when they start off on a bridal tour.

The finest church in Buenos Ayres is called the "Church of the Recolletta" (remembrance). It is of pure Roman architecture, in Italian marble, beautifully carved, and cost about $250,000. It is the property of Señor Don Carlos Guerrero, a wealthy citizen, who erected it as a memorial to his daughter, who was murdered by a rejected lover about ten years ago. She is buried under the altar, and the magnificent stained glass window imported from Florence represents incidents from her life.

The cathedral is a very large and costly building, but it looks more like a bank or Government palace than a church. Within the walls is the mausoleum of General Saint-Martin,

THE CATHEDRAL OF BUENOS AYRES.

the George Washington of the Argentine Republic, who liberated the country from the Spanish yoke and was then turned out to die in exile and poverty. In 1880 the remains of the Liberator were brought with great pomp from France, where he had died in 1850, in banishment, and were entombed under a costly and imposing sepulchre, which, however, looks very little like a tomb, and is entirely without sacred emblems. Four statues in marble guard the grave; not Faith, Hope, and Charity, but "Agriculture," "Industry," "Justice," and "Liberty." It looks rather queer to see the emblem of Industry with hammer and saw over a tomb in a church, but the Argentines evidently have not noticed the incongruity.

Besides the twenty-four churches belonging to the Catholics, the Protestant community is pretty well supplied with religious advantages. There are a Church of England society, a Scotch Presbyterian, an American Presbyterian, a German Evangelical, three Methodist churches, and a Jewish synagogue— the only one in all Spanish America. Jews are not allowed to live in some of the countries; but in the Argentine Republic, where religious as well as civil liberty is protected, they are numerous, and worship every Saturday. In 1884 the Methodists celebrated the twenty-fifth anniversary of their missionary work in the country, and it was emphasized by an incident which attracted a great deal of comment, and was significant as showing the religious toleration that exists. Formal invitations were sent as a mark of courtesy to the

President and all the prominent officials, but there was no expectation that they would attend, as the great majority of the people are Catholics and the public men are naturally politic. Just as the services were about to commence, however, the managers of the affair were astonished to see the President, followed by his Cabinet, walk into the church. Conspicuous seats were given them, and they seemed to take great interest in the exercises. After the Rev. Dr. Wood, the Superintendent of Missions, had concluded his address, in which he reviewed the history of Protestantism in the Argentine Republic, he invited President Roca to speak. The latter promptly responded; and as every one knew he had been born and reared in the Catholic Church, the audience were amazed at the eulogy he pronounced upon the Protestant missionaries, and the enthusiasm with which he complimented the work they had done. To their influence he attributed much of the progress of the republic, and urged them to enlarge their fields and increase their zeal. The President's speech was commented upon in the newspapers the next day with a great deal of vigor, the Liberal press approving it, but the Conservative editors censuring what they considered an attack upon the prevailing religion of the people.

There is a peculiar order of monks in the Argentine Republic which is not found elsewhere. Its members are known as "Lazarists" (from Lazarus), and they live, as he is said to have done, on the crumbs that fall from the rich man's table. They travel about the country like tramps, having no apparent aim or purpose, barefooted and bareheaded, eat what they beg from door to door, and sleep wherever night overtakes them. They are supposed to be members of the other orders of friars, who have sinned and are doing penance as Lazarists.

There is a place called Washington and another called Lincoln in the Argentine Republic, but the newest thing in the way of towns is La Plata, the capital of the province of Buenos Ayres. Until within a few years that province, having more than half the population of the entire country, has considered itself entitled to rule the rest, as far as the Government was concerned, and the outlying provinces have had nothing to say about it, being regarded as insignificant dependencies of the city and State of Buenos Ayres. They tried to secede, but were whipped into the Union; but as immigration has come into the country the population of other provinces outnumbers Buenos Ayres, and often in Presidential campaigns the contest depends upon a geographical issue. Roca, the recent President, is an outside man, and the Buenos Ayrians determined to prevent his inauguration or overthrow his government; but to mollify them he announced a great scheme of building a new capital at Government expense. There was no time to lay out a town site and let it grow up in the ordinary way, so the President sent to the United States and had five hundred houses manufactured to order and shipped down here, like a box of toys, all ready to put up. A location was selected on the pampas, all the revolutionary leaders were let into the speculation, war was averted, and a brand-new city sprang up on the prairie, like a bed of mushrooms, almost in a single night. Two or three millions of dollars were spent by the Government, but the President considered that the cost of the town was much less than would have been the cost of the war that was averted; plenty of money was put into circulation, all the laboring men in the country got lucrative employment, and, as in the old-fashioned storybooks, everything came out happily in the end. These houses were made in Brooklyn and Chicago: a New York firm got the contract. There was so much haste and carelessness in their construction that they do not wear very well, and are no credit to their builders.

THE GAUCHO.

The gaucho (*gowcho*) of South America is the most interesting character on the continent, and if the writers of tales of adventure could get at him, he would afford them as much material as the Crusader of the Middle Ages or the North American savage. The Spanish colonies have produced no Fenimore Cooper or Mayne Reid, and such a writer as Ned Buntline is unknown to South American literature. Buffalo Bill and Texas Jack would die of mortification if their horsemanship and endurance were placed in comparison with that of the genuine gaucho of the pampas, and even the centaur of mythology would blush with envy.

The gauchos are the descendants of the aristocratic Spanish dons and Indian women; for the grandees and hidalgos who once ruled these colonies did not hesitate to seek the society of the Pocahontases of the Guarani race. They are at once the most indolent and the most active of human beings; for when they are not in the saddle, devouring space on the back of a tireless broncho, they are sleeping in apathetic indolence among their mistresses or gambling with their chums. Half savage and half courtier, the gaucho is as polite as he is cruel, and will make a bow like a dancing-master or thrum an air on the native mandolin with the same ease and nonchalance as he will murder a fellow-being or slaughter a steer. He recognizes no law but his own will and the unwritten code of the cattle-range, and all violations of this code are punished by banishment or death. Whoever offends him must fight or fly, and his vengeance is as enduring as it is vigilant. The statute of limitations is not recognized by him, and he will kill an enemy he has not seen for a quarter of a century. He never shoots or strikes with his fist, and his only weapons are the short knife, which is never absent from his hand or his belt and is used at short range, and the lasso, which is not only an implement of his trade but an instrument offensive and defensive.

A fight between gauchos always means murder, and it is the duty of him who kills to see that his victim is decently buried and the widow and orphans cared for. The widow, if she pleases him, becomes his wife or his mistress, and the orphans grow up to be gauchos under his tutelage. He is as superstitious as a Hindoo, and an inveterate gambler. When he is not asleep or in the saddle he is always engaged at quaint games of chance that are his own invention, and are known to no other race in the world. He is peaceable when sober, but a reckless dare-devil, regardless of God and man. When he is drunk he is a fiend incarnate, for a howling savage is like a prattling child when compared to a drunken gaucho. As brave as a lion, as active as a panther, with an endurance equal to any test, faithful to his friends, as implacable as fate to any one who offends him, he has exercised a powerful influence upon the destiny of the Argentine Republic, and kept that nation back in civilization until his influence was overcome by an increased immigration of foreigners. The gaucho has never taken any part in politics except as a soldier, and as such, under a leader that he will obey, he is without an equal in either civilized or savage fighting.

The Argentinians once had a gaucho President, Don Manuel Rosas, who ruled the country with a despotism of iron and blood for twenty-two years (from 1830 to 1852), and even now is seldom referred to without a shudder, for the marks of his cruel hand are still visible, and the ancient aristocracy still feel the sting of blows he inflicted upon them. He was the son of a wealthy Spaniard of the same name, who exercised a patriarchal sway over the peons that looked after his flocks and herds; and as the young Rosas grew up, the old man gradually yielded to the stronger will of the son, until the latter became a sort of gaucho leader, and commanded a regiment of them in the war of 1829 against the Indians. So powerful did he become that it was an easy step from the chieftainship of the gauchos to the Presidency of the Republic—a self-appointed Dictator, the head of an absolute despotism which existed for nearly a quarter of a century, in defiance of the constitution and the laws.

Rosas was a compound of the arrogance and stubborn superstition of the Spanish race and the cruelty and craft of the Guarani Indians, whose blood he inherited through his mother. He maintained his power by the loyalty of the gauchos, of whom the people of the towns lived in terror. With an inflexible will, with the cunning of a fox and the courage of a lion, with egregious vanity and arrogance, and a perpetual distrust of every living being except his daughter Mannileta—the only person to whose influence he ever

GENERAL ROSAS.

submitted or for whom he ever showed any affection—he ruled like a savage chieftain over the entire southern half of the continent, from Paraguay to the Strait of Magellan, relying solely upon the terror which his own cruelty and that of his gaucho lieutenants had inspired among the people. Blood flowed by his command as freely as water, and the extermination of those who opposed him was the policy under which he perpetuated his power. No citizen of the Argentine Republic or Uruguay felt himself safe. No man went to bed at night with any confidence that he would be alive in the morning; for neither friendship, relationship, nor even obscurity, was a shield from assassination. Rosas only ceased to murder when the great fear he had inspired paralyzed the people and rendered them absolutely prostrate to his will. He spared neither age nor sex. Even his oldest friend, a man who had been more than a father to him, and was supposed to be his confidential adviser, was murdered in cold blood by the *masorqueros*, the secret assassins or Danites on whom he relied to execute his atrocious designs. The official history of Buenos Ayres gives the following estimate of the numbers who died through the caprice or vengeance of the tyrant Rosas: poisoned, 4; executed by the sword, 3765; shot, 1393; assassinated, 722; total, 5884. Add to this the number slain in the constant struggle to overthrow his despotism, 16,520, and we have an aggregate of 22,404 victims to the ambition of a gaucho chief.

An idea of the arrogance and conceit of the man can be formed from the fact that the money coined during his administration was stamped with his portrait and the inscription "Eternal Rosas." But he was not eternal, and was overthrown in 1852 by General Urquiza, escaping from the country with his daughter at night, both in the disguise of English sailors, and finding refuge on board the *Centaur*, an English man-of-war.

But the day of the gaucho is passing. Immigration and civilization have driven him to the extreme frontier, where nowadays he can only be found in his full glory. Like the North American Indian, he decays when domesticated, and a tame gaucho is always a drunkard, a loafer, and a thief. Civilization saps his vitality, quenches his spirit, and lowers his standard of morals. In his native element he will not steal nor do a mean act, but when he becomes a resident of a town he will rob a dog, and there is no end to his maliciousness. Few of the race have ever acquired land, and even at the present day he despises the *estanciaro*, who will not depend upon the public domain for pasturage. So the gaucho has to keep moving, faster and faster, to get out of the way of barbed wire fences and the restraints of civilization. A few years hence he will disappear or assume more of the character of the North American cow-boy. Even now, in the more settled portions of the country, the word gaucho has become a word of reproach, and is applied to worthless characters who live by cattle-stealing, and correspond to the rustlers of the United States.

PALACE OF DON MANUEL ROSAS.

The language of the genuine gaucho is a mixture of Spanish and the Guarani Indian tongue, and his food is beef and *yerba mate*. At every *rodeo*, or "round up," there is a great feast, at which many good things are set forth; but the ordinary diet of the race consists of ribs of beef roasted on a spit before the fire, and eaten without salt or bread, while the ordinary drink is the Paraguayan tea, which is sucked through a tube. The gaucho lives like the Indian—gorges himself when he has plenty of food, or goes for days without eating; but he always has his mate cup with him, and the yerba contains a great amount of nutrition. He usually has a habitation in a hut at the headquarters of the estancia upon which he is employed, and there he keeps his family and goes on feast-days, for he is enough of a Catholic to keep as close a reckoning of the ecclesiastical calendar as the archbishop himself. He has no regard for the Sabbath, but recognizes every religious anniversary of the Church by leaving his cattle on the range and going to headquarters, where he spends the day in drinking, dancing, gambling, confessing his sins to the padre, cock-fighting, and testing horsemanship with his companions. These feast-days never end without a murder, and often more than one.

When dressed in his full regalia the gaucho's appearance is picturesque; with his swarthy face, long hair, and long mustaches, he would create a sensation in any guise, for his physique is perfect, and his swagger as bold as that of a buccaneer or a bandit chief. The gaucho woman is said to be beautiful when young, but at twenty-five or thirty she is a dirty, unkempt slattern, with bleared eyes and tangled hair, and wears nothing but a soiled and faded gown, and perhaps a pair of brass or silver ear-rings. When she is a maiden the gauchos will kill each other out of jealousy, but when she becomes a wife or a mistress she is kicked about the camp, beaten, and abandoned at her master's will.

All the finery in the family goes on the husband's back and saddle. In place of trousers he wears a chiropa and calconcillas. The former is a square piece of cloth, drawn about the thighs and fastened around the waist with a belt. It descends as far as the knee, from which the rest of the leg is covered with the calconcillas—a wide pair of cotton drawers, handsomely and gaudily embroidered, and ornamented with two or three wide frills. The feet are incased in a pair of *botas de potro*, made of the skin of the leg of a colt rubbed until it is as soft as buckskin. The heels are decorated with a pair of immense iron or silver spurs weighing a pound or so each.

Instead of the sombrero and velvet jacket of the Mexican cavalier, the gaucho wears a hat of pita fibre—such as is commonly known as a Panama hat, and which may have cost him as much as would a dozen cattle—and a poncho. But in his saddle lies his wealth, for all his savings and gambling gains go to decorate that emblem of his trade. Silver ornaments for bridle and saddle are legal tender in exchange for anything salable wherever the gaucho goes, and what is his seat by day and his pillow by night he always uses as a sort of savings-bank. I have seen saddles worth a thousand dollars, with solid silver stirrups, pommels, and ornaments weighing as much as a man. A pair of silver spurs are worth anywhere from fifty to one hundred dollars, according to their size and the workmanship upon them. Stirrups of solid silver, made in the form of a heelless slipper, are very common, and the belles of the cities of the Argentine Republic consider them essential to a riding costume. Stirrups are often made of brass, and when highly polished add a unique feature to the accoutrements of an Argentine caballero. His belt is usually covered with a string of silver dollars, and all his buttons are of silver.

The Argentine poncho is a great institution, and if some fashionable swell in New York would set the style by wearing one, it would add greatly to the comfort of our people, as well as to their convenience. There never was a garment better adapted for out-of-door use, and particularly for plainsmen or those who are much in the saddle. It is a blanket of ordinary size, with a slit in the centre through which the head goes. It rests upon the shoulders, and its folds hang down as far as the knee, allowing free use of the arms, but always furnishing them and the rest of the body with protection. In summer it shields the wearer from the heat of the sun, while in winter it is as warm as an ulster, and in rainy days takes the place of an umbrella. The native is never without it, summer or winter, afoot or on horseback, at home or abroad. It stays by him like his shadow, and serves him as an overcoat by day and as a blanket by night.

Ponchos were formerly made of the hair of the vicuña, an animal which is a sort of cross between the camel and the antelope, and is found in the Bolivian Andes. Before the Conquest vicuña skin was the royal ermine of the Incas, and none but persons of princely blood were allowed to wear it. A vicuña poncho is as soft as velvet, and as durable as steel. You can find plenty of them in the Argentine Republic and in Chili that have been, like grandfather's clock, in the old families for two centuries or more, and have been handed down with the family jewels as heirlooms. They never wear out, and, like lace, improve with age. But genuine vicuña ponchos are hard to get, and very expensive, costing often as much as a camel's-hair shawl, as the animal is becoming scarce. The color is a delicate fawn, and will not change when wet, which is a sure test of its genuineness. Most of the fine ponchos worn nowadays are made of lamb's-wool in Manchester, England, and cannot be distinguished from vicuña except by experts; but tons after tons of a common sort, made of cotton and wool, of gaudy colors, are now imported annually, and answer the purpose of the gaucho just as well, while the bright tints please his taste better.

The gaucho always carries tobacco, cigarette paper, flint, and steel. He is an inveterate smoker, but confines himself to cigarettes, which he rolls at full gallop. He does everything on horseback, when he chooses—eats and sleeps, catches fish, carries water from the well in a pitcher or urn on his head, and even attends mass on horseback—at least, the nearest he ever gets to the altar is to ride up to the door of a church and sit in the saddle while the service is being celebrated.

A gaucho child is put into the saddle at as early an age as an American child is put into breeches. When he is eight or ten years old he will ride anything less than a tornado; and after he reaches his growth, if he is thrown from a horse he is disgraced forever; nothing he can do will recover for him the respect of the community. He is an ostracized and despised creature, as hopelessly lost as a fallen star.

The animals the gauchos ride are splendid native stallions, as swift as the wind and as enduring as time. Fifty or sixty miles a day is a gentle jaunt, for a well-bred pampa horse will gallop from sunrise to sunset without throwing a fleck of foam. During the recent war against the Patagonian Indians a gaucho courier made six hundred miles in forty-eight hours with only four changes of horses.

One of the sports of the gauchos is "breaking horses," cruel and dangerous, like all their amusements. Two gauchos mount, and taking positions forty or fifty yards apart, at a given signal start at a full run and come together breast to breast, like two battering-rams, with a shock that often kills the animals, and nearly always unseats one or both of the riders. Another is called "crowding horses." Two mounted gauchos place their stallions side by side, and crowd them against each other to see which will yield. A third game is to place across the entrance to a corral or other enclosure a bar about as high as a horse's head. The gaucho mounts, retires to a distance of forty rods or so, rushes to the entrance at full gallop, and, without checking the speed of his horse, leaps out of the saddle when the bar is reached, throws himself under it, and regains his seat, passing under the bar without touching the ground.

The skill with which the gaucho handles the lasso is an everlasting source of wonder. While at full gallop he can throw a coil of raw-hide with as much accuracy as an expert rifleman can crack a glass ball, and will catch a running cow or sheep or hog, lassoing the horn or foot or head at will. Duels with the lasso are often fought, the contestants throwing nooses at the heads of each other, sparring and dodging like pugilists, until one or the other is caught and dragged out of the saddle. If the duel is an earnest one, as often occurs, and the gauchos are determined, the man who is caught is often dragged, with a noose around his neck, behind a galloping horse until the life is choked and pounded out of his body.

The Argentine Republic will some day become a formidable rival of the United States. It has vast natural resources similar to ours, and is developing them rapidly. It has a magnificent fluvial system like that of the Mississippi, fertile plains like those of Illinois and Iowa, boundless pampas stretching for twelve hundred miles to the mountains, and affording pasturage for millions of cattle, horses, and sheep, like the prairies of Kansas, Colorado, Nebraska, and New Mexico. Towards the north, into Paraguay, which, although an

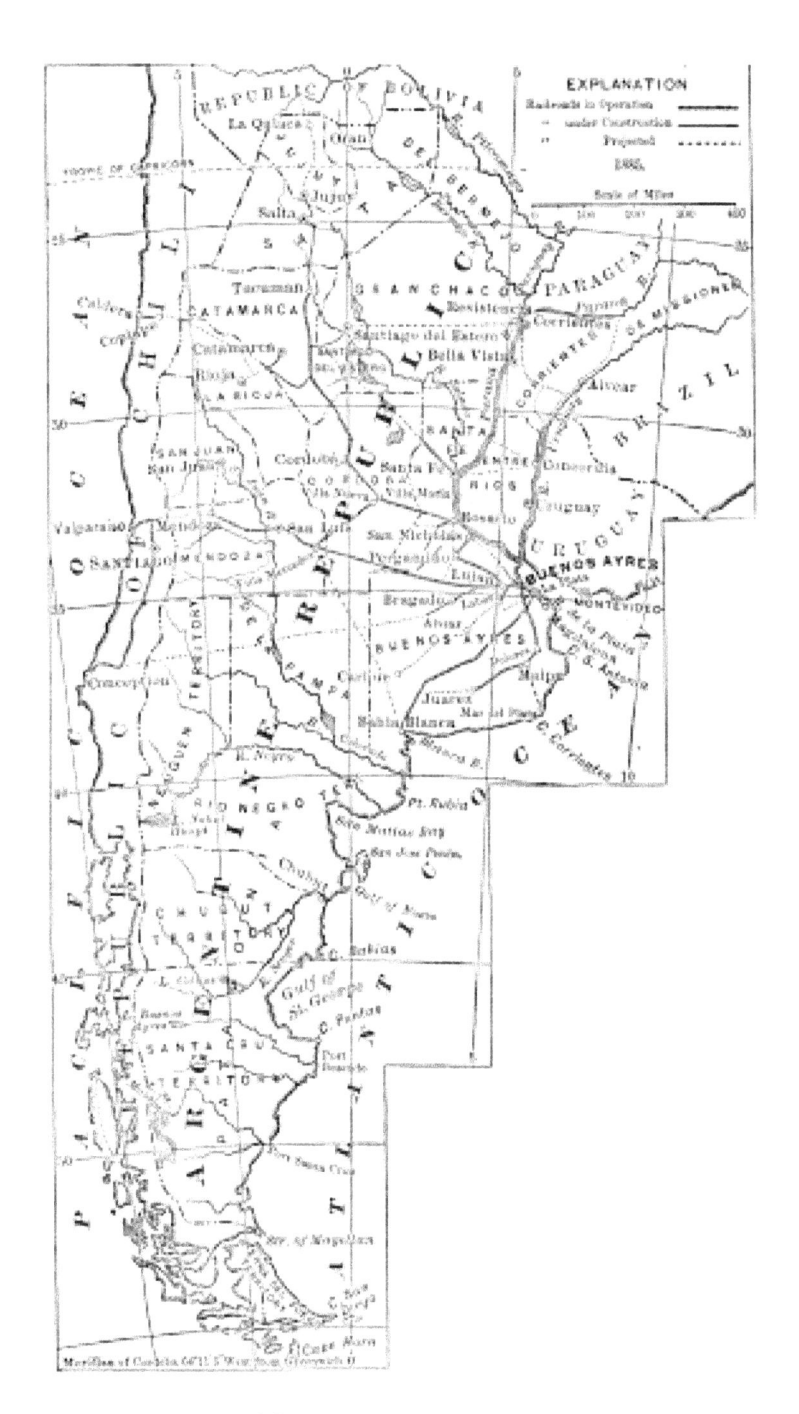

MAP OF THE ARGENTINE REPUBLIC.

independent State, is a tributary to the Argentine Republic, are lands that will produce sugar, cotton, rice, and other semi-tropical staples like those of our own sunny South. There is also an almost unlimited supply of timber, hard and soft woods, easy of access, within reach of mighty streams; and the forests are greater than man knows, for they have never been measured. The latitude of the Argentine Republic corresponds with that of the United States; its climate is similar to that of our great West, and the people have an activity, an enterprise, and a patriotism that remind the North American of home.

Where rivers do not run the people are pushing railroads, and in a few years they will have a railway system second only to that of the United States. They are offering tempting inducements to settlers, and immigration is very large. The increase in population during the last fifteen years was one hundred and fifty-four per cent., while that of the United States was seventy-nine per cent. From Germany, Norway, and Switzerland, but especially from Italy, come ship-loads of hardy, thrifty, industrious men every week, and the passenger mole at Buenos Ayres resembles Castle Garden. The Government aids and encourages immigration more than does ours. The immigrant vessel that arrives at New York is required to pay "head-money" on every passenger it brings. At Buenos Ayres the vessel receives "head-money" from the Government as an inducement to bring passengers. The fare from Europe to the river Plate, or the Rio Plata, that great stream which divides the continent, is about the same as to the United States; and although I do not believe that the class of immigrants which arrives there is equal in intelligence and the other qualities that constitute good citizens to that which comes to the United States, every family arriving means so many more acres developed and an increase of population. They do not at once become citizens, as in this country. This is particularly the case with the Italians, who seldom take out naturalization papers. Foreigners are allowed to vote at municipal elections, and therefore the temptation to citizenship is not so strong; but nevertheless they go to make up the body politic, and as they are exempt from military service, the country is always sure of having its fields tilled and its crops gathered, whether there is a war or not.

In 1882, 51,503 immigrants arrived at Buenos Ayres from Europe; in 1883 the number increased to 63,242; in 1884, to 92,700; in 1887, to 138,000. In 1888 it was estimated that over 600,000 foreigners had settled in the country during the preceding ten years, and it is known that the population of the city of Buenos Ayres has doubled since 1872.

The greater portion of these immigrants are Italians, who go directly into the agricultural regions, take up land, and cultivate small but increasing farms. Some are Germans and Scandinavians, but more are French. The latter usually settle in the cities, and become small tradesmen or servants. Large numbers of English, Scotch, and Irish capitalists are securing estancias, and raising sheep and cattle upon a large scale. It is estimated that ten million dollars have been invested in this way within the last three years, and one Englishman alone has expended a million. The usual plan, as in the United States, is to organize companies, with headquarters in London, Glasgow, and other large cities, and send out capable superintendents. The cattle interests of the Argentine Republic, like those in our country, will ultimately be controlled by a few large corporations.

The colonization plan is popular there, and so far quite successful. Within the last five years 1,126,000 acres of land have been taken up by colonies, representing a population of 82,000 souls, mostly Italians and Swiss. The English and German immigrants will not colonize. The railroad development of the country is very rapid, and lines are now being constructed in various directions from Buenos Ayres and other commercial centres.

The result of the internal improvements made under this policy is plain to be seen. Within the last five years the cattle have been driven back gradually upon the pampas, towns have sprung up, and farms have been opened in territory that was inaccessible before the railroad improvements began. There is a natural tendency to overbuild, as has been the case in this country; but so far only the needs of the present have been met, and the roads have become at once self-sustaining. The prospective roads, however, are very numerous, and concessions for thousands of miles have already been granted on the most liberal terms. Two of these concessions are held by citizens of the United States.

Five years ago the Argentine Republic was importing wheat and flour from Chili and the United States, and Uruguay only raised enough for her own consumption. The wheat crop of Uruguay in 1878 was 2,000,000 bushels; in 1880, 2,600,000 bushels; in 1882, 3,000,000 bushels; in 1884, 4,000,000 bushels; and the increase in the corn product was equally rapid. In 1854 only 375,000 acres were under cultivation in the Argentine Republic; in 1864 the cultivated area was 506,000 acres; in 1874 it was 825,000 acres. In 1879 the boom commenced, and in 1884 there were 4,260,000 acres under cultivation—an increase of 3,435,000 acres in ten years. In 1874 there were 271,000 acres in wheat; in 1884, 1,717,000 acres—an increase of 533 per cent. In 1874 there were 554,000 acres in other crops; in 1884 the area jumped to 2,543,000 acres—an increase of 360 per cent. The average yield of wheat throughout the republic in 1884 was eight and one-half bushels to the acre, and the total crop was nearly eleven million bushels. It was in 1880 that the importation of wheat ceased, the amount purchased of Chili that year being 11,330 bushels. It is estimated that the area in wheat the present year is as large as 5,000,000 acres, but no official returns have been received.

Wheat and flour are not the only agricultural products exported by the Argentine Republic. In 1884 the exports of corn were 1,160,000 bushels; of barley, 70,000 bushels; of baled hay, 11,460,000 kilograms; of linseed, 23,061,000 kilograms; of peanuts, 2,617,292 kilograms; of potatoes, 100,000 bushels. The production of sugar is becoming a very important industry, and is now almost sufficient to supply the domestic demand, the yield last year amounting to nearly 50,000,000 pounds. The increased area under cultivation and the improved methods of reducing the cane will soon make sugar an article of export. There are a number of Cuban exiles in the northern provinces and in Paraguay cultivating sugar and tobacco on the Cuban system with marked success.

COUNTRY SCENE IN THE ARGENTINE REPUBLIC.

It is estimated that the extent of agricultural land in the Argentine Republic equals six hundred thousand square miles—an area equal to Louisiana, Mississippi, Alabama, Georgia, Tennessee, Arkansas, Kentucky, Illinois, Indiana, Ohio, Missouri, Iowa, and Wisconsin, and capable of producing every crop in those States; and if the increase of population continues at its present rate they will hold a population of seven millions by the close of the century. The market which we shall first lose by Argentine competition in breadstuffs will be Brazil, where we now sell about $5,000,000 worth of flour annually. The Argentine Republic will also become our rival in the West India trade, which now absorbs most of its meat product; and we will soon feel the effect of the cheapness of Argentine products in the European market, where considerable beef, mutton, and grain, is now sent in exchange for manufactured merchandise. But in pork, lard, and dairy products the Argentinians cannot compete with us. The country does not seem to be adapted to hog-raising, and while there is always fresh pork to be had, the supply of bacon, hams, and lard is included in the imports. Nearly all the cured pork comes from the United States, but most of the hams and bacons are disguised under English trade-marks. The merchants here say that American packers do not prepare their meats in a proper way to get this market, and that our cured pork first goes to England, and there receives some treatment and a particular style of wrapping which make it salable in the River Plate country. There is some native butter made, but none is exported, the climate not being suitable to the dairy business. Most of the imported butter, as well as the cheese, comes from Holland and Copenhagen. The butter is packed in one-pound tins, hermetically sealed, and will keep any length of time if properly handled. There is no American butter or cheese to be had there, not even oleomargarine, an article that is unknown to the people. A comparatively small amount of lard and butter is consumed, however, as oil is commonly used for cooking. Most of the cooks are French and Italian, in both private and public houses, and use the same methods they were accustomed to in their respective countries.

The wool product of the Argentine Republic is not so valuable as that of Australia, although larger, because it is coarser, and contains a much greater percentage of dirt and grease. The people complain that our duty on wool, being levied by weight, is an unjust discrimination against their product, and in favor of the product of Australia, which is true. The only shipments to this country are of the coarser varieties, to be used in the manufacture of carpets, and we take annually about a million dollars' worth. The great bulk of the product goes to Belgium, and is consumed in the Brussels carpet mills, the export to that country in 1883 amounting to $12,148,000. Some attempt is being made to improve the quality of the wool by grading up the flocks with imported bucks, but the judgment of the sheep-growers is generally against it, as the present quality is in demand for carpet manufacture.

The sheepskins go to Germany and France, but many of the hides come to the United States, being our largest item of import from the Argentine Republic. The same objection that is made to improving the sheep is made against the improvement of the breeds of cattle, as the native hides are heavier, and command a better price than the Durhams, Herefords, and Jerseys that have been introduced. The imported breeds yield a better quality of beef, but a less valuable hide, leaving the profit from the animal about the same. The number of hides exported in 1885 was less than usual, because of the demand for stock for new ranches; and the amount of jerked beef was smaller.

This jerked beef is the flesh of the animal cut into thin strips and dried in the sun, a weak brine being commonly used to hasten evaporation and arrest decay. It is packed in large bales, and sent to Brazil and the West Indies, where it is the staple food of the slaves and the laboring classes. We have nothing to compare with it in the United States except the jerked buffalo meat of the Indians, which is prepared in a similar manner. Of this product $1,710,000 worth was sent to Brazil last year, and $1,143,000 worth to Cuba.

No attempt has ever been made by our beef-producers to compete with the Argentine Republic and Uruguay—the only exporters of jerked beef—and it would undoubtedly be difficult for them to do so, as the cost of the cattle is so much greater in this country. Their transportation facilities to the West Indies are better than ours, notwithstanding the difference in distance, and a steamer leaves Buenos Ayres for the Brazilian ports every day. Various endeavors to introduce jerked beef into Europe have proved unsuccessful, but the attempt has not been abandoned. Samples are prepared with more than ordinary care, and the article is sold for five cents a pound, but it does not seem to be popular.

The Argentinians are beginning to ship large quantities of fresh beef to Europe in refrigerator ships, one or more leaving

JUAREZ CELMAN—PRESIDENT OF THE ARGENTINE REPUBLIC.

Buenos Ayres every week, and the new steamers of the English and French lines contain compartments built especially for this purpose. They do not use ice, but have a cooling process similar to that adopted on transatlantic steamers. Companies are already formed to slaughter and ship beef in this way, and the business is growing so rapidly that it will soon be felt by our exporters. The whole carcass is shipped, and only choice beef is selected. They cannot now compete with us in quality, but their cattle are so much cheaper, and are being graded up by the introduction of improved stock from England. Their cattle are not sold by weight, but by the head, being graded according to size and condition, prime steers bringing only fourteen or fifteen dollars, the next quality twelve dollars, and the poorest ones ten dollars per head. Within a radius of fifty miles from Buenos Ayres are ranches larger than any in Texas, and cattle can be driven almost on the steamers in the harbor, so that the cost of transportation and shrinkage is merely nominal, while our ranches are from two to four thousand miles from the sea.

Fat steers can be set down at the slaughter-houses, not fifty miles from the harbor of Buenos Ayres, at a maximum price of fifteen dollars a head, and they are high now because of the demand for cattle to stock new ranches. The cost of transportation from the ranches in the Argentine Republic to Covent Garden market in London is never greater, and often less, than from Kansas City to New York; so that our producers, in addition to the difference in the price of beef, will have the freight from New York to Liverpool against them.

Sheep are also killed and frozen for exportation to Europe, a single *saldero* or slaughter-house, at Campana, fifty miles from Buenos Ayres, shipping five hundred carcasses daily. They are hung for an hour after killing, and then removed to a chilling-room, where the temperature is slightly above the freezing-point; from this they are taken to a still colder chamber, where they are left until as hard as stone. Then they are packed in canvas bags, and sent to the steamer in refrigerator cans. Live sheep in condition for killing are worth only three or four dollars for the best quality, and ordinary mutton is sold in the city market for seven cents a pound. In 1879 we exported ninety million pounds of dressed beef. In 1884 this total had been nearly doubled, with a fair prospect of continued increase. In 1884 the Argentine Republic exported sixty-five million pounds of dressed beef, with an increase quite as rapid as ours. In 1884 there were 49,000,000 head of cattle in the United States, and 30,000,000 in the Argentine Republic. The single province of Buenos Ayres has just twice as many cattle as Texas, and as many as Texas and all the territories of the United States combined. Then across the River Plata is the little republic of Uruguay, about as large as Iowa, with 500,000 people and 8,000,000 cattle, and presenting about the same ratio of increase.

The cattlemen of the Argentine Republic and Uruguay are going into the business of canning meats, and will soon compete with us in that line. It is not generally known that Liebig's extract of beef, so largely used in hospitals as a tonic, is made in Uruguay, for the jars in which the tonic reaches the market bear trademarks to make it appear to come from England. The extract was invented by Dr. Liebig, the celebrated chemist, nearly half a century ago, but its process passed into the hands of an English company in 1866, which then removed the establishment from Antwerp to Fray Bentos, Uruguay. This company is now erecting buildings for the purpose of canning meats, and have Chicago men in charge of the work.

Although horses are very cheap, there is a good deal of profit in raising them, and the stock is being improved very rapidly by the introduction of thorough-bred English stallions. The native Argentine horse is almost the counterpart of the North American broncho, tough, swift, and enduring, and when crossed with better blood loses none of his good qualities, but improves in size and appearance. They are usually kept in droves of five hundred, and run wild the year round, the stallions being turned loose among them at the proper season—about one to twenty mares. When the colts are two years old they are taken from the drove and kept separate until three or four years old, when the fillies are turned back with the mares, and the stallions broken for service. Mares are never broken, but run wild on the range from the time they are foaled until they are driven to the saldero at the age of twelve or fifteen years. A three-year-old mare is worth seven or eight dollars for breeding purposes—not as much as a heifer—while a fifteen-year-old brings three or four dollars at the saldero. Her hide is shipped to Europe, her bones turned into bone ash, and her hoofs sent to the glue factory.

The best kind of an improved saddle-horse, such as would bring two hundred and fifty or three hundred dollars in the States, can be bought in the Argentine Republic for seventy-five dollars, fine carriage-horses for fifty dollars each, and work-horses for twenty or twenty-five dollars. The street-car companies pay about ten dollars a head for their stock. Everybody rides; even the old adage about a beggar on horseback is realized there.

There is a curious story about an island in the River Plata which was a horse ranch in early Spanish times. The animals became so numerous that there was not grass enough to feed them, and no demand for their export. The owners decided to reduce their stock in a barbarous way, and when the grass was dry they set fire to it. Every horse on the island was burned to death except those that ran into the river and were drowned. The stench was so great that navigation was almost entirely suspended on the river. The result of this method of reducing stock was a little more complete than the owners anticipated, so when the grass grew up again they had to buy stallions and mares and start anew. Singularly enough, every animal placed on the island since that fire has died of a mysterious disease, and no colt has been foaled there for one hundred and fifty years. Various breeds of stock have been tried, but never a hoof has left the island alive. Three months there finishes them. The island was unoccupied for fifty or sixty years, but is now used as a cattle ranch, and horned stock do not appear to be subject to the mysterious malady.

MONTEVIDEO.

THE CAPITAL OF URUGUAY.

SOON after General Garfield became President, an ex-member of Congress, since the governor of a western State, came into a correspondent's office in Washington, and sitting down with a discouraged and disgusted air, asked, "Where in Tophet is Uruguay? I have been offered the honor of representing the United States in that country, and before I accept I would like to find out where it is."

THE CITY OF MONTEVIDEO, LOOKING TOWARDS THE HARBOR.

Not three out of four men in the Congress of the United States could have answered the question correctly; and if the embryonic diplomatist had entered into an inquiry about the resources of the country, and the number and character of the people, he could not have found a man in our National Legislature, on the Supreme Bench, or in the Cabinet, who could have given him the information correctly, and he might have sought in vain for it in our modern school geographies. Yet Uruguay is one of the most enterprising, progressive, and prosperous nations on this hemisphere, growing faster in proportion to its area and population than the United States, and is beginning to be a formidable competitor of ours in the provision markets of Europe.

The country which appears on the map as Uruguay is known in South America as "the Banda Oriental," with a strong accent upon the last syllable, which, being interpreted, means "the Eastern Strip," as it was once a part of the Argentine Republic, which in those days was known as "the Banda Occidental." Uruguay is the old Indian name, and the legal one, being recognized by the Constitution. The inhabitants are known as "Orientals," with a strong accent on the "tals." Uruguay is the smallest independent State in South America, and in its agricultural and pastoral resources the richest, with undiscovered possibilities in the mineral way. In the good old colony times the Viceroy of Spain and the Jesuits used to get a great deal of gold and silver—placer washings—from the interior of Uruguay, but during the long struggle for independence, and the sixty years of revolution that followed, the operation of the mines was suspended, and their localities forgotten or obliterated by the people, who were mercilessly robbed of the wealth they gathered in that way. They found it economical to do nothing, for as fast as they accumulated a few dollars they were robbed of it, and those who were suspected of knowing where the gold and silver came from were persecuted until they disclosed the secret, or else died with it concealed in their breasts.

No country ever suffered more from war than Uruguay, as for almost a hundred years a struggle of arms, under one excuse or another, has been going on within her borders, and until the present despotism—which makes only a mask of the nominal democracy it pretends—came into power, there was a change of government, or an attempt to secure one, under almost every new moon. Although Uruguay is as much of an absolute monarchy to-day as exists on the face of the earth, her people have peace and prosperity, her development is being hastened by large works of internal improvement, her population is increasing rapidly, her commerce is assuming immense proportions, and she is making more rapid strides towards greatness than any other country in South America, except her neighbor across the River Plate. With a republican form of government guaranteed by the constitution, with civil and religious freedom as the foundation-stone of the nation, the will of the President has been usually as absolute as was that of the ex-King Thebaw.

HARBOR OF MONTEVIDEO.

Maximo Santos, who was for many years to Uruguay what Guzman Blanco has been to Venezuela, and Rufino Barrios to Guatemala—its nominal President, but its *de facto* dictator—was a man of immense energy, broad views, and an ambition to lift his nation to the standard of modern civilization. Although an autocrat, to a certain degree he was a wise one, and as long as a citizen did not interfere with his management of the Government, nor criticise with too great freedom his disbursement of the public revenues, Santos gave him every encouragement and all reasonable concessions. His methods were rude, cruel, and arbitrary; his ministers were the instruments of his will, the Congress simply one of the fingers of his right hand, and the army his weapon of offence and defence, without regard to the Constitution, the laws, or the rights of the people, while the courts were puppets to perform at his pleasure. Occasionally he went through the form of holding an election, but the soldiers always had charge of the polls and counted the votes. No candidates but those favored of the President were ever elected in Uruguay, and whenever any public expression was called for by him the leaders of public opinion were always careful to discover his preferences and anticipate them. If a true and complete history of his administration, and his military career preceding his assumption of the Presidency, could be written, it would be as remarkable a document as the events of the nineteenth century in any land could justify.

Santos was what they call "a barrack dog." That is, his father was a soldier, his mother a rabona—one of that class of homeless women who are encouraged by the Government to follow the army—and he was born in a barracks. From birth until he was able to bear arms he was kicked about without care or education, generally housed and fed in a military garrison or camp. He entered the army as a private when not more than fourteen or fifteen years of age, and within twenty years, by reason of his brains and force of character, became its commander-in-chief. It was a short step to a dictatorship, during one of the revolutions that were epidemic in Uruguay, and then after a form of an election

MAXIMO SANTOS.

(President of Uruguay from March 1, 1882, to November, 1886.)

he was declared "constitutional" President. When he came into power Uruguay was going backward, and had been for several years; the country was gradually becoming depopulated, property was greatly depreciated in value, everybody was living from hand to mouth, and there was no commerce of consequence. Although Santos was a brutal tyrant, the magnificent results of his progressive policy are to be seen on every hand, and he should be judged accordingly. The results he accomplished should be permitted to obscure his methods. It was in 1887 that Santos was finally overthrown, and to "let him down easy," as the saying is, his successor in the Presidency gave him credentials as an Envoy Extraordinary and Minister Plenipotentiary to all the courts of Europe, where he has since remained. Twice he has attempted to return to Montevideo, and once got as far as the harbor, but was not permitted to land. After spending a few months in Buenos Ayres, he became convinced that his power was broken, and he returned to Europe to remain the rest of his days and draw a salary or pension that is paid him by the Government as the price of his absence.

The President of Uruguay in 1889 is Gen. Maximo Tajes, a man of education, culture, and liberal tendencies, but not so much of an autocrat as Santos.

The country is enjoying great prosperity and much-needed peace. Immigration is very large and increasing, the newcomers being mostly from Italy and the Basque provinces of Spain—a frugal, industrious, and law-abiding people. They bring a good deal of property with them; in fact, according to the statistics during the last ten years, only 1335 people were lodged and fed at the expense of the Government even for a day. There are some German, Swedish, and Swiss colonies which are small but immensely prosperous; but the Government has not encouraged the formation of colonies, preferring individual immigrants.

It is said that there is not an acre of unproductive land in all Uruguay, and that its area of seven thousand square leagues—a little more than that of England—is capable of sustaining as large a population as England, Scotland, and Wales together. The soil and climate are of such a character that any grain or fruit known in the list of the world's product can be produced in abundance. Coffee will grow beside corn, and bananas and pineapples beside wheat; sugar and potatoes, apples and oranges, in fact all things that man requires for food or clothing, are capable of being raised within the boundaries of the republic at the minimum of

ONE OF THE OLD STREETS.

labor. There are medicinal plants, and forests of useful timber, plenty of grass of the most nutritious quality for cattle, and so abundant that ten times more can be fed upon the same area than in the Argentine Republic. There is plenty of water for mechanical purposes, and the geologists say that much of the surface of the northern provinces is underlaid by coal-beds. Nearly all sections of the republic may be reached by navigable rivers, and natural harbors are frequent along the coast. Besides coal and silver and gold, there are said to be many other rich mineral deposits, and the report of a Geological Commission, recently intrusted with an examination of these resources, reads like a fable of Eldorado. Even if these glowing recitals are exaggerated, there is no doubt of the agricultural and pastoral possibilities of the country, and all Uruguay needs is permanent peace to become a rich and powerful nation. Her population has doubled within the last few years, not only by immigration, but from natural causes, and her statistics show a larger birth-rate and a smaller mortality than any country on the globe. The vital tables show a net increase of births over deaths of eighteen in a thousand of population, the birth-rate averaging forty-five and the death-rate twenty-seven per thousand during the last five years.

It is quite remarkable, and the facts deserve the study of scientists, that the excess of males born in Uruguay is so great, the statistics showing that of every 1000 births 561 are males and only 439 are females. In the United States the ratio is 506 males to 494 females; in England, 485 to 515; and on the Continent of Europe, 402 to 508. Another remarkable fact, which is attributed to the climate, is that there is less insanity in Uruguay than in any other country, the ratio of insane being only 95 per 100,000 of population, while in the United States it is 329, in Great Britain 322, in France 248, and in other countries equally large in comparison.

It is said, too, that living is cheaper in Uruguay than anywhere else. Beef is three to five cents a pound, mutton and other meats about the same price, fish five cents a pound, partridges and similar birds ten cents each, chickens and ducks fifteen cents each, and vegetables are sold at proportionate prices. Labor is scarce and wages are high, consequently the public wealth is increasing very rapidly, being estimated in 1884 at $580 per capita of population. Taking the foreign commerce of Montevideo alone, the statistics show a ratio of $240 for each citizen, and the increase is very rapid. But a still greater increase is shown in the agricultural and pastoral development of the country. With a population of 500,000 Uruguay produces 5,000,000 bushels of grain annually, or an average of ten bushels per inhabitant, and this with only 540,000 acres of ground under cultivation, including vegetable gardens as well as wheat and corn fields. It is claimed there that no other country can show so high an average.

The increase in cattle, sheep, and horses is astonishing, there being now 7,000,000 cattle, 700,000 horses, and 11,000,000 sheep in Uruguay, valued at $86,000,000. This valuation is very small when considered by the side of the estimate placed upon such stock in the United States, being less than five dollars per head for sheep, horses, and cattle, all taken together. The horses alone, if estimated at the average value of $100, would be worth $70,000,000, and if the cattle were valued at only twelve dollars each, which is a low estimate in the United States, the 7,000,000 head owned in Uruguay would be worth alone the amount at which the whole livestock interest of the country is valued.

A large proportion of the wealth of Uruguay is in the hands of foreigners. The aborigines are totally exterminated. It is the only country in South America where "civilization" has been thorough and complete in this respect, and it might be searched from end to end without discovering a single representative of the Indian race which originally occupied the land. The descendants of the Spanish Conquistadors are called natives, or Orientals, while foreigners are those who were not born in the country. Of the 500,000 population, 166,000 are said to be of foreign nativity, and most of them have come in within the last ten years. This class holds about $237,000,000 of property, or $1440 per capita.

The interior of Uruguay is being rapidly developed by the construction of railways under the control of the Government, and representing an investment of about $12,000,000. Besides the lines already in operation, extensions are in progress which, when completed, will give the country a system of about 1500 miles of road, at a cost of something like $50,000,000! Railroad building is cheap in Uruguay, as grades are light and easy, and ties are plenty and accessible. The commerce of the country now amounts to $58,000,000 annually, with $29,500,000 of imports and $28,500,000 of exports. The imports are unusually large of late years, because of the vast amount of railway supplies and other merchandise used by the Government. The bulk of the trade is with England and France, the United States having but a very small share, which consists chiefly of lumber, kerosene-oil, and agricultural implements. Uruguay ships to Europe annually about $4,300,000 worth of hides, $7,000,000 in wool, and $6,000,000 in beef. There are twenty-one lines of steamers connecting Uruguay with Europe, and sending from forty to sixty vessels each way every month, while there is no direct communication with the United States except by occasional sailing-vessels.

The foreign commerce of the country is increasing with great rapidity. In 1875 it was $25,000,000; in 1878, $33,000,000; in 1880, $39,000,000; in 1881, $38,000,000; in 1882, $40,000,000; in 1883, $45,000,000; in 1884, $51,000,000; in 1885, $52,000,000; in 1886, $55,000,000; and in 1887, $58,000,000, having increased $33,000,000 in thirteen years, during which time the exports have run up from $12,000,000 to $28,500,000, and the imports from $12,000,000 to 29,500,000.

The great wealth of Uruguay is at present in cattle and sheep, and its chief exports are wool and beef, but the agricultural resources of the country will be the basis of its future greatness, and it will enter into competition with the United States in supplying the world with breadstuffs and provisions. When a total population of only five hundred thousand, including men, women, and children, carries on a foreign commerce of nearly sixty million dollars annually, it can be inferred that there is energy and industry at work, and a productive field for it to engage in. It is claimed that Uruguay has greater natural resources than any other South American country, and it is probably true. It is also claimed that the profits on labor and capital are greater there than elsewhere on the continent, which the statistics demonstrate.

The largest export of Uruguay is wool, 20,000,000 sheep making a clip worth over $10,000,000 for exportation. The increase in sheep has been 310 per cent. in ten years. The next article of export is beef, valued at about $6,000,000, being the product of about 8,000,000 cattle, which are also rapidly increasing. The third export in value is hides, of which $5,000,000 worth are annually shipped. Then come about $4,500,000 worth of wheat, $1,000,000 worth of corn, and $2,500,000 worth of other agricultural products. All of these have more than doubled within the last ten years, and are now increasing like compound interest.

We are accustomed to regard Uruguay as an obscure and insignificant country, worth not even a thought, but the commercial strides she is making show that she means competition with the United States in the near future. Chili has taken the flour market of the west coast of South America away from California, and Uruguay and the Argentine Republic are soon to meet our Dakota, Illinois, and Kansas wheat in the markets of Europe, while they threaten an even greater danger to our cattle interests. With 100,000,000 sheep in the Argentine Republic, and 20,000,000 sheep in Uruguay; with 30,000,000 cattle in one country and 8,000,000 in the other, and only about 4,000,000 people to furnish domestic consumers between them, it is easy to see what the supply of beef and wool and mutton will soon be for exportation. There is more cause for alarm in the ranches of Uruguay and the Argentine Republic than in the manufactures of England and Germany. We can compete with foreign industries in the quality and price of mechanical products, but we cannot compete with ranchmen who can put beef cattle into the market at ten and twelve dollars per head.

One of the greatest advantages the cattle producers of Uruguay and the Argentine Republic will always have over those of the United States is the nearness of their ranges to the sea. The present supply of beef in both these countries for the export market comes from within a radius of one hundred miles from an ocean harbor in which can be found the steamers of every maritime nation on earth except our own. Ocean vessels can go two thousand miles up the River Plate and five hundred miles up the Uruguay River into the heart of the cattle country, and almost tie up to the trees on the ranches, while our cattle have to be carried fifteen hundred to four thousand miles on the cars. The geographical and navigable conditions of these countries are such that ours would only equal them if ocean steamers could visit Denver and Fort Dodge. Any man of business can calculate the difference in the value of the product and the difference in profits. It is claimed that the cattle companies of the countries of which I have been speaking can sell marketable steers at ten and twelve dollars a head, and declare thirty per cent. dividends. We will not have the native Spanish population to compete with, but Englishmen, Irishmen, and Scotchmen, who are going in large numbers and with an immense amount of capital into the River Plate countries to establish ranches and raise beef for the European market.

Montevideo, the capital of Uruguay, lies upon a tongue of land which stretches out into the River Plate, nearly the shape of Manhattan Island, on which New York City stands, except that it has the Atlantic Ocean on one side and a river sixty-five miles wide on the other. This strip is of limestone formation, with very little soil on the surface, and rises in the centre to an apex like a whale's back or the roof of a house, so that the streets running northward and southward are like a series of terraces rising one above the other, not only affording perfect natural drainage, but giving almost every house in town a vista of the river or the sea from the upper windows. As you approach Montevideo the city seems much larger than it really is, and Yankee Doodle could not complain of it as he did of Boston when he said he could not see the town because there were so many houses.

MONTEVIDEO—THE OCEAN SIDE.

There is no city more delightfully situated than the capital of Uruguay, and viewed from any direction the prospect of Montevideo is a lovely one. Were it not for those dreadful pamperos, which during the winter season sweep the whole southern half of the continent from the Andes to the sea, searching every nook and crevice for dust to cast into the faces of the people, and parching the skin, this place might be made an earthly type of Paradise. But nothing can afford shelter from these searching winds, and even strawberries the year round are no compensation.

The old Spaniards had a queer way of naming places. When the catalogue of saints was exhausted and duplicated and triplicated, and all the holy fasts and feasts had served to christen colonies and towns, they "dropped into poetry," as it were, and gave their imaginations a chance at nomenclature. For example, the Rio de la Plata means the "silver river," so called, I suppose, because its waters have not the slightest resemblance to silver, but are of the color of weak chocolate, like our own Missouri. Then, again, the Argentine Republic means the "land of silver," and was so called, not because mines were found there, but to attract colonists in the expectation of finding wealth.

The real name of Montevideo is San Felipe de Montevideo, which does not sound quite so poetical when translated into English, for it means "I see the hill of St. Philip." The name of the saint has been dropped, and now the place is known as "I see the Hill." The hill which the discoverer saw used to be called after the Apostle, but now is called the "Cerro." It has a picturesque old fortress on its crest, which is innocently supposed to afford protection to the capital and the harbor. If the place were ever attacked, the guns of the fort would furnish no more protection than so many pop-guns, as it stands back so far behind the city that half of the balls would fall on the roofs of the houses, and an assaulting force be landed under the shelter they would give. As the location of a light-house the Cerro does very well, and the fortress is useful now only as an arsenal and prison. The old city formerly surrounded the fortress, and it was closely besieged for nine years, from 1842 to 1851. In those hard years a new city sprung up around the besieging encampments, with shops and stores and churches and factories. After the coming of peace the intermediate space was laid out by French engineers, and the two cities rapidly grew into one, on the best ground and after the most approved models of modern times. This space is now the most beautiful and desirable part of the consolidated city.

It is claimed that Montevideo is the most healthy city in the world, and there is no reason why it should not be, as the natural drainage is perfect, and the climate is about like that of Tennessee, the cold weather of winter being moderated by the Gulf Stream from the ocean, and the heat of summer by the sea-breeze that seldom fails to perform its grateful service. When it is not June in Uruguay, it is October—never too hot and never too cold. There is not such a thing as a stove in the whole country, but some of the foreigners have fireplaces in their houses, to temper the winds for the tender feet. What Montevideo most needs, like Buenos Ayres, is a harbor, for during a pampero the ships at anchor in the river are without protection, and at all times the landing and the shipping of merchandise are conducted with great difficulty in lighters, as at the latter place. A contract has been made with a French company to construct two breakwaters or piers in triangular form, and the work, already commenced, is expected to be completed in 1890.

Around the curve of the bay, fronting the water, are a series of beautiful villas, or "quintas," as they are called (pronounced *kintas*), the suburban residences of wealthy men, built in the ancient Italian style, with all the luxury and lavish display of modern extravagance, and reminding one of the Pompeian palaces, or the Roman villas in the golden age which Horace pictured in his Odes.

These residences are of the most picturesque architecture, and would be attractive anywhere, but here they are surrounded by a perpetual garden, and by thousands of flowers which preserve their color and their fragrance winter and summer, and give the place an appearance of everlasting spring.

One of these beautiful retreats belongs to a Philadelphian, Mr. W. D. Evans, who has a romantic history, and is the friend of every naval officer and every skipper that enters the port. Thirty years ago Mr. Evans shipped as mate on a sailing-vessel bound for Uruguay. She was wrecked off the coast by one of the ill winds which seamen meet, and he was cast ashore, penniless and friendless. All the property he had in the world were an ordinary ship's boat, which he had saved from the wreck, and the clothing which he wore. But he had a strong reserve in the form of muscle, courage, and manliness, and with his boat he commenced life as a *cargador*—that is, a longshoreman—and offered his services to the public to convey passengers and baggage to and from the ships in the harbor. About a week after he had entered his new employment he was caught in a gale outside the harbor. His boat was capsized, and he floated around for four hours clinging to her keel, until rescued by the crew of a steamer which happened to be coming in. He thanked his saviors graciously, but declined their invitation to go on board the steamer, only asking assistance to right his boat, in order that he might sail back to town. He was jeered at, and advised to let the old tub drift, as it was worthless; but he told the sailors that while it was not much of a boat, it was all the property he owned in the world, and he intended to make a fortune out of it yet. They liked the spirit of the man, and helped him put his boat in sailing trim, wishing him goodluck as he started back to Montevideo.

In the centre of the finest private park in the River Plate country is a handsome bronze fountain which must have cost several thousand dollars. In its basin, casting a shadow over myriads of gold-fish and speckled trout, floats Mr. Evans's old boat, the most precious piece of property he owns, and he is said to be worth millions. He never allows a day to pass without visiting the fountain, and no guest ever comes to the Evans *quinta* who is not brought to bow to the idol. There is something pathetic in the affection and reverence which the millionaire shows for the rotten old tub. "She has saved my life twice," says Mr. Evans to everybody, "and when I was flat broke she was my only friend. You gentlemen may not notice anything pretty about her, but she is the most beautiful thing I ever saw."

There never comes to Montevideo a distressed seaman of any race, worthy or unworthy, who does not find a snug harbor through Mr. Evans's bountiful generosity, and there is not a man in all the valley of the River Plate who does not feel a pleasure in grasping his hand.

There are many beautiful residences and fine stores in Montevideo, and everything that can be bought in Paris can be found there. There are three theatres and an Italian opera, a race-course and any number of clubs, a university, a public library, a museum, and all the etceteras of modern civilization. The ladies dress in the most stylish of Paris fashions, and among the aristocracy the social life is very gay. The people are highly educated, are making money quickly, and spend it like princes. The Hotel Oriental is the best in South America, being built of Italian marble, and luxuriously furnished. There are hospitals, asylums, and other benevolent institutions supported by public and private charity; two Protestant churches, Protestant schools, fifty-five miles of street railways, carrying nine million passengers a year—which is a remarkably high average for a city of one hundred and twenty thousand population—boulevards and parks, gas and electric lights, telephones without number, and only now and then does something occur to remind a tourist that he is not in one of the most modern cities of Europe.

The vestibules of the tenement-houses, and the *patios*, or courts, in the centre of each, which invariably furnish a cool loafing-place, are commonly paved with the knuckle-bones of sheep, arranged in fantastic designs like mosaic-work. They always attract the attention of strangers, and it is a standing joke to tell the gullible that they are the knuckle-bones of human beings who were killed during the many revolutions which occurred in that country.

The ladies of Uruguay are considered to rank next to their sisters of Peru in beauty, and there is something about the atmosphere which gives their complexion a purity and clearness that is not found among ladies of any other country. But, like all Spanish ladies, when they reach maturity they lose their grace and symmetry of form, and usually become very stout. This is undoubtedly owing in a great degree to their lack of exercise; for they never walk, but spend their entire lives in a carriage or a rocking-chair. Native ladies who have married foreigners, and gone abroad to France or England, and there adopted the custom of those countries, preserve their beauty much longer than their sisters who live indolent lives at home.

SCENE IN MONTEVIDEO.

The Government offices occupy a rather plain and insignificant structure, which does not compare in architectural beauty with the private residences and business blocks. Most of the merchants reside in the upper floors of their business houses, so that there are but few exclusively residence streets. The best houses are three and four stories high, and are quite ornamental in their exterior decorations, resembling those of Italy, and naturally, as most of the architects and builders are Italians.

In the centre of the city are two large public squares. One, the Plaza Constitution, is a military parade-ground, and upon it fronts the Government building and military barracks. The other is the Plaza Washington, named in honor of the Father of American Liberty. Crossing Calle de Washington, and going north a block, one comes to "Calle Veinte y Cinco de Mayo" (the Twenty-fifth of May Street). This seems odd at first, but it is sanctified in the minds of the Uruguayans by the story of their valor and patriotism. It commemorates the national independence. Turning west on this street towards the point of the promontory on which the city is built, the traveller stands before one of the best buildings in the city—the Hospital de Caridad (Charity Hospital). It is three stories high and three hundred feet long. It covers an acre of ground, and has accommodations, or beds, for three hundred patients. Of course the Sisters of Charity are supreme in these wards, and large numbers of patients are treated here every year.

The Hospital de Caridad has become popular by the manner in which the money is raised for its maintenance. It is supported by a public lottery. This finds favor everywhere. One meets many men, women, and boys on the streets of South American cities selling lottery tickets, as he would see newsboys selling papers in North American cities. Not far from Charity Hospital is the British Hospital. It is a fine, substantial building, and worthy of the people who built it. It cost nearly forty thousand dollars, and can accommodate sixty patients.

The cemetery is a long way off, around on the south side of the city, and is a place of beauty. The entrance is tasteful, and much more elaborate and expensive than any cemetery entrance in the United States. The chapel down the walk in front of the entrance, with its ornamental dome and marble floors and ornaments, is worth seeing. The ground is occupied with private or family vaults much more elaborate and expensive than those one sees in North America. There are individual tombs in North American cemeteries far more elegant than any in Uruguay; but, taken as a whole, this city of the dead is of a higher order. The streets are too narrow, and the surface is nearly all utilized. It is common to have glass doors back of the iron gates, so one can look into the little rooms above the vaults. The walls of these are covered with pictures and curious wire and bead work ornaments. There are crucifixes and candles everywhere. In one tomb is to be seen a picture of Mary seated on an island or floating raft, pulling souls out of the flames of purgatory. The poor things are stretching up their hands pleading for help, and Mary is watching the prayers on earth and choosing accordingly. Back of these tombs, and forming a high wall twenty or twenty-five feet high, is a long series of vaults one above another, each with an opening large enough to receive a casket shoved in endwise. These vaults are either owned, or rented for a term of years, or as long as the friends pay the rent. In case of default, the remains are taken out and dropped into deep pits, and the vaults rented to the next comer.

The standing army of Uruguay consists of five thousand men, mostly concentrated at the capital. Their uniform, with the exception of that of the President's bodyguard—a battalion of three or four hundred men, dressed in a novel and striking costume of leopard-skins—is of the zouave pattern. There are connected with the army several fine bands, which on alternate evenings give concerts in the plazas. These concerts are attended by all classes of people, and furnish good opportunities for flirtation.

Everybody rides; no one thinks of walking. Each family has its carriage, saddle, and other horses, and even the beggars go about the streets on horseback. It is a common thing for a person to be stopped on the street by a horseman and asked for a centavo, which is worth two and a half cents of our money. These incidents are somewhat alarming at first, and suggest highway robbery; but the appeal is made in such a humble, pitiful tone that the feeling of alarm soon vanishes. "For the love of Jesus, señor, give a poor sick man a centavo. I've had no bread or coffee to-day;" and receiving the pittance, the beggar will gallop off like a cow-boy to the nearest drinking-place.

The national drink is called *caña*, and is made of the fermented juice of the sugar-cane. It contains about ninety per cent. of alcohol, and is sold at two cents a goblet; so that a spree in Uruguay is within the reach of the poorest man. But there is very little intemperance in comparison with that in our own country. On ordinary days drunken men are seldom seen on the streets, but on the evening of a religious feast-day the common people usually engage in a glorious carousal.

The policemen in Montevideo are detailed from the army, and carry sabres instead of clubs, which they use with telling effect upon offenders who resist arrest. A few years ago there was no safety for people who were out late at night either in the city or country; robberies and murders were of frequent occurrence, and yet the prisons were empty. But President Santos rules with an iron hand, and after a few highwaymen and murderers were hanged, there was a noticeable change in the condition of affairs, and now a woman or a child is as safe upon the streets or highways of the country as in their own homes.

One of the curious customs of Uruguay is the method of making butter. The dairy-man pours the milk, warm from the cow, into an inflated pig or goat skin, hitches it to his saddle by a long lasso, and gallops five or six miles into town with the milk-sack pounding along on the road behind him. When he reaches the city his churning is over, the butter is made, and he peddles it from door to door, dipping out with a long wooden spoon the quantity desired by each family. Though all sorts of modern agricultural machinery are used on the farms of Uruguay, the natives cannot be induced to adopt the wooden churn. Some of the foreigners use it, but the butter is said to be not so good as that made in the curious primitive fashion. Fresh milk is sold by driving cows from door to door along the principal streets, and milking them into the jars of the customers.

During the last year religious and political circles have been in a state of the greatest agitation, owing to the resistance of the priests to the arbitrary policy of the Government. For several years the Church has seen itself stripped of its ancient prerogatives, and its occupation and income gradually restricted by the enactment of laws conferring upon the civil magistrates duties which were formerly within the jurisdiction of the priests alone. Under the constitution, the established religion of the country is the Roman Catholic, and the archbishop was formerly a greater man than the President, being the final authority in matters political as well as spiritual.

The Romish Church, like the Spanish kings, ruled very unwisely in the South American dominions, and instead of keeping pace with the progress of the people, endeavored to enforce fifteenth century dogmas and practices in the nineteenth. The result is the same everywhere. The Liberal element, representing the progressive and educated, have denied the authority of the Church, and defied its mandates. The Liberals have been growing stronger and the Church growing weaker each year, until the former are in power everywhere except in Ecuador, and have given the priests repeated and bitter doses of their own medicine. Santos, the President of Uruguay, cares no more for the curse of Rome than for the bleating of the sheep upon his estancia, and has been arbitrary and merciless, carrying on a war in which the Clerical party has been driven to the wall, the parish schools closed, the monks and nuns expelled, and the pulpits silenced. The first step was to take the education of the children out of the hands of the Church by establishing free schools and a compulsory education law, under which the parish schools were not recognized in the national system of education. The money which formerly had been given to the Church is devoted to the school fund. Then the registration of births and deaths was taken from the parish clergy and placed in the hands of the civil officials. Formerly the legitimacy of a child could not be established without a certificate from the priest in whose parish it was born; and the cemeteries were closed to heretics. The next thing was the passage of the civil marriage law, similar to that of France, which required every couple to be married by a magistrate, in order that the legitimacy of their offspring might be established. This was a serious blow at the revenues of the Church, as its income from marriage fees was very large. It formerly cost twenty-five dollars to get married, and very few of the peons, or laboring classes, could afford the luxury. Now it costs but one dollar. The Church submitted to all assaults upon it until the marriage law was passed, and then it openly defied the civil authorities, and threatened to excommunicate all members who obeyed the statute.

President Santos is not a man to quietly endure defiance of his authority. He ordered the police to arrest and imprison every priest who preached such doctrine. Three or four arrests were made, when the archbishop addressed a letter to the President declaring that the Church could not and would not recognize marriages formed without its benediction, and that the police authorities had no right to determine what subjects should be discussed in the pulpit. The President took no notice of the protest, further than to direct the police to carry out their previous orders. The Papal Nuncio, legate from the Holy See, interfered and entered his remonstrance, whereupon he was given forty-eight hours to leave the country. The archbishop then instructed the priests not to preach any sermons whatever, but to confine their spiritual offices to the celebration of the mass. Then a law was passed abolishing all houses of religious seclusion, and forbidding secret religious orders within the territory of Uruguay. The excuse for this was that the monasteries were the hot-beds of political conspiracy, which was probably true. An edict was issued expelling all monks and nuns from Uruguay, and many of them at once left the monasteries, some taking refuge in private families, others going into hospitals and almshouses, but more left the country.

On the first of August, 1885, all the convents, except one, were closed. This one had for its Mother Superior a sister of President Santa Maria, of Chili. She was a woman of pluck, and determined to defy the law. When the first of August arrived, the inspectors of police went to her place, called "The House of the Good Shepherd," and being denied admittance, burst in the doors. The Mother Superior was found alone, and when asked what had become of the Sisters, refused to answer the question. A search was made, and forty-five terror-stricken women were discovered concealed in the loft of the chapel and under the altar. They cried pitifully, and falling before the cross of Christ, begged for His protection; but the police dragged them out and gave them orders to leave the country at once. Some of them took refuge in private houses, and the Mother Superior, who, it was supposed, would be imprisoned, found an asylum in the house of an Irish Roman Catholic named Jackson, who raised the English flag over his roof. They soon after disappeared, however, and quietly left the country.

This ended the supremacy of the Roman Catholic Church in Uruguay. The next movement of Santos towards its extermination will undoubtedly be the confiscation of its property; but as yet no steps have been taken in that direction. Except among the women, there is very little sympathy for the priests. Men are seldom seen in a church except on notable feast-days, but the women go to mass every morning, and perform the duties of their religion with ardent devotion. Protestantism is making considerable progress in Uruguay under the direction of the Rev. Thomas Wood, formerly of Indiana, who has been superintendent of Methodist missions in the River Plate valley for many years. There are in Montevideo two Protestant churches, and several schools for ordinary as well as religious instruction. One of the churches is under the care of the Established Church of England, and is the fashionable place of worship for foreigners. No mission work is done by it, but it has a Sabbath-school, and there is regular preaching on Sundays. The success of Mr. Wood's labors is very marked, particularly among the natives. He receives encouragement, but no financial aid, from the Government. His work is supported by the Missionary Board of the Methodist Church of New York, and all he asks of the Government is its non-interference. This it agrees to, and gives him full protection besides. Mr. Wood is an active, energetic, and enthusiastic man, and the Methodists could not have placed their work under a better superintendent.

Standing on the Plaza Constitution, one sees towering up, one hundred and thirty-three feet above, the great cathedral, a large, plain, and somewhat imposing structure. It was dedicated eighty-two years ago, but time and the fortunes of war have dealt kindly with it. On entering this building, at first the visitor wonders at its tawdriness; next he feels its coldness, and then he is impressed by the dominating importance given to the Virgin Mother, and the inferior position assigned to the Son. This is so in all the Catholic churches of South America. Over the great altars always may be seen some huge and coarse representation of Mary. She is dressed after the modern style, in some rich material and an abundance of lace. The stiff wax form and awkward wax hands would make a sad appearance in a collection of wax-figures like the moral show of Artemus Ward. The form of the Saviour is pushed away off to one side in some obscure alcove. The supremacy of Mary in these papal lands is wrought into all the life of the people. She has every sort of name. Every conceivable relation in the Virgin's life is named, and that name bestowed upon men and women alike. There is "Maria Remedia"—that is, Mary of Remedies; "Maria Dolores," Mary of Griefs; "Maria Angustos," Mary of Anguish; "Maria Concepcion," Mary of the Conception; "Maria Mercedes," Mary of Mercy; "Maria Anunciacion," Mary of Annunciation; "Maria Presentacion," Mary of the Presentation; "Maria Carmen," Mary of Blood; "Maria Purificacion," Mary of Purification; "Maria Trinidad," Mary of the Trinity; "Maria Asuncion," Mary taken from earth; "Maria Transitu," Mary going into heaven—and so on indefinitely. In the Montevideo cathedral, and in many others, stands a statue of a black saint—St. Baltazar—among many classes of people, one of the important saints of the catalogue.

Montevideo, with a population of one hundred and twenty-five thousand, has twenty-three daily papers—more, in proportion to its population, than any other city in the world; three times as many as London, and nearly twice as many as New York. Buenos Ayres has twenty-one daily papers for a population of four hundred thousand. Other cities in South America are equally blessed; but in those of the republics of Ecuador, Bolivia, and Paraguay no daily papers are issued. The South American papers are not published so much for the dissemination of news as for the propagation of ideas. They give about six columns of editorial to one of intelligence, and publish all sorts of communications on political subjects, furnish a story in each issue, and often run histories and biographies as serials. One frequently takes up a daily paper and finds in it everything but the news, so that last week's issue is just as good reading as yesterday's.

The principal reason and necessity for having so many newspapers is that every public man requires an organ in order to get his views before the people. The editors are ordinarily politicians or publicists, who devote their entire time to the discussion of political questions, and expect the party or faction to which they belong to furnish them with the means of living while they are so employed. Each of the papers has a director, who holds the relation of editor-in-chief, and a sub-editor, who is a man-of-all-work, edits copy, looks after the news, reads proof, and stays around the place to see that the printers are kept busy. There is never a staff of editors or reporters as in the United States, and seldom more than two men in an office. The director usually has some other occupation. He may be a lawyer, or a judge, or a member of Congress, and he expects his political sympathizers to assist him in furnishing editorials.

At the capital of each of the republics in Central and South America there are usually one or more publications supported by the Government for the promulgation of decrees, decisions of the courts, laws of Congress, and official reports; and usually the paper which sustains the Administration that happens to be in power expects and receives financial assistance, or a "subvention," as it is called, from the Government. This comes in the form of sinecures to the editors, who receive generous salaries from the public treasury for their political and professional services. Every president or cabinet minister, every political leader, every governor of a province, every *jefe politico* (mayor of a city), and often a collector of customs, has his organ, and, if he is not the editor himself, sees that whoever acts in that capacity is paid by the tax-payers.

Except in Montevideo, Buenos Ayres, Santiago, Valparaiso, Rio de Janeiro, and other of the larger and more enterprising cities, there are no regular hours of publication; but papers are issued at any time, from eight o'clock in the morning until ten at night, whenever they happen to be ready to go to press. It seems odd to have yesterday's paper delivered to you in the afternoon of to-day, but it often occurs. As soon as enough matter to fill the forms is in type, the edition goes to press. In the cities mentioned and some others there is a good deal of journalistic enterprise and ability; news is gathered by the editors—there is no reporter in all Spanish America. Telegraphic despatches are received and published, including cablegrams from Europe furnished by the Havas News Agency; news correspondence regarding current events comes from the interior towns and cities; meetings are reported, fights and frolics are written up in graphic style, and even interviews have been introduced to a limited extent. The newspapers of Valparaiso and Buenos

Ayres are the most enterprising and ably conducted, *El Comercio*, of the former city, and *La Nacion*, of the latter, ranking well beside the provincial papers of Europe.

The editors of papers in the tropics are seldom called upon to report fires, as they are of rare occurrence. The houses are practically fire-proof, being built of adobe, and roofed with tiles. No stoves are used, and as there are no chimneys such a thing as a defective flue is unknown. All the cooking is done upon an arrangement like a blacksmith's forge, and charcoal is the only fuel used. The delight of the South American editor is a street fight, and although an account of it may not appear for several days after the occurrence, the writer gives his whole soul to its description. It is always recorded in the most elaborate and flamboyant manner. The following is a literal translation of the opening of one of these articles:

"A personal encounter of the most transcendent and painful interest occurred day before yesterday in the street of the Twenty-fifth of May, near the palatial residence of the most excellent and illustrious Señor Don Comana, member of the Chamber of Deputies, and was witnessed by a grand concourse of people, whose excitement and demonstrations it is impossible to adequately describe."

A dog-fight or any other event of interest would be treated in the same manner. Everything is "transcendent," everything is "surpassing." The grandiloquent style of writing, which appears everywhere, is not confined to newspapers, nor to orations, but you find it in the most unsuspected places. For example, in a bath-room at a hotel I once found an *aviso* which, literally translated, read as follows:

"In consequence of the grand concourse of distinguished guests who entreat a bath in the morning, and with the profound consideration for the convenience of all, it is humbly and respectfully requested by the management that the gentlemen will be so courteous and urbane as to occupy the shortest possible time for their ablutions, and that they will be so condescending as to pull out the plug while they are resuming their garments."

Papers often quote from one another. They select their news as ship-builders select their timber—when it is old and tough. Compositors are not paid by the thousand ems, as in the United States, but receive weekly wages, which are seldom more than eight or ten dollars. Six or seven compositors are a sufficient force for the largest office, as the type used is seldom smaller than brevier, and more often long primer. The printers are mostly natives, although a few Germans are to be found. There are no typographical unions or trade organizations in South America. The laborers and mechanics are called peons, and are in a state of bondage, although not so recognized by law. In the larger cities the papers are delivered by carriers, and sold by newsboys on the streets; but in the smaller towns they are sent to the *correo*, or post-office, to be called for, like other mail, by the subscribers. The price of subscription is inordinately large, being seldom less than twelve dollars per year, and often double that amount; and single copies cost ten cents in native money, which will average about seven and a half cents in American gold. The paper which has the largest circulation in South America is *La Nacion*, of Buenos Ayres, which is said to circulate thirty thousand copies; but twelve or fifteen hundred copies is considered a fair circulation for the ordinary daily.

Most of the offices are very cheaply fitted up. A dress of type lasts many years, and stereotyping is almost unknown. The presses used are the old-fashioned elbow-joint kind, such as were in vogue in the United States forty years ago. In Chili and the Argentine Republic there are some cylinder presses run by steam; but the people generally through the continent are very far behind the times in the typographic art. Modern equipments might be introduced very easily, but the printers down there know nothing about them, and when a perfecting press that cuts and folds is described to them, they are apt to accept the story as a North American exaggeration.

The advertising patronage is very good nearly everywhere, particularly that of the Government organs; but small rates are paid, and the rural system of "trading out" is practised to a considerable extent. The same patent medicine "ads." that are familiar to the readers of the newspapers in the United States appear in the South American journals, and are eagerly scanned by homesick travellers, although they look very odd in Spanish, and usually can only be recognized by trademarks and other well-known signs. Most of the advertising in South America is done through the newspapers. Very few posters or dodgers or almanacs are used, and the patent medicine fiend has not used his brush so extensively upon the fences and dead walls as in the United States. Not long ago the manufacturers of a popular specific sent their agent in Peru a box of handsomely illuminated advertising cards. The custom officers seized them, and the druggist to whom they were consigned was obliged to pay a heavy penalty for trying to smuggle in works of art.

The South American editor is not allowed the same liberty to criticise public men that is enjoyed by his contemporary in the United States. He speaks with moderation during political excitement, and uses great precaution in his comments upon public affairs. Last winter the Secretary of the Treasury of one of the Spanish-American republics absconded with every dollar in the vaults at the expiration of his term of office. The Administration organs contained no allusion to the event, while the Opposition paper announced it in this innocent language: "The Treasury on Saturday last was the scene of a violent raid on the part of Minister Pena, of the Treasury Department. He entered the cashier's office late in the afternoon, and demanded all the money that was in the vaults. In spite of the protest of the cashier, he carried away what is said to have amounted to nine thousand dollars. It was the last act of the retiring Minister of Finance. The motives that prompted the procedure are unknown, and the disposition of the money has not been explained."

In some of the republics there is a censor of the press, to whom a copy of each edition is submitted before it is published. This causes some inconvenience and delay at times, for if the censor happens to be out of town, or at a dinner-party, or otherwise engaged, the issue is withheld until his august signature and rubric are placed upon each page of the copy submitted to him. This copy is filed away for the protection of the editor, in case any article creates trouble. In 1885 the editor of *El Campeon*, of Lima, Peru, published an attack upon the Congress of that republic, which was very mild compared with articles that are frequently directed at our law-makers; but it was considered a sufficient reason for his imprisonment for six months, and the confiscation of his machinery, type, etc., which were sold for the benefit of the Government.

The most popular names for the newspapers in South America are *La Revista* (The Review), *La Nacion* (The Nation), *La Republica* (The Republic), *La Tribuna* (The Tribune), *La Libertad* (The Liberty), *La Voce* (The Voice), *La Union* (The Union), *El Tempo* (The Times), *El Diario* (The Diary), *El Eco* (The Echo), *El Correo* (The Post), *El Puebla* (The People), *La Verdad* (The Truth). There is a habit of naming streets and parks and towns in honor of great events, and this sometimes includes newspapers. For example, there is a daily in Montevideo called *The Twenty-fifth of May*, which corresponds to our Fourth of July—the Independence-day of that republic. There are only three dailies printed in the English language in all Central and South America. Two of them are published in Buenos Ayres—*The Herald* and *The Standard*—the other at Panama—*The Star and Herald*. There is a weekly printed in English at Valparaiso, and there was formerly one at Callao, Peru, but it was suspended during the war and its publication has not been resumed.

It is not generally known that "Liebig's Extract of Beef," which, like quinine, is a standard tonic throughout the world, and is used by every physician, in every hospital, on every ship, and in every army, is a product of Uruguay. The cans in which it comes are labelled as if their contents were manufactured at Antwerp, where the original extract was invented by Professor Liebig, the famous German chemist, and the preparation was formerly made there; but in 1866, the patent having passed into the control of an English company, the works were removed to Uruguay, where cattle are cheaper than elsewhere, and the entire supply is now produced at a place called Fray Bentos, about one hundred and seventy miles above Montevideo, on the Uruguay River, whence it is shipped in bulk to London and Antwerp, where it is packed in small tins for the market. An attempt was made to do the packing in Uruguay, but the Government of that republic imposed so high a tariff upon the tins that the scheme was abandoned. The chemical process by which the juice of the beef is extracted and mixed with the blood of the animal is supposed to be a secret, but as the patent has long since expired, it could be easily discovered, and thus the manufacture of an almost necessary article would become general.

ASUNCION.

THE CAPITAL OF PARAGUAY.

THE population of Paraguay and its products to-day are less than they were one hundred years ago, when the present half-ruined city was the capital of the southern half of the continent, and from it had been issued the ecclesiastical and vice-regal edicts for over two centuries. Then Asuncion was a gay and busy capital, and Buenos Ayres, with the rest of the continent, paid tribute to the viceroy there. After the war of independence, a Jesuit by the name of Francia secured control of the Government, and nothing but death was ever able to loosen his grip. Although the constitution was republican, Francia established himself as "Perpetual President," maintained a despotism as absolute and cruel as any that ever existed, and erected around the country a wall that prevented immigration and kept the people in ignorance. Foreign commerce was monopolized by the President, and he exacted in the shape of tribute from the people the products he shipped away. The revenues of the Government went into his pocket, and public expenditures were made at his will. His policy seemed to be to isolate Paraguay from the rest of the world, for the good of its people; and being a religious fanatic, he taught them nothing but obedience to the will of the Church. For thirty-two years he ruled peacefully, and when he died, in 1840, he was sincerely mourned.

His successor was Lopez I., a man who had all the bad qualities of Francia, but none of his good ones. Selfish, lustful, brutal, his only motive was to perpetuate his power, and enjoy the opportunities it gave for the gratification of his passions. He continued the policy of exclusion which Francia inaugurated, but for entirely different reasons, considering it necessary for his own safety that the people should be kept ignorant and isolated, lest they might learn that there were justice and liberty elsewhere in the world. He ruled twenty-two years, until death took the sceptre from him and gave it to his son.

GASPAR FRANCIA,

First President of Paraguay.

If the father was bad, the son was worse, and Lopez II. seemed to be inspired with an ambition to excel his sire in every crime the latter had been guilty of. Filled with passion and lust, there was no form of cruelty he did not practise, and no act of brutality that he did not commit. He murdered his mother and brother, like King Thebaw, lest they might conspire against his authority. He had men pulled to pieces by horses, and invented a form of capital punishment before unknown to the catalogue of horrors. People who offended him were sewed up in green hides, which were hung up before a fire to dry. As the hides dried they shrunk, and the victim was slowly crushed to death by a pressure that human bones and flesh could not resist. The wives and daughters of his subjects were his playthings, and his agents were busy in all parts of the country collecting beautiful maidens to sacrifice to his lust. He resisted immigration, and, like his two predecessors, kept the foreign commerce of the country in his own hands. When steamers began to ascend the Parana River, he chained logs together and obstructed navigation, and when foreigners entered the country he drove them out.

STREET IN ASUNCION.

The only outlet for the interior provinces of Southern Brazil is through Paraguay, and the people of Brazil resented the obstruction to their commerce. The Argentine Republic and Uruguay also had grievances, and in 1868 the three great nations, representing about half the population of South America, called the tyrant Lopez to account. Then began a war which has no parallel in history. For six long years the little State of Paraguay held at bay the three combined nations whose territory surrounded it. The war did not end until the population of Paraguay was wellnigh exterminated, the country laid waste, and the tyrant Lopez driven to the mountains, where he was finally killed in a cave in which he sought refuge. The war cost Brazil, the Argentine Republic, and Uruguay two hundred and fifty million dollars and twenty thousand lives, while it cost Paraguay everything. There were scarcely enough survivors to bury the dead. The entire country was practically destroyed and depopulated.

LOPEZ, THE TYRANT.

AFTER THE WAR.

During the reign of the two Lopezes, father and son, the most intelligent and the best men in the country were banished. Exile was the penalty of all whose views differed from those of the tyrant, and who would not submit to his exactions. More were murdered than banished, and their families fled from the country. On the downfall of the despot the exiles returned with enlarged intelligence, broader views, and an education received in foreign lands which fitted them to restore their almost ruined country, and to establish something like a liberal and wise government. After the death of Lopez and the occupation of the country by the allied armies, a junta was formed, consisting of three citizens of Paraguay, two of whom had returned from banishment, and had taken part in the war against the tyrant. Their powers were provisional, and similar to those of the consuls of old Rome. These men called a constitutional convention, which organized a permanent government, based upon the plan of that of the United States. The constitution guarantees religious and civil liberty, security of person and property, prohibits the re-election of Presidents, endows the Congress with authority much more extended than that of ours, and in every possible manner provides against the repetition of the old dictatorships.

ASUNCION, FROM THE WEST.

One of the first steps taken by Congress was to encourage immigration, and agents were sent to Europe to organize colonies and offer inducements to settlers. There was a strong effort made to secure German colonies, but it was difficult to divert them from the United States. In Italy and the Basque provinces of Spain the emigrant agents were more successful, and about twenty thousand people from these countries have settled in Paraguay during the last four years. Their prosperity and the treatment they have received have been so encouraging that a steady stream of immigration is now flowing from all the European States towards

ASUNCION—THE PALACE AND CATHEDRAL.

Paraguay; and the German Government has lately sent a commission to explore the territory and report upon its advantages for the establishment of colonies. Liberal inducements are offered to all immigrants. The lands of the republic have been resurveyed and divided into three classes—timber, pastoral, agricultural. At the end of five years' residence, each adult immigrant is entitled to a deed of eighty acres of the latter class as a gift from the Government, and is reimbursed from the public revenues to an amount equal to the cost of his passage to Asuncion, the necessary farming implements, and a yoke of cattle. In addition to these he has also the right to purchase not more than four extra lots of agricultural lands of forty acres each. The grazing lands are not given away, but are sold by the Government at the price of eight, twelve, and fifteen hundred dollars per square league, according to location, or are leased for a term of years at a nominal rental. The timber lands are sold at higher rates, but as yet there is little demand for them. The emigrants from Continental Europe usually settle upon the agricultural lands, but large areas of the pampas are being taken up by English, Irish, and Scotch, some of whom purchase upon their own account, while others represent companies of considerable capital. The British will soon monopolize the pastoral industries of the La Plata countries, and Paraguay will be full of their cattle.

An enumeration made of his subjects by Lopez in 1857 showed the population of Paraguay to be 1,337,439; at the close of the war in 1873, a census demonstrated that this number had been reduced to 221,079 souls, of whom only 28,746 were men, 106,254 were women over fifteen years of age, and 86,079 were children, the enormous disproportion between the sexes, as well as the vast decrease of population, telling the results of the war. In 1876 there were 293,844 inhabitants, showing an increase of 72,765 in three years; and in 1879 the total was increased to 318,018, two-thirds of the adults being women. It is said that there are but three citizens of the United States in Paraguay—one white man who keeps a drug store, and two negroes, both of whom are reported to be fugitives from justice.

The Rio de la Plata, or the River Plate, as it is better known, is the widest stream in the world, and, with the exception of the Amazon, empties more water into the ocean than any other, draining a region of 1,560,000 square miles. With its tributaries, it affords more miles of navigation than all the rivers of Europe combined, and more than the Mississippi and its branches. The tide from the Atlantic reaches up a distance of two hundred and fifty-eight miles, and there is a depth of water sufficient to carry vessels of twenty-four feet draught one thousand miles into the interior.

Above the mouth of the Uruguay River, which forms the

WRECK OF THE OLD CATHEDRAL.

boundary line between the republic of that name and the Argentine Republic, the River Plate is known as the Parana, and is so called as far as its source, which lies not far from that of the Amazon in the interior of Brazil, and is fed through a thousand channels by the rains of the tropics and the melting snows of the Cordilleras. The Parana flows for one thousand two hundred miles through a country—the interior of Brazil—that has never been explored, and is inhabited by a race of savages who have so far resisted all attempts to invade their domain. As far as the river has been explored it is deep enough for navigation, although at present the steamers only run to Cuyabá, a distance of 2500 miles. At Corrientes the Paraguay River enters the Parana, and the two great streams form the western and eastern boundaries of the republic. At Asuncion the Paraguay divides again, the main stream flowing through the centre of the State, and the Pilcomayo continuing as its western boundary. The Paraguay River is navigable for 1200 miles, and the Pilcomayo for nearly as great a distance, almost to the mountains of Bolivia. The chief affluents of the Pilcomayo are the Pilaya and Paspaya; and the only city on its banks is Chuquisaca. With the removal of obstructions which offer no obstacles to engineering skill, it is said that the Pilcomayo might be put in such shape as to afford an easy and convenient outlet for the products of Bolivia to the Atlantic ports, and investigations are already in progress looking to that end.

Whoever obtains control of these natural lines of communication, and supplements them by railways, will hold the key to the treasures of the heart of South America, whose value has furnished food for three centuries of fable. A section of country as large as that which lies between the Mississippi River and the Rocky Mountains lies there practically unexplored. On its borders are rich agricultural lands, fine ranges, unmeasured resources of timber, the diamond-fields of Brazil, and the gold and silver mines of Bolivia and Peru. What exists in the unknown region is a matter of speculation, but the farther man has gone the greater has been his wonder. The tales of explorers who have attempted to penetrate it sound like a recital of the old romances of Golconda and El Dorado; but the swamps and the mountains, the rivers that cannot be forded, and the jungles which forbid its search, the absence of food, and the difficulty of carrying supplies, with the other obstacles which now prevent exploration, will be overcome eventually, and the secret which has tantalized the world for three centuries will be disclosed by scientists. Almost every year expeditions are sent into the wilderness by the Government of the Argentine Republic, and each one goes farther than the last, so that the prospect of a thorough exploration is encouraging.

STATION ON THE ASUNCION RAILWAY.

The commerce of Paraguay is small, although rapidly increasing, and at present is absorbed in that of Uruguay and the Argentine Republic. There is one railroad in the country, which was built by Lopez II. for the transportation of troops, and runs a distance of forty-five miles, from Asuncion to Paraguay, an interior town of some importance. In 1877 the railroad was sold to an English corporation for a million dollars, but has not been well maintained. A street-car line connects the railway-station with the steamboat landing at Asuncion. There are two lines of steamers to Asuncion, one from Buenos Ayres and one from Montevideo. It is a journey of 1700 miles, and usually requires about fifteen days, as the stops along the route are numerous, and a great deal of time is taken up in loading and unloading. The steamers on this route are as good as any that ever floated upon the Mississippi River, and are fitted up in the most elegant style. They compete actively for passengers and furnish excellent meals and accommodations. One line sails under the French flag, and the other belongs to an Argentine company.

A VISIT TO THE SPRING.

The Government is making an honest and patient effort to educate and enlighten the people, and in comparison with its poverty and scanty revenues, is expending a large amount of money in maintaining a system of free schools; but until teachers are imported from abroad little progress will be made, as the native instructors are incompetent.

The change from the tyranny of Lopez to the present liberal, enlightened, and progressive administration was as sudden and radical as a change from darkness to light. The people have accepted the blessings with a genuine appreciation of their value, and have devoted themselves assiduously to the restoration of their country, and are happy in the enjoyment of peace.

The President of the republic is Dr. Caballaro, a man of education and broad intellect. He has travelled in Europe, and during the reign of Lopez II. was an exile, spending most of his time in the Argentine Republic. He has a Cabinet of three ministers, and his Secretary of State was educated in the Methodist Mission at Buenos Ayres. The latter gentleman is a Protestant, understands English well, and is a man of the most progressive ideas. It is largely owing to his efforts that Paraguay is making such rapid progress; and as he is the ruling spirit of the Government, he will probably be the next President.

THE PARAGUAYANS AT HOME.

The people are quiet, submissive, and industrious, having a mixture of Spanish blood and that of the Guarani Indians, who were the aboriginal settlers of the country. Their kinsmen across the Paraguay River, in the Argentine Republic, were a nomadic, savage tribe; but the tyranny of Lopez, father and son, took the spirit out of the Paraguay Indians, and they are now domesticated, and live in bamboo huts, cultivate the soil, and raise cattle. There is said to be less crime in Paraguay than in any other of the South American countries, and in 1883 there were but one hundred and twenty-five criminal trials in the entire republic, twenty-one of the defendants being foreigners. But for the tyranny of its rulers in past years Paraguay might have been an Arcadia, for the simple habits, the few wants, and the peaceable disposition of the people made them contented and well disposed towards each other. As nature has provided for all their wants, they have no great incentive to labor, and the enterprise and thrift of the country is generally found among the foreigners, from whom the people are, however, rapidly learning the ways of the world and the value of money. The men and women are of small stature, and the latter are usually very pretty when young, but lose their beauty of feature and figure after maternity. They are innocent, and childish in their amusements, are fond of dancing and singing, and have native dances that are as graceful, and native songs that are as melodious, as are the dances and music of the negroes of the United States.

PARAGUAY FLOWER-GIRL.

PARAGUAY FLOWER-GIRL.

Asuncion, the capital of the republic, is the oldest settlement in what is known as the valley of the River Plate. There were a considerable number of people there, and it was the seat of civil and religious authority, before the city of Buenos Ayres or the city of Rio de Janeiro was founded. There was a time when Asuncion was the greatest city in that part of the world, being the seat of the viceroys of Spain and the centre of a great commercial business. But after the independence of the republic, and during the reign of the despots Francia and Lopez, father and son, who for sixty years exercised despotic sway over the country, all immigration was shut out, and the people of the country were not permitted to leave it lest they should learn ideas of civilization and liberty that would excite them to revolution. At that time Asuncion was a city of seventy-five thousand inhabitants, but during the war it was almost depopulated, and three-fourths of the buildings are now in ruins.

REMAINS OF THE PALACE OF LOPEZ.

REMAINS OF THE PALACE OF LOPEZ.

In all tropical countries nature soon repairs or conceals the traces of man's wanton devastation. Fields corpse-strewn and blood-bathed, blackened with fire and trampled by the hoofs of cavalry horses, within six months' time wave in the golden luxuriance of a harvest; and the villages of the peasants, built of bamboo and palm-leaves, are quite as soon restored. Paraguay's rural territory shows no signs of the nine years' war and devastation; but in Asuncion and other cities the case is different. Its spacious edifices, costly churches, and public buildings are in ruins. Some which still stand are disused and deserted, more are only partially occupied, and are in a state of half neglect, too large for the shrunken populace; others, sad monuments of the vanity of the Dictators, are shattered and shamefully defaced. Whole streets are lined by empty shells of what were once costly dwellings, with here and there open gaps that tell of the pillage and devastation that follow war.

The most conspicuous object in Asuncion is the immense palace of Lopez, which covered four acres, and was completed at an enormous cost of money and labor, wrung from an unwilling people shortly before the fall of the tyrant. It is now an empty, roofless shell, towering, like one of the ruined castles in Europe, over the river. With its long rows of dismantled windows and black, ragged holes, it is as ghastly as the eye-sockets in a decaying skull.

Its shattered towers, shivering cornices, and broken parapets disclose the results of a three weeks' bombardment, and the destruction that followed its capture. The Brazilian plunderers carried off all that was portable; what they could not take away was burned, and what fire would not consume was defaced. The palace is said to have cost two million dollars, and was built exclusively by native workmen. The men are very skilful in the use of tools, and in the manufacture of gold and silver ornaments, and the women make a very fine lace which is called *nanduty*. The lace-making art was taught the women by the Spanish nuns. They do not use cotton thread, but the very fine fibres of a native tree, which are as soft and lustrous as silk. Some of their designs are very beautiful, and the fabric is indestructible. Lopez had his chamber walls hung with this lace, on a background of crimson satin, and the pattern was an imitation of the finest cobweb. It is said to have required the work of two hundred women for several years to cover the walls, and that every one of those women was a discarded mistress of the despot. The lace is fastened to the wall by clamps of solid gold of the most unique workmanship. There are four hundred of these clamps, each worth from twelve to fifteen dollars.

INTERIOR OF THE LOPEZ PALACE.

Near by the palace are the roofless walls of a spacious unfinished theatre, an example of Lopez's extravagance. The cathedral, and the Church of the

Incarnacion, where Francia sought, but did not find, a final resting-place, are heavy, ungraceful constructions of Spanish times. Nor have the Government buildings—many of which sheltered the terrible Dictator, for he continually shifted from one to another, for fear, it is said, of assassination—any pretension to beauty. Neither are the remains of the old Jesuit college, now converted into a barrack, anyway remarkable. The streets, wide and regular, are ill paved and deep in sand, while the public squares are undecorated and bare. On the other hand, the dwelling-houses—at least such of them as are constructed on the old Spanish plan, so admirably adapted to the requirements of the climate—are solidly built and not devoid of beauty. They have cool courts, thick walls, deeply recessed doors and windows, projecting eaves, and heavy, protected roofs.

THE CATHEDRAL, ASUNCION.

The furniture of the dwelling-houses is of native wood-work, solid, and tastefully carved. The pavement is generally of marble local or imported. The hard woods of the native forests are susceptible of high polish and delicate work, and the marbles, of various kinds and colors, are not inferior in beauty to any that Italy herself can boast of; and these will, when Paraguay is herself once more, take a high place on the list of her productions and merchandise.

MARKET-PLACE AT ASUNCION.

The majority of the houses are one-storied; but in some localities, where a mania for European imitation, encouraged by Lopez, prevailed, some uncomfortable and ill-seeming dwellings of two or three stories, flimsy, pretentious, and at variance alike with the climate and the habits of the people of Paraguay, have been erected.

The most cheerful, and almost the only active part of

A PARAGUAY HORSEMAN.

Asuncion is the market-place, which is situated near the centre of the town. It is a large square block of open arcades and pillared roofs, to which the natives from the suburbs daily bring their produce, intermixed with other wares of cheap price and of every-day consumption, the vendors being almost exclusively women. Maize, watermelons, gourds, pumpkins, oranges, mandioca flour, sweet potatoes, half-baked bread, cakes, biscuits, and sweets—the chief articles of food—are here offered for sale, together with tobacco of dark color and strong flavor, and yerba, the dried and pulverized leaf of the Paraguayan tea. Alongside of these are displayed a medley of cheap articles, for use or ornament, mostly of European manufacture; and here may be found matches, combs, cigarette paper, pots and pans, water-jars, rope, knives, hatchets, small looking-glasses, handkerchiefs, ponchos, and native saddles much resembling Turkish ones, which are very comfortable for riding, and are loaded with coarse silver ornaments. But the chief interest of the scene is the study of the buyers and sellers themselves. The men, who mostly belong to the former class, are from the villages round about, and come mounted on small, rough-coated horses, which are unclipped of mane or tail. The rider's dress consists of a pair of loose cotton drawers, coarsely embroidered or fringed with lace, and over them and around the waist are many-folded loin-cloths, generally of white; or it may consist of a pair of loose, baggy trousers, much like those worn by the Turkish peasants, and girt by a leather belt of generous width. These, with a white shirt often loaded with lace, and over all a striped or flowered poncho, complete the dress. Boots are rarely worn, and the bare feet are sometimes equipped with immense silver-plated spurs. The features and build of the riders present every variety of type, from the light-complexioned, brown-haired, red-bearded, honest manliness of the ancestral Basque, to the copper-hued, straight black-haired, narrow dark eyed, beardless chinned, flattened nosed, and small wiry framed aboriginal Guarani.

PARAGUAY BELLES.

The women are scantily, and in more civilized countries would be considered immodestly, clad, wearing nothing but a white tunic of native cotton, tied around the waist with a girdle of some gay color, often handsomely embroidered. These tunics are usually fringed at the top and bottom with native lace, and are always scrupulously clean. Cleanliness is the rule in Paraguay, and it extends to everything—dwellings, furniture, clothes, and person. Each house in the country has behind it a garden, small or large, as the case may be, in which flowers are sedulously cultivated. Flowers are a decoration that a Paraguayan girl or woman is rarely without. The women are pretty and often handsome. Dark eyes, long, wavy, dark hair, and a brunette complexion most prevail; but the blond

COSTUMES OF THE INTERIOR.

type, with blue eyes and golden curls, indicative of Basque descent, is by no means rare. Their hands and feet are almost universally delicate and small, and their forms, at least till frequent maternity has sacrificed beauty to usefulness, are simply perfect. The people seem to be always good-natured, the women particularly, who laugh, chat, and joke among themselves and with their customers, and are courteous and generous. Unlike many of their South American neighbors, they are as honest as they are gentle. A brighter, kinder, truer, more affectionate, and more devotedly faithful person than the Paraguayan girl exists nowhere. The women are more regardful of their beauty than in other countries, and the Paraguayan girl is never without a bit of decoration, ear-rings, a necklace, a bunch of flowers, or something of that sort; but they all smoke, young and old.

AN INTERIOR TOWN.

Some of the native ceremonies are peculiar and beautiful. When a couple are married, the bridal bed is always covered with flowers, and each neighbor contributes something towards giving them an outfit, even if it is nothing but a wooden spoon or a gourd cup. Their funerals are conducted after the ordinary formula of the Roman Catholic Church, but it is customary to hold a sort of wake over the dead, as in Ireland. Their market-days occur twice a week, and on Sunday there is the largest gathering and the greatest display, the people coming together after mass in the morning, and remaining about the plaza all day, enjoying a sort of festival which invariably closes in the evening with a dance. The dances are usually of the European kind—quadrilles, waltzes, polkas, mazourkas, and lanciers, interspersed with Paraguayan figures—the *cielo*, the *media caña* (a great favorite, and very lively), the *Montenero*, and some variations which were inherited from the aboriginal races. Cigars, cigarettes, sweets, refreshments, drinks—among which last *caña*, the rum of the country, comes foremost—are freely distributed in the intervals of the dances, and the ball is kept up till morning light. The women, seated around the room, each waiting her turn to dance, while the men gossip in groups outside the door, are dressed in Paraguayan fashion, with the long white *tupoi*, or tunic, which is deeply embroidered around the borders, and is often fringed with the beautiful home-made lace of the country; sometimes with silk skirts or brightly colored petticoats, and a broad colored sash; some of them wearing slippers, others barefooted.

HOME, SWEET HOME.

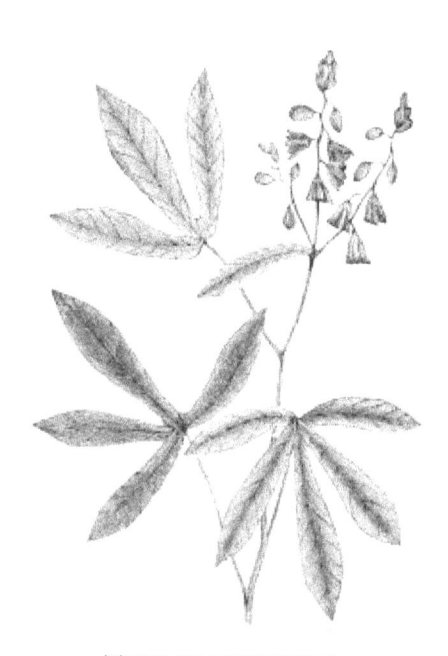

THE MANDIOCA.

The country about Asuncion is the very perfection of quiet rural beauty. The scenery resembles the prettiest parts of New England, enhanced by the richness of the verdure of the palm-trees with which the whole country is studded. The cultivated land is divided into fenced fields, wherein grow maize, mandioca, and sugar-cane, and the cottages dotted about complete the pleasantness of the picture. There are roads in every direction—not kept in first-rate condition, but still good; the cross-roads, which are not so much worked, are beautiful green lanes of considerable width, and for the most part perfectly straight. In some places the country presents the appearance of a splendid park.

The attractions of Paraguay are its agricultural and pastoral resources; and the timber-lands are said to be the finest in the world, the forests being situated in the northern part of the republic, and reaching an unmeasured distance into the heart of Brazil—as far as the Amazon River to the northward, and far into the mountain regions of Bolivia to the eastward.

Between Paraguay and the Andes stretches a vast country known as "El Gran Chaco," a region almost unexplored, and which offers fine grazing land and excellent pasture for cattle, besides the timber along the streams which water it profusely. Several enterprising colonists, English and German, have gone in there and opened sugar plantations, producing enormous crops; and the time will soon come when a large portion of the sugar supply of South America will be derived from this source. The land of Paraguay is said to be unusually good for sugar, but the chief products nowadays are mandioca, mate, and fruit. During the war with Uruguay, Brazil, and the Argentine Republic, nearly all the cattle were slaughtered; but new stock has been introduced, and very large droves are now being pastured upon the ranges. The fruits comprise nearly everything that is grown in the tropical or semi-tropical zones. The oranges are said to be the finest in the world, and the pineapples compare with those of Ecuador, which surpass anything raised upon the western coast of South America. There are other very rich and wholesome fruits, but the country is so far inland that they will never be exported.

The mandioca is a root resembling the yam, from which is produced the tapioca of commerce. Life and death are blended in the plant, but every part of it is useful if properly treated, and is as essential to the domestic economy of Brazil and Paraguay as rice is to China, or as potatoes are to Ireland. It is served at every meal, from that taken from the dinner-pail of the laborer to the banquet of the grandees, just as bread is with us, and is made into as many forms of food as our flour. There are four species of mandioca, but they differ

OX CART ON THE PAMPAS.

only as one kind of apple differs from another, all serving the same general purpose. The plant grows about four feet in height, and resembles the tomato in its foliage. The stalk and leaves are excellent fodder for cattle, and are often dried and used for their medicinal properties by the old women of Paraguay. When eaten raw the root is a deadly poison. Thirty-five drops of the juice were once administered as an experiment to a negro who was under sentence of death, causing speedy dissolution after five minutes of horrible convulsions. This poison is mysteriously removed or neutralized by the application of heat, and the root can be boiled or baked like a yam or sweet-potato. When cooked it is almost pure starch, and contains ninety-five per cent. of nutritious properties, being in fact as well as in fancy the staff of life of the people. The roots are boiled, and are then ground in rude mills, producing a powder about the color of buckwheat flour. Tapioca is a refined mandioca, and is produced by a modern process, the flour being reduced to a paste by boiling, and then allowed to crystallize. Very little tapioca is manufactured in the country, but the raw product is shipped to other parts of the world where the tapioca of commerce is manufactured.

CURING YERBA MATE.

A drink called *chicha* is also made of mandioca by soaking the flour in water and letting it ferment. It has a taste very much like malt or yeast, and one glassful of it will last a lifetime for an American, although the native will drink it by the quart without injury. It is a rapid intoxicant, but leaves no deleterious effect, and the man who goes upon a chicha spree will not wake up with a headache the next morning. The chicha of Peru is made of the juice of the sugar-cane, and the chicha of Chili of the juice of the grape. All these drinks have a similar taste and a similar effect.

A SIESTA.

Although the Paraguayans use considerable chicha, they are not an intemperate people. This is largely due to their excessive fondness for their native tea, the yerba mate, which they prefer to any alcoholic drink, usually taking from ten to fifteen cups of it daily. It is a mild stimulant, but is not intoxicating. The yerba mate is drunk all over the southern half of South America, and is well adapted to the climate and the requirements of the people, having a cool effect in the warm weather, and a warm effect in the cold. The taste is very much like that of catnip tea, as it has a bitter herbal flavor that is disagreeable at first, but one comes to like it very soon. The South American would no more refuse a cup of yerba mate than a German would a glass of beer. Whenever he travels in foreign countries he always takes a supply along, for it cannot be obtained in the United States or in Europe. In the markets, by the road-side, in the gardens, and in the doorways of their homes, as commonly as the Cuban with his cigarette or the Irishman with his dudeen, men and women can be seen at all hours of the day and night with a mate cup in their hands. Instead of having beer-gardens or wine-rooms, the people sit around the public places in Paraguay drinking mate; and it is one of the few cases in existence where a national habit of drinking improves the mental and physical condition of the people.

Yerba mate grows wild in Paraguay in great copses, like hazel or cranberries, but its quality improves under cultivation. Its uses were originally discovered by the Jesuits, those inquisitive fellows who were always prying into the secrets of nature as well as the secrets of State and the souls of men. They were the best mining prospectors in South America, and were constantly exercising their botanical and chemical knowledge for the advantage of the people. The sappy twigs are picked from the bushes, and are hung on frames over a fire to dry. When they become crisp they are reduced to powder by being rubbed between the hands. This powder is packed for export in green hides, which shrink when exposed to the sun, and press the mate into a compact, solid mass. Everybody carries a mate-cup and a tube called a *bombilla*. The cups are usually ordinary gourds, but they are often made of cocoa-nut shells and the shells of other nuts, and are sometimes beautifully carved. The bombillas of the common people are bamboo stems with the pith punched out; but the wealthy people have them made of silver, and often of gold. The bamboo tubes are the most agreeable to use, as they do not conduct the heat so rapidly, and never scald the lips, as the silver ones do. The cups are half filled with powdered yerba mate, then boiling water is poured in. Delicate drinkers always throw away this water, and fill the cup again, as it is too bitter for their taste; but the habitual users of the weed consider the first water as the best, and keep pouring in water and sucking it through the tube until the strength of the powder is exhausted, when the refuse is thrown out and the cup is refilled.

The *yerbales*, or mate fields, of Paraguay are said to cover three million acres in their present state, and to produce an annual crop of thirty thousand tons. During the reign of the tyrants Francia and Lopez the exportation of mate was monopolized by the Government, and every citizen was

A PARAGUAY HOTEL.

compelled to pay as tribute-money a certain amount each year for the benefit of the despots, being driven to it by taskmasters, as were the children of Israel to the making of bricks in Egypt. But under the new regime the tea-forests have been leased to an Argentine firm, which pays a royalty of one dollar a ton to the Government. This concession was given when the Treasury was empty and the Government was greatly in need of money, so that what might have been a very productive source of income was sacrificed for a little cash in hand.

NATIVE PAPPOOSE AND CRADLE.

The export goes to the Argentine Republic, Uruguay, and Chili. Several attempts have been made to send it to Europe, but they were not successful. During early times the Queen of Spain prohibited the importation of yerba mate by her subjects, on the ground that it was productive of barrenness in women, but the rapidly increasing population of the River Plate countries, where it is used to the greatest extent, seems to prove the fallacy of her Majesty's theory. In Uruguay, where the women are scarcely ever seen without a mate-cup in their hands, the vital statistics show a larger percentage of births than in any other country in the world; and there is something curious in the fact before-mentioned, that the number of males born in that country is so much greater than the number of females. No attempt has ever been made to introduce mate into this country, and the consumption of the article will probably always be confined to South America.

Paraguay tobacco is used all over South America. It is rank, black, and full of nicotine, but it makes a very good cigarette, being about as strong as the blackest Turkish tobacco, or "perique." Everybody in Paraguay smokes—men, women, and children—and their cigarettes are made of the native tobacco and corn-husks. During the last few years several political refugees from Cuba have found a resting-place in Paraguay, and have experimented with native tobacco on the Cuban plan. These experiments have shown that, where properly cultivated and properly cured, this tobacco is as good as any raised in the West Indies; but the natives let it grow wild, and take no pains either in its cultivation or in the treatment of the leaves.

A HACIENDA.

The timber of Paraguay is very fine, and includes almost every variety known to arboriculture, from the finest light woods that may replace those of China and Japan to the heavy and tough varieties that sink in water like iron, and are indestructible. For lack of energy and saw-mills, the forests, so far, are almost untouched. The dwellings and other buildings of the country are made of adobe, and the small quantity of dressed lumber used there comes from Canada or from the United States. Two American saw-mills have recently been introduced, and the water-power is sufficient to operate them at a small expense. The timber regions are full of streams, which can be utilized for floating logs and rafts, and nature seems to have provided every facility for the development of their extensive resources.

PEOPLE OF "EL GRAN CHACO."

Along the western border of Paraguay lies an immense territory, in some parts reported to be arid and waste for want of water, but in others filled with a succession of rivers, and destined in time to be one of the most valuable portions of the Argentine Republic. It is called "El Gran

AN ARMADILLO.

Chaco." It extends from the Parana River to Bolivia, and is separated on the east from Paraguay by the river of the same name. It is divided by the river Vermijo into two almost equal parts, one called the "Chaco Austral" and the other "Chaco Boreal," the latter extending to latitude 20° south, and bounded on the north by the Bolivian province of Chiquitos. The "Chaco Boreal" is an uninterrupted plain, elevated about four thousand feet above the level of the sea, and divided into the most beautiful forests, with intervening meadows, as if made purposely for the raising of cattle. The Austral or Southern Chaco lies between the Vermijo on the north, the Parana on the east, and the province of Santa Fé on the south. It is completely level, and is richly endowed by nature, not only with a deep soil, but with most magnificent forests. As yet these vast regions are almost exclusively occupied by wild Indians. A large portion has never been explored, and hence but little is yet known of the interior, or of its treasures of vegetable wealth. Only where it skirts along the Parana and Paraguay rivers, with here and there a small clearing and settlement, the nucleus of a number of agricultural colonies, has anything been scientifically determined in reference to its timber resources. The region possesses an immense advantage in great water-courses flowing along its eastern borders, and the smaller streams which penetrate its interior, and are navigable for many hundreds of miles. Thus all its vast wealth of precious woods and valuable timber is rendered accessible not only to Buenos Ayres, but as ocean ships can load along its banks, it is also accessible to the markets of the world, without the necessity of transshipment. The wood-choppers are at work, and the quantities of all kinds of precious woods shipped down the rivers are becoming greater and greater every year.

A RANCH ON EL GRAN CHACO.

The number of horned cattle in Paraguay is now estimated at six hundred thousand, and there is said to be pasturage for several million within the limits of the republic, and an unlimited area in El Gran Chaco beyond the timber regions on a plain similar to New Mexico, rising in great terraces or steppes to the foot-hills of the Andes. The elevation of this area above the sea is from four to eight thousand feet, and although it borders upon the tropics, it is said to be an excellent range, and the ranchmen of the Argentine Republic are contemplating it with covetous eyes. No industry pays so well in Paraguay as cattle-raising. The severe frosts and droughts which at times annoy the ranchmen of the Argentine Republic are unknown there; the streams are numerous and perennial, the cattle fatten quicker, attain greater weight, and afford a better quality of beef, owing to the nutritious grass and abundance of water. Young cattle, as before stated, may be bought in the Argentine Republic and transported by river steamer to Paraguay for twelve or thirteen dollars per head, and land can be purchased at about twenty cents an acre from the Government.

RIO DE JANEIRO.

THE CAPITAL OF BRAZIL.

THE name of the capital of Brazil means "River of January," and in the native tongue is pronounced *Reeo-day-Hay-nay-ray-oh*. When the ancient mariners who discovered the Brazilian coast passed through the narrow gateway to the harbor, and saw the beautiful bay in the amphitheatre of mountains surrounded by eternal verdure, they supposed they were entering the mouth of a river that would lead them to the Enchanted Land; and when they found out their mistake they despised the place so much that they did not even have the good-nature to christen it after a saint, but marked it on their charts simply the river discovered in January.

The bay around which the city lies is famous for its beauty, and rivals that of Naples or the Golden Horn. The panorama is ever changing with the shifting clouds, and in this country everything is intense. Nowhere is the contrast between sunshine and shadow so strong, and the outlines of the clouds lie distinctly upon the landscape where their shadows fall, changing the tint of the foliage and flowers. The mountains, which furnish a noble background for the picture, are so steep, so rugged, and so high as to exaggerate the peace of the water, and furnish another striking contrast in their dark and frowning lines to the white buildings of the city and its countless towers. These mountains seem to enclose the town and the bay like a wall, and leave no passage in or out except at the entrance to the harbor, which is scarcely wide enough for two vessels to pass. Along their base lies the city, like a lazy white monster, sleeping under the shade of imperial palms in a garden of never-failing colors and eternal loveliness.

BAY OF RIO DE JANEIRO.

Viewed from the deck of a ship in the harbor, the city of Rio looks like a fragment of fairy-land—a cluster of alabaster castles decorated with vines; but the illusion is instantly dispelled upon landing, for the streets are narrow, damp, dirty, reeking with repulsive odors, and filled with vermin-covered beggars and wolfish-looking dogs. The whole town seems to be in a continual perspiration, and the atmosphere is so enervating that the stranger feels an almost irresistible tendency to lie down. There is now and then a lovely little spot where Nature has displayed her beauties unhindered, and the environs of the city are filled with the luxury of tropical vegetation; but there are only a few fine residences, a few pleasant promenades, and a few clusters of regal palms, which look down upon the filth and squalor of the town with dainty indifference. The palm is the peacock of trees. Nothing can degrade it, and the filth in which it often grows only serves to heighten its beauty. Behind some of the residences of the better classes are gardens in which grow flowers that baffle the painter's skill, and foliage that is the ideal of luxuriance and gracefulness. They are little glimpses of green and gold in a desert of misery and dirt. A few years ago there was not even a sewer in Rio, and all the garbage and offal of the city was carried through the streets on the heads of men, and dumped into the sea. Now there are drains under the principal streets, but they seem to be of little use, as the main thoroughfares are abominable, and one wonders what the less pretentious ones may be. The pavements are of the roughest cobble-stone, the streets are so narrow that scarcely a breath of air can enter them, and the sunshine cannot reach the pools of filth that steam and fester in the gutters, breeding plagues.

A STREET IN RIO.

The city is in the shape of a narrow crescent, lying between the mountains and the bay, nowhere more than half a mile wide, and stretching for a distance of nine or ten miles. It can never be any wider, but grows at either end. The chief residence street lies along the edge of the water, but the business houses are crowded into the lower portion of the town, damp, gloomy, and dismal, the streets being so narrow that carriages are forbidden to enter them during the busy hours of the day. A fire that would burn out the older portion of the city would be a blessing, and might redeem Rio from some of its filth and ugliness.

THE CITY OF RIO FROM THE BAY.

The public buildings are quite as ugly and unpretentious as the commercial houses. The city palace of the Emperor fronts the market-place, in which donkeys and carts are unloaded daily, and where the fish-boats land. It is impregnated by the stench of decaying vegetation, and has an ancient and fish-like smell. The structure looks more like a warehouse than the shelter of imperial power, and Dom Pedro will not live in it. He has two beautiful palaces in the country, in which he resides, and only comes to the city palace on occasions of public importance. The only presentable Government buildings are the post-office and printing-house, and many of the private residences are superior in every respect to anything the Government owns. The building in which Congress sits is a gloomy old pile, without a single redeeming feature, and a great empire like Brazil ought to be ashamed to house its Parliament in such a place.

The Rue Dineta is the Wall Street of Rio de Janeiro, and during the morning hours, while the Coffee Exchange is open, presents quite an animated appearance. Brokers and commission men, merchants, planters, agents of transportation lines, speculators, men of all ages and nationalities, assemble there to trade and gamble; and one can hear a dozen different languages in half as many groups. Most of the speculation is done in coffee, and in the buying and selling of exchange on London.

Nothing in Rio strikes an American as more singular than the nomenclature of the streets. Many of them, such as the "Seventh of September" and the "First of March," are named after days on which something (no one seems to know exactly what) has taken place. There is one thoroughfare called the "Street of Good Jesus," and the names of the saints are freely used. It seems a trifle queer to be directed to "No. 20 First of March Street," or for a man to live at the corner of "St. John the Baptist and St. John the Evangelist Streets," but the Brazilians do not mind it.

The principal street in Rio is the celebrated Rua do Ouvidor. It is a narrow little alley-way, in which two carriages could not pass each other. In fact I never saw a carriage in

AQUEDUCT AT RIO.

the street, and doubt if a driver would be bold enough to venture there. Here are the shops of the principal merchants, and the gorgeous stores of the artificers of feather flowers, and the dealers in gold and silver and precious stones. The street, from one end to the other, is filled at night with people, not on the narrow sidewalks only, but completely filling the thoroughfare from wall to wall. Officers of the army and navy, and soldiers and sailors, all in uniform, mingle with the crowd, and flash their gold lace in the bright light that floods the street. Everywhere, too, are the elaborate mulatto gendarmes, the police of the city. From the *cafés chantants* come the sounds of music and the clinking of glasses. At little tables in the cafés the Brazilians sit, drinking strong coffee or other beverages, talking, gesticulating, and never for a moment completely at rest. Catching a weasel asleep is easy compared with that of catching a Brazilian when some portion of his body is not in motion. This is owing to the amount of strong black coffee they drink. A Brazilian proverb says that coffee, to be good, must be "black as night, as bitter as death, and hot as sheol."

THE AVENUE OF ROYAL PALMS—RIO.

The total abstinence cause has few if any supporters in Brazil. Everybody drinks—men, women, and children. The police records show that men do get drunk here, but they are very seldom seen. The laboring classes drink a vile beverage called *casasch*, which is made of the juice of the sugar-cane in the regular distillery fashion. But moderate as the Brazilians are in the use of liquors, they are decidedly immoderate in the use of coffee. It is coffee the first thing in the morning and the last thing at night, coffee at meals and coffee between meals, and all of it made according to the proverb.

Rio is a succession of disappointments. The only really pretty place is the Botanical Garden, which serves to illustrate what the whole city might be with the exercise of a little taste and the expenditure of a trifling sum of money. Here are colonnades of palms which surpass anything on the globe, and which are worth a journey to Brazil to see. Here are all the plants and trees that the country produces, and no land is so rich in vegetation as Brazil. Flowers of the most gorgeous hues, orchids that are wonders of color, and a representation of the virgin forests of the Amazon, a tangled mass of wild, luxuriant vegetation, full of birds of the most brilliant plumage, bugs that look like animated gems, and flowers of scarlet, purple, and yellow, that make the forest appear as if it were ablaze. Every color is intense.

THE PRETTIEST THINGS IN BRAZIL.

There are no delicate tints and no gentle hues. The flowers have no perfume, and the birds no songs. The whole country seems to be painted yellow and red.

Strangers always visit the fish-market, where all sorts of shiny creatures are to be found, most of them peculiar to the waters of Brazil. The whole business is conducted by auction, and the fish are sold by the basket to the highest-bidder men, who have retail places throughout the city, or who peddle them in the streets. All varieties of food are peddled about the town, and the venders attract attention by clapping pieces of wood together and uttering peculiar cries. There are drinking-booths along the street at which all sorts of beverages can be obtained, from goats' milk to brandy, and casasch is sold by the bucketful. There are plenty of street-car lines, and all the population ride. The cars are always crowded, and everybody reads a morning paper as he goes down-town, and an evening paper on his way home.

Foreigners are generally puzzled to know why the horse-cars in Rio are called "bonds." It happened in this way: When the first horse railroad was built in Rio bonds were issued to pay for it. There was a great talk about these bonds, and the uneducated were at a loss to know what the English word meant. When they saw the first car they thought they had found a solution of the question, and all exclaimed, "There is one of those much-talked-of bonds." So all over Brazil a horse-car is a "bond" to this day.

It is noticed that every ox-cart in Brazil creaks with the most soul-reaching sounds. I asked a cartman why he did not grease its wheels. He replied that the creaking stimulated the animals, and they would not work without it.

Humming-birds are plenty as flies about Rio, and the natives call them *be aflores* (kiss flowers). At night the air is full of myriads of fire-flies that look like a shower of stars. To one who makes a tour of South America before going to Brazil, it seems as if all of the homely women on the continent had emigrated there, for pretty ones are extremely scarce. Their complexions are sallow, and they all have a bilious look. Another oddity is that the women are invariably fat and the men are invariably lean. Their complexions are ruined by the climate, and the lives of indolence they lead give them a tendency to obesity, which is augmented by the excessive use of sweetmeats. The women are munching confectionery from morning till night, and scarcely eat anything else, and their time is divided between dozing in a

A BRAZILIAN HACIENDA.

rocking-chair or peeking through the blinds to see the people on the streets. One can ride about Rio all day without seeing a Brazilian lady, and the only glimpse a man ever gets of them is during the evenings at the cafés or at the playhouses, unless he gets out early in the morning and sees them on the way to mass.

At six o'clock every morning the streets are full of women on their way to church, at seven o'clock they are on their way to their homes, and at half-past seven there is not one to be seen. In the evening, when the gas is lighted, they pour from the houses into the streets, the parks, the ice-cream booths, and the theatres. There they appear in their Paris finery, overloaded with jewellery, munching candy, nibbling ices, and gossiping.

Next to her complexion, the ugliest thing about a Brazilian woman is her voice. It sounds as if the parrots had taught her to speak, and when you hear it behind the blinds, as one often does, it is always a matter of doubt whether

"Polly" or her mistress is talking. But the Brazilians do not call their parrots Polly, as we do. The common name is "Loreta."

A Brazilian woman never goes shopping. Servants are sent for samples; and if it is a bonnet the señorita wants to buy, a box or basket containing all the latest Parisian styles is sent up for her inspection. Most of the purchasing is done in this way, and a woman is seldom seen in a shop. But in all of these remarks the negroes are excepted. The streets swarm day and night with gorgeously dressed Dinahs, wearing turbans that would shame a passion-flower for color, and usually yellow or red gowns. They chatter like magpies, and seldom seem to be going anywhere or to have any object in life beyond gossiping with the friends they meet.

More attention is now paid to female education in Brazil than formerly. At one time it was only necessary for a señorita to know how to read her prayer-book and to embroider, but of late seminaries for females have been established, and the nuns compelled to enlarge the curriculum of convent study. The Brazilian woman is now beginning to receive the respect that modern civilization demands for her, and is no longer kept as a plaything for man. She is intelligent, learns readily, and has considerable wit, but never reads anything except the fashion papers and translations of French novels. A bookseller told me that the demand for the last named was increasing largely, and that where he sold only one ten years ago he sells a hundred nowadays. Education in music and the lighter arts is also becoming popular, as the increased sales in music and painting and drawing materials show. The Brazilian woman has always been famous for her embroidery, and her house is full of the most beautiful work, the doing of which she has learned from the nuns.

THE OLD CITY PALACE.

In Rio social restrictions are being removed, the two sexes are allowed to mingle with greater freedom than formerly, and society is beginning to assume a new phase. Occasionally grand balls are given, and within the last few years the natives have acquired the habit of occasionally visiting one another's houses socially with their wives—something that was unknown a few years ago. The etiquette of modern society was reversed in Brazil not many years ago. If a man bowed to a female acquaintance, or addressed her, except in the presence of her husband, father, or brother, it was considered an insult, to be punished with a blow, but now it is considered entirely proper for ladies and gentlemen to converse together. There remains, however, the old system of formal calling or exchanging visits. Ladies never go out alone to call on their friends, and no gentleman will be received at a house when the husband or father is absent.

IN THE SUBURBS.

The theatres of Rio are numerous and well attended, but are neither handsome nor well arranged. There are French, Spanish, and Portuguese performances, and during the winter season an Italian opera two or three times a week, which is liberally patronized by the upper classes. The performances at the opera as well as at the theatres are considered only an adjunct to social conversation, however, and because of the talking going on around him during the play, one can scarcely hear what is said by the performers. Connected with every theatre is a garden and café, and between the acts the people repair to these places. Ice-cream and all sorts of beverages are served, and confectionery of course. They have recently built the great Theatre Dom Pedro Segundo, larger than La Scala or San Carlo, and said to have a seating capacity of eleven thousand. In building this theatre the matter of size has rather been overdone, for a large portion of the audience is unable to hear the opera. The Emperor has two boxes in the opera-house—one a small private box, and one a great and gorgeous box of state. When the venerable gentleman is out spending the evening somewhere, and wishes to visit the opera quietly for a moment, he goes into his private box, and sits there without causing unusual attention; but when he goes in state he occupies the large box. Then he dashes up to the theatre with his guards, equerries, and gentlemen-in-waiting. As he enters the box the orchestra strikes up the stirring imperial hymn, the people rise, and shout, "Viva Dom Pedro Segundo!" the Emperor bows, smiles, takes his seat, and the opera proceeds.

COTTAGES IN THE INTERIOR.

The hotels in Brazil are very bad. There are two or three small ones, which furnish tolerably good rooms and good living, but they are usually crowded, and a stranger coming to the city finds it difficult to procure rooms. The city might support a very fine hotel, such as is found in Montevideo and Santiago, but at present there is nothing to compare with the accommodations found in those cities. Rio is about as badly off for hotels as any city in the world. The meats and fish served are usually of a poor quality, but the fruits are excellent. There is no such fruit to be found anywhere, either for variety or for deliciousness of flavor, and the wines are usually good. Good wine can always be procured throughout Spanish America. If a Spaniard were limited to a crumb of bread and a drop of water per day, he would always expect a bottle of wine to go with it. The strawberries and grapes of Brazil are unusually fine, and are grown the whole year round. The peaches are also very good; but the principal fruits are bananas, oranges, pineapples, chirimoyas, sapotes, and some other things that we do not find in temperate climates.

So far it has been found impossible to raise good cattle in Brazil, although the province of Rio Grande de Sul, being the most southerly, has a cooler temperature, and ranchmen have been utilizing the ranches to be found in the interior on the border of Uruguay. Cattle-breeding is chiefly in the hands of the natives, and the horses come over the Uruguay border. The stock cattle sell for from five to six dollars a head, while fat cattle are worth about twelve dollars. The larger amount of the beef and mutton supply of Rio de Janeiro comes by steamer from the Argentine Republic.

The native dishes are peculiar, and are not palatable to those who do not care for an unlimited amount of garlic. In fact, a stranger going into the interior cannot find anything to eat but boiled eggs, for these are the only articles the native Brazilian cook cannot spoil. Grease and garlic do not penetrate the shells; but even eggs are unreliable, for the natives seem to have no idea of any difference in them, and use them in all conditions of age, and often in the transition stage of being.

Among the important articles used for the table is jerked beef. Immense quantities of it are imported from the Argentine Republic and Uruguay, and it is shipped here by the ton. It is said that thirty thousand tons of it are annually imported into Brazil, and it furnishes the staple food for the slaves on the plantations and the common people in the cities. Jerked beef and beans are always to be found on the table, and both mixed in a stew with plenty of garlic compose the omnipresent national dish. *Bacalao*, or codfish, is considered a great delicacy, and about seventy-five thousand tubs are annually imported from Nova Scotia and the United States. The people in Brazil are so fond of it that they will use it at any time in preference to the fresh fish of their own waters; but the Yankee would not recognize either the codfish or the beans in this country, mixed up as they usually are in an *olla podrida* of yam, cabbage, and garlic.

THE IGUANA.

The foreign commerce of Brazil is in the hands of the English, and the retail commerce in the hands of the French and German. In fact, nearly nine-tenths of the commercial community of Rio de Janeiro is composed of foreigners. There are very few Americans there, however, and that is one reason why our trade with that country is so small. The native Portuguese are usually the land-owners, the planters, and professional men; and there is a very large body of officials, composed to a great extent of the decayed aristocracy.

At all the public gatherings in Rio these people appear in uniforms or court dresses, decorated with stars and crosses so numerously and inappropriately bestowed as to border on the ridiculous. Many boys, apparently not more than fourteen or fifteen years of age, can be seen at these gatherings, wearing tawdry silk and velvet dresses, and stars which have been obtained by inheritance or by purchase. There used to be a custom under which patents of nobility, with stars and crosses, and "the insignia of the order of Christ," which was the highest decoration, could be obtained by purchase, and the rage for these decorations attained a greater height in Brazil probably than in any other country. At one time almost every petty shopkeeper in the empire might be seen on the streets on holidays with a "habito de Christo" on his breast. These purchased honors were worn by the dignitaries of the Church as well as by civilians of all degrees, and being handed down from the generation that lived when such

A BRAZILIAN LAUNDRY.

things could be procured by purchase, still exist in great numbers among the people of the country. In the present generation the decorations of the empire are given to those only who have performed some service for the State, and cannot be secured by purchase.

A COUNTRY SCHOOL.

The prevailing costume of the people in the country is just as it was a hundred years ago. They wear broad-brimmed hats with low crowns, tied with a ribbon under the chin; velveteen jackets, and waistcoats of gay colors, with metal buttons; linen or cotton drawers; high black gaiters buttoning up to the knee, and a sort of mantle similar to that used in Portugal, generally lined with red, thrown negligently over the shoulders; but on the sea-coast people dress in the European style. In Rio there is a great deal of rivalry in toilets among the ladies. As in other cities of South America, the gentlemen usually dress in broadcloth suits, patent-leather boots, and black silk hats, or in white duck or linen.

The school system is very meagre, but is improving. There are in the empire 2000 public schools for a population of 12,000,000 people, and the State expends annually $8,000,000 for public instruction. During the last few years, at nearly every session of Parliament, the Government introduced a compulsory education bill; but the bill has never become a law. The upper classes have an inclination for education; but nothing is ever done by the Government towards educating the slaves. The little learning which they acquire is received from the priests.

There are several institutions for higher education, several schools of medicine, of law, civil engineering, and mining; a normal school for the education of teachers, a conservatory of music, a school of fine arts, an institute for the blind, and another for the deaf and dumb, several reformatory schools, and an Imperial Industrial School founded by Dom Pedro upon the plan of the Cooper Institute of New York, the suggestion for it having been derived from his visit to that place while in the United States. There is also a bureau of colonization and immigration in the Department of Agriculture, and as an inducement to settlers, the Government offers them free subsistence and shelter at the boarding-house in Rio de Janeiro during the time that it is necessary for them to wait, as well as free transportation for themselves and baggage from Rio to any part of the country. They can purchase land on credit, the first payment to be made at the end of the second year, and four payments during the succeeding four years, and for cash they receive a discount of twenty per cent. For the first season the Agricultural Department gives them a donation of necessary implements and seeds, and an allowance of twenty-five cents a day for each adult, and ten cents for each child, during the first six months after settlement, until the land they occupy can be made to produce. The cost of the land is now from eight to sixteen dollars an acre. There are under the care of the Department of Agriculture twelve colonies, comprising a population of sixty-two thousand people, mostly German. The number of immigrants arriving in the country amounts to from forty to fifty thousand a year.

BRAZILIAN COUNTRY-HOUSE.

The immense area of Brazil, stretching as it does from 4° 30′ north to 33° south latitude, and from the thirty-fifth to the seventy-third degree of west longitude, affords almost as great a variety of climate and soil as can be found in the United States, and the two countries are of very nearly the same area. A glance at the map will show the extensive fluvial system of Brazil. The many large rivers that traverse the interior in all directions are navigable, and afford unequalled facilities for commerce.

Independent of the agricultural resources which the climate, situation, and productiveness of the soil afford, the mineral treasures which nature has stored in the interior are very abundant. Gold, together with diamonds and various other precious stones, is found in many localities, and the resources of the interior of the country, which has never been explored, are only a subject of speculation. The population now consists of about twelve million people; and it has not increased any during the last twenty-five years. Of this population there are about two million slaves and five hundred thousand Indians; but neither the moral character, social habits, nor intellectual attainments of this class afford material of value wherewith to build up an enlightened and progressive government. The natives are neither enterprising, thrifty, nor industrious. The system of slavery has taught them idleness, and the fact that they have gained their living without work has taught them habits of extravagance. There are a few men of wealth among them who have earned by their own efforts the money which they have, but nearly all have either inherited it or secured it as the result of slave labor. Brazil will never be a great or prosperous country until its population is increased by immigration.

Considerable progress has been made, and great interest taken, in railroad development. There are now about 2500 miles in operation, 800 of which are owned and operated by the Government, and 1700 by private corporations. In addition to this, about 1400 miles are under construction, and there are many prospective enterprises. The Government guarantees an annual income of seven per cent. upon the construction bonds of all railroads, and has so far paid this guarantee promptly. Recently a loan of thirty-four million dollars has been made in London for the construction of additional railways, and this is also secured by the Government. The rails are all imported from England, but a part of the rolling stock is brought from the United States. The roads are surveyed

UP THE RIVER.

and built by Brazilian engineers, but the principal machinists and locomotive drivers are Scotchmen. The principal railroad in Brazil is the one named in honor of the present Emperor, Dom Pedro II., and it is familiarly known as the "Pedro Segundo" road. This line runs from Rio Janeiro to the most important towns, and through a country which produces coffee, corn, and cattle. There are now about 500 miles of track in operation. It is a favorite route for tourists, and affords a view of the finest mountain scenery in the empire.

DOM PEDRO II.

The prevailing opinion among the practical men of Brazil is that Dom Pedro II. is a lovable old humbug. Everybody regards the Emperor with a feeling of reverence, and his character and motives are universally respected; but he leaves the cares of State entirely to the direction of his ministers and his half-brother, the Baron de Capanema, who has more influence with the Cabinet than the Emperor himself. The old man is wrapped up in philanthropic movements, and is

ON THE WAY TO PETROPOLIS.

constantly engaged in doing something for the amelioration of his fellow-men; but he is so easily imposed upon, and his ideas are so impracticable, that not only are his efforts wasted, but a large amount of money with which a great deal of good might be accomplished is expended upon chimerical projects; and the only result is the gratification that the Emperor enjoys in performing what he considers to be a duty. He is credulous, ingenuous, and trustful, and no matter what the reputation of the men who come to him with schemes is, he never fails to be interested in anything that will tend to the improvement or welfare of his people. He devotes almost his entire time to entertaining impostors and developing schemes that are suggested to him by the people who take advantage of his philanthropic disposition to accomplish their own ends.

A little beyond the city of Petropolis is the imperial hacienda, which is known as Santa Cruz. Here Dom Pedro II. used to live, but his first-born and only son died in the palace, and since that time, which was many years ago, neither he nor the Empress has ever entered its walls. Some twenty years ago he devoted this hacienda, as he does almost everything else, to philanthropy, and attempted a grand philanthropic experiment which has demonstrated nothing but the Emperor's own lack of ability as a manager.

The Princess of Brazil has three children, two sons and a daughter; and besides these the Emperor has three other grandchildren, orphans of a deceased daughter, who live with their grandparents and are a great source of comfort to the Emperor, who is very fond of children.

The Empress is a woman of rare traits, being noted for her womanliness, her charity, and her lovely character; and those who became acquainted with her while she was in the United States will remember her with the greatest affection. There is nowhere in the world a couple more devoted to each other, or with a kindlier disposition towards their fellow-creatures, or having a more earnest desire to accomplish something for the good of mankind, than Dom Pedro and the Empress. She is much more practical in her charity than he, and it is said that she frequently chides the Emperor for being so easily humbugged. The Empress is a fine-looking old lady, with white hair and a kindly face. She has not the force

THE EMPRESS OF BRAZIL.

and energy of her daughter, but is of a more retiring disposition, and prefers to interest herself in the affairs of the household rather than in matters of State. Every week or so the Emperor gives a reception, which is attended by all the nobility and by such strangers of sufficient dignity to receive royal attention as happen to be in the country. The Emperor is particularly fond of Americans, and he considers the United States the model country of the world. He has introduced into Brazil a great many ideas that he received during his visit to this country, and has organized an Agricultural Department and a Geological Survey, and several other branches of the Government, in imitation of what he found in the United States.

The Emperor had a great friend in Dr. Gunning, who left a high place in the medical college in Edinburgh about twenty years ago, and came to Brazil for his health. He had an ample fortune, and determined to devote his time and money to the abolition of slavery. With this object in view he bought thirty-five or forty slaves and a tract of land. The negroes for miles around him were earning large wages for their owners, but the doctor had a theory that they would pay for themselves, and buy their own emancipation, if they had an opportunity. So he commenced a system of bookkeeping, charging each slave with his original cost and the expense of his maintenance, and crediting him with the amount of labor he performed. When the accounts balanced, the slave was to be set free. But they never balanced.

Dr. Gunning impressed the Emperor with the great benefits of this system, and succeeded in inducing him to adopt it on his plantation. But the negroes are not fools. They understand very well that they are better off with such masters as Dr. Gunning and the Emperor than they would be in the condition of freedom, and they work so unprofitably, and make the expenses of their maintenance so great, that they never yet made enough in any one year to pay for their keeping.

The Emperor spends most of his time at Petropolis, and the only thing that can induce him to visit the city of Rio is a debate in Congress on the slavery question. It is nearly four centuries since Brazil was discovered, and it has always been governed by the same family. This part of the continent was given to the Portuguese by the Pope. When they began to quarrel with the Spaniards over the possession of the discoveries in America, the Pope drew a line along the sixty-fifth parallel of longitude and decided that the Portuguese should have all that part of the world lying east, and the Spaniards all that part lying west of it. Therefore Brazil became a viceroyalty of Portugal, and remained so until 1807, when the two countries changed relations, Brazil becoming the seat of government and Portugal becoming a colony. Portugal temporized with Napoleon, and when he made a raid upon that nation the royal family of Briganza took a step which astonished all Europe. In order to save the nation from the bloodshed and devastation that followed

Napoleon's avarice, Dom Joao fled from Lisbon to Rio, and left Napoleon in peaceable possession of Portugal.

DOM PEDRO'S PALACE AT PETROPOLIS.

For many years Joao preferred to remain in Rio de Janeiro, and govern his subjects with delegated power. Finally, Napoleon having vanished from the face of Europe, the Emperor returned to Lisbon, leaving his son, Dom Pedro I., upon the throne of Brazil; but the people were ill satisfied with this, and a bloodless revolution soon after occurred, in which Dom Pedro I. was compelled to abdicate, and in 1831 he fled to Portugal, leaving his son, Dom Pedro II., then a boy of fifteen, as Emperor, who governed through a regency until he became of age. His authority has been recognized in Brazil ever since, and he is loved by the people as few monarchs have ever been.

The Emperor's power is limited, and is infinitely less than that of any of the Presidents of the South American republics. He has the right to veto acts of the national legislature, but it requires only a majority vote to override it, so that it practically amounts to nothing. The senators are elected for life, are endowed with titles, and their duties are similar to those of the peers of Great Britain. The Emperor receives from the State an income of four hundred thousand dollars per annum, but he is a poor economist, and spends it all, the greater part in mistaken charity.

There is a small party called Republican, which proposes to unseat the Emperor, do away with all the titles and all insignia of royalty and nobility, and to take, as the rest of the South Americans have done, "the great republic of the north" for its example. In theory they are for upsetting the throne and tumbling the Emperor off, but they recognize his goodness and benevolence, and have the wisdom to see that they are a great deal better off under the administration of such a man than under a President who would be an autocrat. When the Emperor dies Brazil will become a republic. The Liberal party believe in republican principles; and the ideas of civil and religious liberty have so permeated the people, from the nobles to the slaves, that it will be impossible to continue the empire under the daughter of Dom Pedro when she comes to inherit the throne.

The Emperor had but one son, and his only living child is the Princess Isabella, wife of the Count D'Eu, a grandson of Louis Philippe, a cousin of the Count of Paris, and a Prince of the House of Orleans. This French husband of the Brazilian princess is said to be an uncommonly good fellow, and a man of considerable ability. He holds the rank of major-general in the army, and is an aide-de-camp, or grand marshall, under the Emperor. The princess and her husband live in the city of Rio de Janeiro in a very ordinary way, the palace they occupy and their style of living being a great deal inferior to that of many merchants and foreign residents of the country. They have a plantation near Petropolis, and spend the unhealthy seasons of the year at that place.

The princess is now about thirty-five or forty years of age, and takes a great deal more interest in the affairs of State than her distinguished father. She is far from being good-looking, and is rather masculine in disposition. She has intelligence and firmness, and is often compared to Queen Elizabeth. During the absence of the Emperor in the United States and Europe in 1876 and 1877, she assumed his authority, and upset matters so generally that she brought on a revolution that would have overturned the empire entirely had it not been suppressed in time.

In dealing with this outbreak she showed an ability and determination that gave her a great reputation among political leaders; but the condition of Brazil is changing so rapidly that by the time the princess comes to the throne by the death of her father, the Liberal element will be so large and powerful that they will prevent her from assuming authority. If her character and disposition were other than they are she might be tolerated on the throne; but their experience with her during her father's absence has taught the people that she is not such a ruler as they want, and the contrast between her rigorous rule and the political indifference of the Emperor is so great as to aggravate the dislike of the people for her. In addition to this, the princess is a great Church-woman, and attends mass every morning in her house, spends a great deal of time in religious devotion, supports a large retinue of priests and friars, who are said to be the only people who have any influence with her, and does a great deal to strengthen the Catholic Church in Brazil.

The Emperor does not seem to know of the unpopularity of his daughter. He does not seem to be aware that she possesses traits and a disposition in striking contrast with his own. With that generous charity with which he regards all human beings, he believes that she is as liberal-minded and as philanthropic as himself, and his dreams are never disturbed by any thought of what may occur after his death.

As everywhere else in South America, the Liberal element in Brazil has been making an active war against the Roman Catholic Church, and as long ago as 1870 a law was passed abolishing monastic institutions in the empire; but that legislation was more liberal than that passed and carried out in other South American countries, for it gave the religious orders ten years in which to dispose of their property and close up their affairs. This period expired in 1880, and very little has been done by the monks and nuns towards complying with the law. In 1881 an attempt was made to forcibly close their institutions, but an appeal was made to the courts, and it was only recently that a decision was rendered sustaining the constitutionality of the act of Congress and imposing a tax upon all real estate owned by the religious orders, and proceedings were commenced to confiscate and sell their property for the non-payment of taxes.

The religious orders refused to recognize the right of the civil power to dispose of their property. They claim that the Pope alone has authority over it; and their writers fill the papers with thrilling accounts of what terrible visitations have fallen upon all those who have taken the property of the Church, or in any way acquired real estate which once belonged to it, in other lands.

It may be said, however, that the general public takes very little interest in the dispute. There is no affection or respect felt for the monastic orders, which are in a condition of

THE COLORED SAINT.

decay, and their approaching extinction by the death of the few monks and nuns remaining is viewed with indifference; but the clergy take a different view of the case. They expect to inherit the revenues derived from the Church property, and they do not want to see it pass into the hands of private parties. Until ten or twelve years ago the political leaders encouraged the superstitious observances of the Church in order to secure the loyalty of the priesthood, but the growth of Liberal sentiment has been so great that the Church has been robbed of the terror it formerly inspired and of the influence which it possessed, and there has been much encouragement given to Protestants who have come into the country and engaged in missionary work.

One of the great holidays in Brazil is the feast of St. George, the patron of the empire. Each city and province has a sort of deputy patron, whose worship is duly celebrated on a particular day. Saint Sebastian has charge of the city of Rio de Janeiro, and in his honor a celebration is held once a year; but when the annual feast of St. George returns, every town and village from the northern to the southern boundary of the country has the grandest procession and demonstration of the season. This is not the same St. George who is supposed to have formerly had England under his protection, but an entirely different individual. Formerly this saint held the rank of colonel in the army, and was entitled to a yearly pay of thirty-five thousand dollars, which the priests drew for him and pretended to invest in jewels and dresses. A few years ago he used to be taken through the streets on horseback on his anniversary day, surrounded by a bodyguard—a regiment composed of the greatest swells of Rio de Janeiro, who acknowledged him as their commander, and were known as the "Imperial Order of St. George." An old resident told me about an instance that occurred some years ago, when the attendant who had charge of the image buckled Colonel St. George's sword on so carelessly that it dropped from his belt and wounded a priest. The aide-de-camp and the saint were both tried for the offence, and both found guilty. The officer was punished with imprisonment, and the saint fined a large portion of his salary.

The anniversary of Corpus Christi is always celebrated with great pomp in Rio, and with a procession which marches through the principal streets. At its head is usually carried an effigy of the Saviour, preceded by bands of singing priests and bearers of incense, and covered with a canopy carried by the Emperor and the Count D'Eu, his son-in-law, and the principal ministers of state. The participation of the

STATUE OF DOM PEDRO I.

Emperor in this ceremony has existed from time immemorial, and is supposed to illustrate the obedience of the civil to the ecclesiastical power; but Dom Pedro hates the nonsense, and last year he declined to participate.

The money used in Brazil is liable to give a stranger the nightmare. Imagine yourself presented with a bill for thirty thousand reis after eating a dinner and drinking a bottle of wine at a café. One is apt to indulge in some expressions of astonishment, even if he is too honest to attempt an escape by the back door. But composure is restored when it is discovered that a "reis" is worth only the twentieth part of a cent, and at the present discount of Brazilian money such a bill amounts only to about seven dollars.

The book-keepers of Brazil have a hard time of it, however, as the reis is the standard value, and the long lines of figures which represent the commercial transactions of the ordinary mercantile or banking house each day are a severe tax upon the mathematical accuracy and ability of the people. For example, $1,000,000 equals about 4,000,000,000 reis, and the paper currency of Brazil represents 488,000,000,000 reis. The commercial statistics of Brazil look very formidable; but the people simplify matters somewhat by using the term millreis, which means a thousand reis.

The currency of the country consists of irredeemable paper shinplasters, the smallest denomination being five hundred reis, which is equal to about thirteen cents in gold. Nickel and copper coins are used for change below that sum, the reis being a very minute disk of copper. There is no gold or silver in circulation; and as the balance of trade has been largely against Brazil of recent years, there is not coin enough in the country to pay the interest on the public debt, and the bondholders are given bills on London.

There is no wharfage at any of the Brazilian ports; vessels are compelled to anchor out in the harbors, which are usually good, and be loaded and unloaded by means of lighters. Passengers are carried to and fro in *bongoes*, managed by a noisy and naked boatman, who inspires alarm in the breast of the nervous passenger, who imagines this gang of savage-looking maniacs are cannibals howling for his blood. The wardrobe of a bongo usually consists of a dilapidated straw hat and a pair of cotton drawers amputated at the thighs. These drawers are a degree farther from decency than the bathing-trunks small boys wear at the sea-side. The bongoes are shrewd fellows, and make bargains easily, but are hard to settle with when the work is done. They agree to take you and your trunk ashore for a dollar, but when you reach the custom-house they demand twice as much, with an additional dollar for Pippo, who helped carry the trunk down the gangway. People who remain on the vessel amuse themselves by throwing small coins into the water for the boatmen to dive after. If you toss a silver quarter overboard, a dozen or more will plunge after it, and one of them will have it in his mouth before it reaches the bottom.

CARRYING COFFEE TO THE STEAMER.

MARKET-PLACE IN COUNTRY TOWN.

The most noticeable thing that strikes one when he lands at one of the Brazilian ports is the extraordinary economy observed in the matter of wearing apparel. The children in the streets up to eight or ten years are usually entirely naked, playing in groups around the door-ways, and in the corners sheltered from the sun. Nearly every woman you meet has a big basket of something or other on her head, or a naked baby in her arms; the number of babies to be seen at the windows or in the streets is astonishing. The yellow-fever and other epidemics carry off a large percentage of the population every summer, but the increase from natural causes more than keeps pace with the mortality. When the girls get to be eight or ten years of age they put on a white cotton tunic, which hangs loosely from the shoulders, and the women wear a plain white chemise, with the arms and shoulders bare. The boys and men have cotton trousers or drawers, and, if they are prosperous, add a speckled shirt to their wardrobe, which hangs loosely over the pantaloons, and flaps in the breeze with cheerful *négligé*. A society for the encouragement of modesty among the men, women, and children of Brazil would find a fruitful field for missionary work. They act and live like animals; but the younger women show some sense of shame, and gather their scanty drapery around them as the stranger passes. Among their own kind they are as regardless of the proprieties of civilization as the mangy dogs which stretch out in the sun at their feet. The priests, under whose control they yield an absolute submission, and whose authority here is even greater than in Rome, are said to teach no lessons of chastity or modesty, but to practise a licentiousness which makes one shudder when he hears common anecdotes told.

The sun always rises and sets very suddenly in the tropics. There is no "rosy blush of morn to herald the coming of a newborn day," and so on, nor is there a gorgeous glow in the west when the twilight comes; but old Sol gets up in the morning and goes to bed at night without any ceremony, and with a startling suddenness. You awaken at the noise of carts in the street, find it dark as midnight, with the stars more brilliant than you ever saw them at home, turn over, doze a little, and in a few moments jump up, supposing it to be noonday. The sun jumps into the air out of the darkness and drops below the horizon as if he had been shot. There are only two periods in the twenty-four hours—midnight and high noon. There is gas in most of the large towns, but it is seldom used in any except the finest modern residences. Candles or kerosene lamps throw light upon domestic circles, but there are always plenty of gas-lamps in the streets, and they light them in an odd way. One fellow goes ahead with a long stick and turns on the gas; another follows him with a torch and gives it light. Sometimes the latter stops to gossip on the corner, and the consequence is a strong odor of gas all over the town.

On every block is a policeman or watchman, whose business

"SERENO-O-O-O-O! SERENO-O-O-O-O!"

is to sing out at certain intervals to inform the inhabitants what o'clock it is, and that all is well. Like the fakirs in the streets during the day, they have a most melancholy tone in their voices, and to the stranger their announcements sound like the cry of a lost soul—"Sereno-o-o-o-o; Sereno-o-o-o-o; Las diez y media y Sereno-o-o-o-o!"

The text-books on oratory that were used in old times gave the statement that Demosthenes could make an audience weep or laugh at will by simply uttering "Mesopotamia," but he could not have put more pathos, more lingering agony, than the tropical policemen in these simple words—"All's serene; all's serene! It is a day and a half-midnight, and all's serene!"

The stranger never fails to hear these announcements, for two very good reasons; first, because his bed is as hard as the racks upon which the Roman tyrants used to torture early Christians; and, second, it is always occupied by a colony of the most vigorous pests that ever drank human blood. At the hotels all the servants are men. They do the work of chamber-maids, cooks, porters, and dining-room waiters, wash the dishes, and everything but washing and ironing.

The Brazilian rises early in the morning, to do the greater part of his work in the cool of the day. He drinks a cup of strong coffee, eats a roll, and perhaps an egg, and then goes to his store or office, from which he returns at twelve to his breakfast—the most elaborate meal of the day. It begins with soup and ends with cheese, dulces, and coffee, like the dinner of the temperate zone. He has a fish, a chop or steak, an omelette, and a salad, but no vegetables. Then he lies down for a nap, after which, about four o'clock, he returns to business, and remains often as late as eight or nine o'clock. His dinner is a repetition of his breakfast, except that he has vegetables and a roast or fowl. He takes a walk in the plaza with his family after dinner and retires early, if he does not go to the club or gaming-table. The people are inveterate gamblers. There is no more disgrace attached to attendance upon the faro-table or the roulette-board than attends stock gambling in New York. He calls upon the Holy Mother when he tosses his chips upon the cards, and says an "Ave Maria" when he wins a stake. At every religious festival the cathedrals and churches are surrounded by gambling-booths, and the priests always go to the cock-fights after high mass on Sunday. Some of them breed game chickens, and carry them to the pit under their priestly robes.

SLAVE QUARTERS IN THE COUNTRY.

The great problem for Brazil to solve in the future is that of labor. With the gradual emancipation of the slave the labor system of the country is becoming disorganized and demoralized. It has been demonstrated beyond a doubt, even in the minds of the most radical abolitionists, that the emancipated negroes are neither disposed nor competent to take care of themselves. They are different in this respect from the freedmen of the United States because their ignorance is much greater. Their dependence is much more absolute, and they never received the kind treatment and instruction that was enjoyed by so many of the slaves in the United States. From one end of Brazil to the other there is scarcely a negro slave, or one who has ever been enslaved, that can read and write. Their ignorance is so dense that they scarcely know anything of the work outside of the cabin in which they live; and the policy of the slave-holders, aided by the priests, has been to keep them in this condition as far as possible. As long as they have attended mass, and said so many prayers a day, the priests have been satisfied with their condition, and their owners and masters have never thought of anything but to get as much work out of them as was consistent with their strength.

THE POLITICAL ISSUE IN BRAZIL.

The political issue in Brazil to-day, as has been the case for many years, is the abolition of slavery. Ten years ago the two political parties were as wide apart on this question as the Abolitionists and Democrats were in the United States in 1860; but the emancipation policy has been rapidly growing in favor, the necessity and justness of the movement have become almost universally recognized, and the two political parties differ only upon the measures by which the result shall be accomplished. There are very few people in Brazil to-day who, when asked the direct question, will advocate the perpetuation of human slavery; but those who have property in slaves naturally resist any movement that will deprive them of its value without some compensation.

A law was passed in 1881 which declared free all negroes and their children who should be imported into the empire after that date; but it was never executed, and in spite of it the slave-trade increased, reaching prior to 1851 enormous proportions. Fifty thousand negro slaves were imported in a single year when the trade was at its height. The effective intervention of the British Government in 1851 broke up the foreign trade, and from that time the friends of the slave in Brazil were able to make some headway against their opponents.

The first legislation enforced towards the abolition of slavery was enacted in 1871, in what was known as the "Free Birth Law," which was framed by the Emperor himself, and adopted by Congress largely through his own personal efforts. This laid the axe at the root of the tree, and provided that human bondage in Brazil should end with the present generation. Every child born since the passage of the act is free, but the owner of its mother is required to educate and support it until twenty-one years old, being entitled to the results of its labor during the same time. The law also provided that slaves should be credited with their labor, and all service performed over and above a given maximum should be considered as a surplus and credited against the value of the slave, in order that those who had energy and ambition might in this manner earn or purchase their own freedom; and by a further provision all slaves reaching the age of sixty-five were free, but could look to their old masters for support in case they were in a condition of disability.

This law, however well intended, proved impracticable, and could not be generally enforced. Forgeries were committed upon the records of birth, both by the slaves and their masters. The latter refused, or fixed so high a valuation that very few were able to earn their freedom; they neglected to educate the children as required by law, so that even if a young man gained his freedom he was not fitted to enjoy it or exercise the right of citizenship. The old men and women were turned off the plantations to beg or find refuge in the public almshouses; and the planters, feeling no longer any interest in the health and welfare of their slaves, neglected their sanitary condition and ill-treated them. The result of the law was to demoralize the laboring element. It proved a disaster to the slaves as well as to their masters, and disturbed the political condition of the country.

There is no slave-market in Rio Janeiro, nor has there been one for several years, all the transactions in human flesh being conducted privately; but there are agents who buy and sell on commission, like the real estate or cattle dealers of the United States.

MILITARY MEN.

There is a small number of negroes in Brazil from Minas, a territory on the west coast of Africa, who differ from all other blacks. They are of immense frame, capable of great endurance, display a remarkable degree of intelligence, are very clannish, speaking a language among themselves unintelligible to others, and practising religious rites similar to those of Mohammedanism, from which they have never been allured by the tempting ceremonies of the Catholic Church.

As slaves the Minas natives are valued at more than double the price of ordinary negroes, and as freedmen they are useful, industrious, and excellent citizens, and will work of their own accord. No other blacks exercise the regular Yankee thrift in saving their earnings and in economizing their resources. They are ingenious as well as intelligent, and make first-class mechanics as well as laborers. These Minas have frequently purchased their freedom and returned to Africa, but those that go invariably come back to Brazil. Several instances are reported in which they have chartered vessels for this purpose, and have even brought over friends and kinsmen of their own across the Atlantic to settle in Brazil. The wisest thinkers of the country advocate the organization of immigration companies for the purpose of bringing cargoes of these people from Africa, not as slaves, but as freemen, to supply the demand for labor in the country. They are much preferable to the Chinese or the coolies as laborers, and are particularly adapted to the Brazilian climate.

There are a great many Germans going into the country, forming colonies in the interior, opening up sugar plantations, planting coffee, gathering rubber, and engaging in all sorts of agricultural employment; but the climate is so enervating that after an experience of two years the German colonist will be found by his Portuguese predecessor sitting in the shade of the fig-tree and hiring a negro to do his work. Everywhere in hot climates the people become enervated, and Brazil will scarcely form an exception to other countries in the same latitude. In the more southern provinces and on the higher levels white colonists may succeed if there is nothing but climatic differences to oppose them. There has been a small number of immigrants from the United States to the southern provinces of Brazil; and after the war a great many Confederates flooded in there for the purpose of establishing plantations and raising sugar and coffee, but their success has not been great. Most of the colonies have broken up, and the members have been scattered over different parts of the country. Some engage in one undertaking, some in another, but many have succumbed to the influences of the climate and died of fever.

THE END.

www.ingramcontent.com/pod-product-compliance
Ingram Content Group UK Ltd.
Pitfield, Milton Keynes, MK11 3LW, UK
UKHW032028070225
454812UK00005B/421